SURVEY OF WORLD CULTURES

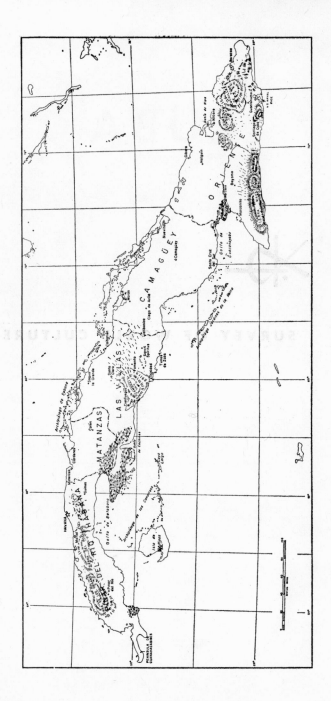

SURVEY OF WORLD CULTURES

A Series

Perhaps at no other time in history has so much been written about the behavior of peoples in the different countries of the world. While there remain critical areas of ignorance about motivation and behavior, the dynamics of society, culture and its power, there do exist quantities of recorded observations and information, and of highly detailed analyses of this or that aspect of life as it is lived by given groups of people. Observations, information, analysis—all usually are scattered, available but separate. The books of this series represent an endeavor to gather together and interpret the separate pieces.

This series, in short, presents a different kind of book, one that is concerned with the relationship of parts usually studied separately. The focus of each book is a society as it functions, the interrelationship of its parts and of the parts to the whole. Emphasis is on the dynamics of that interaction, on constants of attitude and behavior, abiding values, the presence and impact of forces for change.

Volumes in the SURVEY OF WORLD CULTURES already published or scheduled for publication are listed on the back of the jacket.

SURVEY
OF
WORLD
CULTURES

CUBA

its people   its society   its culture

Wyatt MacGaffey
Clifford R. Barnett

IN COLLABORATION WITH

Jean Haiken and Mildred Vreeland

prepared under the auspices of
The American University

HRAF PRESS

NEW HAVEN

Already Published in this Series

LIBRARY OF CONGRESS CATALOG CARD NUMBER: 62-13516

© COPYRIGHT 1962
HUMAN RELATIONS AREA FILES, INC.
NEW HAVEN, CONN.
ALL RIGHTS RESERVED
MANUFACTURED IN THE UNITED STATES OF AMERICA BY
UNITED PRINTING SERVICES, INC.

PUBLISHER'S NOTE

THE SURVEY OF WORLD CULTURES, of which *Cuba* is the tenth in the series, is one of several means by which the Human Relations Area Files seeks to promote and facilitate the comparative study of human behavior and a greater understanding of cultures other than our own.

These surveys, though augmented by original research, are primarily a collation and synthesis of the best and most authoritative materials, published and unpublished, on the societies selected. For many of these societies excellent specialized studies exist, but the materials are often so widely scattered as to be virtually unavailable to all except the most determined scholar. It was to meet the need for a comprehensive readable volume, bringing together all those aspects of a country and culture usually studied separately, that these books were undertaken.

Unlike earlier volumes in this series, *Cuba* was prepared independently of the Human Relations Area Files by members of the research staff of American University (see title page). We wish to thank American University for permission to include this study in our Survey of World Cultures and to express our appreciation to the individual authors for their assent to the editorial changes that were necessary to ensure general conformity to the series format.

PREFACE

THE ATTENTION GIVEN TO CUBA SINCE 1959 by the world at large has been out of all proportion to its area, its population, and even to its significance as the world's largest producer of sugar. It also contrasts strangely with the relative neglect of Cuba in the years before the Castro revolution. In the United States in particular the proximity of the island and the familiarity of many individual Americans with Havana meant that Cuba was generally taken for granted. Political developments since 1959—the replacement of one authoritarian government by another, the change from a nominally individualistic society to a loudly proclaimed collectivistic one, the adoption of an entirely new posture in world affairs—have commanded startled attention. To some, they represent hopeful departures and an example to be widely imitated; to others, a triumph of the imperialist designs of the Soviet Union and a threat not only to Latin America but to the heartland of democracy.

Personal and national reactions, feelings of hope or of betrayal, have governed many published efforts to repair the neglect of years past and adjust opinion to the new face of Cuba. This book, on the other hand, endeavors to understand the revolution of 1959 as a Cuban phenomenon, examining its local antecedents and its relation to Cuban values and problems, with a minimum of direct reference to its significance in the international scene. Objectivity is a rare virtue, which the authors do not claim; but at least they have consciously sought an independent point of view. Their principal concern has been the pattern of political leadership—its values, goals, and techniques; inevitably, many aspects of Cuban life are slighted which others would have stressed.

The authors wish to express their thanks to their Cuban informants, some refugees and others not; to Michael Kenny of the

Catholic University of America for specific information; to Howard J. John, Archibald G. MacArthur, and Frederica Muhlenberg, all of the American University staff, and to G. A. Mellander and Randolph Carr, also in Washington, for drafts prepared by them and used in the book; and to Ernest A. Will, who was responsible for the maps. They gratefully acknowledge a special debt to four books—indispensable to students of Cuban affairs—among others listed in the bibliography: C. E. Chapman, *A History of the Cuban Republic* (1927); the Commission on Cuban Affairs of the Foreign Policy Association, *Problems of the New Cuba* (1935); Lowry Nelson, *Rural Cuba* (1950); and the International Bank for Reconstruction and Development, *Report on Cuba* (1951). The use made of these materials is however the sole responsibility of the authors.

Washington, D.C.   WYATT MACGAFFEY
April 1962   CLIFFORD R. BARNETT

CONTENTS

LIST OF PLATES

LIST OF TABLES

INTRODUCTION

PLAYING ON THE HISTORIC FEARS and prejudices of Latin Americans, Fidel Castro has boasted that Cuba is the first country in the Western Hemisphere to have broken away from the tutelage of the United States, to have friendly dealings with the Communist world, to offer social justice to its ethnic minorities, and to have begun the rational exploitation of economic resources for the benefit of the people.

The economic and social innovations in Cuba since 1959 have been carried out in the name of a personified revolution, "that great teacher," as President Dorticós called it. "The Revolution knows what it is doing," said Raúl Castro. In the first two years the revolution, while avoiding a public commitment to international Communism, was explicitly Marxist in its interpretation of its task. Economic and political reform were related aspects of a single process which could not be entrusted to individual enterprise and the social institutions remaining from an earlier time. By May 1, 1961, when Castro announced a "socialist Cuba," the regime had nationalized all major economic enterprises, all instruments of public information and education, and all representative institutions, including the labor unions and the professional associations. Of elections Castro said that the revolution, having substituted direct government by the people for pseudo-democracy, had no time for such foolishness.

The Tyranny, as the regime of Batista from 1952 to 1958 was known in the language of the revolution, inspired an almost universal opposition whose militant arm was Fidel Castro's 26th of July Revolutionary Movement. The revolutionaries agreed on the general outline of necessary reforms, but as a political agency in the day of success the Movement, divided into the competing factions characteristic of Cuban political life, failed to agree upon the manner of its execution or to provide a political base from which reform could begin. It also failed to provide Castro personally with the reliable support his continued supremacy required.

Between May and November 1959, Castro turned to the only faction which promised to satisfy his needs—a group including Raúl Castro, Ernesto Guevara, and the Communists. In so doing he alienated and eventually eliminated the members of the 26th of July Movement, many of whom followed the Batistianos into exile, and committed his regime to an authoritarian course not envisioned by the majority of his original supporters. The material benefits offered by his new course, however, ensured the continuing loyalty of the majority of the peasants and unskilled workers, who had formerly been the last to benefit from economic and political opportunities, and of some sections of the professional class.

Castro castigated his opposition as agents of United States imperialism and equated efforts to "save the revolution" with a hypocritical attachment to the discredited values of the old social order. The revolution, though in effect the policy supported by Castro and his immediate colleagues, was presented, with Marxist arguments, as the logical continuation of a social revolution begun in the early nineteenth century. The upheaval of 1958 and 1959 was, in fact, the latest in a series of drastic changes, some political and some economic, which had marked the history of the preceding two hundred years.

The myths, ideals, and opportunities of revolution are the frontier and horizon of discontent in Cuba. Reformers place their hope in new departures, guided by personal convictions, attracted by the call to greatness. They have little or no faith in the institutional restraints that conservatives regard as the necessary fabric of civilization. Revolutionary leaders have nearly all been drawn from the younger generation of the middle sector; according to their own account, by indignation against social injustice and the mortgaging of the national potential. In many cases their actual motivation seems to have been equally the frustration of their personal economic and political ambitions, but no simple distinction can be made between the two.

The revolution of 1898, which prepared the way for the Republic, was carried out by a fairly small group of intellectuals and landowners. The revolution of 1933, which gave the government precedence over the upper class in the structure of patronage, was the work of a larger group including the newly formed army and the newly organized labor unions. On both occasions, however, paternalism was accepted without serious question as the dominant principle. All governments, however constituted, maintained themselves in power by balancing the major interest groups.

Castro's innovation was to build his regime on a single national political organization. Within this structure many traditional features persisted. Law still originated from the leader, who provided all necessary and proper benefits for his followers. The personal loyalty of these followers constituted the bond of national unity. Some 100,000 of the upper class had emigrated by mid-1961; their powers and privileges had been assumed, in the name of the peasants and of social justice, by a successful minority of middle-class revolutionaries.

Since June 1961, when the chapters of this book were completed, the trend toward Communist control of the totalitarian government has advanced methodically; the main development has been the appointment to senior positions of men publicly active in Communist party leadership since the 1930's. In July the merging of the 26th of July Movement, the Communists, and the Revolutionary Directorate, which had effectively occurred some time before, was made official by the announcement of the new ruling group known as the Integrated Revolutionary Organizations. Its principal officers were Blas Roca, Aníbal Escalante, Lázaro Peña, Carlos Rafael Rodríguez, Severo Aguirre, and Fabio Grobart. In November Lázaro Peña became secretary-general of the labor confederation.

In December Castro announced the transformation of the Integrated Revolutionary Organizations into the United Party of the Socialist Revolution, whose membership was to be made up of selected adepts of revolutionary theory and practice. The party would work through the mass organizations to form a dictatorship of the proletariat looking toward a Communist society in thirty years or more.

In a speech on December 2 explaining the character of the new party and the need for it, Castro for the first time accepted explicitly the name of Marxist-Leninist. At the university, he said, he was sympathetic to Marxism but influenced against the Communist party by his bourgeois education, and later he had hoped to establish "utopian socialism" without the scientific discipline which the "socialist party" alone could provide. He had read some of *Das Kapital* and intended to read more.

In view of the country's deteriorating economic condition Castro may have hoped by making this confession to influence the Soviet bloc to be more generous. The reports were contradictory, but it appeared that labor difficulties as well as bad management, shortage of parts and supplies, and lack of technical help were contributing to reduced productivity. A poor sugar harvest was expected. Castro warned of still more extensive rationing. However, during 1961 the Soviet bloc readily cited the United States base at Guantánamo as an imperialist outrage but showed little enthusiasm for admitting Cuba into the socialist camp.

The remarkable feature of the December speech, however, was Castro's virtual renunciation of the role of *líder* in favor of collective leadership, and the indebtedness he expressed toward the Popular Socialist Party for rescuing the revolution from its amateurish confusion. If he refrained from calling himself a Communist it was largely from apparent deference to professional Communists. Castro explained that there would be renewed emphasis on revolutionary education through the UPSR, the National Printing Office (controlled by PSP members), and the schools. The elevation of senior Communists continued with the appointment in January 1962 of Juan Marinello as head of the University of Havana, and in February of Carlos Rafael Rodríguez to replace Castro as head of the National Agrarian Reform Institute.

Despite the very evident success of the PSP effort to assume the publicly commanding position in the government, political friction within the regime had not ended and threatened to increase in the face of the apparent failures of the agricultural program. There remained possibilities for further conflict between what remained of the non-Communist radical left and the PSP and within the PSP. Castro himself appeared less than happy about the possibility that his power would be collectivized. In March 1962 he won a round by denouncing Aníbal Escalante for introducing the cult of personality; Escalante left the country. Castro did not appear to be courting a full scale battle with the PSP but, taking advantage of party disputes, to be demonstrating once more his own essential role.

The nation's income and that of a majority of the people is derived from sugar production. After a period of high prices and greatly expanded production following World War I, Cuba found itself competing with other countries to meet a reduced world demand for sugar. The need to limit production brought about international regulatory agreements and strengthened the traditional concept of the government as patron rather than servant of the people. Wage labor, capitalists, the managerial class, and the chambers of commerce all depended on the government, which regulated so much of the economy, to regulate it in their favor. The support of particular economic interest groups helped to relieve the government of dependence on the electorate.

Until 1959 government was rarely honest and frequently staggeringly corrupt. Dictatorship was always a possibility, in several periods a fact. When it existed it was based more upon the structures of patronage than upon military force, as in many instances elsewhere in Latin America. Social and economic conditions combined to prevent the fulfillment of the democratic system provided for by the constitution; the excessive power of the president enabled him to disregard or pervert many constitutional provisions. People tended to understand democracy as benevolent dictatorship; a feeble executive, no matter what its legitimation or how honest its administration, earned little support.

Batista as *jefe supremo* ruled as much with the assistance of his clients in the business world and the labor unions as by military force. Their benefits were secured at the expense of the rural population and the unorganized, semiemployed sector of the urban lower class whose political loyalties were attached to patrons at a much lower level—the landlord, the merchant, the local political organizer. The benefits returned for loyalties at this level included security of employment, extension of credit, freedom from petty persecution.

The upper class as a whole played the part of patron to the lower class. It was distinguished by its self-conscious avoidance of manual labor, its ostentatiously urbane standard of living, and its education. Almost everyone with any wealth or education lived in cities where he had access to managerial and entrepreneurial positions and especially government office. The law called for free and compulsory education up to the age of fourteen, but in 1953 almost one-fourth of the population was illiterate. Most of those able to obtain higher education came from upper-class families. The content of education—literary, speculative, legalistic, formalistic, with special stress on rhetorical skills—conformed to the upper-class formula for social leadership.

Within the upper class, economic considerations distinguished a small but growing middle class from the true upper class. There was, however, no ideal middle-class way of life; many families with middle-class incomes found it hard to meet the upper-class standard of living they felt was expected of them. They were trained by their class background to expect roles of political and managerial responsibility, an income capable of providing the appropriate standard of living and the accompanying social prestige.

Political activity as the chief means of enlarging one's share of the inadequate national income was the particular domain of the middle sector of society which extended from the leaders of organized labor upward on the social scale to include those whose political success had placed them securely in the higher ranks of the upper class. The heart of the middle sector, however, was the underemployed professional group of the middle class. The middle sector was not an integrated and self-conscious group analogous to a class, but an area of social competition often tending to violence and at the same time a phase in the career of many men who began as impecunious university graduates inclined to revolutions and ended as relatively wealthy, nationally-known upholders of the existing order.

Beliefs in personal potential, the integrity of the soul, and destiny provided justification for the revolutionary tradition. In the words of the national hero, the nineteenth-century revolutionary leader José Martí, "whoever is capable of greatness and dies without being summoned to fulfill his promise, dies in peace, for he knows that somewhere his hour will come. And if it does not come, well and good; there is greatness enough in the capacity for greatness."

In practice, for the majority this attitude placed a high value on conspicuous ability, power, and distinction and a low value on steady effort, caution, and strict adherence to an external code. Those who did not have the opportunity or the capacity for greatness were content, for the time at least, to seek advantage by attaching themselves to the strongest available patron.

The masses whose discontent gave the opportunity to Fidel Castro found in 1962, if not before, that their chosen leader was inadequate to the demands of greatness. No revolutionary enthusiasm could conceal the disappointments of the expected new society. For others in the Western Hemisphere his failure was more disturbing for the advancement it offered to an alien ideology and a threatening imperialism.

For those who are aware of the existence in other countries of similar discontent and are concerned for the future, the background and career of Castro's revolution have special relevance.

CUBA

THE ISLAND AND ITS HISTORY

CUBA, THE LARGEST AND MOST WESTERLY of the Caribbean islands, has an area of 44,278 square miles (about the size of Pennsylvania) and an estimated population of 6,744,000 (January 1960). Lying only 98 miles from the Florida keys, astride the entrance to the Gulf of Mexico, it commands the sea approaches to Mexico, the Mississippi Valley, and western Florida. Its strategic location gave it prominence in the struggles of the colonial powers for mastery in this part of the Americas and assures its continuing importance in world politics, while the narrowness of the several straits separating it from neighboring countries has been a major influence in Cuba's political history and economic orientation.

Surrounding the mainland are numerous islands and keys, the largest being the Isle of Pines, 59 miles to the south. Some of the islands and keys are completely uninhabited, some support a few charcoal makers and fishermen, the latter making a living from the numerous varieties of fish, sponges, and crustaceans found in the coastal waters.

The terrain of the mainland, about 40 percent mountainous, is unusually varied for a small island. The most important mountain ranges are the Sierra de los Órganos and Sierra del Rosario in the west, the Sierra de Trinidad which, together with the Sierra de Sancti Spíritus, is also known as the Escambray in the center, and the Sierra Maestra, the highest mountainous region, in the east.

The surrounding ocean gives the country a moderate and stable climate which, with the exception of the higher mountains, is basically the same everywhere. The mean temperature is 77°F. in winter and 80° in summer. July and August, the hottest months of the year, register a median temperature of only slightly over

80°F. Lying in the trade wind belt, the island receives breezes from the northeast in summer and the southeast in winter, as well as the perpetual breezes created daily by the difference in temperature between the land and the sea.

There are two distinct seasons based on rainfall. During the rainy season from May to October inclusive, with some abatement during August, there are almost daily afternoon storms of considerable violence, especially inland. The dry season corresponds to winter, from November to April, with December and February the driest. Average rainfall ranges from 8.16 inches in June to 1.48 inches in February.

The most notable and destructive aspects of the climate are the tropical hurricanes which afflict the island, most frequently in August, September, and October. Pinar del Río and La Habana provinces suffer most, especially on their south coasts where wind-driven flood waves sweep over the low coastline. The soils are extremely varied, although a few types occur over extensive areas, among which the Matanzas red clay, covering much of the plain in the western region and in Camagüey, is the best for sugar cane. The sandy soils such as are found in the central plain of Camagüey are poor for crops unless abundantly fertilized but support grasses for cattle.

The island is a natural botanical garden. Situated in the path of tropical cyclones and of north and south bird migrations, both of which encourage dispersal of seeds, it boasts an estimated 8,000 different species of trees and plants, among which are tobacco, pineapple, and yucca, all native to the island. In addition, the country is particularly well endowed with iron, nickel, copper, manganese, tungsten, naphtha, asphalt, and perhaps petroleum.

Cuba under Spain

Columbus landed on Cuba during his first voyage in 1492, but the first permanent Spanish settlement was made in 1496 on the neighboring island of Hispaniola, which now contains the Dominican Republic and the Republic of Haiti. From Hispaniola the growing colony expanded, conquering and settling Jamaica, Puerto Rico, and, in 1511, Cuba. During the ensuing thirty years, Cuba became a prosperous and lively outpost of empire, but gradually the settlers were drawn on by the greater promise of new regions in Central and South America.

1. *The Island and Its History*

Spanish expeditions to the New World were privately financed ventures authorized by a royal contract defining the authority and the revenues to be divided between the Crown and the conquistadors. At first the explorers were given great power to govern the areas they conquered, but as the extent of the New World became known in Europe, the Spanish Crown reserved more powers to itself.

The first organization of Cuban government and economic institutions was modeled on the experience of Hispaniola. The island was divided into seven municipalities—a unit found throughout the empire and derived from the medieval organization of the Kingdom of Castile. In the towns of Baracoa, Bayamo, Puerto Principe, Trinidad, Sancti Spíritus, Santiago de Cuba, and Havana, each the seat of government for the surrounding territory, the governor appointed a municipal council (*cabildo*) consisting of three *regidores* (councilors) and two *alcaldes* (magistrates). Certain intermediate supervisory functions were performed by an *audiencia*, a court of appeal with some administrative authority, resident in Hispaniola, and by the Viceroy of New Spain in Mexico. Either directly or through these officials, depending on the issue, island government was responsible to the councils in Spain and to the Crown.

Officials divided land and Indian laborers among the colonists, basing their allotments, as well as governmental appointments, upon the individual's capital investment and military risk in the enterprise. A man's legal status as a citizen and his opportunity for wealth depended on his possession of land and laborers. The recipients of land grants, *vecinos,* had the right to fully participate in municipal affairs. Indian laborers were allotted under a system known in Cuba and throughout the empire as the *encomienda,* theoretically a nontransferable grant of from forty to two hundred Indians, which might be revoked at any time and was legally distinct from landholding rights. Actually titles to Indian labor were often sold along with the land on which they lived.

Economic decline and the exhaustion of the gold supply were instrumental in bringing about the eclipse of Cuba. Despite orders from the Crown and the efforts of many individuals, the Indian population steadily declined from disease and maltreatment. Although the first Negro slaves were imported in 1517, their numbers were not sufficient to prevent a labor shortage. Cortes' expedition to Mexico in 1519 was organized in Cuba and drew heavily on the

Spanish population. Hernando de Soto's expedition to Florida (1539-1541) was the last of the major ventures to embark from Cuba. By mid-century the population had declined to about twelve hundred Spaniards, two to three thousand Indians, and a few slaves.

From about 1540 until the late eighteenth century, Cuba remained a neglected, underpopulated backwater of the Spanish empire, subsidized from the Viceregal treasury in Mexico. The island's chief importance to Spain lay in its position at the entrance to the Gulf of Mexico, whose shores were all Spanish territory, making it an outpost against impinging Portuguese, French, and English interests in the Caribbean. Pirates, smugglers, and buccaneers—mostly Portuguese and French in the sixteenth century, Dutch, French, and British in the seventeenth century—made sporadic raids, from which the almost defenseless inhabitants usually fled inland.

Against these threats the Spanish Crown, in the mid-sixteenth century, devised the fleet system of protecting its commerce. Havana increasingly supplanted Santiago as the commercial center of the island and in 1589 became the official capital. From the late sixteenth century, island governors usually were military men with the title of captain-general, defense appropriations were larger, and great fortresses were built to guard the entrances to Havana and Santiago harbors. The general decline of Spain during the seventeenth century, however, enabled other powers to gain permanent strongholds in the Caribbean: the French in Haiti and the British in Jamaica.

Disappointed in their hope of mining gold in quantity, the Spaniards turned during the sixteenth century to cattle raising, for which much of the island was ideal. In Spanish law all land belonged ultimately to the sovereign, but *cabildos* were empowered to confer grazing rights which were in effect freehold grants (*mercedes*) of land. The first such grant was made in 1536 in Sancti Spíritus (in the modern province of Las Villas), a district which remained a center of the cattle industry and of traditional Spanish attitudes.

Although the political system was corrupt, the island was not prosperous enough for the accumulation of great fortunes. Offices were sought as much for their perquisites as for revenue. The church added moral and spiritual sanction to the dictates of government, and provided, as well, nearly all existing social services. By the seventeenth century, Franciscans, Dominicans, and Jesuits were active in the maintenance of hospitals, care of orphans, and provision of rudimentary education for children, some of whom went on to universities in Santo Domingo or Mexico.

During the eighteenth century Cuba gradually became more prosperous. Piracy abated after the last great buccaneer, Sir Henry Morgan, who raided Camagüey so thoroughly that the inhabitants moved the city inland in 1668, retired to a life of respectability as governor of Jamaica. Immigration of Spaniards from Jamaica and some new immigration from Spain gave impetus to new agricultural pursuits, particularly the growing of tobacco. Sugar cultivation also expanded. With the increased production of tobacco and sugar, the breakup of the enormous cattle ranches was begun, a process which continued well into the nineteenth century. The founding of the navy yard at Havana in 1723, where ships of the Spanish navy were constructed for the rest of the century, gave a boost to the city's economy. But the colonists chafed under the repressive trade policies of the Crown and smuggling continued. Early in the eighteenth century, three unsuccessful local revolts occurred against the Crown's enforcement of a monopoly on tobacco exports, the first signs of colonial resentment against Spain's exploitative trade policy.

During this period society consisted of the predominantly white Spanish group, the Negro slaves, and, in an ambiguous intervening position, the diminishing native Indian population. Within the white group, an incipient class distinction between peninsular Spaniards and Cuban-born Spaniards (*criollos*) appeared at an early date. From the first, because of the shortage of white women, white-Negro and white-Indian sexual unions were common, so that the *criollo* group contained a mestizo element. Serious conflicts between *peninsulares* and *criollos,* however, did not arise until the prosperity of the late eighteenth century was well established.

The Seven Years' War (1756-1763) between Great Britain and France (the latter aided by Spain under the terms of the Family Compact of 1761 between the two Bourbon dynasties) opened a new era in Cuba. The British captured Havana in 1762. During the ten months of their occupation, trade restrictions were relaxed and North American markets opened to a rapidly expanded trade. The Treaty of Paris returned Cuba to Spain in exchange for Florida, but the impact of the defeat on Spain, and the quick succession of revolutionary changes in North America, France, and Latin America, opened the way to creation of a new society in Cuba. The subsequent era was one of rapid economic expansion, moderate governmental reform, and relatively free exchange of goods and ideas with Europe and North America.

The accession of Charles III of Spain (1759-1788) inaugurated a period of governmental reform and intellectual freedom in Spain. French advisers influenced many administrative changes and introduced the intellectual currents of the French enlightenment. The first academy of natural sciences was founded in 1760, and Charles III later sponsored expeditions of natural scientists to the colonies. Finding the Jesuit establishment too powerful, he expelled the order in 1767 and in the same year the first secular school was founded.

In colonial administration Charles III effected reforms intended both to tighten the administrative system and to prevent the abuses which drained revenue from the royal treasury. The intendancy system, patterned in part on French administration and already implemented in Spain, was first tried in Havana in 1764 and during the next twenty years was extended throughout Latin America. In Havana the intendant, ranking equally with the captain-general, was appointed to oversee the two departments of treasury and war. His primary function was to enforce trade laws, collect revenues, and encourage all agricultural and other economic measures that would increase prosperity and revenue. Trade restrictions were liberalized, the monopoly on the import of slaves abolished in 1791, some products freed of export duties, and Havana and Santiago opened for free trade within the Spanish empire. Incentives were offered to encourage immigration. New immigrants from Europe, Martinique, and Haiti, and Spanish refugees from the revolutions elsewhere in Latin America made possible rapid economic development at a time when the American Revolution greatly increased the North American market for coffee and sugar.

The labor demands of these growing industries caused a tremendous increase in the importation of slaves. In 1763 there were only about 32,000 in Cuba but the trade expanded rapidly after 1790, reaching a peak in 1817 when Spain agreed in a treaty with Great Britain to prohibit the slave trade after 1820. Although the treaty was not fully enforced the number imported declined. Manumission was quite frequent and carefully regulated by law; slaves often worked for pay and could purchase their freedom in installments.

1. *The Island and Its History*

The 1827 census estimated the population at 311,051 white, 286,942 slaves, and 106,494 free colored.

The liberalism and prosperity of the period were reflected in the development of a more lavish social life and greater interest in the intellectual life of Europe. Wealthy Spaniards and native-born Cubans enjoyed a leisurely pursuit of social and cultural activities. A number of unusually capable Spanish officials sponsored or encouraged cultural societies modeled on those in Spain, new schools, and reform in the university curriculum to include modern philosophy and science. The Sociedad Económica de Amigos del País, founded under Governor Luis de las Casas' patronage in 1795, remained the focus of economic and political liberalism through most of the nineteenth century. It sought greater freedom of trade, sponsored technical experiments and publications (particularly on agriculture), maintained libraries, and exchanged publications with other groups in Europe and North America. The educational section, established in 1816, assumed the direction of a number of free schools.

Napoleon's invasion of Spain and the deposition of King Ferdinand VII in favor of Joseph Bonaparte in 1808 found Cuba, like most of the other colonies, loyal to Ferdinand and to the provisional government of the junta of Seville that led the Spanish opposition to Napoleon. The apparent liberal ascendancy in the junta aroused great hope for colonial reform and freer trade, especially after the junta promised colonial representation in the Spanish legislature. Three Cubans participated in drawing up the Spanish Constitution of 1812, which became the symbol of liberal hopes for the rest of the century. On one point at issue, slavery, they successfully opposed the abolitionist proposals of the Spanish liberals. On most other articles of political reform, the goals of the colonial representatives were identical with those of the Spanish liberals, including separation of civil and military authority in Cuba, a free press, and continued representation in the Cortes (Spanish parliament). In 1814, upon his restoration following the defeat of Napoleon, Ferdinand abrogated the constitution. Six years later the Spanish revolution of 1820 restored it and the Cubans once more were allowed to elect representatives to the Cortes, but in 1822 the French army assisted Ferdinand in freeing himself from all constitutional restrictions. Meanwhile revolution broke out in the colonies and, while Spain was caught up in internal turmoil, swept the South American continent. By 1823 only Cuba and Puerto Rico remained in the empire. Alarmed that Ferdinand, backed by the conservative coalition of the Quadruple Alliance, would attempt to reconquer the colonies, the United States with the support of Britain promulgated the Monroe Doctrine. This pronouncement assured the continued independence of the rest of Latin America, but in Spain's two remaining island possessions the liberal era was over.

During this period several small groups of intellectuals in Cuba had been actively working for independence but had received little support. One such group, taking its inspiration from Simón Bolívar, was accused of participation in a revolutionary conspiracy in 1823. Two members, José María de Heredia (1803-1839), a poet, and Father Félix Varela y Morales, known as one of the first educational reformers and Cuban representative at the Spanish Cortes in 1823, were the first of many literary and intellectual leaders of nineteenth-century Cuba to be exiled.

The colonial government gradually became more despotic after 1823, and by the middle of the century all distinctions between civil, military, and fiscal authority had been removed. The governor-general, provincial governors and intendants, lieutenant-governors of districts, and captains of *partidos* were all Spaniards, each vested with military, administrative, and some judicial authority. For the Cubans, the turning point was the harsh administration of Governor Tacón (1834-1838), who in one of his first reports wrote that "the nastiness of the streets is horrifying, and laziness, excess, and dissipation are the paramount attributes of many of the people." In 1837, during his tenure, the 1812 Constitution was again proclaimed in Spain, but the colonies were denied representation in the Cortes.

Following Tacón's administration, political lines were drawn that were to prevail throughout most of the century, and the distinction between Spaniard and *criollo* as one of political identification and loyalty was solidified. The *peninsulares* came to include not only the officials and the officers of the garrison but also Cubans who were loyal to Spain or cultivated the Spaniards for political or economic reasons. Some Cuban-born members of the *peninsulares* bore Spanish titles of nobility, often purchased, which besides social status carried privileges including special rights in the courts. The *peninsulares* had their own clubs, such as the Casino Español in Havana, and usually belonged to the Volunteers, a militia first organized in 1811. The Volunteers became increasingly the adjunct of the Spanish police and spy systems, and in time of insurrection, worked with the army.

Leadership in the reform movements came from among the *criollo* intellectuals, and during the long struggle the country produced two generations of prominent men who were at once poets, philosophers, teachers, publicists, and sometimes conspirators. Although the leadership was united in demanding political rights, more freedom of trade, freedom of education from state and clerical control, and self-government, some were loath to give up hope that liberalism would triumph in Spain. Throughout the century they remained divided into autonomists, or reformists, looking toward self-government within the empire, and separatists, or radicals, working for independence, often from exile.

Especially in the years before the Civil War in the United States, the slavery question played a major part in discussions of the Cuban future. There had been occasional slave revolts, and many advocates of reform remained loyal to the existing order because they feared a repetition of the Haitian example, where revolution had led to Negro supremacy and massacre of the whites. A few Cubans sought annexation to the United States as a means of gaining political and economic freedom while preserving slavery. Although several offers by the United States government between 1845 and 1860 to buy Cuba from Spain were rejected, private Southern interests aided annexationists. The leader of the most important of such attempts, Narciso López, landed a small force in Cuba in 1850 but received little support there. In 1851 he tried again in cooperation with a local group in Puerto Principe, but he was captured and executed.

In the period beginning in 1865 and continuing to the winning of independence in 1898, Cuban history was primarily a chronicle of political woes interspersed with rebellion. The Crown recognized the need for reform, but each step was made reluctantly and with little evidence of good faith. The first attempt at revolution, led by Carlos Manuel de Céspedes, began with the reading of a declaration of independence from Spain (known as the Grito de Yara) at Yara in Oriente province, October 10, 1868. Céspedes, a wealthy lawyer and sugar planter who had freed his own slaves, was soon joined by a force that included planters, a large number of students, Negro freemen, and recently freed slaves.

This rebellion, known as the Ten Years' War for independence, was initially successful, gaining military control of half the island.

A provisional government was organized which included Tomás Estrada Palma, later first president of the Republic, and a constitution was adopted. Spain responded by sending reinforcements and using the Volunteers as police and spies. The war was marked by atrocities on both sides, crops were burned, and the eastern part of the island devastated. As the Spaniards regained territory the war degenerated into guerrilla fighting. Cubans were by no means unanimously behind the movement, and with defeat the rebels relied increasingly on hired soldiers who proved better looters than fighters. Céspedes was killed during the fighting, and finally, both sides exhausted, the Pact of Zanjón was concluded in 1878. Spain made a number of concessions and promised widespread political reform. A general amnesty was declared, applying to exiles as well as to participants in the rebellion; Negroes who fought in the rebellion were not to be returned to slavery; and Cubans were assured representation in the Cortes and some elective institutions at home.

A few of the promised reforms were carried out: an emancipation law was enacted in 1880 ending slavery six years later; Cubans were represented in the Cortes but the franchise was so restricted that the Conservatives (the Spanish party) won nearly all of the regionally distributed seats, while the Autonomists regularly elected only members from the Sociedad Económica. The amnesty was short-lived. José Martí, later to take a leading role in the independence movement, was one of several who returned in 1878 only to be exiled again the same year after making inflammatory speeches. In 1880 a rebel leader of the Ten Years' War, Máximo Gómez, launched another abortive revolution (The Little War).

After this failure the center of political action shifted to New York where the Revolutionary Junta made contact with groups of Cubans in the major cities of the United States and coordinated efforts to collect money, arms, and recruits. Among their strongest supporters were the Key West tobacco workers. José Martí (whose life and literary career are discussed in another chapter) became the leading figure in the Junta, which by 1892 also included Tomás Estrada Palma, Benjamín Guerra, and Gonzalo de Quesada.

In Cuba in the years after 1880 conditions were even more conducive to revolt. The economy had been unstable ever since the Ten Years' War, from which the coffee and tobacco industries of the eastern end of the island had never recovered. More important was the dislocation within the sugar industry. In 1868 the sugar crop had been produced by slave labor mainly on moderate-sized Cuban-owned plantations, each with its own mill. The crop accounted for over 80 percent of total exports. In the 1870's, however, the growth of the beet sugar industry in northern Europe began to offer serious competition to Cuban producers, forcing the price down. At the same time, the devastation of the Ten Years' War, followed by the emancipation of the slaves, forced many owners to sell their land as larger-scale production became essential for economy. The number of mills in Cuba declined from nearly 1,500 in the 1860's to 400 in 1894. Shifts in Spanish and United States tariff policies caused further instability, and in 1894 the price paid producers for the first time fell below $.02 per pound.

In 1895 Martí recognized that the time was propitious to launch a final rebellion. The Junta was ready, communications and smuggling systems were organized from Florida to Cuba, and the revolutionists had the sympathy and support of many Americans. Military command for the invasion was vested in Máximo Gómez and the mulatto general Antonio Maceo, another hero from the Ten Years' War, who together with his father and ten brothers was to lose his life in the rebellion. Martí and Gómez landed in eastern Cuba in April 1895. Determined to counteract criticism that he was more willing to risk words than his life, Martí joined the fighting personally and was killed in May. But the revolution had been his creation and Martí became the greatest martyr and hero of Cuban history, the symbol of the struggle for independence.

When the war began, Cubans were still not united in the desire for independence; moreover, in 1895 Spain had finally approved a new law granting considerable home rule which the majority of the autonomists were prepared to accept. Many of their sons joined the fighting, but it was only the revolution itself that finally forced large sections of the older generation to take sides on an issue they would have preferred to avoid.

Although at all times vastly outnumbered, the revolutionaries gradually gained throughout 1896. Following the general pattern of operations used in the Ten Years' War, they started in Oriente where their support was greatest, and remained largely in the rural areas, while the Spanish forces were concentrated in the towns. During 1896 they moved west, taking no major cities but raising rebellion in every province as they burned sugar cane to destroy Spanish wealth and drive the unemployed into their ranks. The Spaniards brought in reinforcements, and, after the death of Maceo in December 1896, they began to regain ground, but government repression and the suspicion with which all *criollos* were treated led to increased support for the revolution. Finally the policies of General Weyler, sent to take command of the Spanish forces in 1896, turned the entire population against the Spaniards. Because the rebels controlled many rural areas, Weyler forced the people into *reconcentrados* (concentration camps) in and near the towns. With no means of livelihood, many thousands died of starvation and disease.

The policies of Weyler, known as The Butcher, were equally effective in drawing United States support to Cuba. Until 1898, the administrations of Cleveland and McKinley had pursued a course of nonintervention despite great pressure in Congress and from much of the press, especially the Hearst and Pulitzer papers in New York. The Revolutionary Junta kept an office in Washington and lobbied constantly to obtain United States recognition of Cuban belligerency, which would have eased the supply situation for the rebels. On the other side, pressure was exerted by Spain and by United States sugar interests, dependent on the Spanish forces for protection of their plantations, to prevent recognition.

Finally, the sinking of the United States battleship *Maine* in Havana harbor, after an explosion whose source was never discovered, led to intervention. The sensationalist press played up the situation and there was considerable agitation for action within the executive branch, led chiefly by Under Secretary of the Navy Theodore Roosevelt. On March 27, McKinley sent an ultimatum to Spain, demanding among other things an armistice, relief measures, and recognition of the United States as arbiter if agreement was not reached by October 1. Spain in effect rejected the ultimatum, and although a later message met most, but not all, United States conditions, on April 11, McKinley asked for a declaration of war. By Joint Resolution of Congress the President was authorized to use United States forces to terminate the war in Cuba. The Teller Amendment specified that after pacification the United States would "leave the government and control of the island to its people."

The Spanish-American War lasted less than four months. The armistice in August was concluded by the Treaty of Paris, effective April 11, 1899, by which the United States acquired Puerto Rico, Guam, and the Philippine Islands. The conclusion of the war left considerable confusion both in Cuba and Washington regarding United States intentions. The revolutionaries were not wholly enthusiastic, having desired recognition of belligerency rather than the sending of troops. Spain suggested annexation by the United States, and some Cubans favored the proposal. President McKinley resisted annexationist pressure from United States business interests but was not prepared to recognize the government proclaimed during the revolution. Military government, first under General John R. Brooke and then General Leonard E. Wood, was instituted and was not terminated until May 20, 1902.

As governor of Oriente province and subsequently of the entire island, General Wood showed great ability in reorganizing government and economic life. Disease and starvation were rife, the sugar mills were largely destroyed, and the population had declined by an estimated twelve percent. After distributing food and medicine and completing basic sanitation measures, Wood gave special attention to education and improved health standards. He appointed Dr. Walter Reed to direct the experiments that proved the validity of Dr. Carlos Finlay's theory of mosquito-transmission of yellow fever and incidence of the disease was nearly ended within a year.

Roads, bridges, hospitals, communications, the post office, and customs were put in order. A public school system was established and 1,500 Cubans were sent to Harvard for a summer of teacher training. Wood reorganized the judicial system, placing the judges on salary for the first time. The revolutionary army was disbanded, not without arousing some enmity, but many of the men were incorporated into a system of rural guards. What criticism Wood received was for the rapidity with which he sought to create new institutions on United States models and for his inflexible honesty.

Preparations for the creation of a Cuban government began in 1899. After consultations with Cubans, General Wood proclaimed an electoral law that gave the franchise to adult males who were literate, owned a small amount of property, or had served in the revolutionary army. The first elections for municipal officials were held in June 1900, and in September thirty-one delegates were elected to a Constituent Assembly. Out of the three political parties that were important contestants, the two representing factions of the revolutionary army won nearly all seats.

The Constituent Assembly convened in November 1900 and completed its work in February 1901. The delegates agreed to adopt a presidential system of government similar to that of the United States, with a bicameral legislature and distribution of power much as in the United States. The constitution incorporated a lengthy Bill of Rights with particular emphasis on the separation of church and state (a detailed discussion of the constitution will be found in a subsequent chapter).

The United States government had made specific stipulations concerning relations between Cuba and the United States which the Cuban delegates resisted including in the constitution, but which were eventually made the price of independence. Enacted as the Platt Amendment to the Army Appropriation Bill of 1901, they were at length accepted by the Constituent Assembly as an appendix to the Cuban constitution and were incorporated into the Permanent Treaty between the United States and Cuba in 1903. They provided the basis for later United States intervention and became a focus for nationalist reaction against the United States. The Platt Amendment stated:

I. The government of Cuba shall never enter into any treaty with any foreign power which will impair or tend to impair the independence of Cuba nor permit any foreign power to obtain lodgment in or control over any portion of the island.

II. The government shall not assume or contract any public debt for the ultimate discharge of which the ordinary revenues of the island shall be inadequate.

III. The government consents that the United States may exercise the right to intervene for the preservation of Cuban independence, the maintenance of a government adequate for the protection of life, property and individual liberty, and for discharging the obligations with respect to Cuba imposed by the Treaty of Paris on the United States, now to be assumed and undertaken by the government of Cuba.

IV. All acts of the United States in Cuba during its military occupancy are ratified and validated.

V. The government will execute and, as far as necessary, extend the plans already devised or other plans to be mutually agreed upon for the sanitation of the cities of the island.

VI. The Isle of Pines shall be omitted from the proposed constitutional boundaries of Cuba, the title thereto being left to future adjustment by treaty.

VII. To enable the United States to maintain the independence of Cuba, and to protect the people thereof, as well as for its own defense, the government of Cuba will sell or lease to the United States lands necessary for coaling or naval stations at certain specified points, to be agreed upon with the President of the United States.

Conservatives in Cuba approved of the provisions, but the delegates to the Constituent Assembly opposed them strongly. Few objected to the first or fourth provision and feeling was not especially strong on the second or fifth. Articles III, VI, and VII, however in the Cuban view were clear impairments of sovereignty.

The Isle of Pines provision apparently was included as insurance that the United States would preserve a military base in the area, and it gave rise to much controversy. United States real estate companies featured it as a tropical paradise, and within a few years Americans owned most of the island. By 1903 a treaty was signed by which the United States recognized Cuban sovereignty over the island, but since the Senate failed to ratify it, a new treaty was signed in 1904. Ratification was not achieved until 1925, but the island was administered by Cuba throughout the period.

Article VII was implemented in 1903 by a treaty in which Cuba ceded small territories at Guantánamo Bay near Santiago and at Bahía Honda west of Havana for United States naval use. In 1912, in return for an additional cession at Guantánamo, the United States relinquished the territory at Bahía Honda.

After acceptance of the constitution, including the Platt Amendment, on June 12, 1901, the country went on to choose the Congress and President. Both the Nationalist and Republican parties endorsed Tomás Estrada Palma for the presidency after Máximo Gómez refused to run. Palma had been a prominent figure in the Ten Years' War and the representative of the revolutionary government in the United States after 1895. He returned to Cuba to take office, and the Cuban flag was raised on May 20, 1902.

First Years of Independence, 1902-1930

Palma's administration, from 1902 to 1906, successfully carried on the work begun by Wood in sanitation, roads and public works, and education. He had the confidence both of the United States and of the Cubans. Immigration laws were liberalized, and this period marked the beginning of the sizable Spanish immigration that continued until the 1920's. The sugar crop reached prewar totals, and plantations, formerly concentrated in Santa Clara and Matanzas, developed rapidly in Oriente and Camagüey. The Reciprocity Treaty of 1903 provided for a 20 percent reduction in United States tariffs on all Cuban exports entering the United States. A similar reduction was made by Cuba on United States goods entering its ports. The apparent stability of Cuba and the benefits to be gained from reciprocity attracted large United States investments after 1902.

Party realignments before the 1905 election resulted in the nomination of Estrada Palma for a second term by the Moderate Party. By using laws left from the Spanish era, the Moderates took control of a number of municipalities, and neither side was free of illegal and extralegal pre-election maneuverings. After the Moderate victory, the Liberals appealed to the courts to annul the election, and failing in that, in August 1906 launched an open rebellion. Faced with the choice of civil war or making concessions to the Liberals, Estrada Palma asked for United States intervention under Article III of the Platt Amendment.

President Roosevelt sent an American mission to investigate. Secretary of War William Howard Taft and Under Secretary of State Robert Bacon concluded that the elections had been dishonest and suggested a remedy but Estrada Palma refused any compromise and resigned. The Moderates then refused to attend the meeting of Congress to choose a new government. Without a quorum, nothing could be done, and the United States intervened the next day, September 29, 1906.

Taft became provisional governor of the island but was soon succeeded by Charles E. Magoon, who drew the extreme criticism of later Cuban historians. Magoon was selected because he had gained a knowledge of Cuban law while working in the War Department and the United States government conceived the main purpose of intervention to be the enactment of laws that might prevent the recurrence of civil war. Magoon's administration drew up an organic body of law for the executive and judiciary and for local provincial and municipal government. An electoral law was provided as well as laws for a civil service and for municipal taxation and accounting. A military penal law and regulations for military procedure were also passed. Feeling that much of past difficulties had stemmed from control of office by the Moderates, Magoon appointed Liberals when offices became vacant until a balance of both parties had been secured. Cubans, therefore, have often attributed to Magoon the origin of the *botella* (bottle), the name applied to sinecures.

New elections were held for municipal and national offices in 1908. A new Conservative party, replacing the Moderate party, nominated for president General Mario García Menocal, a United

States-educated engineer who managed one of the larger sugar mills, and for vice-president Rafael Montoro, a widely respected, former autonomist. The Liberals were divided into two factions for the municipal, but collaborated in the national elections, nominating José Miguel Gómez and Alfredo Zayas. The election produced a solid Liberal majority, and on January 28, 1909 (Martí's birthday) the United States withdrew.

Leadership in political life and government henceforth became the special province of a relatively small group of men who had achieved prominence in the war of independence; many of them had been elected delegates to the 1900 Constituent Assembly. Their main political support came from those who had served with or under them; and their chief political interest lay in gaining and keeping control of the spoils of office. Their retention of power was facilitated by the social system and the events of the recent past, which made it difficult for those who had opposed independence to win political office. Other groups which did not actively pursue politics included the new immigrants from Spain and the Canary Islands, and those prerevolution Spaniards who preferred to retain Spanish citizenship.

The political aspirants were grouped into two political parties, Liberal and Conservative. The Liberals adopted a more critical attitude toward the United States than the Conservatives and their electoral platform usually called for abrogation of the Platt Amendment. The Liberals, who tended to attract the urban vote, appealed to the Negro population and emphasized their revolutionary inheritance. The Conservatives had the support of business interests and the rural population and admitted into their ranks a few prominent men who had been autonomists. Individuals at the top of each party, however, shifted their allegiance according to the relative advantages of alignment with one party or the other. A man who could deliver the vote of a province or municipality was in a strong position to barter with both sides.

Of the six national elections between 1908 and 1933, each party won three. With each change of the party in power, however, the victor had the support of the outgoing administration. President Gómez (1908-1912), a Liberal, gave his support to Mario Menocal (1912-1920), a Conservative, who in turn gave his support to Alfredo Zayas (1920-1924). Zayas, who as a Liberal had been vice-president under Gómez but was elected as a Conservative, gave his support to Gerardo Machado (1924-1933) a Liberal, whose dictatorship led to revolution. Each man was an effective organizer and used the various available techniques to gain and keep power –the distribution of patronage, especially by means of the national lottery and government jobs, cultivation of the army, well-timed amnesties and pardons, vote buying, and appeals to the United States government. Each retired from political life in considerable comfort.

Political change posed peculiar problems because of the Platt Amendment. United States business interests in Cuba sought to use it to protect their investments, and Cubans at times appeared to regard it as the final weapon in their political arsenal. When, for example, the Liberals revolted in 1917 after Menocal was elected to a second term they did so on the assumption that the United States would intervene as it had in 1906 and that new elections would then be held. United States Latin American policy had, however, gradually shifted. The United States now took the position that it should intervene to prevent loss of life and property rather than wait until the government had disintegrated—a policy that came to be known as dollar diplomacy. At times it was enough for the United States to notify the Cuban government that it regarded a situation with concern, but in a few instances Marines were landed to guard United States property. The Wilsonian policy of refusing recognition to governments established by other than constitutional means served to deter the use of violence and worked to the advantage of the government in power.

When the Liberals had recourse to arms in February 1917, the United States made clear that it opposed revolution and landed Marines at Guantánamo. Although they took no part in the fighting, their presence prevented the burning of cane, always the main weapon of antigovernment insurrectionists. The entry of the United States into World War I in April increased concern for the safety of the sugar crop, but Menocal immediately declared war on Germany and accused the rebels of pro-German proclivities. The government won a number of military victories over the rebels, and by May the rebellion had declined into occasional forays in Camagüey and Oriente.

Menocal's second term of office was an era of strong personal government and also of unprecedented prosperity. During World War I the European beet sugar industry was nearly destroyed, and demand for Cuban sugar rose accordingly. The price in the United States was fixed at $.055 per pound, of which 25 percent was profit to the producers. More land was planted to cane, and the crop increased from 1.38 million tons in 1911 to 5.1 million tons in 1925, most of the increase occurring in the war years. Total trade quadrupled, government revenues more than doubled, United States investments increased, and immigration reached new peaks. As labor remained in short supply, workers led by Spanish immigrants with syndicalist experience organized and won higher wages. The island appeared a haven of prosperity for all. Heavy indebtedness was incurred by thousands who hoped to benefit, and banking services multiplied as the demand for credit rose.

After the end of the war and the removal of price controls, sugar prices soared, reaching a peak of $.225 in May 1920. During this time, known as the Dance of the Millions, huge fortunes were made in sugar and in speculation. The great palace in Havana and luxurious clubs, casinos, and country clubs were built. Cuba became a winter tourist haven for wealthy Americans. Then it became apparent that the world was oversupplied with sugar, and in December the price fell to below $.04. By October panic began to develop in Havana. A run on the banks was stopped by the declaration of a moratorium on October 11.

When Zayas was elected president in 1920, largely as a result of a political deal with Menocal, the opposition protested and succeeded in obtaining a degree of United States intervention. The Harding administration sent General Enoch Crowder to investigate the elections. Zayas' election was validated but, because of the economic crisis, Crowder remained as financial advisor until 1923, and forced the appointment of an "honest cabinet." After his retirement to the position of ambassador, however, the Zayas administration became even more corrupt than its predecessors.

Gerardo Machado, a Liberal active in politics since 1900, won the 1924 election by promising honest government and a single term of office, but in 1927-1928 he obtained constitutional amendments lengthening the president's term to six years, abolishing the vice-presidency, and extending congressional tenures. To silence opposition he deported or caused to be assassinated a number of labor leaders, political opponents, and students critical of his regime. As a consequence he was re-elected in November 1928, without opposition, to a six-year term.

His second term coincided with the world depression. The sugar market, after fluctuating for a few years, collapsed in 1930 following the enactment of a higher United States tariff. Machado's efforts to spur economic revival included a program of agricultural diversification, and a public works program requiring large new loans from United States banks. Convinced that sugar production must be regulated to prevent wild fluctuations, the government joined in the Chadbourne Plan for world-wide control but the plan failed in its main purpose of restoring the price to a profitable level, while decreased production in Cuba led to further unemployment and a decline in commercial activity.

Revolution and Reaction, 1930-1935

The difficulties of the economic situation together with the dictatorial methods of the President gave rise to political dissatisfaction and unrest to which the government responded with further suppressive and terroristic measures. In 1930, Machado declared martial law, which remained in effect most of the time until he was forced out in 1933. The University of Havana became a center of opposition, and was permanently closed in 1930, along with all high schools and normal schools. Machado's strong-arm men, the *porristas*, murdered hundreds of suspects. The underground ABC revolutionary group, composed mainly of students and professional men organized in cells for terrorist activity, led the opposition. Reprisal begot reprisal, the exile community swelled, and by 1933 the island was near civil war.

The election of Franklin Delano Roosevelt brought a change in United States policy that aided the rebels. Sumner Welles was appointed ambassador and arrived in May 1933 with instructions to attempt mediation. Cubans hoped that intervention would ensue, and revolutionary activities were stepped up, guerrilla warfare in some rural areas was added to widespread urban terrorism. In August a strike among bus workers spread until it became a general strike. On August 11 the army commanders withdrew their support from Machado, "to save Cuba from foreign interference . . . ," and Machado fled the country. Carlos Manuel de Céspedes, son of the hero of the Ten Years' War, was named president and selected a Cabinet including four prominent members of the ABC.

With the 1933 revolution a new generation of political leaders emerged who were to remain prominent in public life until 1958. The new political aspirants, among whom the dominant group were usually termed leftwing nationalists, were concerned with economic and social problems, and convinced that the government must take the initiative in raising the economic, social, and cultural levels of life. Their nationalistic and economic orientation led them to make the United States the chief target of their resentment over island conditions. Foreign business interests were attacked as both non-Cuban, therefore threats to nationalism, and as exploitative, therefore threats to progress. The difficult economic conditions prevailing during the depression also fostered resentment against free immigration policies, especially against the many thousands of Spaniards who resisted assimilation, controlled retail trade, and associated primarily with other Spaniards in regional associations. Labor, first organized during the 1920's under anarcho-syndicalist leadership, had also developed into an organized force in which socialists and Communists competed for leadership.

The revolution neither brought to power a united group nor removed all of the older political leaders. A few leaders prominent before 1933 immediately re-entered political life while many others retired only temporarily. The ABC, dominant in the first postrevolution government of Céspedes, included men of many political leanings and never was successfully transformed into a cohesive political organization. A radical group of students and professors, centered around the leadership of Ramón Grau San Martín, a physician and professor at Havana University, formed the Directorio Estudiantil (Student Directorate). A similar group of young men gathered around Antonio Guiteras, leader of the Young Cuba Party. The Communists, unable to ally with any of the more powerful parties, concentrated on the labor organizations, where they met sharp opposition from socialist organizers, who tended to favor Grau San Martín. Céspedes vacillated among the many political groups, referred often to Ambassador Sumner Welles, and quickly obtained a reputation for indecisiveness. Rumors flew that a Menocal *coup d'état* was imminent. The policy of the United States government, though clearly supporting Céspedes, remained a major question in relation to the possible alternatives.

In the prevailing circumstances of intrigue and near-chaos, a group of army sergeants under the leadership of Fulgencio Batista Zaldívar were the first to take decisive action. Whether Batista actually organized the move or whether, as some claimed, the sergeants made him their spokesman because he was a "persuasive talker," he quickly became the most powerful figure in Cuba. Born of poor parents in Oriente province in 1901, he received some education in a local school, and, after working at odd jobs for a time, joined the army in 1921. He learned typing and shorthand and read law, and in 1928 was promoted to sergeant-stenographer and assigned as a court reporter. Sometime after the unsuccessful 1931 revolt he joined the ABC, to which, as a reporter at political trials, he supplied useful information.

At Camp Columbia, where noncommissioned officers had complete charge of the troops, Batista and others agreed to oust the senior officers, many of whom had served under Machado. In the early morning of September 4, the sergeants took over Camp Columbia and appointed sergeants to command army units throughout the country. A five-man commission, headed by Ramón Grau San Martín, was appointed to form a government.

The main lines of the new government's program were nationalistic and reformist. It immediately enacted progressive labor legislation, including provisions for an eight-hour day and a minimum wage; issued statements promising social justice and equality for the Negro population; and declared its independence from the United States Embassy, at the same time vehemently criticizing the United States government for not recognizing it. The United States refrained from recognition because of the government's radicalism and inability to restore order.

The growing unrest and lack of support from both the Right and the extreme Left strengthened Batista's hand. Now a colonel and head of an army officered largely by former sergeants, he alone appeared capable of restoring order. After a period of conflict with the Student Directorate, Batista managed, on January 15, 1934, to force Grau San Martín to resign. After a two-day tenure by Carlos Hevia, Colonel Carlos Mendieta, Batista's original choice for the job, was made provisional president. One of the few politicians who had consistently opposed Machado, Mendieta headed the Nacionalista party and was regarded as honest and conservative. The United States recognized the new government on January 24.

The Batista Era

Civilian groups who had supported the revolution were opposed to Batista's growing power and after the advent of the Mendieta government they became increasingly desperate. The ABC withdrew from the government in the summer of 1934 and Mendieta, left with the support of only conservative groups, became more and more dependent on Batista. Radical opposition took many forms, and constitutional guarantees were suspended during most of the period. Conflicts within the Cabinet over civilian versus military control led to several resignations.

During February and March 1935 the opposition was able to call a general strike, the major leadership coming from Antonio Guiteras and his Young Cuba followers and from Grau San Martín's party. The Communists joined early in March; and on March 10 President Mendieta suspended all constitutional law and the struggle became a direct one between the army and the radicals. Guiteras was killed in May and gradually the strength of the opposition was broken. The army was used to break strikes, thousands of suspected terrorists were jailed, and a semblance of order was restored.

Much of the history of Cuba between 1934 and December 31, 1958 revolved around the figure of Batista. As army chief of staff from 1934 to 1940, he was stronger than the president; from 1940 to 1944 he was president. After a lapse of eight years, he returned to power in 1952 in a *coup d'état* and remained in power, using increasingly despotic methods, until overthrown by Fidel Castro. The problems of Cuban economic and social life that the Castro revolution hoped to solve had not changed from those faced by the Grau government in 1933. Batista, after some early efforts, had ended by using them to perpetuate his power.

Batista shared and, to some extent, used the growing sense of nationalism in Cuba. Like many other Cubans, he resented United States interference under the Platt Amendment, and one of his first popular successes was the Mendieta government's negotiation of the end of the Platt Amendment on May 29, 1934. Good relations were further enhanced by the signing of a new Reciprocity Treaty in August making possible tariff reductions. Problems stemming from the complex economic relationships between Cuba and the United States were more difficult to solve. Although many Americans sold their land in Cuba during the depression years, the dependence on the United States market continued, and Cubans tended to blame the problems of the industry on the United States. Large United States private investments in Cuban mining, public utilities, and banking were similarly resented because profits were remitted to the United States.

Almost half of the national income was derived from sugar exports, and the total dependence of the economy on the fluctuations of an industry in trouble throughout the world posed problems which no government was able to solve. Other outstanding problems concerned land tenure, the tax structure and administration, and the government's failure to achieve a reputation for honesty. Neither the tax system nor any other function of government could be administered honestly as long as government employment was viewed as a gigantic spoils system.

The elections, promised for the end of 1935 were held on January 10, 1936, and for the first time women voted. Because most of the radical leaders were in jail or exile, the contest was among former President Menocal, former President Carlos Manuel Céspedes, and Miguel Mariano Gómez, son of the earlier president and himself a very popular political leader who had served capably as mayor of Havana despite open opposition to Machado. Gómez and Laredo Brú were elected president and vice-president, with the support of Gómez' Republican party, the Nationalists, and the Liberals. They took office in May 1936.

Gómez announced a program of general social and economic reform, re-establishment of civil rights, and a reduction in government expenditures; some 1,500 political prisoners were amnestied, and exiles began to return. Gómez, however, quickly came into conflict with Batista, who had firmly consolidated his army support and had had considerable influence in the nomination of congressional candidates. His favorite project was the development of rural schools taught by members of the rural guard stationed throughout the island. Gómez, as part of his attempt to restore civilian supremacy, vetoed a bill levying a special sugar tax to support Batista's rural school program. As a result he was impeached. Vice-President Laredo Brú took office in December 1936, and Batista's power was secure.

By the late 1930's, Batista was the most powerful man in Cuba despite his lack of official position outside the army. His rural education program, organization of mobile health units for rural areas, and patronage of labor brought him some popularity. He had restored order in the country and therefore had the support of the business community. Although basic economic problems remained, sugar production was regulated and some diversification encouraged. There was at the same time a decline in petty graft.

Batista wanted, however, to legitimize his position, and in April 1938 announced his intention of convening a Constitutional Assembly before the 1940 elections. In July 1940 the first elections under the new constitution were held with Batista as the candidate of a Democratic-Socialist coalition made up of his own Democratic party, the Liberal party, and the Communist party (legal since September 1938). The Cuban Revolutionary party (formed of Grau San Martín's supporters), the ABC, and the Republican party, all nominated Grau San Martín. The election was considered relatively honest, and Batista won with a large majority.

The new constitution was scarcely functioning when Cuba entered World War II, and emergency legislation conferring war powers on Batista enabled him to institute political and economic controls. Although Cuba did not send troops into action, the government cooperated in intelligence operations against German espionage and granted several bases to the United States for patrolling the Caribbean. Internally the government cracked down on Falangist organizations, which had some support among the Spanish population and had actively espoused the Fascist cause.

Despite material shortages early in the war and serious injury to the tobacco trade because of the loss of the European market, the economy benefited as always from the wartime expansion of the sugar industry. Batista, as required by the constitution of 1940, did not seek re-election in 1944. He backed Carlos Saladrigas against Grau San Martín, the opposition candidate. Somewhat to the surprise of everyone, since Batista had been expected to control the election, Grau won the presidency by a large majority.

The administrations of Grau San Martín and of his successor Prío Socarrás formed a critical period of expectation and disillusionment. Grau's victory had to a large extent put the "outs" into the government, and the tremendous patronage powers at his disposal were fully exploited. Labor unrest arising from wage demands was intensified by struggles for union control between Communist and non-Communist leadership. Much of the progress made by Grau in the areas of health, education, and housing was obscured by an increase in graft and a decline in public order. Grau himself was later charged with misappropriation of government funds, but the charges were eventually dropped. In the 1948 elections Prío Socarrás, Minister of Labor in the Grau Cabinet and his chosen successor, ran successfully on a platform combining promises for reform and progress and opposition to Communism. His administration differed from that of Grau San Martín's primarily in the greater effort made toward essential economic and some political reforms, but there was no improvement in public order, prevalence of graft, or use of government patronage.

As the 1952 elections approached, the major issue was political reform. The 1940 constitution had been in effect for twelve years; gradually many of the institutions which it had been hoped would enforce governmental responsibility had been created, some progress had been made in planning more rational economic policies, and the island was benefiting from the prosperity induced by the Korean war. The government had pursued pro-labor policies and had strong labor support. The government's main point of vulnerability was corruption. The candidates for the presidency were Carlos Hevia, of Prío Socarrás' party, Roberto Agramonte, of a new reformist party (Ortodoxo) that had split from Prío's, and Batista. Agramonte was expected to win.

On March 10, 1952 Batista, convinced that he had no chance to win the election, returned to power in a quiet, bloodless *coup d'état* that depended entirely on army support, the element of surprise, and Batista's ability to cement his success by rapid political manipulation. Although university students declared a strike, and several political leaders issued critical statements and appealed to the courts to denounce the action, there was no effective opposition. Batista promptly dismissed the Congress and dissolved all political parties; depending upon the army and organized labor, he ruled as virtual dictator until elections were held in 1954.

The major achievement of Batista's second period of rule was the creation of the Sugar Stabilization Fund to prevent economic collapse after the end of the Korean war. The 1950's were relatively prosperous, although the standard of living of most of the population remained low. Batista sponsored some needed public works, including the construction of a good water system for Havana, the promise of generations of political leaders.

The first revolt against Batista, a year after he took power, was led by Fidel Castro, then a twenty-seven-year-old lawyer. In 1952 he had been a congressional candidate of the Ortodoxo party, and after Batista's *coup* Castro presented a long brief to the Supreme Court protesting its unconstitutionality. On July 26, 1953 with only a hundred and sixty-five supporters, he directed a suicidal attack on the Moncada army post at Santiago de Cuba. Many of the attackers were killed, but most, including Castro, finally surrendered.

Batista increased his restrictions on the press and the suppression of civil liberties, but, in 1954, attempted to legalize his position by holding elections. Grau San Martín was again the opposition candidate but several parties refused to participate, and, convinced that Batista's control would prevent a fair vote, Grau withdrew before the elections. Batista took office as an elected president in February 1955. In spite of sporadic violence, Batista felt secure enough to declare a large amnesty later in 1955 in which hundreds of his enemies were released from prison, including Castro, while others, including Prío Socarrás, returned from exile.

Although Batista believed he could keep power by becoming the elected president, he was prepared, when the growing opposition refused to accept his election as a legitimate mandate, to retain it by force. The last three years of Batista's regime were in large part a repetition of the last years of Machado. Opposition centered among the students and intellectuals, and in 1956 there were sporadic bombings. Castro in the year since his release from prison had organized a small force in Mexico, and in December 1956 he landed with his followers on the coast of Oriente. They had expected immediate mass support but were joined only by students from Santiago and were forced to withdraw into the Sierra Maestra where government troops hunted them unsuccessfully. Until February 1957, when Herbert Matthews of the *New York Times* published a long interview with Castro in the mountains, most Cubans believed government reports that Castro was dead and the rebellion quelled.

The rebels called themselves the Twenty-sixth of July Movement (after the abortive attempt on the Moncada fortress). Like the rebels of 1895, they conducted raids on police and military expeditions, attacked isolated army patrols, and burned sugar cane. Like the students in 1933, they also conducted urban terrorism. Batista suppressed all opposition ruthlessly and his increasing use of terror and violence did more than any action of Castro to draw support to the revolutionary movement. His downfall, however, occurred much as had Machado's, when the most important institutions on which the government relied withdrew their support. On January 1, 1959, Batista and his Cabinet fled the country. Castro and his army reached Havana on January 8.

ETHNIC INFLUENCES
AND SOCIAL PATTERNS

ACCORDING TO THE 1953 CENSUS, Cuba had a population of 5,829,029 and a population density of about one hundred thirty-two persons per square mile. The population was estimated at 6,744,000 in January 1960. In Latin America, only Haiti, El Salvador, and the Dominican Republic have higher average densities.

The rate of growth has declined since 1907 although the population continues to increase and the birth rate has risen since World War II (see Table 1). The average age of the population has been gradually increasing since 1899 largely because of improved sanitary conditions, particularly the eradication of yellow fever at the beginning of the century. Cuba is one of the few countries in the world with more men than women, the 1953 census showing 51.2 percent men as against 48.8 percent women. Ethnic origins are varied; the 1953 census classified 72.8 percent of the total population as white, 12.4 percent black, 0.3 percent yellow, and 14.5 percent mestizo. Intermarriage among various groups has always been common and the census classification, based upon the subjective impressions of the census takers, does not adequately show the mixture that has occurred. Other estimates, for example, indicate 30 percent white, 20 percent mestizo, 49 percent Negroid, and 1 percent oriental.

In Cuba, the term "mestizo" indicates someone of mixed parentage. The most common mixture is Negro-Spanish, but the term also refers to Negro-Chinese and white-Chinese mixtures. This usage differs from that in many Central American and Andean countries with large Indian populations, where the term "mestizo" is used to denote physical and cultural traits resulting from Indian-Spanish mixture. The lack of a significant Indian population and heritage has not, however, deterred the Castro government from presenting itself as the leader of "Indian America."

Whites outnumbered Negroes 6 to 1 in the island as a whole in the 1953 census, but their relative strength was weaker in urban districts (5 to 1) than in rural (7 to 1). In some provinces and districts, the relative proportions of whites and Negroes also differed considerably from the national average (see Table 2). In La Habana province where there were 11 city dwellers to every rural resident, whites outnumbered Negroes by 24 to 1 in rural areas. In Las Villas province (primarily a tobacco-growing region), whites outnumbered Negroes 9 to 1, but in Oriente province (primarily a sugar-growing area) their preponderance was only 4 to 1. In Oriente the mestizo population, elsewhere considerably less than the Negro, was twice as large; in two districts (Alto Songo, Cobre) Negroes slightly outnumbered whites.

Most of the white population is of Spanish extraction. The word *criollo* denotes someone who identifies himself with Cuba in nationality and outlook. It may refer to persons who appear Negroid, Chinese, or predominantly white. Although a *criollo* is simply any-one born in Cuba, the term has had complex cultural and political significance since colonial days, indicating a sharp division between those who by birth and the primary focus of their interests consider themselves Cubans and those, born either in Cuba or in Spain, who consider themselves Spaniards. During the colonial period native Cubans were excluded from important governmental posts and were in addition discriminated against in the awarding of commercial privileges. Occasionally, *criollo* is used to refer to the white Cuban leadership that has provided the ideology for *criollo* nationalist movements but which has always appealed, from necessity, for the support of colored Cubans against the dominant foreign-oriented group (originally Spanish, then Spanish and American) which was characteristically and self-consciously white. In 1960 Fidel Castro asserted that all true Cubans were mestizos, in spirit if not in fact.

Cuba has always had a large number of persons born abroad, many of whom retain foreign citizenship. In 1953, seventy-three different nationalities were represented. The internal composition of the population has thus been closely bound up with problems of foreign relations. In 1953, 230,431 persons, or 4 percent of the population, were born abroad. Of 149,327 who retained their foreign citizenship, 94,000 were Europeans, 32,000 were from other parts of Latin America, 13,000 from Asia, 3,000 from the Middle East, and 7,000 from Canada and the United States. The bulk of the foreign-born, whether immigrants or transients, were concentrated in La Habana province. With the exception of the English-speaking group, the older Spanish families, the Jews, and to a lesser extent the Chinese, most of the immigrant groups have shown little desire to maintain a separate identity. Ethnic issues have been largely obscured by political divisions between *criollos* and Spaniards, English-speaking North Americans, or other foreigners.

Since the conquest, there has been a constant traffic of Spanish emigrants to and from Cuba. In the seventeenth and eighteenth centuries, many came from Andalusia as government agents and military personnel. In the nineteenth century, large numbers of Asturians, Galicians, Catalans, Basques, and Canary Islanders arrived, most of whom engaged in agricultural and small-scale commercial activities. Regional differences among these immigrants persisted and were expressed in the regional designations of the mutual benefit societies they founded. During economic depressions, substantial numbers returned to Spain, and workers were sometimes transported across the Atlantic and back solely for the Cuban sugar harvest. Upper-class children were often sent to Spain for their education.

A new type of Spanish immigrant, refugees from the Spanish Civil War, began arriving in the late 1930's. They included a high proportion of men with urban backgrounds, industrial-technical training, and radical political inclination. Some of this group were later useful to the Castro regime as political organizers and operators of the nationalized industries.

Under the constitution of 1901, Cuban-born children of foreign parents were automatically foreign citizens but could register as Cubans on their twenty-first birthday. Since 1934, such children have been considered Cuban but have been able to opt for registration as foreigners. The retention of choice in the 1934 law has permitted some Spanish families to maintain their sense of separate, non-Cuban identity. In the everyday lives of long-time residents of the island, distinctions are made such as, "I am a Cuban but my husband is Spanish."

As they achieve financial security and move up the social ladder, many Spanish families merge with the *criollo* upper class. Others

2. Ethnic Influences and Social Patterns

maintain social and economic interests in Spain. Elements of Spanish culture, of which the language is the most obvious example, permeate the whole of Cuban society, but it is in their social and economic interests that the Spanish group emerge most distinctly. Not all members of the Spanish group, however, have had dominant economic positions. The 1934 law requiring employers to maintain 50 percent native Cubans in their work force confined many poorly educated Spaniards to such jobs as small traders, taxicab drivers, waiters, and domestic servants. Lower-class immigrants of this type were collectively known as Gallegos (literally, natives of Galicia) and were stereotyped as closefisted, stolid, and ambitious.

According to the 1953 census, 12.4 percent of the population were Negro and 14.5 percent of mixed race, but these figures grossly underemphasize the extent of Negro physical and cultural influence. There has never been any legal prohibition against interracial marriage, nor have there been legal supports for racial segregation. The first Negroes arrived as slaves in the early sixteenth century. By 1817 Negroes slightly outnumbered whites and Havana had become an important international slave market. The slave trade was officially abolished in 1820 in a treaty between Great Britain and Spain but an estimated 200,000 Negroes were brought in illegally during the next fifty years.

The Negroes came from all parts of West Africa—from Senegal, the Congo, the coastal areas, inland—but those who retain their ancestral customs think of their homeland as a semimythical land called Guiné and there is no general identification with Africa. It is impossible to ascertain the tribal origins of most of the groups because the old slave records list no tribal names, only ports of embarkation. But the largest and most influential Negro group in Cuba, as in Trinidad and Brazil, are undoubtedly the Yoruba, originally from southwestern Nigeria. The Yoruba, called Lucumí in Cuba, are distributed throughout the island. Striking similarities exist between the Lucumí and the modern Yoruba in Nigeria in such matters as posture, gestures, the hairstyles of women, and agricultural practices. Some typical Cuban dishes are of Yoruba origin.

The second largest group of Negroes, concentrated in La Habana province and in the cities of Matanzas and Cardenás (Matanzas province), are known as Carabalíes, from the port of Calabar in southeastern Nigeria, and come from various tribes, such as the Efik (known as Efi in Cuba) and the Ibibio (called Bibios).

Other Negro groups represented are Dahomeyans, Congolese, Haitians, and Jamaicans. The Dahomeyans (called Araràs) are more numerous in Matanzas than in La Habana province. The groups known as Congos or Bantus, who include some of Cameroun and Angola origin as well as Congolese, are largest in the east, particularly in the cities of Santiago de Cuba and Guantánamo. Haitians and Jamaicans have been imported in the past to work the sugar harvest, and some have settled permanently in Cuba, preserving many elements of their own culture, but no information is available on the size of any of these groups, their exact distribution, or the extent to which they consciously maintain separate identity.

It is commonly stated by Cubans that Cuba has no racial problem; nationalists assert that white Cubans, remembering the achievements in the struggle with Spain of such Negro heroes as Antonio Maceo, regard all Negroes as brothers. Discriminatory hiring practices and exclusion of Negroes from upper-class hotels, resorts, and clubs and from public parks have been blamed on American and Spanish financial interests in alliance with Cuban dictators. Opponents of Castro maintain that he invented the racial issue. It is, however, an old problem which has always become more serious in times of political crisis—e.g., at the end of the nineteenth century, when anti-Negro feeling among supporters of independence was one of Martí's greatest difficulties (and even in that era was blamed on the American example). Many wry Negro proverbs commenting on the relations between Negroes and whites refer unmistakably to home-grown attitudes of long standing: "The black fought the war, the white enjoys the peace"; "If you see a black and a white together, either the white man needs the black, or else the black has won a lottery."

Before 1959, Negroes were excluded from most of the better hotels, beaches, and places of entertainment patronized by Americans and upper-class Cubans. This segregation was primarily economic but became explicitly social in many ordinary resorts, such as the public squares and parks where Cubans congregate in the evenings. It was alleged that systematic discrimination was practiced in the government service, the diplomatic service, the legal profession, and many private undertakings. Most of the social clubs were exclusively white, but there were also a few that were exclusively for Negroes. Segregation was generally less marked in Oriente province, more marked in Camagüey. Racial antagonism between Negroes and mulattos is often sharp, for according to the proverb, "One Negro may harm another, but a mulatto will do worse." In some districts mulatto societies excluded persons considered too dark and did not allow members to enter occupations regarded as degrading. The size and variety of the mestizo population and the number of whites in the lowest social groups helped to forestall the development of a corporate Negro consciousness. Among better-educated and more prosperous Negroes, however, racial discrimination has long been an important concern.

Indians were long thought to have disappeared from Cuba, but a few families strongly Indian in appearance and culture were discovered by Núñez Jiménez (since 1959 a major figure in the Castro regime) during expeditions into remote regions of Oriente province. Although they speak Spanish (mixed with a large Indian vocabulary) and dress like other Cuban peasants, these Indians have been relatively untouched by the modern civilization of Cuba and in several recent instances openly resisted the incursions of strangers into their territory.

When Columbus landed in Cuba, the sparse Indian population (perhaps 200,000) consisted of several different peoples, the oldest of which were the cave-dwelling Ciboney Indians. The Ciboney had occupied the whole island before the arrival of successive waves of Taíno-speaking Arawak Indians from Haiti. By 1492 the Ciboney were restricted to the modern province of Pinar del Río and to several offshore islands, and some had been enslaved by the Taíno, who had a more advanced technology. The Ciboney were hunters and fishermen using stone implements, but the Taíno practiced agriculture and lived in the thatched house (*bohío*) which is still a prominent feature of Cuban rural life. In the extreme east of Cuba the most recent Taíno immigrants remained in contact with their Haitian homeland, from which they drew reinforcements for fighting the Spaniards. Carib Indians, fierce fighters and cannibals, originally resident in the Lesser Antilles, were invading the Greater Antilles at the time of Columbus' arrival. They probably raided Cuba but did not settle there.

In 1550, after several decades of the brutal *repartimiento* system, the Indians were officially declared free. Many of them lived in towns and reservations of their own (generally associated with Spanish settlements) adopting Spanish culture to a large extent and developing in time a certain prosperity. The process of assimilation was speeded by the scarcity of Spanish women, which resulted in many mixed marriages. Thereafter the Indian population slowly lost its identity and merged with the predominantly white *criollo* agricultural class. The Indian element was reinforced during the nineteenth century by the importation of some thousands of laborers from Yucatan though most subsequently proved unable to survive the conditions of their employment.

Recently it has become fashionable among nationalists to point to various Indian chiefs as the first heroes of the centuries-old struggle against foreign domination and to try to identify indigenous Indian traits in modern Cuban culture. The best-known Indian resistance hero is Hatuey, a name better known as that of a popular beer. Indian culture survives in place names, plant names, and in the rural *bohío*.

Chinese are found throughout Cuba, but only in Havana do they form an important distinct community. Coming to Cuba in the second half of the nineteenth century as indentured laborers, they steadily advanced to a position of prosperity and considerable commercial influence. In 1960 the Chinese community was estimated to number 35,000 people, of whom 12,000 resided in Havana. Because of the small number of Chinese women in the island, mixed Chinese-white and Chinese-Negro marriages have been common, with a steady decrease in the proportion of pure Chinese. Marriage to a white, preferably a Spaniard, has carried high prestige in the Chinese community, constituting successful social climbing. Chinese-Negro unions occur largely in the lower class.

The many Chinese political clubs were devoted to the worldwide concerns of Chinese rather than to Cuban affairs; in 1959 the Chinese Nationalist Party (Kuomintang) maintained an extensive organization with centers in the principal cities. The national federation of Chinese associations, the Centro Chino, had its headquarters in the Chinese (Taiwan) consulate. But as part of their struggle to succeed in an alien environment and to be accepted as Cubans, Chinese leaders have stressed the part played by Chinese heroes in the War of Independence (a monument in Havana memorializes their devotion) and the existence of a common tradition has been upheld in the assertion that Sun Yat Sen is "the Martí of China."

During 1960, Communist influence among the Cuban Chinese became increasingly noticeable. Opening a China-Cuba People's Friendship Week, Peking representatives placed wreaths at the monument and redefined the common tradition: "Now the real China is linked with the real Cuba." Questionnaires regarding family connections with China were circulated. The government assured the Chinese colony that the revolution had ended forever whatever racial discrimination might have existed under the previous regime, but a number of Chinese, particularly those with substantial investments, were reported to be trying to leave the country.

The Jewish population of Havana numbers between 7,000 and 8,000; some 3,000 more Jews are distributed throughout the island, principally in Las Villas, Camagüey, and Oriente provinces. The Jewish community in Havana forms a distinct group, with a life and culture of its own, and little marriage with other Cubans. But despite its small size, no single representative organization has been created, and major rifts, arising principally from the heterogeneous origin of Cuban Jews, continue to divide it.

It was estimated in the 1950's that about 75 percent of the working Jewish population were engaged in small-scale retail trade, 15 percent owned larger stores, and 10 percent were engaged in the production of consumer goods. There were many Jewish commercial and professional associations and a Jewish Chamber of Commerce. Jews also had long been active in the island's principal labor unions. Jews encountered no special difficulties arising from the Castro revolution. The few Jewish labor leaders who were prominent Castro supporters were not closely associated with the Jewish community.

The members of the large English-speaking colony in Havana, which was predominantly American but included British and Canadians, were sometimes referred to as the "ABC's." Most were executives of foreign companies, and others were permanent residents with property in Cuba. Close social contacts of the ABC's with Cubans were largely limited to the upper class, which itself affected American ways. The names "yacht club" and "country club" were always left in their English form, and the newest and most fashionable residential suburb of Havana was known simply as El Country, from the typical social institution of those who lived there. Since 1959 this district has been renamed Cubanacán and most of the ABC's have left.

Between 1900 and 1925, when it was widely believed in the United States that the Isle of Pines would become United States territory, Americans settled there in some numbers and bought up most of the island. It has remained noticeably North American in character, although many Americans returned home when their expectations were not fulfilled. There is in addition in the southern part of the island a colony of Lutheran, English-speaking farmers who came from the Cayman Islands south of Cuba. They live like *guajiros* and consider themselves Cubans. In 1960 an educational mission was sent from Havana to teach them Spanish.

Traces of other nationalities can be found. During the period of the Haitian revolt (1789-1804), many French families fled to Cuba, settling mainly in the east. Most were coffee-planters, who for a time during the nineteenth century formed a distinct community operating plantations somewhat different in type from those of the rest of Cuba. French names survive in parts of Oriente and in Cárdenas. The Spanish element has always included a number of Irish Catholics, Spaniards by adoption. Some Spanish colonial officials were Irish and several of Havana's thoroughfares—for example, O'Reilly and O'Farrill—still carry their names. Syrians and Lebanese, known inclusively as "Turks," are found in some numbers, but they do not form a distinct group. Most of them are Maronite and Orthodox Christians. Mexicans are found particularly in the Regla district of Havana, and there is a small Japanese colony on the Isle of Pines.

Language

Spanish is the national language, spoken by everybody except a few recent immigrants. As written by educated Cubans it is identical with standard Spanish everywhere but the spoken tongue is full of highly idiomatic and elliptical expressions and has a distinctive accent similar to that heard throughout the Caribbean region and sometimes reminiscent of Andalusia, the Spanish province from which many of the early immigrants came. African influence is considered to be responsible for some of the special characteristics of Cuban Spanish. Several African languages introduced by slaves are used principally in the rituals of religious cults, from which many expressions have passed into general usage.

Taíno, the language of the original Indian inhabitants of Cuba, is no longer spoken in Cuba, but many words and names survive. It is a branch of the Arawak language group still spoken elsewhere in the Antilles and in northern South America.

The proximity of the United States and the constant pressure of

2. *Ethnic Influences and Social Patterns*

its culture on Cuba have introduced a multitude of English words into everyday speech. One class of words includes those accepted as good usage—though perhaps not by purists—because there is no exact Spanish equivalent or because the English expression has gained international currency. Most words of this class refer to international affairs, politics, and economics. Castro, for example, is referred to as *líder* (leader), a word widely used in preference to such a word as *caudillo,* which suggests primarily a military dictator.

Another class of words, referring mostly to athletics and popularized by sports writers, is not accepted as good usage because Spanish equivalents exist or because in many cases the construction and transliteration are bizarre. *Beisbol* itself is accepted by the Spanish Academy but *balconesto* is preferred to the usual *basquetbol.* The increasing use of English expressions has been opposed, without effect, both by upholders of the purity of standard Spanish and by nationalists who resent the Americanization of Cuba. Many of the American-owned enterprises nationalized in 1960 were given names considered more meaningful to the people. English is usually the first foreign language learned. Since the turn of the century many upper-class Cubans have studied in the United States; others use it extensively in business or in tourist services.

Of the many African languages introduced by slaves, only three—Yoruba, Fon, and Efik—are of any importance today. Occasional words and phrases of other African languages, including Ijaw, Ibo, and even Arabic, are found embedded in the liturgies of the numerous religious cults. Yoruba and Efik are Nigerian languages; Fon, a language of Dahomey. All three belong to the widespread Niger-Congo language family of West and Central Africa.

In all these languages, as in Chinese, words are distinguished from each other partly by raising or lowering syllables to a different musical pitch. This feature has been partly abandoned in Cuba, but the languages are still intelligible to African speakers. Unwritten and lacking standard forms, these languages depend primarily on their religious use for survival. The fact that pronunciation and usage vary from region to region has led many Cuban writers to assume that they ceased long ago to exist in coherent form.

Command of language, especially of spoken language, is the mark not only of the educated man but of the able man of affairs, above all the politician. Training in rhetorical skills is an important part of education at all levels. In ordinary life, speaking ability is an essential part of the public bearing of every successful man and most women. Declamation is more persuasive than statement, and some distrust is felt for taciturn individuals and those who express themselves simply, without repetition or flourish. Poetry is frequently quoted by people in all walks of life, and many of Cuba's best known political heroes have been noted poets.

Social Structure

The social order before 1959 was based on a division of society into upper and lower classes, distinguished by the privileged access of the upper class to political authority and capital resources. The terms "upper class" and "lower class" were not used; instead Cubans generally distinguished social groups according to cultural and functional characteristics. Of special importance was the distinction made between those who performed menial tasks and those who hired others to do them.

In early colonial times there was a clear distinction between those who were slave and property owners and those who were not; later, the structure of the economy changed, but left the control of economic resources, principally land, in the hands of a relatively small group. Socially, class differences were expressed in forms largely derived from Spanish tradition, which emphasized the superiority of the educated over the uneducated, and by certain kinds of ostentatious refinement. Responsible people (*los hombres responsables* or *los dirigentes*) and people of culture were phrases equivalent to upper class. References were made to the "conservative classes," contrasting them with the "popular classes" (*las clases más humildes* or *populares*).

On the basis of economic criteria, three classes could be distinguished in the years before Castro: a lower class, consisting mainly of unskilled, uneducated wageworkers, city and country; a middle class, almost entirely urban, consisting of skilled workers and self-employed and salaried persons with some education, small proprietors, and landowners; and an upper class made up of those in the upper ranks of government service or in the professions and owners of large estates, mills, and businesses. In terms of social identification, however, the only important division was between the upper and lower classes, commonly referred to as the "rich" and the "poor." The upper class included those who employed labor and did not themselves work with their hands. Their wives and daughters were provided with domestic help, or at least would not themselves go into domestic service. Similarly, an office worker considered his social status to be higher than that of an industrial worker and would feel obliged to hire a servant, although the industrial worker, who might be making more money, would not. The rich recognized an obligation, social as much as religious, to make charitable gifts to the poor; such giving was done publicly, emphasizing the difference in status between donor and recipient. Family pride and tradition also played a part; those whose parents were of the upper class might continue to regard themselves as belonging to the same group although their material fortunes had declined.

The middle class lacked both a substantial foundation in moderate-scale capital investment and a set of ideals and traditions differentiating it from other classes. When delineated by economic criteria, the middle class was small; in terms of self-identification, it scarcely existed.

But in every historical period since the late eighteenth century, there has been a middle sector definable in political terms, consisting of a sharply divided aggregate of self-seeking factions, drawn from a wide range of occupations and income groups, including notably the better educated and more prosperous elements of the lower class and the younger generation of the upper class. The middle sector, recognizing only goals denied to them by the upper class, was perennially the seedbed of revolutionary movements intended not to overthrow the social order but to accelerate their admission to secure membership in the upper class.

The principal scene of social conflict was the urban areas. These included not only the cities but the plants which processed the products of the rural economy, which were in effect urban concentrations in a rural environment. Chief of these in the nineteenth century were the cigar factories; in the twentieth century the sugar *centrales* replaced them in importance.

The strikingly high level of urbanization (57 percent) was given still greater significance by the predominance of the capital as the center of administrative, political, and economc power. From the beginning of the nineteenth century Havana, more than any other part of the island, was the seat of the upper class and the area in which the struggle of the lower class for upward mobility was sharpest. In rural areas the population belonged almost entirely to the lower class; the social advancement of individuals began with their emigration to the cities and abandonment of the rural economy.

Toward the end of the nineteenth century a cluster of technological and other developments initiated the era of the great landed estates (*latifundios*) supporting large-scale industrial sugar mills. The last of the *haciendas comuneras* disappeared, while the expropriation of small landowners was facilitated by the legal entanglements and ambiguities remaining from the sixteenth-century system of *mercedes*. By 1930 the vast expansion of the largest enterprises, partly at the expense of smaller ones, and a shift from individual to corporate ownership had rendered the rural upper class insignificant and greatly reduced the size and independence of the middle class. Many estates were run by professional managers representing either corporations or absentee owners. Small-scale investment in distributive and service enterprises as well as in agricultural production, hampered by the weakness of a one-crop economy and restricted by the predominance of very large enterprises, showed a relative decline.

An increasing amount of protective legislation halted an early trend toward the virtual disappearance of the small landowner and producer but was ineffective in regard to diversifying the economy, broadening the investment base, or promoting a prosperous middle class. A middle class, consisting of the owners and operators of farms large enough to require hired labor and of managers, schoolteachers, shopkeepers and the like, could be distinguished from the much larger mass of wageworkers and *colonos* employing only family labor. But the distinction did not point to clearly defined groups conscious of their corporate interests. Independent farmers, in particular, were steadily reduced by the chronic depression of the rural economy to the level of dependence on large enterprises that characterized the lower class—the *campesinos* or *guajiros* (peasants) who made up the bulk of the rural population as defined by living conditions and by the government.

Merchant moneylenders, industrial workers, technicians, absentee landowners, lawyers, government officials—all played important parts in the economy and organization of rural society, but their values and their places of residence, whether in towns or in the industrial communities (*bateyes*) of the sugar estates, were entirely urban in character. The relationship between these urban elements and the rural lower class was one of patronage in which credit was extended, tenure disputes were settled, and employment opportunities were offered in exchange for political support. On occasion the patron—perhaps the owner or manager of the local sugar mill—made up deficiencies in a government service, for example, by equipping the local school. Similarly, some operators of *colonias* built churches for their workers.

Land tenure was an important element in the pattern of capital investment underlying the class structure, but other factors such as the provision of seed, equipment, and housing, and, in the case of nonowners, the length of their contract, were also criteria. The distinction between those who worked with their hands and those who had sufficient means to own land and equipment or to hire labor formed the dividing line between the upper and lower classes. In general, the larger the scale of the operation and the greater the independence of the operator, the higher his status, whether he was an owner or not. Owners were more advantageously placed than cash renters, but share renters were scarcely better off than laborers.

In 1953, 231,000 persons were listed as farm operators, including 9,000 (4 percent) who were managers of the estates of others; 489,000 were wageworkers (*trabajadores agricolas, remunerados*) and 67,000 worked unpaid for their families. No further analysis of the 1953 farm-operator group was available, but in 1945 the relative proportions of the principal tenure classes were: owners, 30 percent; managers, 6 percent; renters, sharecroppers, and others, 64 percent. Because of the scale of their operations some renters belonged in the upper class, but, on the other hand, most of the owners did not. Of the total number of farms, owned and rented, 8 percent employed 65 percent of the permanent wage labor; 70 percent were of 25 acres or less and employed only 11 percent.

Standards of living and education provided other guides to social status. In 1953, 2.3 percent of rural homes had inside piped water; 85 percent were supplied only by rivers and springs. Fifty-four percent were without sanitary facilities of any kind; only 3 percent had modern equipment. Rural illiteracy was as high as 50 percent in Oriente province, with 42 percent as the national rural average. In 1943 nearly 60 percent of all Cubans engaged in agriculture earned a monthly income of less than $60, and less than one-half of one percent made more than $300. Many landowners, such as the family of Fidel Castro, were Spanish immigrants; other families, particularly in the cattle districts and

Camagüey province, though settled in Cuba for several generations clung to old Spanish traditions.

In sugar areas most of the cane-producing land belonged to the *centrales,* but (in 1945) only about a tenth of the cane was grown under direct mill management (administration cane). The rest was grown by *colonos,* either owners or renters, who assumed the management and the risks of production. Some land registered as *colono*-operated was actually managed by subsidiary companies set up by the mills to take advantage of laws favoring *colonos* over administration lands in the allocation of quotas.

There were an estimated 40,000 *colonos* of all classes in 1950. Among *colonos,* the principal beneficiaries of the laws were the middle- and upper-class *colonos,* whose interests were defended by the Asociación de Colonos de Cuba and the Instituto Cubano de Estabilización del Azúcar. Many small *colonos* were chronically in debt to the mills and independent in name only.

Settlement patterns, like class structure, varied somewhat according to the economy of the region. In most areas the rural population was widely dispersed with very few substantial villages. The principal social centers were found in towns, to which farm people made visits when they could to collect mail and see friends. Roads and other communications facilities were poorly developed and one of the strongest complaints of the peasants was their isolation, which deprived them of social and educational opportunities and created major economic obstacles.

The typical peasant's house (*bohío*), providing only minimal protection from rain and sun, contrasted sharply with the solid Spanish architecture of some of the old city residences. Constructed entirely from local materials, it consisted of a skeleton of poles, enclosed with lumber or strips of royal palm bark, which supported a canopy of *caña* or royal palm leaves. The floor was usually hard earth. A simple *bohío* could be constructed for as little as $200. The more elaborate ones had interior partitions and a separate, but connected, area for cooking. Furnishings were limited to a few stools, a cot or two, and a kerosene stove. A few independent farmers were well enough off to build small cement or wooden houses roofed with tile.

Small farmers lived with their families on the land they owned or rented. Unnamed hamlets consisting of a store or two and a few houses were common. In areas dominated by *latifundios* (great landed estates) farmers had to depend upon the company store.

2. *Ethnic Influences and Social Patterns*

Occasionally the location of the administrative headquarters of a *barrio* (township or ward; subdivision of a *municipio*, district) formed the nucleus of a village. A typical settlement of this kind, numbering some 800 inhabitants, included a bar, seven stores, a restaurant, a saddlery shop, and quarters for the military, together with an unfinished church and a hospital lacking staff. The most imposing building was the social club. Near cities many more small enterprises were found—producers of vegetables, milk, and fruit—and a better developed market economy prevailed. The better established villages of farm workers (*bateyes*) were located only on fairly large size *colonias*, which usually were provided with some social, educational, and medical facilities. Large estates provided barracks (*barracones*) to house temporary workers during the harvest, but more permanent workers lived in *bohíos*. As a rule each *bohío* had its own plot of land and some employers, particularly the large American companies, encouraged the growing of a diversity of crops. On many estates, however, tenants and laborers were forbidden to produce food for their own use lest they compete with the company stores.

As in the cities, squatters (*precaristas*) were a major problem. Many peasants built their *bohíos* either on public land, such as the margins of highways, or on unused private land. The squatters included many of the poorest of the lower class but also a few who operated enough land to hire labor and who belonged in fact to the middle class. This situation was made possible by the confused state of land claims and by the abundance of unused land. Although it was difficult to buy small farms, a number of large estates (1,500 acres or over) were not put to any productive use. Squatters could acquire title to their land after thirty years' occupation but were usually evicted before then.

In Latin America only Argentina and Chile show a proportion of urbanization higher than that in Cuba. Urban growth in Cuba, unlike much of Europe and the United States, does not stem from the development of heavy industry. Rather, it is chiefly a product of the Spanish colonial system in which land was considered not as a place to establish homesteads but as a source of raw materials for the European markets. The best way to exploit this land was to have large plantations worked by slave labor. The city, usually a port, became a link in the economic chain, the center of culture and of European influence. Wealthy landowners established homes in the cities on income from the plantations. As the population grew, laborers, unable to procure small holdings, were attracted to the mills and cities by the prospect of better wages. Accordingly, a dual movement of the upper and lower classes gave a special impetus to urban development. This pattern outlived not only Spanish rule but many laws intended to diversify the rural economy and broaden the social base of capital investment.

The 1953 census considered as urban dwellers all persons who lived in population clusters of 150 persons or more, if such clusters were provided with electricity and medical, legal, and recreational services or were adjacent and functionally related to other clusters which were so provided. These criteria placed in the urban category many communities with an essentially rural character. But according to the census authorities, they serve to distinguish a way of life which is in fact markedly different from the rural.

There are two kinds of urban settlement: the ordinary city or town and the industrial *batey* of the big sugar mills. In 1951, by law, all *bateyes* were considered urban if a *caballeria* (33.16 acres) or more of land next to the *batey* had been designated for the development of an urban center. The population of a *batey* is commonly between 2,000 and 3,000 and consists mostly of unionized industrial workers and administrators permanently employed by the mill and housed near it. The agricultural field workers live near the outlying canefields (*colonias*) which are linked by railroad to the mill.

The towns and cities have a more independent economic and political origin. The total number of urban units as defined by the 1953 census were: 22 under 5,000 population; 20 from 5,000 to 25,000; 23 from 25,000 to 100,000; and 35 of more than 100,000. In the past several decades there has been a particularly marked growth of urban centers in the range of 25,000 population, but the metropolitan area of Havana, which together with its satellite cities, Guanabacoa, Regla, Marianao, and San Antonio de las Vegas, includes 21 percent of the total population, far surpasses all other cities in size and importance.

As in other parts of the Spanish empire, cities in Cuba were planned to suit a social and administrative structure controlled by the king and his representatives. Streets forming a rectangular grid surrounded the central plaza, on which faced the principal public buildings and the churches. The latter were included, among other reasons, because the Roman Catholic Church shared with the government the task of supervising the people and also the revenues collected from them. The higher the social status of residents, the closer to the plaza they lived. The plaza also served as a social center by providing space for the citizens' evening promenades. Social status was indicated by the segregation imposed upon the promenaders. In some cities the circuit of the plaza reserved for Negroes was one step lower than the one reserved for whites, a situation that still prevailed in the 1950's and probably persisted through 1960. The homes of the poor were located on the outskirts of the city, ignored alike by fashionable society and by the authorities, which did not extend municipal services to them. This also is characteristic of modern cities where public housing and the provision of utilities has lagged further and further behind the growth of the population. The inadequacy of local government and the public works program has limited the paving in most towns to the main street, which is also the chief highway of the region, and a few adjacent streets parallel to it. Modern towns, therefore, have a straggling, elongated outline. Houses abut directly onto neighboring houses, with no interval between them and the street except that provided by the porch of each house, supported on tall pillars. The windows of older houses often are heavily barred.

Until 1959 at least, the majority of recent arrivals in the cities lived in suburbs of shacks with such names as Llega y Pon ("come and squat," a name often applied to squatters in general). Frequently, luxurious new homes were interspersed with slum dwellings, some of whose inhabitants found domestic employment in the homes of the rich. These residents of the slum suburbs governed themselves, electing their own mayors.

More typical of the lower class was the *solar* or tenement house, a rundown mansion divided into small units. Negroes predominated in the *solares*, but the better rooms were commonly rented by whites. In 1953 nearly a fifth of the urban dwelling units consisted of a single room housing an average of five people.

The upper class consisted of the wealthiest landowners and professional people, the higher ranks of the government service, and a number of representatives of foreign commercial and industrial interests. In their political activity the members dealt directly with the government in power, rather than with the political parties and the popular vote. Americans, British, Canadians, Dutch, and French were freely admitted to upper-class society, but people of color were rigidly excluded. A few families considered themselves to be Spanish descendants of aristocratic colonial families; some claimed Spanish titles of nobility. Articles on genealogical topics, written by members of the Cuban Genealogical Institute, appeared frequently in such periodicals as *Habana Yacht Club*. More recent arrivals include the families of those who had been middle-class insurgents in the later nineteenth century and who formed the new governing class of the period 1900-1930. Most recent and most numerous were those whose success was related to the careers of Batista, Grau San Martín, and Prío Socarrás; such groups continued to participate to some extent in party politics and to give at least nominal support to radical programs.

The typical social institutions of the upper class were the country club and the yacht club, avowedly imitative of similar resorts in the United States. Associated with these in the minds of most Cubans were the expensive nightclubs and hotels catering chiefly to visitors from the United States, many of whom came for business contacts with the government and the upper class. The members of this group lived principally in a series of suburbs west of Havana, successively vacating each one to the middle class as a new neighborhood was built on the outskirts. Just as the lower class sought public schooling for their children and the middle class private schooling, the upper class frequently sent its offspring to the United States. Much of its capital was invested abroad or in foreign-controlled interests in Cuba, with the result that the upper class appeared to many other Cubans partly foreign in composition and largely foreign in the orientation of its social and economic interests. It was inordinately wealthy by Cuban standards and appeared to devote much of its wealth to dissolute living.

The upper class was also associated, especially in the invective of nationalist leaders, with the Roman Catholic Church, even though there were many agnostics in its ranks. Much of the strength of the Church was based on the traditional standards of respectable behavior, which were essential to the recognition of upper-class status. Only the financially secure could participate in charitable works sponsored by religious organizations and could afford both the fees charged for baptisms and marriages and the elaborate social ceremonial regarded as an indispensable feature of such occasions.

Members of the middle class observed or thought they ought to observe the standards of living and the attitudes that distinguished the upper class socially from the lower class. Their social ambitions often imposed an artificial burden on families whose income might not be adequate to the required expenditures.

2. *Ethnic Influences and Social Patterns*

An important economic and political distinction existed between the commercial and professional segments of the middle class. The commercial segment, in which Spanish influence was strong, drew its income from businesses large and small which benefited from conditions of prosperity and stability; for its contacts with government it relied on informal channels and commercial associations. Its politics were conservative, expressed not in the campaigns of the political parties but in general by abstention from overt political debate. In this respect the commercial middle class was linked with the upper class, especially the pre-Batista generation of the upper class, but in other respects it regarded the upper class with a mixture of hostility and jealousy, suspecting its members of political irresponsibility.

The professional segment of the middle class, on the other hand, was dependent upon a salary. Members of this group, many of whom came from commercial families, had benefited from private school and university education, one of the largest items in the typical middle-class budget. Their education, emphasizing mastery of ideas rather than of techniques, was consistent with the class division of society, in which to be educated was to be civilized and urbane, a philosopher rather than a technician. The prestige of a certain kind of education and the relative stagnation of the economy combined to produce a surplus of doctors, lawyers, architects, and engineers (except industrial engineers, for example, and others whose profession lacked the dignity of white-collar employment). Underemployment characterized this group in the same way that unemployment characterized the lower class and nonemployment the upper. There were, for example, approximately 1,000 Cubans per physician in the 1950's, as compared with 800 per physician in the United States, but approximately half of the Cuban population lived in rural areas that were defined partly by the absence of medical services. Doctors, like other professional men, had two or three jobs in order to provide incomes adequate for their social aspirations; journalism and university teaching occupied many of them, either full time or part time. The biggest employer of the professional middle class was, however, the government. The Ministry of Public Health, for example, employed many physicians as administrators; teaching appointments were extensively made for patronage purposes; most newspapers were subsidized by the government. The IBRD mission in 1950 reported that an estimated thirty to forty thousand government employees did not actually work and that the efforts of thousands more were at best token efforts.

Control of the industry of government was the reward of political success. In the Spanish tradition, public office was considered properly to benefit primarily the holder; despite the efforts and public protests of many distinguished Cubans, this tradition was consistently observed in republican practice. The perquisites of the governing faction included not only the distribution of government jobs but, notably, the control of the national lottery, the awarding of government contracts, and the manipulation of economic regulations. Skillful use of these powers meant not only the present enrichment of individuals but the promise of continued political support. As a result, the active politicians were drawn largely from the salaried, professional segment of the middle class. This group was motivated not only by its material ambitions but by the social values of its educational background, which emphasized leadership as an admirable quality and the opportunity to exercise it as a prerequisite of social and personal success. University-educated middle-class men formed the core of the middle sector of political life, a sector characterized by intense competition for political and economic privileges; by radical reformist policies, socialist programs, and a tendency to resort to violence; and by the success of many individual members in advancing themselves from a precarious position on the lower margin of the middle class to a position of great wealth and influence—though often of uncertain political security. The middle sector included prominent members of labor unions who saw in politics a means of social advancement and whose position as intermediaries between the government and organized labor gave them special privileges in the distribution of government patronage. It also included the younger generation of the upper class, men whose own efforts had raised them to economic and political independence but who were not wholly able to dissociate themselves from party politics. The lower class provided the middle sector with the mass support necessary to win elections and to undertake other forms of political struggle, including mob violence, general strikes, and public demonstrations.

The armed forces, including the police and the rural guard, were a means to advancement for both the lower and the middle class and hence an instrument of political control. The poor could expect at least a uniform, quarters, and regular pay; all ranks could hope for more or less rapid advancement and many opportunities for private graft. There was no particular social pattern for recruitment, apart from some discrimination against Negroes; all classes and all regions were represented, but personal recommendations were useful in obtaining appointments. Before 1933, the officers were mostly members of wealthier families. The sergeants' revolution led by Batista substituted a lower-class group who were thereby promoted socially as well as professionally. Batista's second *coup d'état* in 1952 effected a similar, smaller-scale promotion into the officer class, which was accordingly strongly loyal to him.

It was in the middle class that color was given particular importance as a criterion of social status. Batista, a mestizo, would not in ordinary conditions have achieved high military rank; at no time could he have been considered a member of the aristocracy. In general, the middle class considered itself white, in accordance with the view—frequently contrasted by Cubans with that prevailing in the United States—that a man with some white ancestry is not Negro. A certain degree of social segregation was practiced: friendships with Negroes were not sustained publicly; private schools and the newer residential areas were closed to them. But there were a few exceptions: individual Negroes with exceptionally high standards of living and education were accepted in white schools and neighborhoods; Negroes who were old family servants often became almost like members of the family, although the manifestations of affection never obscured the difference in status. The ambiguity of color attitudes was particularly pronounced in the case of a mulatto family rising generation by generation to higher status, its progress marked by successive diminution of the proportion of Negro ancestry. A well-known poem asks, "But your grandmother, where is she?" in reference to the Negro grandmother of a middle-class family kept discreetly out of the public view.

Typical middle-class institutions are the social and insurance societies or clubs (*centros*), of which the oldest and best known were Spanish. With the relative decline of the purely Spanish element in the Cuban population, the *centros* lost much of their Spanish character. During the 1950's, the 90,000 members of the Centro Asturiano included an estimated 30 percent Spanish-born, 10 to 15 percent Spanish by inclination, and the rest *criollo* Cubans. Some non-Spanish foreigners were admitted, but Negroes and Chinese were excluded. Many other *centros* of similar type were founded, offering similar benefits, particularly the hospital facilities.

Some, such as the Anglo-American Association, the Centro Chino, and those for Negroes and mulattoes, were based on ethnic divisions; others catered, at least originally, to certain occupational groups. One or two, such as the Casino Español in Havana, showed an upper-class rather than a middle-class character. The *centros* were not politically active except on rare occasions when government decrees threatened their interests.

Neophilanthropic international clubs including Rotary, Odd Fellows, and Kiwanis were very active. Smaller groups within the middle class founded more narrowly representative associations of social and professional character and of remarkable number and variety. Many of them were frankly political pressure groups, providing their members with steppingstones to political office. Their meetings and the journals many of them published showed a similarly ambiguous character; articles written under solemnly academic titles often revealed themselves after a few paragraphs as political diatribes. Such associations also obtained for their members, especially for their officers, benefits from the government in the form of pensions, exemptions, subsidies, and other concessions. In return for their privileges, they, like the labor unions, submitted to a degree of government supervision, commonly exercised through a national federation or front whose officers were political clients of the chief of state. When the government changed, the elected committees of the associations also changed.

The members of the urban lower class, including the industrial workers of the sugar *centrales*, were much better organized than their rural counterparts and enjoyed a higher standard of living. Although the entire economy followed to some extent the seasonal rhythm of the sugar industry, employment was steadier in the cities and there was a greater choice of occupation. Furthermore, women could find wage labor in the cities but not on the farms. Legislation regulating wages and benefits was more effective in urban areas, and union organization was given particular importance by the relative preponderance of large enterprises.

A long history of organized action in support of social and political objectives has characterized urban labor. In 1933 the concerted action of workers throughout the island helped to overthrow Machado. Thereafter, represented chiefly by the Confederation of Cuban Workers (CTC), industrial labor exercised a strong influence in national politics. Batista depended on its support; decrees promulgated by him increased the privileges of the workers and in effect authorized featherbedding on a large scale. Labor, including its Communist elements, developed a conservatism of its own, supporting Batista. Party politics did not deeply concern the lower class as a whole; only the Popular Socialist Party (Communist) had any pretension to being other than a party of the middle class. But skilled workers and foremen sought educations for their sons and showed a relatively high upward social mobility, contrasting specifically with the rural lower class in this respect. Leadership of trade unions in particular provided means of social advancement; Negroes and Jews, both denied normal opportunities, were conspicuous in this role.

The professional and cultural associations of the middle class were found also among the lower class, but the typical social center, exceeded only by the family in importance, was frequently simply a meeting place or club where people could gossip, play dominoes, gamble, and entertain their friends. The first goal of any small community was to build a clubhouse, as large a one as possible.

Family

The family is the most important social institution not so much because of its own strength and scope as because other institutions—church, school, community—have been weak. In urban areas, however, particularly among the middle and upper classes, men traditionally have spent much time away from their families in clubs and informal groups. In the rural areas, particularly those more isolated, family ties are more extensive, and neighborhoods may be made up of related families.

At all social levels in pre-Castro Cuba the special claims of relatives were recognized and often determined the choice when privileges were distributed. In the lower class the cooperation of relatives was limited to sharing food and houseroom; in the upper class nepotism was not only possible and permissible but expected. Those who attained positions of influence in politics, government, or business favored their relatives as a matter of course. Those who were better off assisted their relatives lest the public spectacle of their indigence damage the family's reputation and its collective claim to upper-class status.

The Castro government has reaffirmed the value of the ideals of family life upheld by its predecessors and has shown itself conservative in its policies toward family life, although outside the home—in business, government, and law in particular—the former network of family connections was disrupted by the new regime. In 1960 a rumor was current among anti-Castro elements in Havana and Miami that the revolutionary government planned to take all children away from their mothers and place them in state-run institutions. Apparently the rumor originated in the government's proposals to take over and expand the institutions for the care of destitute children, formerly supported chiefly by the private charity of the upper class.

Certain actions of the government eventually may have some effect on family life and structure. The government has championed women's rights and has taken many women into the militia; it has also encouraged women to take jobs. Plans were announced for the establishment of a number of child centers. The functions and scope of these centers were not clearly defined, but apparently included looking after children to enable their mothers to work. The first, named the Lenin Child Center, was opened in May 1961 with the Soviet ambassador attending the ceremony.

According to the constitution of 1940 and the Fundamental Law of 1959, civil marriage is gratis and must be performed by officials designated by law. Religious ceremonies by themselves have the validity of common law marriage and impose binding obligations upon the parties. The legal age for marriage is fourteen for boys and twelve for girls but the parents' consent is required if the parties are under twenty-one. Parents are obliged to support, aid, train, and educate their children whether or not they were married when the children were conceived. The law provides that no record of the marital status of the parents be entered on birth certificates and similar documents. Legal marriage was practically universal in the upper class, but rare among the very poor, partly because of the cost of the ceremony. Despite the constitutional stipulation that civil marriage should be free, payment was expected by the officials concerned; but the fee was not the chief deterrent. A formal marital commitment required a certain stability and a closer association with the authorities than many couples were willing to assume. Popular attitudes distinguished sharply, however, between common law marriages and casual affairs. Legally, common law marriages imposed obligations similar to those of regular unions, but in practice few of them were submitted to judicial scrutiny. A common law marriage, therefore, was in effect more binding upon the woman than on the man, as is indicated by the remark sometimes heard, "I am single, and here is my wife." In rural areas, common law marriages were slightly more numerous than legal marriages, while in towns nearly three times as many people claimed to be legally married as said they were married by consent.

The Castro regime made strong efforts to reduce the number of common law marriages. The Ministry of Justice formed committees in every district to marry common law couples, in some areas by mass ceremonies. By late 1960, 20,000 couples had been married, and it was anticipated that by the end of 1961, 400,000 marriages would be completed. The regime offered a more positive inducement for marriage by refusing land title to unmarried peasant couples, but it is not known how rigorously this policy was enforced.

The average size of the family has decreased during this century, but because census figures are not strictly comparable, no exact measure of the decline is available. In 1953 the average size was reported to be 4.86 persons, with 4.35 the urban average and 5.75 the rural average. The family generally consisted of husband, wife, and their children; only 14 percent of the family units, largely high-income families, included grandparents or other relatives.

Before 1959 upper- and lower-class families differed considerably. The upper-class ideal was drawn from aristocratic tradition which emphasized the authority of the father and the gentility of the whole family, particularly of the women. Spanish law subordinated a wife to her husband; without his permission, for example, she could not engage in any business transaction. This tradition has been growing weaker in Cuba; the Fundamental Law of 1959, repeating the constitution of 1940, specifically guaranteed equality of rights and a married woman's control over her own property and wages.

Equality of status as decreed by law is gaining wider acceptance as an ideal, but the tradition of paternal authority remains strong. Husbands are usually four or five years older than their wives, and some feel it advisable to maintain a certain severity toward their womenfolk in the interests of discipline. In farm families in the 1940's women commonly served meals to the men but did not eat with them. Family life in Havana, especially in the upper class, was strongly influenced by American manners and fashions, but in Camagüey, for example, a relatively staid and conservative Spanish outlook prevailed.

Since the turn of the century women have been increasingly

prominent in public affairs, but their participation does not demonstrate their elevation to full equality with men. Social visiting in the home continues to be limited chiefly to relatives, and men still tend to seek male company. The café is a favorite gathering place for men, although it is becoming more usual to see women there also. Since 1959 women have been encouraged to participate more actively in life outside the home. They have joined the militia and their contribution as guerrillas to the success of the revolution has been emphasized.

Husbands, in the traditional view, are not expected to be faithful to their wives. Some, who can afford to, keep one or more mistresses; others, particularly in the urban areas where there is an excess of women, have recourse to the large number of prostitutes—a major social problem. The ideal woman, on the other hand, is a subservient figure, not only chaste, but preferably sexually innocent. In republican times, however, women have been less and less inclined to accept this ideal.

In the urban lower class, women have always provided at least part of the income of the average family, either in domestic service or, increasingly since 1930, in industry or commerce. In general, a woman could more readily find work in the city, particularly during the slack season, than a man. One effect of this was that women predominated in the general population drift to the cities. In 1953 the urban population included 1,631,000 men and 1,694,000 women; the rural population, 1,354,000 men and 1,150,000 women.

The lower-class urban household frequently consisted of a woman and her children. The woman might have a more or less permanent lover resident elsewhere who contributed to the support of the family, but she was its head and center. In rural areas women have had little opportunity to earn, since they rarely did agricultural work. In La Habana, the most urban province, 10 percent of all women over the age of fourteen were heads of households, as compared with 6 percent in Pinar del Río, the most rural province.

Children are generally pampered. When they are very young their mothers commonly baby them, sometimes to the extent of discouraging them from walking; it is alleged that this and other independent endeavors are likely to be physically harmful to the child. In upper-class families (before 1959) the pampering included total exemption from household tasks. Specifically youthful activities, social events, and styles of clothing were not valued;

2. *Ethnic Influences and Social Patterns*

upper-class parents were anxious that their children assume the dress, manners, and accomplishments of adults as soon as possible. Boys were expected to show familiarity with the classical themes of Cuban history, politics, biography, and literature and to be able to speak in public; girls in the 1930's and 1940's took piano lessons and in the 1950's studied ballet.

In the lower class, on the other hand, the fondness of parents for their children often was subordinated to their recognition of the difficulty of providing for them. Placing a child in one of the institutions for the care of poor children often was the chief hope of a lower-class family. Other children might have to go to work at an early age shining shoes, running errands, shoplifting and the like, disregarding the nominally compulsory school attendance law. An American observer of Cuban society in the 1940's (Lowry Nelson) considered that "almost the entire childhood population in the lower-class urban families might be classified as 'neglected' in a better-regulated society." Shoes were rare, and boys to the age of about seven often wore no clothes at all.

Children are required by law to respect and aid their parents and are customarily regarded as under parental tutelage until they marry. Spanish tradition requires strict chaperonage of daughters, but it was not a strong pattern in the lower class and now is very rare. Even after marriage a woman remains a member of her father's family as is partially indicated by her continued use of her family surname, to which her husband's surname is added in formal contexts: for example, Vilma Espín or Vilma Espín de Castro, but not Sra. Raúl Castro.

Under old Spanish law, adultery by a woman was one of the few grounds admissible for divorce; adultery by the man was not, unless it caused a public scandal. The 1919 law of civil marriage, however, recognized legal divorce on other grounds, including that of mutual disagreement. The Roman Catholic Church and its supporters campaigned against this provision without effect. During the 1930's additional legislation, reaffirmed in 1940 and 1959, enlarged the grounds for divorce. The Church maintains its disapproval, but only a minority of Cubans heed it; both Batista and Castro have been divorced, and the proceeding is accepted at all levels of society with little or no stigma attached.

AN ECONOMY OF SCARCITY

THE OUTSTANDING FEATURE OF THE ECONOMY is its dependence on sugar exports. The sugar industry, the principal source of livelihood, employs almost a quarter of the labor force, uses over half the cultivable land, and accounts for over eighty percent of the nation's exports. The country is ideally suited to the easy cultivation of sugar and, when sugar prices are high, no other activity is so rewarding. Before 1959, this prospect attracted large-scale foreign investment, primarily from the United States, and since most foreign trade was also with the United States, American influence on the economy was strong and served to reinforce the dominance of sugar.

Cuba ranks fifth among industrial countries in Latin America (after Brazil, Argentina, Mexico, and Chile), an industrial prominence directly related to agriculture and especially sugar. Sugar production accounts for about 50 percent of all industrial output and foodstuff processing (which includes sugar) for some 66 percent of the total value of manufactures. Approximately 327,000 workers, or 40 percent of the workers engaged in industry in 1953, were employed in foodstuff processing industries. Sugar production reached five million tons in 1925, dropped to two million during the depression in 1933, and surged to an unprecedented seven million, or 18 percent of total world production, in 1952 during the Korean war (see Table 3).

Statistics on over-all industrial activity are scanty and conflicting, but an estimate in 1950 by the IBRD placed the total number of industries at between 12,000 and 13,000 with total assets of around $300 million. Investments in the sugar industry exceeded by a wide margin all other forms of industrial investment. Concentration on the manufacture of sugar derivatives and industries requiring sugar was urged by the IBRD as the most efficient and promising use of resources with the dual objective of encouraging a larger export trade and supplying the domestic market with processed food now imported. Little was done, however, to develop the potential production of sugar derivatives and byproducts and only about five percent of the annual sugar crop has been consumed domestically.

Although sugar is the backbone of the economy, it is also the economy's greatest weakness. World prices for sugar fluctuate, and production is a highly seasonal activity, throwing thousands of cane cutters out of work at the beginning of every summer. In the years between 1925 and 1950, sugar came to dominate the economy to such an extent that the fortunes of other enterprises rose and fell with sugar prices and the sugar seasons, not only because incomes and earnings fluctuated but also because many domestic firms depended upon sugar exports to pay for their imports of fuel, machinery, and materials.

The central problem has been, therefore, to reduce this dependence by developing a broader, more diversified productive base in both agriculture and industry. There have been brief periods of prosperity in recent history that would have afforded the means to expand the economy, but these opportunities were not seized. Cubans sought rather to act during periods of depression, which provided the motives but not the means for change. The country is well endowed with human and natural resources and, until 1959, also had the capital needed for growth. A large internal market, dependent on imports, could be filled in part by domestic produce and manufactures. American markets, particularly the great United States consumer market, are close, as are international trade routes. The soil is exceptionally fertile, suitable for a variety of agricultural products for export and home consumption, and there are undeveloped metallic and nonmetallic mineral resources. Although literacy and skills are at a low level by United States standards, the labor force is large and accustomed to working for wages and producing for a market.

Over the years, however, dependence on sugar so influenced the psychology of investors, attitudes of labor, methods of commerce, government finances, and even the network of roads that resources and capital were never exploited to their fullest potential. A general indifference to everything but sugar meant that the conditions necessary for diversification—competitive industry, technological improvements, research, high production standards, low labor costs, vocational training, better transport facilities, and an improved distribution system—were never developed.

Cubans tended to view the material benefits of economic activity as fixed quantities, incapable of expansion, and available to individuals and groups through political rather than economic effort. The distribution of the national wealth was determined by government decree, political deals, and other artificial devices, rarely by economic forces. No reliable economic information was available to either the producer or consumer, except perhaps in the sugar industry, a deficiency that opened the door to all types of private manipulation in such matters as price fixing, wage fixing, and inflated contract bids. The influence of political forces and the tendency of the government to form economic policies without reference to factual data discouraged even further the creation of new wealth and employment.

The accumulated problems of a static economy, which had reached the limits of its capacity to absorb a growing population and still maintain living standards, fell on the Castro regime. The institutional changes which the new government made in attacking the problem were so broad and deep that certain areas of the economy could probably never be restored to their previous norm. Many of the changes—though not necessarily the manner in which they were made—had long been recommended. The International Bank for Reconstruction and Development (IBRD) had suggested in 1950 that agrarian reform—not the wholesale redistribution of land among the landless but the use of idle land to diversify agricultural production—be effected by buying up idle land or taxing it heavily. Castro, however, merely expropriated it. In 1961 it was not yet clear what beneficial effect his program would have, but the potential of the economy is so great that productivity could be expected to grow in response to any constructive effort.

In the years before Castro there were repeated attempts to limit sugar production in order to maintain prices. Cuba has always been at the mercy of fluctuations in the world price of sugar and has also had to face increasing competition from other sugar producing countries and restrictive quota arrangements. In addition to the instability caused by the world sugar market the seasonal nature of sugar production itself has raised almost insoluble problems. Economic activity and employment were greatest during the brief *zafra,* the cane cutting and milling season, which lasts usually from January to about June, and lowest during the long *tiempo muerto*, or "dead season," between the harvests. There was a difference in this respect between the cities, particularly Havana, and the countryside. Rural areas suffered the most, the effects of seasonal fluctuations being all the more marked since there was little self-sufficient subsistence farming which would enable farmers to withstand market and employment changes. Cities, where most new investment in nonsugar industry, construction, and services took place, had a more varied economic base, and in addition public works spending was concentrated in and around large urban centers. But because so much of the national income depended on sugar, even the cities did not escape the influence of sugar seasons and prices. Commercial and transport industries, harbor activity, consumer industries—all profited from the increased prosperity of the *zafra* and were depressed during the *tiempo muerto*. Moreover, much of the tourist trade, which provided a livelihood for hotel workers, taxi drivers, servants, and entertainers, took place between January and April.

Violent political changes and the unpredictable application of laws weakened popular confidence in economic ventures and encouraged the gambling instinct evident in the national enthusiasm for the weekly lottery. People were interested in short-term methods of obtaining as much economic security as possible and reluctant to take the risks or make the concessions necessary to increase investment and productivity; they hoarded their savings, if any, or invested them in safe real estate or ventures offering a quick and spectacular return. Many of the wealthy kept bank accounts and investments overseas. A lack of confidence in the future encouraged the high price markup and low volume sales characteristic of domestic trade; it motivated the search for quick commercial profits and the effort to stifle competition by protective tariffs and monopoly arrangements. A large part of the country's productive facilities were underutilized; industries were handicapped by inefficient production practices; even the transport network handled less traffic than it was capable of bearing.

The need for development had become urgent by 1950 and critical by 1959. An indication of the extent of the problem was the IBRD's suggestion in 1950 that much more was needed than the addition of new industries to replace imports. Because so many incomes were tied to sugar, even new industries would continue to be affected by its fortunes. To overcome this difficulty two concurrent developments were required—vigorous promotion of efficient, nonsugar export industries and greatly increased development of industries producing for the home market. These changes would have required a concerted effort in many areas, heavier direct taxation, increased labor productivity, and temporarily reduced living standards as more of the nation's resources were shifted from consumption to development.

Because of the absence of interest on the part of private investors, either Cuban or foreign, Cubans looked to the government to exercise economic leadership such as was called for in the 1940 constitution. Government economic programs, however, were most often confined to short-term public works projects rather than directed to long-term needs, and even the provision of public utilities, education, and roads was spotty and inadequate in relation to the amounts spent. Although institutions established to control government finances and maintain monetary stability—the General Accounting Office (Tribunal de Cuentas) and the National Bank of Cuba—were well staffed and respected, their promise of leadership and economic stability was never fulfilled.

The Economic and Social Development Plan of the Batista regime was larger and more ambitious than any previously adopted. It called for the expenditure of $350 million over a four-year period beginning in 1954, for the broad purposes of reducing unemployment and increasing production. Tax incentives and credits were offered to private investors. There was some diversification and new investment in these years, but at no time were the changes introduced by the government and private enterprise of such a scope as to overcome the dominance of sugar in an otherwise static economy. Government spending on public works did not improve the productive capacity and had little effect on the chronic unemployment but managed to maintain the average per capita income between 1953 and 1957. The average income figures were largely meaningless, however, as they included a small number of great fortunes on the one hand and widespread poverty on the other. Even the average was lower than that of the poorest southern region in the United States, but in Latin America it was among the highest. The middle-income group was also among the largest in Latin America.

Sugar

During the 1950's annual sugar production averaged about 13 percent of total world production, making Cuba the largest producer and exporter of sugar in the world. Actual production is no measure of capacity, however, because market forces have persistently checked production and successive governments have placed controls on the amount of cane that could be planted. The island has optimum conditions for growing sugar cane, except that rain is not always sufficient and irrigation could sometimes improve the crop. Cane will grow from the same root structure year after year and requires only infrequent replanting. The first crop after a new planting yields the most sugar and is called plant cane; subsequent crops or ratoons have diminished yields. Replanting is carried out every five to twenty years. Planting consists of plowing the land and placing pieces of cane in furrows, from which new shoots grow; only a small proportion of a canefield is replanted at one time. Cane is normally planted between September and November (before the dry season) and is ready for harvest fifteen months later. After that, it is cut every twelve months from January to March.

The cut cane is stacked in oxcarts, hauled to the nearest railroad spur, and transported to the mill. Before 1959 the sugar industry operated around the *central* (large sugar mill), which together with surrounding canefields usually represented a capital investment of $3.5 million and up. Technological innovations in the late nineteenth century led to the mechanization of sugar milling and required heavy concentrations of capital. The large modern sugar mills, the first of which was built in 1902, rapidly replaced the small family mill. The number of mills became progressively smaller as their size increased. By the 1920's, when the industry reached its peak, there were about 180 mills. The number decreased to 161 in 1957, a marked contrast with the 2,000 mills of the 1850's. Matanzas and Las Villas provinces had the greatest concentration of mills until the 1920's when a sugar boom led to frenzied development in Camagüey and Oriente (see the map, Major Crop Areas). These two eastern provinces soon surpassed the others in production. Only a small percentage of the industry was in individual hands. Ownership, both Cuban and foreign, normally was corporate. In 1940 there were 174 *centrales* owned as follows: Cuban, 55; American, 67; Spanish, 33; Canadian, 10; French, 3; English, 4; Dutch, 2. American participation in Cuba's sugar production had diminished following the depression of the 1930's, but up to 1958 United States companies still accounted for about 40 percent of the raw sugar produced and owned nine of the ten largest sugar estates.

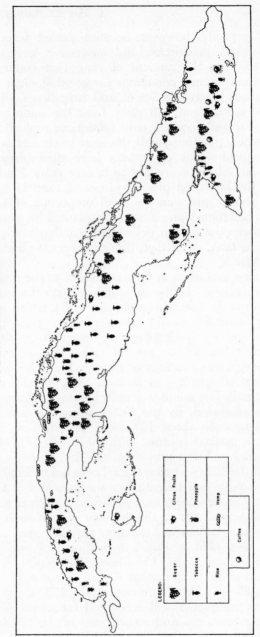

MAJOR CROP AREAS

LEGEND:

Sugar		Citrus Fruits	
Tobacco		Pineapple	
Rice		Hemp	
	Coffee		

3. *An Economy of Scarcity*

The establishment of large sugar mills after 1900 was accompanied by increases in the amount of land each mill owned. By the 1920's the largest sugar estate contained over 160,000 acres, with the average holding between 30,000 and 40,000 acres. Where formerly both the growing and grinding of cane had been handled largely by the individual owner-farmer, the *centrales* came to control both parts of the operation. Most of the sugar cane was grown by the *colonos*, individuals who either rented land from the *central* or who depended upon the *central* to buy their cane. The rest of the cane, called "administration cane," was produced by the *central* itself with hired labor.

In 1944 it was estimated that only 10 percent of all the cane produced was administration cane. This low proportion resulted from a sugar quota law in 1937 which allotted *colonos* larger quotas in an effort to favor the small cane producer. Many *centrales* gave up producing their own cane and rented all their land to *colonos*. The rent charged by the mills was tied by law to the price of sugar.

The *colonos* often were large operators who in turn hired their own labor. The task of cutting sugar cane during the annual *zafra* is an entirely manual operation that requires a vast labor pool, and wageworkers greatly overshadowed the *colono* group. Cane-cutting machinery has been tried in other countries, but to date none of the experimental machines is as efficient as hand labor.

The role of government in the agricultural life of the country assumed importance after the great sugar depression of 1925-1941. The Ministry of Agriculture and specialized agencies began to regulate agricultural production which heretofore had been controlled solely by the market. Controlling sugar production and prices, imposing tariffs to encourage development of food crops in Cuba, and granting aid to small farmers were the main functions of the Ministry of Agriculture after that time.

Beginning in 1926 the Verdeja Act reduced sugar production in an effort to maintain its price. The 1927 crop was limited to 4.5 million long tons (in 1925 sugar production had reached a peak of 5.1 million tons) with each sugar producer being given a quota based on his previous performance. The Act helped bolster sugar prices but was only a first step toward effective control of production.

In 1927 protective tariffs on agricultural imports were established to stimulate diversification. Farmers began to supply the domestic market with larger quantities of meat, dairy products, and potatoes, but the most phenomenal development was in coffee. The high tariff so stimulated domestic production that in eight years, from 1925 to 1933, coffee imports dropped from 28,538,400 pounds to 128,920 pounds, making Cuba virtually self-sufficient in this commodity.

More sugar controls were passed beginning with the Sugar Defense Act of 1927, which established a National Sugar Defense Commission whose job was to analyze foreign markets and to fix production quotas. A Sugar Export Company, owned by the mills, was authorized by law to act as selling agent to countries other than the United States, and quota agreements were made with several European countries. In 1929, a special government agency, the Cooperative Sugar Sales Agency, was organized with the purpose of disposing of the entire 1930 crop. Despite these measures, producers resorted to private selling and sugar surpluses continued to plague the economy.

Throughout the depression, legislation was enacted (usually under the initiative of American sugar interests) with the twofold purpose of securing sugar markets and stabilizing prices. The Chadbourne Plan of 1930, codified in the Cuban Sugar Stabilization Act, established a Sugar Export Corporation to help dispose of old surplus crops. The government bought the sugar outright and secured the purchases by floating a bond issue backed by a government guarantee and by the income from taxes on future sugar production. Export quotas were imposed, and agreement was reached with American sugar interests regulating the share of the United States' market. The president of Cuba was given authority to fix the amount of cane that could be grown, provided agreements on quotas first were reached with foreign customers. In 1931 the International Sugar Agreement attempted to lower sugar output among the major cane and beet sugar exporting countries. Results were disappointing, and prices reached an all-time low despite a 60 percent cut in Cuban and Javanese production.

The most significant piece of legislation was the Ley de Coordinación Azucarera (Law for Sugar Coordination) of 1937, an impressive program that could have materially affected agriculture had it, and succeeding legislation, been fully implemented. This law, which remained in effect through 1958, established minimum wages, production quotas, prices for grinding cane, and rent ceilings based on the value of sugar. Small farmers were given sugar quotas taken away from the large growers and were guaranteed protection from eviction provided they produced their quota of cane. This legislation was intended to protect the small farmer and increase his share in the profits of agriculture. The 1940 constitution, going even further, called for the break-up of large landholdings and the elimination of foreign influence in agricultural affairs. As in so many programs, however, the laws were not implemented since the persons most likely to be hurt were also the most influential.

Cuba enjoyed temporary respite from its agricultural depression during the Korean war. Prices for sugar were high, and the demand was great enough to absorb a large share of Cuban production. But by 1952, with a record crop of over seven million tons, the country was again faced with marketing problems. The long-range Economic and Social Development Program, discussed above, was instituted in 1954. The agricultural sector of the program called for immediate improvements in storage and refrigeration facilities; increased mechanization, fertilization, and irrigation; and intensified research by agricultural experiment stations. It proposed more production of meat, milk, fowl, eggs, fish, rice, beans, fruit, vegetables, coffee, and oleaginous plants. On the social side, the program called for agrarian reform, including regulation of the tenancy system and provision of technical and economic assistance to small farmers through agricultural cooperatives and trade and credit organizations.

This ambitious agrarian program, which had counterparts in the industrial and trade fields, demonstrated a desire for a change in economic orientation and a diminished dependence on sugar. The program never had a chance to prove itself, however, since many of the measures were of a long-term nature and the Castro rebellion upset its operation soon after it got started. Like many previous efforts, the program was subject to corruption and graft within the administration and might have foundered even without the change of government.

Sugar mills are modern and efficient industrial establishments but are inactive for most of the year. Grinding only lasts about 120 days a year during peak harvests, after which the mill is shut down. Cuba's 161 mills, distributed throughout the island at the sources of the cane, have grinding capacities ranging from 634 short tons of cane per 24-hour day to 12,677 tons. The cane is first crushed, converting it into juice and a woody residue called bagasse. Evaporation of the juice leaves a mixture of raw sugar crystals and molasses which are then separated by centrifuges. Alcohol and other industrial chemicals can be made from the molasses but most Cuban molasses has been exported to the United States for use in cattle feed. Most of the raw sugar is also exported, although twenty-one mills have refineries, and, in addition, two refineries have operated independently of sugar mills. Bagasse is consumed as fuel to operate the mills and most modern mills are designed to use this fuel exclusively. It is a cheap, readily available source of energy, particularly useful since natural fuels are scarce. Sugar and bagasse are produced in about equal tonnages during milling operations. Thus, as long as sugar is being ground, there is always fuel to run the machinery, plus a substantial surplus of bagasse for other uses.

In 1957, five new paper and paperboard manufacturing plants, using bagasse as raw material, were either in the construction or planning phase. By 1960 four were operating. These were a newsprint plant at Cárdenas in Matanzas province, whose daily capacity filled all of Cuba's newsprint requirements; a large paper plant at Trinidad; and two paperboard factories, one at Cruces in Las Villas and one at Camagüey. Another paper plant was under construction at Damují (near Cienfuegos). The Trinidad factory, Papelera Pulpa-Cuba, was the largest bagasse paper plant in Latin America. Investment in this plant was almost $12 million. Together with a tile factory using bagasse fiber as a bond, these several factories represented a total investment exceeding $30 million. Private Cuban capital financed much of this development. Other contributors were the Batista government, private United States interests, and the United States Export-Import Bank.

Research on the use of bagasse in the production of cellulose, plastics, activated charcoal, and industrial chemicals was undertaken by pre-Castro governments and some sugar mills, but on a scale incommensurate with its potential importance. Under Castro the desire to expand research on sugar derivatives and bagasse contrasted with the general apathy that had characterized previous regimes. From raw sugar, cane juice, and molasses, Cuba now produces the following derivatives: refined sugar, table syrups, glucose, leavening, fuel alcohol, alcohol for synthetic rubber, drinking alcohol, invert syrups and molasses, cane wax, fertilizers, greases, combustibles, acetone, carbon dioxide, glycerine, and citric, lactic and aconitic acid. These products use only a small proportion of the total sugar produced, and the economy would be substantially aided if their production could be expanded.

Until 1960 the largest sugar mills were American-owned, although since the 1920's the trend had been toward increasing Cuban ownership. The temporary high market and the false hopes of 1920 caused the industry to be overexpanded and overcapitalized, by American interests in particular. Subsequently, the industry was reorganized and American investors sold out to Cubans, retaining for themselves only the larger, more efficient mills. In 1958 Cuban-owned mills accounted for about 60 percent of the total sugar output compared to only 20 percent in 1939 (see Table 4).

The major reason for the decline in foreign ownership was a sharp drop in profit opportunities caused by government controls. There were fifteen different types of taxes on sugar and sugar products alone, which, according to the IBRD, risked sapping the vitality of the industry. Opportunities for tax evasion, not as great for foreign firms, also favored Cuban companies.

Labor laws designed to keep employment high also hurt the mills and discouraged foreign investors. Long paid vacations, social benefits, the security of tenure enjoyed by laborers, labor's objection to any technical improvements, and higher wages, although not ruinous to the millowners, appreciably decreased the profits to which they had been accustomed. Between 1941 and 1947 mill-workers' wages alone were raised 185 percent. When mills developed their efficiency to a point where they were able to grind cane in fewer days, a law was passed to compensate the workers for the decreased working time. All these measures, designed to protect labor, tended to work against the operation of the modern sugar mill as an efficient industrial enterprise.

Other Agricultural Activities

In addition to sugar cane, which grows practically everywhere, Cuba's uplands can grow coffee or cacao; its fertile mountain valleys make good tobacco lands; poorly drained lowlands can be turned into rice fields; grassy plains can support livestock. Fruit, vegetables, and industrial fibers such as henequen and, recently, cotton also benefit from the ideal relationship of climate and soils. Compared with sugar, however, other crops are considered as *frutas menores*, or lesser fruits.

According to the Agricultural Census of 1946 the first and only such census made, of the total land surface of 28,287,428 acres, 79.3 percent, or 22,420,402 acres, was devoted to farmland (see Table 5). The portion of the total surface not in farms, about 20 percent, was largely mountainous or swampy. Las Villas province had the highest percentage of land in farms (90 percent), mountainous Oriente the lowest (70.9 percent).

Only about 22 percent of the total farmland was under cultivation, much of the remainder being wasteland or pasture. Pasture areas represented about 43 percent of total farmland, including both natural and seeded pastures, and was chiefly concentrated in the provinces of Las Villas, Camagüey, and Oriente, the major areas of cattle production. Many of the large mills held a considerable acreage in fallow, either for rotating cane crops, as an alternative to the use of fertilizers, or for planting sugar cane in the event of a boom. Land use is not appreciably affected by climatic conditions, but erosion is a much neglected problem, aggravated by the extensive denudation of forests.

The system of landownership and allotment has changed several times during the years since the island's discovery. First, land grants awarded by the Crown to Spanish colonists were based on the supply of Indian labor rather than on specific land measurements. With abundant land and few colonists, this practice caused no problem. Another form of early land distribution was allotment by regions or topographical features. Again no measurements were made other than purely visual ones. Around the middle of the sixteenth century, however, a kind of land measurement came into use which, though practical when land was abundant, had serious drawbacks later. This was the circular *merced,* a grant of land given to colonists upon petition to the colonial municipal councils. The circular shape, with the hacienda or ranch house located at the center, made surveying difficult and, in order to facilitate measurement, the circle was often turned into a polygon of 64 or 72 sides. The lack of any good land survey made any title to land a dubious affair in which graft, bribery, or sheer confusion predominated. In time heirs or purchasers received an interest in the use of the land instead of a share of it. The original *merced* would then become a *hacienda comunera* (communal ranch). In the eighteenth century as crops, especially sugar and tobacco, replaced cattle ranching in importance, the *haciendas comuneras* broke up into their constituent parts, that is, each person with a share claimed a physical part. The circular ranch was thus divided into innumerable pieces, this time in irregular angular shapes. A large class of small landowners arose, but their titles to land suffered the usual handicap of being inadequately measured or surveyed. The use of several different land measurement systems—metric, English, and others purely Spanish—aggravated the confusion.

Disputes over land were settled in the courts, which considered occupancy, payment of taxes, public testimony, and other factors to determine ownership. By the time of the Castro revolution, however, most farm lands had fairly well-fixed boundaries, often fenced. The odd circular shapes of previous centuries had been largely supplanted, and rectilinear properties, although of varied sizes and shapes, were more the rule than the exception. In 1945, 20 percent of the farmed area was divided among less than 0.1 percent of all farms. Seventy percent of the farms were of twenty-five hectares (about sixty-three acres) or less and accounted for only 11 percent of the land; 39 percent of all farms, comprising less than 4 percent of the land, were of twenty-five acres or less. Only about 30 percent of farms of all sizes were operated by their owners. Exact descriptions of the situation in 1958, on the eve of the Castro revolution, are not available, but there probably had been little change. These facts point to the concentration of large landholdings among a few owners, most of the concentration occurring in sugar, tobacco, coffee, and livestock.

About 70 percent of all farms were managed or worked by people with no ownership interest in them: managers, 5.8 percent of all farms; renters, 28.8 percent; subrenters, 4.4 percent; sharecroppers, 20.6 percent; squatters, 8.6 percent; and a small percentage, 1.3, with usufructuary rights or other arrangements. Ownership could not always be equated with wealth. The groups most well-off economically were not necessarily the owner-operators or managers, since a renter of a large property was often richer than an owner of a small farm who worked it himself. He paid cash as rent, furnished his own equipment, and had virtual freedom in choosing the crops to plant. Cash renters were found particularly on dairy, sugar cane, and coffee farms; owners were found mostly in dairying and mixed farming. Sharecroppers, mostly on tobacco farms, were divided into several groups depending on the amount of responsibility they assumed and equipment they furnished. Squatters, or *precaristas*, were the lowest class, living a parasitic existence on someone else's land, paying no rent either in cash or in kind, and always threatened with eviction.

Tobacco occupies only about 4 percent of the total cultivated area, but it is the fifth most important agricultural product. Exports, however, declined markedly after World War I, and production was maintained principally for domestic consumption. The plant is grown in small plots in many areas, but the most famous tobacco regions are Vuelta Abajo, Semi-Vuelta, Partido, Remedios, and Oriente. Each region produces a particular leaf, distinct from the others in aroma and texture. The most valued tobacco, used extensively for cigars, is from Vuelta Abajo. Because of the constant attention required by tobacco plants, employment levels do not fluctuate as wildly during the year as they do in sugar production, and more workers are needed per acre under cultivation.

Coffee production became important only after the Haitian slave revolt in 1791. French coffee-growers fled to Cuba and established thriving plantations in the eastern part of the island. For a time investments in coffee-growing equaled investments in sugar, but higher returns from sugar and competition from Brazil, Venezuela, and Costa Rica soon caused a rapid decline in production. After 1860 the industry became insignificant until 1927 and 1930 when high tariffs on coffee imports revived production. In 1946 coffee was grown on about 20,000 farms and formed the principal crop on 9,000 farms.

After sugar and tobacco, the most important export crops are tropical fruits (mostly bananas and pineapples), winter vegetables, henequen, avocados, coffee, and cacao. The major crops consumed domestically include rice, corn, beans, peanuts, sweet potatoes, yams, yuca, malanga, potatoes, squash, tomatoes, and citrus fruits.

Cereals and legumes were the primary source of income for about 17 percent of the farms. Corn is grown universally for home consumption, but more rice is consumed than corn and wheat flour combined. The per capita consumption of rice is about 110 pounds a year, as compared to 6 pounds in the United States. The country still does not produce enough to meet the demand.

In the early Spanish colonial period, Cuba's agriculture was based on cattle raising. In 1946, 18 percent of all farms derived their principal income from livestock. Today, agricultural income from livestock is second only to sugar, even surpassing tobacco. Cattle, for which land and climate are ideally suited, far surpass all other livestock in numbers and economic value. Large expanses of savannah afford a good natural pasture, and the warm climate makes supplementary feeding unnecessary. Both beef and dairy cattle are raised, and several meat-packing and milk-canning plants supply an active export market. Oxen serve as the chief beasts of burden. Horses are used chiefly for rural transportation and rarely as beasts of burden or draft animals. Hogs are not well adapted to the warm climate and, being more expensive than cattle to feed, are much fewer in number. Sheep are not suited to the climate, but goats are often found on poor farms. Poultry is raised mainly on small individual farms, rarely in commercial quantities, despite the potential for large-scale production.

Forests once covered the entire island, furnished excellent hardwoods for export, and provided all the lumber for domestic requirements. Wholesale cutting and burning within the past forty years so depleted them that they are insufficient to satisfy local demand and have virtually ceased to figure in Cuba's exports. Only about 15 percent of the island is forested, and much of this area is located in inaccessible mountain regions. The government possesses over one million acres of forest preserves, largely in Oriente province. They have been poorly managed in the past despite a number of regulations designed to protect them. There is great need for an enforced reforestation program that will put back into productivity between three and four million acres of nonagricultural land, double the present extent of forests, and control indiscriminate cutting.

Fishing is still greatly undeveloped despite an estimated 450 types of edible fish in Cuban waters. Major fishing ports are Havana, Batabanó, Caibarién, Manzanillo and Cienfuegos. Fishing methods are still primitive except at Havana and Batabanó, where large fishing vessels are used. Fish production amounts to about $7 million a year in contrast to imports of $8 million. With better organization and equipment fishing could assume much greater importance in the economy.

Farm equipment is rudimentary; even the two-wheeled cart is found only on the larger farms. There are few tractors—only 13,000 in 1954—although the flat terrain makes their use attractive. The agrarian reform program of 1959 called for a large increase in the number of tractors, to be supplied by the Communist bloc.

Planting and harvesting is done by hand on the small farm as well as on the largest sugar plantation. Field work is done almost entirely by men, but the women sometimes supplement the family income by weaving hats from palm leaves. Farm tools include plows, often homemade from a forked tree; harrows; cultivators; shovels; hoes; axes; picks; crowbars; and, most important of all, machetes. The use of fertilizer is not extensive, primarily because the soil is often rich enough to support agriculture without it.

Before 1957, the Ministry of Agriculture and the University of

Havana were responsible for most agricultural research and education. The University had several agricultural departments, including departments of agronomy, animal industry, and agricultural economics, whose graduates were usually interested in agricultural industries rather than in farming. However, as the IBRD pointed out in 1950, too much emphasis was placed on the sugar industry and not enough on Cuba's main need—crop diversification. Another drawback was the absence of research.

Six provincial agricultural schools, open to sons of farmers, provided free tuition, room, and board, but generally could not operate properly because of a lack of funds. Training was good, but most graduates were reluctant to return to the farms upon completion of the three-year course. Lack of money also hampered operations of the experimental stations which were rarely able to carry out long-term research projects. Many sugar companies operated research stations of their own, but the most extensive experimental and research station in Cuba was operated by Harvard University on the property of the Central Soledad near Cienfuegos. In addition to its research work the Harvard station also grew plant and forest seedlings.

The extension of private bank credit to agricultural enterprise always favored the sugar interests to the detriment of other sectors. Sugar loans in some years made up 50 percent of all loans, whereas nonsugar agriculture never received more than 6 percent of the total, principally distributed to tobacco interests, cattlemen, and large rice growers. Banks were particularly attracted to the sugar industry because short-term loans were self-liquidating after the sale of the crop. In the case of renters and smaller *colonos,* the *centrales* themselves, rather than the banks, often acted as credit agencies. Other agricultural enterprises and small farmers were less fortunate and usually had to rely on merchants and retailers for credit, which was invariably tied to conditions requiring the farmer to buy goods or sell crops under terms set by the merchant.

In December 1950 the government created the Agricultural and Industrial Credit Bank, an autonomous government agency divided into banking and development sections. The banking section, through rural credit associations, handled farm loans up to twenty-five years in duration designed to help improve irrigation; construct buildings; purchase cattle, farm machinery, or heavy equipment; and refinance outstanding debts. The Bank's agricultural development division could grant rehabilitation loans to small farmers, but its main function was to finance rural credit associations and supervise agricultural research. The rural credit associations were intended to function as the rural arm of the Bank, and in very remote areas, local committees appointed by the Bank served the same purpose.

One of the Bank's important functions was to grant loans to farmers against crops already deposited in warehouses and thus enable the farmer to hold his crop until well after the harvest when prices were much higher. It was difficult to ascertain to what extent the Bank had aided the small farmer in bettering his lot, but many of its proposed functions were incorporated in the reforms of 1959.

Other Industrial Activities

Major industrial progress was not made until World War II, when wartime shortages stimulated domestic industrial production; after the emergency was over, many factories were abandoned. Between 1950 and 1959, however, American investments in Cuban manufacturing other than sugar doubled. One of the main reasons for this growth was a more attractive investment climate in the form of government tax relief and other measures intended to promote new industries. Most of the American industries were large-scale subsidiaries of United States corporations in the rubber, chemical, and pharmaceutical fields. Other industry in the nonfood sector included fertilizers, textiles, leather products, building materials, glass, lumber and furniture, rubber and petroleum products, metal products, machinery and matches. In most cases, a few large enterprises supplied the major portion of the output with numerous small and usually inefficent plants, workshops, and handicraft establishments producing the rest.

La Habana province contained about 50 percent of all manufacturing establishments and almost all of the larger plants. Las Villas province with 20 percent of all establishments produced proportionately much less of the total output because most of the plants were small. A survey of 1,840 industries in 1954 showed that only 14 firms employed over 500 persons, over 800 employing five or fewer. American investment was chiefly responsible for making Cuban industry the most heavily capitalized in Latin America relative to population. American and foreign enterprises generally tended to have a corporate structure while among the more numerous Cuban firms individual proprietorships were very common. The law governing business organization was liberal and there was no discrimination against foreign businessmen except in the employment of nontechnical foreign personnel.

Until the Castro revolution, private enterprise was the rule and no industry was directly operated by the government. In cases of serious labor-management disputes the government on occasion "intervened" an enterprise, exercising broad controls over certain phases of its operations but without expropriating it. Intervention became a favorite device after 1959 as the first step toward eventual nationalization.

Government efforts to stimulate domestic interest in industry began with the protective tariffs of 1927. Again in 1950, the government embarked on a program of tax and tariff reforms designed to boost private Cuban participation in industry, a program that was the beginning to show some results by 1959. The Castro regime showed a greater interest than any previous government in developing industries using Cuban raw materials. An effort was made to put back into production some mines that had been dormant for several years. However, the regime was handicapped by the loss of some of its major export markets and by the lack of trained technicians, many of whom fled the country. The prospects for any immediate and radical change were not encouraging.

Generally, the development of minerals suffered from a lack of exploratory work. The early Spaniards mined gold and copper, but not until the beginning of the twentieth century was interest again shown in Cuba's large store of minerals (see the map, Principal Mineral Resources). From 1902 to 1950, total mineral production amounted to around $467 million, equivalent to one sugar crop of the 1950's. Even in 1953, when mineral extraction was at an all-time high, extractive industries represented only about 0.3 percent of the total national income.

American government and private business have been the driving forces behind such development of mineral resources as has occurred and almost all of the island's mining output was exported to the United States. The response to American demand for metallic minerals is reflected in the increase in Cuba's exports between 1951 and 1954, when high prices resulting from the Korean war stimulated greater mining activity. The 1950 IBRD mission suggested that the government create a separate Ministry of Mines, Water, and Forests to handle critically needed research of Cuba's mining

PRINCIPAL MINERAL RESOURCES

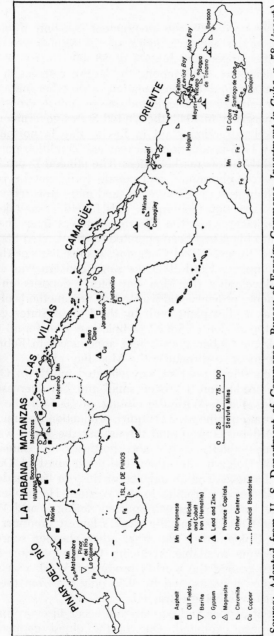

Source: Adapted from U. S. Department of Commerce, Bureau of Foreign Commerce, *Investment in Cuba*, p. 58 (insert).

potential, but until 1959 the government had only a small mining department under the jurisdiction of the Ministry of Agriculture with an annual operating budget of $8,400.

Cuba's nickel ores rank among the largest reserves in the world, but are usually found in association with other minerals which makes their extraction difficult and uneconomical. Prompted by the wartime emergency in 1942, the United States government built the Nicaro nickel extraction plant in Levisa Bay in northern Oriente province. By 1955 production had reached 30 million pounds a year at costs slightly below market prices. The mineral byproducts of the nickel ore—iron, chromium, and cobalt—could not be retrieved in sufficient quantities to defray costs, and more research was needed to improve extraction techniques. This function was taken over by Soviet technicians when the Nicaro plant was intervened in 1959.

The Nicaro plant had been operated for the United States government by the Nicaro Nickel Company, a subsidiary of the Freeport Sulphur Company. Until 1959 the same concern was actively engaged in developing the Moa Bay nickel deposits on the north coast of Oriente province and was testing new methods of separating the nickel at a pilot plant built by the United States government. Following the advice of Soviet technicians, who found the project impractical, the Cuban government announced, in February 1961, that it was going to dismantle the Moa Bay plant.

Despite enormous reserves, concentrated mostly in Oriente province, iron production has been small and has decreased steadily since World War I. With the closing in 1945 of the Bethlehem Steel Corporation mine near Daiquirí, production became negligible.

Chromite deposits are found throughout the island with heaviest concentrations chiefly north and northeast of Camagüey city, northeast of Holguín, and along the north coast of Oriente from Mayarí to Baracoa. The abundance of this ore has made Cuba the largest producer of chromite in the Western Hemisphere. Production for the United States was spurred during World War II to a point where Cuba became the world's largest producer outside of the Soviet Union. After the war, other cheaper sources of this mineral became available, reducing Cuba's position in 1952 to eighth place among the world's producers. Work was stopped on the Camagüey deposits, and by 1955 only ore from the Moa Bay-Baracoa area was being extracted.

Deposits of copper and copper-gold occur in every province but few have been exploited. One of the oldest copper mines, at

El Cobre, northwest of Santiago de Cuba, dates back 400 years and only ceased production in 1927. In 1955, under the stimulus of high copper prices, surface deposits were once more worked. By far the largest and most consistent copper producer was the Matahambre mine of Pinar del Río. Production from this mine alone placed Cuba fourth among Latin American copper producers and accounted for 40 percent of all copper imports by the United States and Canada. The Matahambre mine, which dates back to 1912, was developed by Cubans, but operated by the American Metals Company between 1921 and 1943, reverting to Cuban ownership and control after 1943.

Cuba ranks after Brazil in production of manganese in the Western Hemisphere. Deposits are found in every province and on the Isle of Pines. Oriente province leads in the quantity of known resources and in production. Actual reserves are not known. Manganese mining, started in 1888, reached a peak during the two world wars and the Korean war. During these crises, the United States, sole importer of Cuban manganese, looked to Cuba for the ore normally supplied by Africa and India. In recent years, the value of manganese exports at times surpassed both copper and nickel. United States demand, however, fluctuated greatly.

In terms of the number of persons employed and the value of output, production of nonmetallic minerals—particularly limestones and clays—may easily exceed that of all the metallic minerals combined. Production data figures are poorly reported largely because these minerals are so abundant they have been taken for granted. Cuban limestones cover a wide range of types, from lower grades that can be used in the manufacture of rock wool to high-grade marble. Large quantities are used in building and road construction, but little interest has been shown in developing domestic industries that could use the higher grade limestones—the cheapest source of alkali chemicals—or in exploring foreign markets. The conversion of limestone into lime (by burning in kilns) is the most profitable use that can be made of this mineral. The agricultural uses of burned lime, as a fertilizer and antacid, make its manufacture attractive to Cuba. Large quantities have been used in the sugar industry to clarify sugar juices. Clays, found in inexhaustible quantities throughout Cuba, furnish the raw material for the manufacture of bricks, tile, sewer pipes, and ceramics. Largely because of this abundant resource, Cuba is virtually self-sufficient in basic building materials. Geological features indicate the possible occurrence of several minerals as yet undiscovered in any large commercial quantities. These include magnesite, asbestos, and talc. Silica sand, basic to the construction and glass industries, is scarce.

Lacking commercial deposits of coal, Cuba must look to petroleum for its principal fuel and power needs. Petroleum has been produced commercially in small quantities since 1914; but cumulative production from 1914 to 1955 was only 2,495,000 barrels—roughly equivalent to two months' consumption. Between 1945 and 1959 about $25 million was spent by large American oil companies in search of Cuban petroleum. In 1954 new vigor was given to the quest by the discovery of a substantial field, in Cuban terms, near Jatibonico on the border of Las Villas and Camagüey provinces. It soon surpassed the other fields in production, producing an estimated 294,120 barrels in 1955. Perhaps the greatest significance of the Jatibonico discovery was the indication of potential sources of petroleum in areas heretofore totally unexplored. It is now believed that the most promising sources are not in the north but in the sedimentary formations of the eastern and western coastal plains, southern basins, and marine shelves.

In 1959, the Castro government seized confidential exploration records of foreign petroleum companies, created a Cuban Institute of Petroleum under the Industrial Department of INRA, and passed new petroleum legislation. A new law (November 20, 1959) set the government's share of any oil extracted at 60 percent, based on the value of production at the source. Moreover, the state reserved the right to acquire all or part of national oil production at the prevailing world market price. These measures effectively curtailed the activities of foreign companies, which ceased all operations. The government attached great importance to fostering the growth of this industry since Cuba imports about $50 million worth of petroleum products annually. If oil exists in any quantity, full-scale exploitation could mean substantial savings.

For many years tobacco held second place in the economy, employing the largest number of persons after the sugar industry. In the 1950's it occupied fifth place in agricultural, and third place in industrial output (see Table 6). The industrial phase—the making of cigars, cigarettes, and cut tobacco—employed about 35,000 workers in 1,000 establishments. There were in addition some 1,300 individual cigar makers. Three large, ultramodern mechanized cigar and cigarette factories employed over 500 workers each, but by far the most common type was the small shop employing an average of eight workers.

The labor movement, which began in the tobacco industry in 1865, successfully opposed mechanization of cigar making until 1950 when machine-made cigars for export were finally authorized by the government, immediately increasing exports. Domestic cigars, however, continued to be hand made at high cost, causing Cubans to turn to American cigarettes, which they prefer to their own. Because of the popularity of the American product, nine of Cuba's twenty-four cigarette establishments, some of which are highly mechanized, were not functioning in 1959.

Meat and meat products were produced before 1959 in sufficient quantity—about $75 million worth a year—to provide most domestic requirements. Processed meat—sausages, canned meat, hams, bacon, jerked beef—were produced by some thirty establishments. Of these only a few like Armour y Cía., Swift y Cía., and Oriente Industrial y Comercial, S.A., produced quality products under sanitary conditions.

Most milk production is a sideline to the raising of cattle for beef and milk yield per cow is extremely low. Until tariff legislation in 1927 gave protection to the industry, Cuba was a large importer of dairy products. A large expansion of dairies followed and for a brief period in 1941 Cuba was able to furnish its own needs for condensed milk, butter, and cheese as well as to export a surplus. Domestic demand soon outpaced productive capacity and caused resumption of imports. Misguided policies in 1959 and 1960 reduced the cattle industry to something like a quarter of its former importance and led to serious shortages of meat and dairy products.

Cuba does not furnish her major food requirements but imports, at a substantial yearly cost, large quantities of food products, many of which are canned. Such items as canned tomato paste, canned fruits, and condensed milk could easily be produced at home at a considerable saving, yet there were in the 1950's only some 160 firms, many of them small, engaged in canning. Lack of credit and of technical and managerial personnel, absence of government inspection and grading standards, and the poor quality of agricultural products available operated to curtail the growth of the industry. As about one-half of all canned foods had been imported before the Castro period, shortages were immediately apparent after the new government placed strict embargoes on imports in order to conserve foreign exchange. As a result, expansion of food-processing industries was given a high priority by the regime.

Grain milling is a recent and important development in view of the large consumption of wheat and rice flour. Before 1952 virtually all flour was imported from the United States. Subsequently, one mill, the Burrus Flour Mill, S.A. completed in 1952 at Regla in La Habana province, was able to furnish about 40 percent of consumption requirements. In 1955 this mill produced 52,517 metric tons of flour as against 83,005 metric tons imported. There are sufficient rice mills to handle all of Cuba's imported and domestic rice, and several corn flour mills. In 1956 there were some twenty mills producing feed, chiefly for poultry. Beverages occupy an important place in the food industry, employing some 10,000 workers in about 200 firms.

The chemical industry is perhaps the most modern and efficient enterprise after sugar, rating with those found in advanced industrial societies. With 8,956 persons employed in this sector in 1953, the average work force in chemical plants was larger than in most Cuban industrial enterprises. Sulfuric acid, made from imported United States sulfur, was the principal product. Three factories produced all of Cuba's demand. Superphosphates, caustic soda, chlorine, potassium sulfate, hydrochloric acid, silicate of soda, and carbon bisulfide were among the other inorganic chemicals produced. The chemical industry produced fertilizers to a limited degree from locally produced sulfuric acid, but the most common fertilizer plants were mixing plants using imported raw materials. Four-fifths of Cuba's paint and varnish needs were supplied by home industry. The first paint factory began operating in 1923. In 1930 it was purchased by the American Sherwin-Williams Company.

The pharmaceutical industry was highly developed by a few large American subsidiaries and a great number of small Cuban enterprises. Per capita consumption of patent medicines is one of the highest in the world, making for a very active domestic market. In 1956 Cuba made about half of its own pharmaceuticals.

Until 1931 all textiles were imported. In the 1950's there were some thirty large textile mills producing flat cotton and rayon goods, flat rayon textiles, synthetic cord and fibers, wool textiles, carpets, bedspreads, cotton sacks for refined sugar, hosiery, and towels. The largest cotton-weaving mill on the island, with 72,000 spindles and about 2,000 looms, was the Cía. Textilera Ariguanabo, S.A. at Bauta in La Habana province, which employed more workers than any other factory in Cuba. In 1955, production of cotton goods totaled 42.9 million square yards.

Because very few mills had their own cotton spinning machinery, most of the woven cotton was made from imported yarn. The IBRD pointed out in 1950 that Cuba would do well to increase her cotton-spinning capacity to keep pace with her weaving capacity and save on the cost of imported yarn. Cuba has no cotton production of any importance, but imported raw cotton could be processed on a much larger scale.

The clothing industry was well developed and employed some 30,000 workers in 1956, but the majority of establishments were very small. In 1956 there were five plants producing rayon textiles, often with imported rayon fibers. Cuba's single rayon fiber plant might have better supplied local textile mills with fibers instead of developing its tire cord exports. The only textile industry using domestic raw materials is the cordage industry. Henequen fiber, processed in several large plants, is converted into cordage at four mills, one of which, the Cía. de Jarcia de Matanzas, S.A., is the largest cordage plant in Latin America. Much rope and twine was formerly exported to the United States.

Lumber and wood products have been imported in large quantities because of the extensive depletion of forest reserves early in this century. In 1956 sawmills produced about eighty million board feet of lumber a year for domestic consumption. Beverage crates, cigar boxes, and millwood were produced domestically, but all plywood and veneers were imported. Most furniture is custom-built in shops employing less than five people.

The construction industry has made a major contribution to the economy, especially since the end of World War II. Private building activity has been high since 1946, and public works were stimulated by the adoption of the Economic Development Plan in 1950. Public and private construction since 1951 has averaged about $100 million a year. It evidently suffered an initial setback after the revolution but recovered with the initiation of the government's public housing program.

Petroleum refining capacity increased sixfold—from 9,100 barrels to 59,000 barrels per day—between 1954 and 1957, largely because of government legislation in 1954 encouraging domestic refining of imported crude oil. Two new refineries completed in 1957 (one in Havana with a daily capacity of 20,000 barrels) accounted for most of this increase. Daily consumption of refined petroleum, about 60,000 barrels, was adequately met by the new refineries whose total daily capacity amounted to 80,000 barrels. Until 1959, the refineries were owned and operated by Esso Standard Oil Company, S.A., Cía. Petrolera Shell de Cuba, S.A., and Texas Company (West Indies), Ltd. After nationalization of the refineries in 1960, considerable difficulty was encountered in refining the large quantities of different grades of crude oil imported from the Soviet Union.

About one-third of Cuba's tire and tube needs and most rubber for heels and soles were manufactured domestically. In 1941, the B. F. Goodrich Company established the first tire and tube factory. United States Rubber, Cía. Goodyear de Cuba, S.A., and Firestone Tire and Rubber Company followed in 1945, 1946, and 1956 respectively. All the raw materials for production, excepting rayon tire cord, were imported. Several small factories produced rubber footwear which has largely replaced the handmade cord-soled shoe.

An important function of the metal industry was to supply sugar mills with equipment and parts. Several large iron and steel foundries supplied parts and built mill rolls, vacuum pans, evaporators, boilers, and other heavy equipment. A few smaller foundries processed aluminum, bronze, and copper. A great number of machine and blacksmith shops, some of which belonged to sugar mills, provided parts and repairs. The raw material for this metallurgical industry came mostly from imported pig iron and scrap. Metal products also included a wide range of domestic hardware.

Other manufactures included plastics (buttons, toys, bottle caps, etc.), candles, brushes and brooms, jewelry, and matches. In most cases imported raw materials were used in their production. Most of the machinery utilized was imported. There were assembly plants for automobile batteries, radios, and electric irons but none for passenger cars or trucks. The making of machinery was only a small segment of industry, and the sugar mills were the chief customers.

Electric power is derived mostly from imported fuel oil. There is no abundant source of domestic fuel other than bagasse and the hydroelectric potential is very limited. Ninety percent of public power is furnished by one company, the Cía. Cubana de Electricidad, which until it was nationalized in 1959 was a subsidiary of the American and Foreign Power Company. The private industrial sector in most instances furnished its own power needs. This was particularly true of the sugar mills which used bagasse both in creating steam power for their grinding operations and for producing their electricity. Rather than operate their steam-generating plants the year round, sugar mills often produced electricity only during the *zafra*. During the dead season they utilized electricity produced by the Cía. Cubana de Electricidad.

Article 271 of the 1940 constitution declared the development of industry and agriculture to be a primary function of the nation and economic diversification necessary for the public benefit. Little was done in the way of government promotion of industry, however, until the 1950's, except for some wartime emergency measures. In 1950 the government established the Agricultural and Industrial Development Bank for the purpose of granting credit to industry and agriculture. Other quasi-state institutions were established with much the same purpose, including: the Financial Bank of Cuba, the Bank for Economic and Social Development (BANDES); the Bank for Agricultural Development (BFA); and the Mortage Insurance Institute (FHA). The latter insured commercial bank loans for residential construction. Collectively, these agencies were called the Banca Oficial (BANCA), and they were responsible for a large increase in government spending for development during the latter 1950's (see Table 7).

Industrial and construction projects were often undertaken by means of government concessions to private companies, the government putting up most of the money, the company the remainder. This was the customary method of financing mining projects and large public enterprises. The government also floated industrial development bonds and encouraged commercial banks to increase their loans.

All this financial activity of the late 1950's had a decided effect on construction and industry. In 1952 private construction totaled $53 million and public construction $76 million. By 1957 the figures were $77 million for private construction and $195 million for the public sector. Among the important projects undertaken during this period were the Havana tunnel, a cast-iron pipe factory, a grain-processing factory, a paper plant, a cement pipe factory, a steel rod mill, waterworks in several cities, oil exploration, hotels, roads, and public buildings. The government also purchased the Western Railroad, formerly the Ferrocarriles Unidos de la Habana, from a British concern for $20 million.

Only about a third of the government development loans, however, went into industry; a great part of the money went into monuments, parks, and buildings that were never completed. It was evident that the government's chief concern, as in the past, was to provide jobs rather than increase production.

Domestic Trade

The domestic market is the most highly developed in Latin America largely because, unlike those countries where the rural population consists mostly of subsistence farmers, the rural inhabitants nearly all work for wages. Before Castro the market fluctuated in direct response to the *zafra*, during which railway traffic, banking transactions, and wholesale and retail trade all increased measurably. After the *zafra*, wages dropped, consumer purchases declined and domestic commerce contracted. Installment buying and dependence on merchants for credit were greatly encouraged by this seasonal activity. This yearly fluctuation was more pronounced before World War II than in later years. During the last years of the Batista regime and subsequently, efforts were made to smooth out the erratic yearly cycle of prosperity and depression.

Until the government took over many distribution functions in 1959, island-wide distribution of goods was effected through numerous wholesalers, retailers, commission merchants, and traveling salesmen, and was greatly aided by the good highway and railway systems radiating from Havana, the major port of entry for foreign goods. In all towns and cities, retail shops offered a wide range of consumer goods. The distribution system for imported goods was well developed; in 1955 it was estimated that, of the total value of wholesale trade and services, imported products accounted for about 55 percent and domestic products for 45 percent.

Local markets were generally large old buildings where both wholesale and retail trade were carried on simultaneously. Traders set prices regardless of true market conditions. In the absence of an auction system, different prices for the same produce usually prevailed. There were no published lists of prices, no market information, and no indices that could have given the farmer some idea of the price to expect for his goods. Under these conditions the merchant was in a position to exploit both the farmer and the consumer. There were no standard grading methods, and merchants frequently sold as first-quality goods items purchased from the farmer at second-quality prices. Farmers made trips to towns to purchase goods and services, to market their produce, and to receive their mail. In tobacco regions, especially in Pinar del Río, farmers might make a daily trip, but in the remote coffee-growing regions a trip once a week was more common. Where farmers were particularly isolated, barter between neighboring farms was quite common, although most goods were exchanged for cash.

Retail price markups seemed to follow no consistent pattern. Before 1959 several different stores on the same street might sell identical items at prices varying as much as 100 percent. Local merchants often charged exorbitant prices. Imported United States agricultural machinery was frequently sold at prices 20 percent to 200 percent above the United States retail price.

Domestic manufacturers occasionally pointed to low sales volume as the reason for increasing their prices. When imported items became competitive, they requested higher tariffs but instead of taking advantage of the tariff to undersell foreign competitors they raised their prices, lost the tariff advantage, and then requested still higher tariffs to protect their business. Cartel and price-fixing arrangements among single industries, such as the brick, match, shoe, and textile industries, were sometimes resorted to with government sanction. In other industries, such as milk-canning, producers followed the price policies of the largest firm.

Prices often varied according to the channels of trade from manufacturer to consumer. While some manufacturers sold directly to small retailers, others favored bulk sales to wholesalers, and the consumer price varied directly with the number of middlemen handling the item. Hoarding to corner the market and to speculate on prices was a common occurrence. Unethical business practices such as food adulteration and the watering of milk were frequently practiced, and retail merchants often took advantage of the confusion attendant on the use of both Spanish and English standards of measure.

Until 1959 there was little direct government control of domestic trade. Since 1959, however, most wholesale and retail trade in farm produce has come under state control and operation, and domestically manufactured goods are controlled at the source as the plants have been nationalized. Although the government has stated that it does not intend to drive out the small retailer, many have been forced out of business.

The major trade problems in 1961 were the growing shortage of consumer goods and the increasing difficulty of maintaining controls to keep prices in line with wages. The shortage became particularly acute after the United States established an embargo on all but food and medical shipments to Cuba. Over 70 percent of imports, most of them foodstuffs and other consumer goods, had formerly come from the United States. Industry, already disrupted by sudden changes in management and ownership, could not fill the gap—nor could many of the goods be supplied readily by nations in the Soviet bloc.

The exact scope of government intervention in domestic trade could not be determined. In backward, mountainous areas the government apparently controlled every facet of distribution, from the purchase of the farmer's goods to their sale at Peoples' Stores. In the more developed rural areas, established merchants still did business, but apparently were never certain of their source of supplies since the government had priority on all domestically produced goods.

Cuba's transportation system is the best developed in Latin America, but is still far from adequate. Every town of over 5,000 population is connected either by rail or highway, and nineteen cities have scheduled air transport facilities. The internal transportation system has been relieved of part of the burden of sugar transport by the many excellent harbors around the island. Road and rail construction has been facilitated by the flat or undulating terrain and the small number of streams. The road network, developed largely since 1927, consists of about 5,000 miles of all-weather roads, some 3,500 miles of which are paved (see the map, Transportation System). There are, in addition, about 3,200 miles of roads passable only during the dry season. The most important artery of communication and the chief connecting link between major cities is the Central Highway, built between 1927 and 1931 at a cost of $110 million. Over 700 miles long, it runs from Pinar del Río to Santiago de Cuba, following the central axis of the island except where it turns north to Havana and Matanzas and south to Bayamo and Santiago de Cuba. In 1950 it carried about 70 percent of the island's road traffic.

Highway building has not progressed uniformly however; some areas, especially in the east, have been particularly neglected. The widespread absence of farm-to-market roads is a serious problem that has retarded rural development and agricultural diversification,

TRANSPORTATION SYSTEM

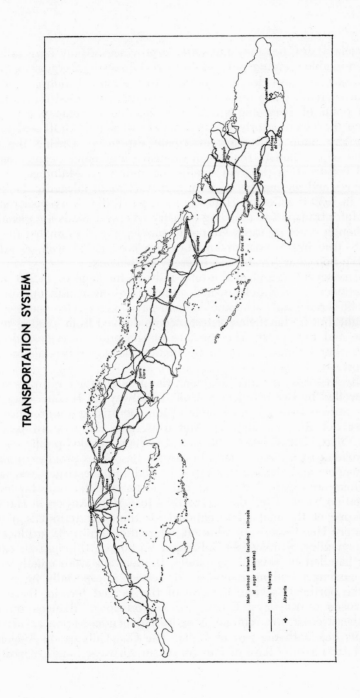

.... Main railroad network (excluding railroads
          of sugar centrals)

———— Main highways

✈ Airports

especially in Camagüey and Oriente provinces. Many farmers have been unable to bring produce to market because, frequently, horse or foot paths provided the only link to the market, railroad, or all-weather road. Once built, roads were often neglected for years to the point of becoming virtually impassable in some places, and often they were poorly planned and constructed. Graft and interruptions made road work extremely expensive. During the last years of the Batista regime an extensive and much-needed repair and construction program finally got underway. Maintenance improved, and the number of farm-to-market roads allegedly doubled, but in 1959 the Central Highway itself was still in very poor repair.

Motor transport is a leading industry wherever roads are passable. Although exact figures were not available, it was estimated that in 1948, trucking companies and bus services carried well over half of the nonsugar freight and intercity passengers.

Sixty-seven percent of the total railroad trackage of 11,256 miles functioned as privately owned adjuncts to sugar mill operations. Public service railways handled both passenger service and general freight, but by far their greatest income derived from hauling sugar cane and raw sugar. The fortunes of the public service railroads were thus intimately tied to fluctuations in sugar production and export.

Except for a very small segment, the public service railways were controlled by two companies. United Railways of Havana operated the entire network west of Santa Clara, comprising the provinces of Pinar del Río, La Habana, Matanzas, and the western part of Las Villas. Consolidated Railroads of Cuba controlled public service railroads east of Santa Clara, in eastern Las Villas province, and in Camagüey and Oriente provinces. United had the largest trackage.

There are excellent domestic and international facilities for transportation by air. Until the end of 1959 José Martí Airport at Havana was one of the major international air transport terminals of the Western Hemisphere. In addition, international airports are located at Camagüey, Santiago de Cuba, and Varadero. Although air cargo was handled by several companies, the airways were chiefly used for passenger and mail service. Air service is especially important in the northeast where, because of the rugged terrain, there are no roads or railways. Except for sea transport, Baracoa on the northeast coast, for example, is entirely dependent upon air service for its link with the rest of Cuba. The Cía. Cubana de Aviación, until 1953 a subsidiary of Pan American Airways, handled most of the island's passenger and mail service. Under Castro the state took over control of this company.

The city of Havana, with its excellent harbor facilities, docks, and warehouses, surpasses all other port cities in volume of trade by sea. Between two-thirds and four-fifths of all imports come through Havana and are distributed to the rest of the island by train and truck. As a port of exit, however, Havana ranks second after Nuevitas in northeast Camagüey province. Because sugar forms the bulk of Cuban exports, ports all along the coast near sugar mills serve as logical shipping points.

For many years coastwise shipping was the principal means of intra-island transport, but the development of railroads and highways caused a decline in coastal trade except for bulk items such as lumber, cement, and sand. In eastern Oriente province, where road building has been retarded by the mountainous terrain, more dependence is placed on coastwise shipping than in other regions. More than half of the coastwise shipping is handled by sailing craft. In the past, Cuban ships handled only 3 percent of the island's international trade; the Castro government expected to spend large sums to develop the island's merchant fleet.

COMPETITION FOR STATUS

CUBANS, LIKE OTHER LATIN AMERICANS, value highly the dignity of the person, the distinctive and innate worth of each individual, but individuality is defined more in terms of personal qualities than of individual rights. The protection of individual rights figures prominently in political speeches and programs, but chiefly as a guarantee of personal integrity, a spiritual quality for which the word "soul" is freely used. The idea of the soul is primarily a secular concept—a means of describing and evaluating personal success and happiness in this world.

Theoretically, material positions and benefits, titular status, and worldly success are not essential to personal dignity; the desire for material goods and successes inhibits the soul. In practice, however, material success is regarded as evidence of spiritual success. Individuality is partly a personal achievement, partly a product of one's home environment, family traditions, associations, and parental inheritance. The ideal person is interesting and valuable because he is unlike anyone else, not because his qualities themselves necessarily approximate to ideal qualities. The concern for personal dignity, together with the complex of political and social attitudes arising from it, is called *personalismo*.

Personal Ideals

Although everybody should be able, in conditions of freedom, to fulfill his spiritual potential, the accepted range of ideal personal qualities tends toward the heroic and implies competition with other people. To be recognized, uniqueness must in effect be achieved by a demonstration of superiority. Unlike the Protestant

Englishman, Robinson Crusoe, whose spiritual fulfillment was ideally achieved in solitude, the Cuban requires a public forum in which to demonstrate and find external supports for his sense of personal integrity.

Success in competition and mastery of one's environment may be demonstrated by a wide range of ideal personal qualities, the most common and admired of which is *machismo* (maleness). The characteristics of the male type (*macho*) in Latin America are summarized by J. P. Gillin (1960):

> The *macho* is expected to show sexual prowess, zest for action, including verbal "action," daring, and, above all, absolute self-confidence. He may express his inner convictions by resorting to physical force, as in the case of bandits and revolutionary military leaders, or he may do so verbally as a leading intellectual, lawyer, or politician. Not all *machos* are caudillos (leaders) but all caudillos must be *machos*.

A husband's virility is considered to be better demonstrated by the birth of sons than of daughters. The ideal of sexual prowess favors extramarital triumphs in which the element of defiance of conventional morality adds luster to the achievement. The implied assertion of the independent right of individuals to justify their own conduct without reference to the prevailing social order has been one of the values characteristic of rationalist insurgent movements. A reputation as a "lady-killer" has accordingly been more important to reformers and revolutionary heroes than to elected officials.

Among conservative people, especially of the upper class, Catholic standards are observed, not only from religious conviction, but also from a more general belief in the importance of law and order. Many of the lower class, however, are out of touch with the concepts of law upheld by the Church, the Constitution, and the courts, although they are familiar with the frequently arbitrary authority of the police, the army, and the civil bureaucracy. Public opinion at this level favors permanent, or at least semipermanent, marital unions out of regard less for the law than for standards of personal responsibility. These standards inhibit women far more than men; a woman who has a series of lovers earns a reputation, not so much for immorality as the upper class understands it as for unreliability and flightiness. On the other hand, colloquial expressions disparage the man whose manly qualities are apparently demonstrated only in sexual exploits.

Manliness may also be displayed in military and athletic prowess. Heroes of this type include the boxer, the baseball player, the cane cutter, and the guerrilla. Not everybody can match the ideal in performance, but most people are enthusiastic spectators, identifying themselves with the boxer or baseball player in his achievements. Batista and Castro both harnessed this enthusiasm to the purposes of the state, Batista by building a Sports City and Castro by providing additional facilities and establishing (in 1961) a Ministry of Physical Education.

The rural sugar worker regards cane cutting as man's work not only because of the muscular exertion required but because of the virile ideal it represents. The cane cutter is a violent, heroic figure, competing to establish records for the number of pounds of cane cut.

The transition is readily made from the cane cutter to the machete-armed peasant defending his rights and finally to the guerrilla. The ideal military type is a hero of hand-to-hand combat, overcoming his enemies by his physical and moral vigor. He is Antonio Maceo mounted on his huge horse, machete in hand; and he is Fidel Castro with his telescopic rifle or swimming to shore with a machine gun on his back. Military heroism is so essential to the ideal leader that José Martí, an intellectual hero in his lifetime but physically frail, felt obligated to risk his life in front-line fighting in order to consolidate his national repute.

Under Castro, the physical training appropriate for a guerrilla has been required for all who carry, or wish to carry, the responsibility for building a new society—defined partly as defending the country against the physical and moral forces of imperialism. To have been in the mountains with Castro is qualification enough for positions of responsibility; the green fatigue uniform of the guerrilla remains the uniform of all true Fidelistas, who, if they were not among the original fighters, wear it as members of the militia. Portly, middle-aged Cubans gird themselves with weapons and ammunition and take up a martial stance in public places, not so much to guarantee public order as to demonstrate their enthusiasm for the new regime.

The idealization of the muscular hero is, however, found chiefly in the lower class. In the upper class the muscular and sexual element, though always present, is muted in favor of intellectual strengths by which the hero overcomes the odds against him. Urbane refinement, transcending the animal heritage of man, is itself an achievement. The intellectual hero, like the military hero, displays his abilities dramatically, especially in oratory. Men of affairs earn respect for an ability to make speeches and publish essays giving philosophical evaluations of current affairs and Cuban social history; many political leaders have also been poets.

The distinctive spirit of an individual is demonstrated by the inexhaustible flow of his eloquence and wit. The splendid, striking gesture has an irresistible appeal. Whatever suggests pettiness of soul is heartily despised no matter how practical it may be. Cuban humor, lively and irrepressible, sometimes broad, often subtly barbed, is applied without inhibition to the most serious issues.

Ironic wit in regard to the nation and its institutions is evident in the national caricature, a cartoon figure called Liborio. Liborio is a nonhero, a vaguely nineteenth-century peasant freedom fighter who has never been glorious. He wears the peasant costume of shirt outside ragged trousers, an unfinished straw hat with a Cuban flag in it, and a droopy mustache; he carries a machete, but somehow has failed to carve a triumphant destiny for himself with it. (Liborio is probably derived from *libertad,* freedom.) Liborio is put upon by braggarts, swashbucklers, politicians, and other self-declared heroes who nevertheless disappear from the scene as suddenly as they come, leaving Liborio eternally hopeful, never at a loss for a wisecrack.

The negative emphases of the Liborio caricature include, besides physical and political ineffectiveness, an unsuccessful air in terms of both status and dress. A Cuban pays close attention to his personal appearance, commonly managing to make a handsome turnout with very small resources and cultivating a solidly built look to demonstrate his prosperity, substance, and self-confidence. Physical defects are often equated with moral defects and can be the subject of a cruel contempt.

For those who can afford it, and even for many who cannot, a conspicuously extravagant standard of living has always been considered essential to the public appearance of success. Expensive cars, hotel entertainments, country estates, clubs, weddings and funerals, clothes, and education were as much marks of distinction in the republican era as noble connections and coats-of-arms in colonial times. High standards of living are characteristically a personal competitive accomplishment; no correspondingly high standards are applied to society in general. Luxurious modern homes, for example, may be located among shacks in areas lacking adequate public sanitation and water supply; the expensive automobile may be driven over unsurfaced and unmaintained roads.

Death for a glorious cause is itself an acceptable achievement as a consequence of the military ideal and as a supreme demonstration of the greatness of a man's soul and his dedication to freedom. One of the slogans of the Castro regime, used by radio announcers signing off and chanted by crowds at public meetings, is "patria o muerte!" (fatherland or death). Similar slogans have always had a strong appeal to Cubans, who have often shown themselves remarkably ready to live up to them.

Death is regarded as the appropriate reward of an opponent—be he an unfaithful lover, a traitor within, or an enemy abroad—who has violated personal confidence. "Paredón!" (to the wall, to the firing-squad) was the fate advocated by cheering crowds in 1960 not only for known perpetrators of atrocities but for all opponents. If a friend or supporter dies, however, it is important to make a martyr-hero of him in order to assert that the physical loss is in reality a gain in the struggle for moral ascendancy. In this mood, generations of teenagers have smuggled arms, defied the police, and planted bombs. Where moral supremacy is at stake and no actual heroism occurs, it is important to invent some; mere competence is not enough.

Death in general, not only violent death, is a major preoccupation. The focus of concern is not so much moral accountability as the strength of the soul; the fate to be feared is oblivion, which is the punishment for inadequacy, rather than hell-fire, the punishment for sin. Strong souls survive the death of the body and continue to be influential in the world, not only through the respect in which their memory is held by the living, but by their continued manipulation of the spiritual forces that made them strong in this life. The world of the dead is ordered hierarchically, like the world of the living. The strongest souls may aspire to become saints, with comprehensive powers in particular fields of human concern, and may act as spiritual patrons to their followers. Beliefs of this kind draw much of their imagery from Catholicism, although the underlying moral evaluations of Catholicism are largely ignored.

Success in life is defined more in terms of the fulfillment of personal destiny or spiritual potential than by the achievement of station. Destiny is thought of as predetermined but is evaluated in terms of the competitive situation and the opportunities that present themselves at any given moment for an immediate improvement in one's personal circumstances. Thus, fatalistic resignation and violently aggressive competitiveness are juxtaposed.

The Cuban is an opportunist; when no opportunity presents itself he is not usually prepared to create one by consistent, methodical effort over a period of time. To be attractive, opportunity must be dramatic; when it occurs, the Cuban's evaluation of his proper destiny is suddenly enhanced, and he finds insupportable all the inadequacies and injustices to which he was formerly resigned.

Destiny is both a product of spiritual forces and a matter of luck. Both aspects are expressed in popular religious beliefs, in which destiny becomes a god. The pervasive gambling impulse springs from the incessant search for a lucky break that will give the necessary special competitive advantage. In the Cuban view, Spaniards rely on hard work to succeed; this is materialism and is despised. Luck, however, is not an external circumstance so much as demonstration of the personal spiritual qualities essential to success. Anybody may discover that it is his destiny to be lucky, to succeed by combinations of fortuitous circumstances.

It is in this spirit that Cubans buy lottery tickets week after week rather than open saving accounts. Similarly, they eagerly wager on the outcome of any event, especially sporting contests and cockfights. In some rural areas almost every household raises its own fighting-cocks. Budgetary thrift inhibits the soul; the possibility of entirely escaping the material limitations of one's present status and environment has far greater appeal than a rational adjustment to those limitations, which would imply acceptance of them as consistent with one's personal destiny.

Luck is vulnerable to the envy of competitors, whose own success is more agreeably attributed to some dishonest trick or device than to superior personal qualities. Among the uneducated, this awareness of the envy of others is expressed as a belief in black magic, against which a charm or other protective device may be effective. Among the educated, the suspected dishonest trick is usually either unscrupulous demagoguery or connivance with imperialists. Even those whose success is not envied are often credited with having access to some special source of power. Fidel Castro was said— more commonly in 1959 than in 1960—to have access to the ageless wisdom of the philosophers, and Batista, according to a rumor widely current in the middle and lower classes, consulted the diviners and deities of the Afro-Cuban religions.

Personal qualities can rarely be realized on an ideal scale. One response to the discrepancy between ideals and reality is to find a hero through whom one can vicariously achieve satisfying dramatic results. Such a leader commands a political following; in 1959 Fidel Castro embodied the ideal qualities to a greater extent than perhaps any previous figure. He was a big man and an excellent athlete, an intellectual and a prodigious speaker. With few resources and from small beginnings he had defied and overthrown all the traditional oppressors—the government, the army, the landowners, the corrupt politicians, the scheming imperialists. His five-hour television speeches demonstrated not only his command of language and ideas but his physical endurance. Opposition to Castro, by both his long-time enemies and those who became disillusioned, was frequently expressed as a personal revulsion from his physical grossness. Upper-class Cubans objected to the beard and Sierra Maestra manners as unrefined and nonurbane. The story that after reading a page he tore it from the book as no longer necessary appealed chiefly to the illiterate. Disillusioned Cubans disparaged the entire self-dramatizing performance by reducing it to the animal component of *machismo*; "He is a horse," they said, gesturing toward the television set.

Pragmatic Compromises

Democracy, permitting people to seek social and material advantages in accordance with their personal destinies, is constantly advocated. But whereas the rewards of transcendent personal greatness are unlimited, the material environment and the benefits it affords are thought of as a fixed quantity. Although designs for an ideal society have been spelled out in a series of detailed constitutions and in innumerable speeches and pamphlets, in practice an hierarchical society is accepted in which, at various levels, those with personal qualifications for leadership, as determined by their "destiny," assume the privileges and status of *patrón*.

Less competent people, compromising between their ideals and the opportunities available, accept provisionally their own lower position in the hierarchy. Part of the compromise is the careful assertion that personal dignity is not infringed by inequality of status; a Cuban, no matter who he is, expects to be treated with individual respect, not as a nonentity. The compromise is also characterized by a search for guarantees. In the social environment guarantees are afforded, not by law or accepted conventions, but by relationships of personal trust and confidence. One does not trust a man because he is a judge, professor, chief of state, businessman, or clergyman, but because one has reached a personal understanding with him.

Relationships of personal trust have two components, both of which are always present, although the particular relationship may exalt one at the expense of the other. The two components are kinship (implying brotherhood, unity of interest, and the absence of competition) and contract (implying a difference in status, lack of reciprocity, and conditional acceptance). In the family, where community of interest is strongest, the head of the family is nevertheless a *patrón*. In the political or economic field, a recognized *patrón*, such as Fidel Castro, whose followers offer their loyalty in exchange for material benefits, is frequently at pains to assert that the bond of unity is actually one of kinship, not of contract. Either kind of agreement establishes an association of people that is of more importance than are organizations and institutions based on laws, principles, or considerations of efficiency. The most conspicuous example of the weakness of law as a binding force is the national constitution itself. Arbitrary and drastic change, such as revolution, is widely regarded as an acceptable political and social process.

The *patrón*, whether he is an estate manager or a political boss (or a guardian angel), provides protection and special favors in exchange for loyalty and service. This relationship is founded upon mutual trust, not on legally defined obligations; in fact it normally operates outside of, and to a great extent in conflict with, formally regulated social and economic structures. The benefits bestowed by the *patrón* are expected but not specifically required of him, and are looked upon as demonstrations of his generosity and magnanimity. Typical examples are the schoolhouse or church provided free by the local landowner, the job preference or political appointment, the Christmas bonus for employees, the alms bestowed at the church door, and the private telephone call to arrange the release of a prisoner.

All such benefits could be guaranteed by law and supported by taxation or other administrative arrangements; in fact, most are provided for in laws that are not carried out. The construction of schools has been repeatedly designated a public responsibility to be paid for ultimately by taxation of the landowners and other

wealthy citizens who would not acquire, through such an arrangement, the personal prestige that is theirs as a consequence of the
patronage system. Nor, in general, would clients and beneficiaries
prefer an impersonal arrangement that would require them to put
their confidence in a law rather than in a person.

Those who benefit from the extralegal privileges of a patronage
relationship do not as a rule question the rights and wrongs of it; if
other individuals, clients of another *patrón,* are seen to suffer a
competitive disadvantage, confidence in the relationship is likely
to be strengthened. This moral relativism is evident in the history of
public reaction to government graft: in general, if one's own
sponsor provides sinecures, this is a demonstration of his magnanimity; but if an opponent does it, it is intolerable corruption.

Demagogues appeal to unanimity and brotherhood in part because these principles deny the envy latent in contractual relationships and the acceptance of hierarchy. Cubans expect to be betrayed
by those in whom they find it expedient to put their trust. Unless
personal confidence remains absolute they are willing to believe
any villainy of former heroes. Entralgo's analysis of the lexicon
(*Apuntes caracteriológicos sobre el léxico cubano,* 1941) notes
particularly the apparent preoccupation with deceit, fraud, public
scandal, and deterioration of character:

> There is presented then the desolate spectacle of a disordered
> mass which seems to clamor desperately for leaders and guides,
> admiring in outstanding individuals the qualities which it lacks
> as a society; sincerity, discernment, and character.

The family is the group within which trust prevails, magnanimity
is displayed, personalities are respected, and competition and envy
kept at a minimum. Relationships of trust are most easily established
with relatives, whose personal qualities, because of community of
interest, common heredity, and similarity of environment, most
nearly resemble one's own. The symbol of this familiar exclusive-
ness is the thick-walled Spanish home with its barred windows,
which protects an individual's honor as well as his property. The
sexual common denominator of social rivalry lends special emphasis
to the defense of the male domain against seducers and against
suitors from families with whom it is not desirable to establish
relationships of trust.

Beyond the family, confidence prevails in associations patterned
after it, up to the widest possible association, the united nation

(*la familia cubana*), which has never existed as more than an ideal passionately or wistfully sought after. The closest pseudokinship relationship is that of the *compadrazgo* which, in its most limited sense, is the link established between a godfather and the parents of his godson. It is also the link between the godfather and other adults with whom the parents may share a *compadrazgo* relationship and so has become the ordinary colloquial term for intimate friendship. It is of greater importance in the lower than in the upper class, where other formulas of friendship have almost entirely replaced the religious original. *Compadre* (often used in the popular form, *compai*) means friend but specifically implies a spiritual kinship between equals.

Wider associations of people spiritually akin include the clients of a particular patron in any field; members of a professional association, union, or pressure group; political parties; and the employees of a particular enterprise. In practice, admission to such a group depends more on sponsorship, that is, on patronage, than on external qualifications; frequently such sponsorship is actually nepotism, so that the group is in part composed of relatives. Even where membership is compulsory and apparently based solely on external qualifications, as in the case of the *colegios* (professional associations) through which the government licenses lawyers, veterinarians, journalists, and the like to practice, protectionist policies have been operative.

Members of a pseudofamilial association have a common material interest, either functional, as in the case of unions, or synthetic, as in the case of political parties. The effectiveness of an association depends upon the maintenance of a common loyalty, frequently the subject of impassioned appeals, which is balanced by an equally passionate refusal to recognize interests shared with groups considered to be competitors. In consequence, an electoral defeat is regarded not so much as the rejection of a party's policy as a slap to its self-respect, a denial of its spiritual validity. It is assumed, usually with reason, that the successful party will exploit the victory to its own material advantage. The role of a loyal and cooperative opposition is inconsistent with the competitive impulse; it becomes the duty of the opposition to point out in dramatic terms the untrustworthiness of the government party, which, it is asserted, must owe its success not to its capacity for leadership but to its perversion of the electoral process. Since acceptable morality is that which prevails within the association, the competing group is presented as utterly devoid of principle. Truth is held to be absolute and proprietary; those who hold another point of view must be wilfully perverting the truth for the sake of obtaining a competitive advantage. Education (the teaching of "truth") has accordingly been an acknowledged vehicle of propaganda and an instrument of partisan recruitment since the early nineteenth century.

Change of opinion is represented by the losing group as defection and abandonment of principle, again for the sake of an immoral ("material") advantage. This attribution of high principles to one's friends and materialism to one's opponents forced Cuban propagandists to make some subtle distinctions in explaining to the people in March 1961 the defection of José Pardo Llada, who was long one of Castro's most violently outspoken propagandists. While he adhered to the regime, his opinions, they explained, were the product of loyalty and dedication to principle; his defection and subsequent opinions were attributed solely to his mercenary acceptance of substantial bribes.

Cuba Libre

When the ordinary processes of compromise, exploitation of the patronage system, reliance on relatives and friends, oratorical appeals, and private arrangements fail to guarantee the Cuban the environment he seeks, he is likely, if he is a member of the lower class, to blame his condition upon the government. The government and authorities in general are an impersonal "they" whom he considers to be properly responsible for the entire state of society. The tradition of centralized, autocratic control of planning and administration, inherited from Spain, discourages local popular initiative. The government, in whose name the police and other petty tyrants act and with which the *patrón* may claim to have some influence, is too remote from most of the lower class for them to feel any personal confidence in it; constitutional guarantees alone mean nothing. If, however, the lower-class Cuban is able to identify the government as a single powerful man, then the relationship between government and people takes on the personal characteristics of relations between individual men. Accordingly, the lower-class citizen does not accept the government's policy in one field and reject it in another; his confidence in the *jefe supremo* or *líder máximo* is either absolute or nonexistent.

For those who have confidence in him, the mandate of the chief of state is his personal stature as a hero. A constitutional mandate is by comparison insignificant; it is even a mark of the hero's greatness that he is able to overcome constitutionally imposed limitations. His conduct defines the law, not the law his conduct. Distrust of a particular leader is always phrased in terms of appeals to humanism, liberty, democracy, and fundamental rights, which are used to describe a Cuban utopia.

In the upper class, dissatisfaction with social conditions and the rewards of individual aspiration may be expressed in several ways. Members of the middle and upper classes whose incomes are drawn from investments and commercial activity and whose interests are best served by stability and institutional continuity, point to a utopia located in the past. Social evils—from alcoholism and juvenile delinquency to Communism and bomb-throwing— will be cured, they assert, by a return to neglected principles. The *jefe supremo* to whom they look is more likely to be a military *caudillo* like Batista than a demagogue like Castro. Lacking a leader, they appeal to law, the democratic process, and, perhaps, as in the 1950's, to the Catholic Church. In 1957, spokesmen for this group deplored the patronage relationship and the values of *personalismo* which lie at the heart of it. To them, *personalismo* was synonymous with the breakdown of confidence in the social system; with the violence of the personal attacks made by politicians against their opponents; with the physical violence and lawlessness of prerevolutionary tension; and with the diminishing public regard for the decencies of behavior. These conditions they blamed on Communist influence.

The intellectuals, union organizers, and public servants of the middle sector—ambitious, educated, salaried, and underemployed men—are more likely to turn to a reformer, one who promises extensive changes with particular benefit to those who support him. Their utopia is located in the future, and their slogan in the twentieth century as in the nineteenth is "Cuba Libre!" (Free Cuba). Their hope lies not in the institutions supporting the existing order—the army, business interests, the law courts—but in specially created instruments subservient to the will of the *líder maximo*. In 1960 these included the militia, the National Agrarian Reform Institute, and the firing squad.

Many members of the middle sector, however, are more interested in becoming heroes themselves than in following another. The competition among them is expressed by arguments concerning the merits of their various programs, but the practical requirements of the common interest are not enough to force the development of a common program. On the contrary, the more pressing the requirements and the more apparent the opportunity for heroism, the greater the disagreement. In 1895 it took all the eloquence of José Martí to unite enough emigré Cubans in Miami and New York to mount an effective invasion. In 1961 estimates of the number of competing counterrevolutionary Cuban groups in the United States ranged as high as 200.

The appeal of dissatisfied groups to universal moral principles does not mean that in the day of success they reject the principles of *personalismo* out of respect for the rule of law. This apparent contradiction was perhaps explained by a Cuban writer in his analysis of the first years of the Republic after the revolution in 1898:

> Between the past and the present there is an immense difference. The former represented the sacrifice of everything on the altar of the ideal; the latter, the shame of the country at the mercy of egoism. The former, the love of Cuba; the latter, the philosophy of the stomach.

Programs for reform are usually a matter of giving power to a single leader who has the confidence of the people. The entire movement is named after the leader—Machadismo, Batistianismo, Fidelismo. When he has achieved power, confidence in him is retained by those who find satisfaction in the new social order. The constitutional reforms of the original program—abolition of corruption in government, of economic monopolies, of race discrimination—are no longer considered necessary except by those who, having lost faith in the leader, are once again appealing to universal moral principles.

It is doubtful indeed whether sound government alone would be sufficient to satisfy a majority and ensure the stability of any regime; Estrada Palma, the only honest president playing a significant part in Cuban history, died in poverty and ignominy. The people are not prepared to wait for long-term benefits. Accordingly, after the first flush of success, governments have resorted to the usual techniques of compromise, rewarding the most influential sectors of the population at the expense of the rest and resorting when necessary to military force.

In such a case dissidents speak of "the revolution betrayed." "Cuba Libre" has never been and can never be any more than a utopian ideal, but its failure is inevitably blamed on traitors, opportunists, and those who exploited the popular trust for selfish ends. If no obvious enemy exists, one must be invented. He may be Estrada Palma or Machado or Batista or Ché Guevara. Since the mid-nineteenth century, however, the most convenient enemy has been imperialism, especially that of the United States—a power sufficiently remote and sufficiently varied that almost anything can be attributed to it with some appearance of plausibility. The culture, government, businessmen, and troops of the United States have been blamed for the poverty of Cuban peasants, the corruption of Cuban governments, the inefficiency of the Cuban economy, the existence of "privilege" and racial discrimination in Cuba, and the perpetration of atrocities by Cuban policemen. Dissidents appealing to nationalist sentiments, that is, to ideals of Cuban brotherhood, assert that such things are contrary to the native morality of the Cuban "family" and can only exist with the support of an amoral foreign competitor.

The values of *personalismo* are applied without hesitation to international affairs. Where confidence exists, compliments can never be too extravagant; where confidence does not exist, abuse and denunciation can never be sufficiently ingenious, histrionic, and comprehensive.

The tradition of comprehensive government responsibility, the direct and indirect personal economic dependence of most Cubans on government, and the importance of conspicuous public action to the ideal type of the successful man have made politics a dominant concern, in a sense not limited to the mechanics of governmental and political processes. In 1946 a sample of farmers asked to list their recreational activities on their visits to town mentioned political meetings more often than any other except social visiting, and twice as often as movies or cockfights. In 1956 a total of 651 books published included 7 on philosophy, 59 on religion, 14 on philology, 97 on the arts and literature, and 106 on pure and applied science; 273 were devoted to the social sciences, geography, and history, which in Cuba are usually pseudonyms for politics.

POLITICAL INSTITUTIONS TO 1958

CUBAN INTELLECTUALS HAVE MUCH DEBATED the nature and means of creating a desirable society, most of them assuming that change must be instituted by the central government rather than left to undirected evolutionary processes. Increasingly they have regarded the root of the country's social problems as economic and, since the twenties, the students especially have accepted Marxist criticism of capitalism, which in Cuba means concentration of ownership rather than individual enterprise.

Idealism appeared to triumph in the writing of constitutions, opportunism in their implementation. Constitutions were statements of national goals rather than outlines of procedure; often the legislature failed to enact the basic legislation called for in them. Despite the considerable efforts of critics and would-be reformers, the government was almost always corrupt, sometimes venal, with political office used as a primary means of economic and social advancement. At times, the government was the prize for which conflicting groups fought, with political weapons or with arms. Usually, however, the government was but the partially successful arbiter of political forces; it was used in many ways by many persons to buy support, to placate opposition, to threaten, and to ensure the support of powerful interest groups. The patronage function of government took precedence over all others. As a result, there was little effective action to remedy the basic social and economic ills. The two most important constitutions were those adopted by elected constitutional conventions in 1901 and 1940. Others were transitional or modifications of the basic documents serving the purposes of dictatorship.

The 1901 Constitution was drawn up during the first United States occupation and reflected United States influence, particularly in the phrasing of provisions for the separation of powers. Also evident, in the individual liberties it guaranteed, were the effects of the recent political struggle. But in general the new constitution followed the pattern of other Latin American constitutions.

After a short preamble stating as the purpose of the Constitution to provide for "an independent, sovereign state . . . capable of fulfilling its international obligations, securing liberty and justice, and promoting the general welfare," the first article defined the territory of the state, declared it to have a republican form of government, and defined the nature of citizenship. The determination of citizenship was particularly important because of the large numbers of Spanish immigrants. Children born in Cuba of foreign parents were not considered Cubans unless they so registered at the age of twenty-one. Children born to Cubans abroad were considered Cuban citizens. Aliens were guaranteed the same rights as citizens except in matters of political participation.

The detailed provisions guaranteeing individual rights mostly concerned equality before the law and protection from arbitrary police power. In cases of serious public disturbance, rights of free speech, press, assembly, and petition might be temporarily suspended. The section on individual rights stated, in regard to religion, that freedom of religion was unconditionally guaranteed, that church and state were to be separate, and that no church might be subsidized. Primary education, to be compulsory and free, was made the responsibility of the state. Suffrage was extended to all male citizens over twenty-one except those in active military service, criminals, or those certified as mentally incompetent.

The Constitution vested executive power in the president, to be elected for a four-year term with tenure limited to two terms. The president was assisted by a vice-president who presided in the Senate, and by a Cabinet of his choice whose members were removable, like the president, only on conviction following impeachment. Besides exercising the usual powers of the chief executive the president might issue executive orders and decrees necessary to carry out the law and for "purposes of administration not at variance with the law." If Congress failed to enact the budget, he was empowered to keep in effect the budget of the previous year. He could suspend the constitution in time of invasion or serious public disturbance either with the prior consent of Congress or without its consent provided that he call it into session within thirty days.

Legislative power was vested in a Congress consisting of a Senate and a Chamber of Representatives. An equal number of senators from each province were elected for eight-year terms, half of the Senate being renewed every four years. The Chamber of Representatives was composed of one representative for each 25,000 persons elected by universal male suffrage for four-year terms, half of the house being renewed every two years. The powers of the two houses were defined much as in the United States constitution.

The judiciary was declared independent, and provision was made for a Supreme Court appointed by the president with Senate approval. The Supreme Court was given the power to declare laws unconstitutional. Regulation of the lower judiciary was left to future legislation.

In practice several provisions in the constitution were made use of to violate the spirit of the constitutional system: constitutional guarantees were suspended to further political control; the requirement that two-thirds of the members of Congress must be present to convene was used to prevent congressional action; congressional power to declare amnesties and presidential power to grant pardons were flagrantly abused, particularly in pre-election periods. A provision that protected a congressman from arrest or indictment unless he were apprehended while committing a criminal act meant that a congressman in effect could not be prosecuted unless Congress voted to waive his immunity, which seldom happened. A congressman employed by a newspaper could by means of his immunity protect the paper from libel suits. There were times when a high proportion of congressmen had criminal records.

Discussions concerning the need for a new constitution occupied an important place in political life after the overthrow of the Machado dictatorship in 1933. The effective life of the 1901 Constitution was widely regarded as having ended in 1928, when Machado amended it in order to perpetuate his power. Many public figures blamed constitutional inadequacies for the failure of successive governments to operate within the law and to meet national needs. Economic stagnation after 1920 also reinforced the conviction of many young intellectuals and the newly organized labor movement that progress could be achieved only through governmental direction.

The convening of a constitutional convention was frequently promised after 1933, but was postponed until 1939. The govern-

ments in power from 1933 to 1936 were *ad hoc* groups which reflected, more than anything else, Batista's increasing power. Each
operated under a constitutional law of its own creation which
vested executive and legislative power in the Cabinet, at times with
the assistance of an appointed consultative body. In 1935, President
Mendieta restored a modified version of the 1901 Constitution—
a major change was an amendment granting the vote to women—
and prepared for national elections. The inauguration of President
Gómez in May 1936 was regarded as a return to constitutional
government even though the reformist and radical groups that
emerged in the early 1930's had been proscribed and did not contest
the elections. In 1936, however, Batista organized the impeachment
of President Gómez, and thus increased the dissatisfaction of all
political groups with the existing system.

Batista's decision to hold elections for a constituent assembly
in 1939 opened a debate in which all of the major political groupings of the 1930's participated for the first time. The move greatly
increased his popularity and advanced his goal of becoming constitutional president. It also afforded the opposition the first real
opportunity to make its views effective in national life. For the first
time, the Auténtico party headed by Grau San Martín was strongly
represented in an arena where major political decisions were made.
The recently legalized Communist party and all the more traditional
parties were also represented.

The Assembly agreed that the new constitution should outline a
new political and social order and that the major political problem
was the dominance of the executive. Remedies proposed for more
than a decade by José Manuel Cortina, Cuba's leading jurist and
president of the drafting committee of the Assembly, were in large
part incorporated into new constitutional provisions outlining a
system of semiparliamentary government to limit executive power.
Detailed attention to governmental procedures clearly reflected the
Assembly's desire to end former specific abuses. Long articles devoted to the government's economic and social responsibilities and
to the guarantee of individual social and economic rights reflected
the philosophy primarily of the Auténtico political leaders, but
also had the support of the Communists, who were engaged in
popular front tactics, and of Batista and his non-Communist supporters.

Of the total of 286 articles in the 1940 Constitution, 61 dealt
with social and economic matters under such headings as "the

family and culture," "labor and prosperity," and "the national economy." The family, maternity, and marriage were given the protection of the nation. Article 47 stated that "culture in all of its manifestations is a primordial interest of the nation." To this end the government was required to provide obligatory and free primary education, secondary and normal schools, adult education to eradicate illiteracy, and training in commercial and technical subjects. All instruction was to be "inspired by a spirit of Cubanism and human solidarity, tending to form in the conscience of students a love for country. . . ."

Most of the provisions dealing with social and economic matters were statements of purpose requiring additional legislation. The section on labor, however, incorporated much legislation already enacted between 1933 and 1940. The right to work was declared to be "an inalienable right of the individual" and the maintenance of full employment a national responsibility. Workers were guaranteed a minimum daily wage; fair payment for piecework, to be made only in legal tender; a maximum day of 8 hours and week of 44 hours; and a month of annual paid vacation. Additional provisions limited the work to be required of minors and women. Social security and protection against disability, old age, and unemployment were guaranteed. Workers were granted the right to organize and to strike.

The provisions on labor, property, and the economy reflected the spirit of economic nationalism prevalent since the early 1930's and the large role intended for the government in regulating economic life. Employers, when hiring, were required to favor Cubans by birth over naturalized Cubans, naturalized Cubans with families born in Cuba over other naturalized Cubans, and all Cubans over aliens. The constitution provided that labor disputes be submitted to conciliation boards composed of equal numbers of representatives of labor and management presided over by a judicial official; decisions were binding but might be appealed to the Supreme Court. Other provisions set forth the principle that economic activity must be regulated in the national interest and that the size of landholdings, by foreigners and Cubans, should be reduced and limited by law. The government was to develop national agriculture and industry, regulate agricultural contracts, prevent the formation of monopolies, and organize a national bank of issue and rediscount.

The individual political rights granted in the 1940 Constitution were very similar to those guaranteed in 1901 though many were modified or outlined in greater detail to meet earlier abuses. For example, provisions against arbitrary arrest and inequality before the law were stated in greater detail than in the earlier document. New provisions prohibited the confiscation of property without compensation and except by competent judicial authority; prohibited the death penalty except in cases of treason or in the military establishment; and recognized the right of political asylum. The revised constitution also provided that "adequate resistance for the protection of the individual rights above guaranteed is legitimate"—a provision popularly interpreted as recognizing the right to rebel.

To meet the problem of domination by the executive, the Cabinet was made responsible to the Congress instead of being removable only through impeachment procedure. The objective of limiting presidential power, however, was vitiated through compromise clauses that forbade raising votes of confidence until six months after a Cabinet took office, or during the last six months of a president's term. A further stipulation was made that neither house could vote on the same issue more than once a year.

The president was required to be at least thirty-five years old. He was to be elected by universal suffrage and might serve a second four-year term only after a lapse of eight years. The provisions regarding the executive authority were similar to those in the 1901 Constitution, but all executive orders required the countersignature of the appropriate minister.

Legislative power was vested in the Senate and Chamber of Representatives. Nine senators from each province were to be elected by universal suffrage for four-year terms. Representatives were elected every four years, one for each 35,000 people, half the house being renewed every two years. Except for their increased control over the executive, the powers of the two houses were much as in 1901.

The judiciary was declared independent. A Chamber of Constitutional and Social Guarantees was to be established within the Supreme Court to consider constitutional and social questions. Each member of the Supreme Court was to be appointed by the president, with the approval of the Senate, from a list of three nominees presented by a special electoral college. Appointment, promotion, and regulation of members of the lower judiciary were vested in a special government section of the Supreme Court composed of the chief justice and six members of the Court chosen annually. Entry into the judiciary was to be by examination; no member of the judiciary or the Prosecution Service under the Ministry of Justice was to be removed without cause.

Three autonomous bodies described in the constitution were intended to regulate areas in which abuses had been common. The Superior Electoral Court, composed of three Supreme Court justices and two justices of the Havana Court of Appeals chosen by their respective members, was given final authority in determining electoral claims and in issuing instructions to the armed forces and police during elections. A Board of Public Offices, to regulate the civil service, was to have seven members, chosen, one each, by the Supreme Court, the president, Congress, the council of the University of Havana, national employees, provincial employees, and municipal employees. The constitution defined carefully the types of positions that were to be considered political and therefore outside the civil service merit system. A third agency, the Tribunal of Accounts, was to be made responsible for the auditing of all accounts of national, provincial, and municipal governments and of autonomous agencies receiving revenues from the government. The Tribunal was required to report to the president and Congress annually or when requested, and to publish its reports.

Suspension of constitutional guarantees, including habeas corpus, was permitted in cases of invasion or serious public disturbance, such suspension not to exceed forty-five days. The suspension could be accomplished by congressional vote or executive decree. In the latter case, Congress was required to meet within forty-eight hours to approve or reject the order. Alternatively, Congress could declare a state of emergency and vest special powers in the Cabinet. During any period of emergency a special commission of twenty-four members of Congress was to meet "to watch over the use of the exceptional facilities granted to the Cabinet."

Partial amendment of the constitution could be initiated by petition of 100,000 literate voters, followed by submission to a national referendum at the next election. If action to amend the constitution were initiated by Congress, the amendment required the approval of a two-thirds majority of the two houses meeting jointly. Complete revision, or revision involving certain articles, required the election of a constituent assembly. Because of the misuse of the 1901 provision by Machado, extending the tenure of any official was made particularly difficult.

5. Political Institutions to 1958

Governmental Structure in Practice

The distribution of powers in practice never followed the outlines of constitutional documents and varied considerably even within brief periods. Outstanding examples of the failure to make the 1940 Constitution fully operative were suspension of constitutional guarantees because of war or internal unrest; failure to enact legislation establishing governmental institutions called for by the constitution; and continued abuse of appointment and patronage powers. The government remained, as it had always been, highly centralized, with little effective authority exercised by provincial or municipal bodies. Critics of the central government tended to regard the 1940 Constitution as a goal still to be reached, and to judge governments partially in terms of their progress in implementing it during the years it was in effect.

When the 1940 Constitution was drafted, it was recognized that the power of appointment was the cause of much of the abuse and graft prevalent in the political system. To remedy this, detailed provisions for the wide distribution of the appointive power were included, but it remained the most common source of corruption. It was almost impossible for an individual to receive an appointment as a teacher, policeman, or civil servant of any kind, without political patronage.

None of the three presidents of the Republic between 1940 and 1952 (Batista, Grau San Martín, and Prío Socarrás) was amenable to parliamentary control. Each at some time violated constitutional provisions concerning executive-legislative powers. During the first two years under the constitution, however, Congress occasionally made effective use of its rights of interpellation and censure. Extra powers voted Batista because of the war then made him less dependent on congressional action.

President Grau San Martín, carrying the Auténtico party into power in 1944 for the first time, at times openly flaunted his independence of constitutional restrictions. The government came closest to conforming to the constitution under Carlos Prío Socarrás (1948-1952). During his tenure four institutions called for by the constitution—the Bank for Agricultural and Industrial Development, the National Bank, the Chamber of Constitutional and Social Guarantees, and the Tribunal of Accounts—were provided for in legislation. The independent Board of Public Offices was never created, and the abuse of patronage powers remained extreme.

Batista's *coup d'état* of March 10, 1952 inaugurated a two-and-one-half-year period during which he governed under a fundamental law incorporating most of the 1940 Constitution but omitting the sections providing for representative government. All functions of Congress were vested in the Cabinet; an eighty-member consultative body provided some contact with public opinion. Political parties were dissolved. Constitutional guarantees were suspended for forty-five days on March 10, 1952 and intermittently after that; for shorter periods censorship also was imposed. In 1953, a law was enacted which provided severe penalties for any disrespectful attack (*desacato*) on the government, effectively stifling criticism of the regime.

Many restrictions were lifted in 1954 as the government prepared to hold elections, and in August Batista resigned to campaign—successfully—for the presidency. With his inauguration in February 1955 and the convening of Congress, the 1940 Constitution was once again in effect. Technically it remained so until shortly before Castro's victory in 1959, but Batista's control of Congress was virtually complete, and from 1956 through 1958 constitutional guarantees were suspended most of the time.

During this period presidential authority was expressed through the Cabinet and the top military personnel—all of whom served at the will of President Batista. Regular ministries included State, Interior, Treasury, National Defense, Education, Public Works, Agriculture, Health and Welfare, Commerce, Labor, Communications, Information and Justice (see the chart, Structure of Government before 1958). Additional members served without portfolio, and the President's secretary also served as Secretary of the Cabinet. One of the ministers was also named prime minister, his main function being to represent the executive before Congress.

Of the regular Cabinet positions that of Minister of Interior was the most powerful. The department supervised relations with provincial and municipal governments, contained the Civil Service Commission, and had administrative control of the national police. The position of Minister of Labor was influential because of the large role played by the government in settling labor disputes and because of the political orientation of organized labor. The ministries of Education, Health and Welfare, Public Works, and Agriculture were described in the constitution as technical departments to be headed by men chosen for technical competence. In practice the heads of these ministries were very powerful political figures because of their large budgets and the patronage they controlled.

Wide authority to regulate the economy was vested in autonomous executive agencies. In addition to the agencies created in the 1930's to stabilize specific agricultural crops, several new agencies—among them the Agricultural and Industrial Development Bank and the Economic and Social Development Bank— were formed in the 1950's to lend capital to persons willing to develop new industries. Although to some extent fulfilling the purposes for which they were designed, these agencies were also used for political patronage.

Under the 1940 Constitution the legislature was expected to

STRUCTURE OF THE GOVERNMENT BEFORE 1958

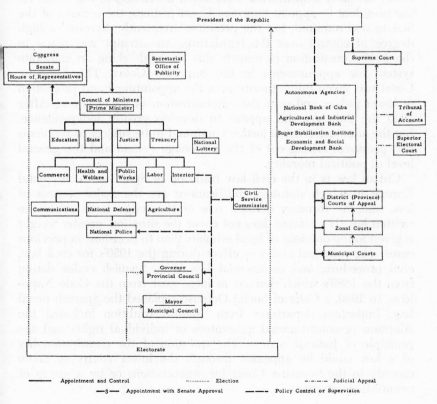

play a larger role in governmental affairs because of the provision for ministerial responsibility, but despite occasional efforts to assert its prerogatives the legislature never developed a permanently strong position. Each house chose its officers and adopted its rules of procedure; each had a large number of committees where bills were always considered before submission to the full house; congressional sessions were often lively and occasionally violent. Frequently, however, lengthy debate ended without action, or proceedings were paralyzed by the absence of a quorum (sometimes arranged by the President). From 1937 until 1949, for example, Congress did not pass a budget.

The judiciary was a frequent subject of debate, criticism, and attempted reform. Each constitution declared the judiciary an independent and separate branch of government. Abuses prevalent under the 1901 Constitution were often attributed to the power of the president to appoint Supreme Court justices; the consent of the Senate was required, but the president frequently exercised a high degree of control over the legislature. An attempt was made in the 1940 Constitution to remedy this by establishing an elaborate system for appointments to the Supreme Court. The Supreme Court was given full authority over the appointment and promotion of lower judges and over the administration of lower courts. After 1940 the judiciary did appear to develop greater independence, but the administration of justice continued to be subject to problems and pressures arising out of the patronage system and the general level of political morality.

Cuban law is in the civil law tradition of Spain and continental Europe in which statutory codifications are the major sources of law, and the formally defined role of the judge is to apply the written law. If a statute does not cover the situation, greater weight is given to the opinions of legal scholars than to decisions in previous cases. The principal codes in effect during the 1950's for civil law, civil procedure, and commercial law were Spanish codes dating from the 1880's which derived in large part from the Code Napoléon. In 1940, a Code of Social Defense replaced the Spanish penal law. Important departures from Spanish tradition included the adoption of constitutional guarantees of individual rights and the principle of judicial review. The question of the constitutionality of a law could be appealed through the lower courts or taken directly to the Supreme Court by organizations or by a group of twenty-five citizens.

Each municipality had one or more municipal courts which dealt with very minor criminal infractions and civil cases where the amount in question did not exceed 500 pesos. Courts of first instance, courts of arraignment, and police courts were organized territorially for each judicial zone (*partido*). Each zonal court had one judge; the senior judge in a zone had some administrative authority over other personnel; and judges of the courts of first instance decided conflicts of jurisdiction between municipal courts. A court of appeal was located in each provincial capital to serve a judicial district coterminous with the province, except in the case of Oriente, which was divided into two judicial districts. Each court, composed of a president and a number of magistrates, was divided into at least three chambers to deal with civil, criminal, and administrative cases.

Assigned to the five chambers of the Supreme Court between 1940 and 1958 were from twenty to thirty-eight justices, each of whom held life tenure. As a whole the Court dealt with major questions of constitutionality, decided on appeal cases of removal of municipal or provincial officials, decided cases of conflict between the Tribunal of Accounts and other government bodies, and had original jurisdiction in criminal cases involving the president, vice-president, or Supreme Court justices. Civil and criminal chambers heard appeals in cassation from lower courts. Other chambers dealt with administrative litigation and with supervision of lower-court personnel and administration. The Chamber of Constitutional and Social Guarantees, established in 1949, was given jurisdiction in questions of constitutionality or the infringement of individual rights and reviewed cases appealed from government labor conciliation boards.

Urgency courts were first established during the Machado dictatorship and were used for summary trials of political offenders. Set up again under a World War II law giving the government expanded wartime powers, they were apparently continued after the war as well. In practice, they came into greater use during the last years of the Batista regime when cases of antigovernment activity were referred to them. Although intended to provide speedy trial in times when constitutional guarantees had been suspended and expanded police powers had produced a large number of arrests, they were often used to confirm the arbitrary exercise of police powers.

The police, in addition to the performance of usual police functions, at which they were considered reasonably efficient, were used extensively for political purposes by every government. In the major cities, particularly Havana, gambling and prostitution were under police protection. Favoritism was shown to officials and their friends by the police, whose jobs were dependent on patronage. The average citizen without influence distrusted the police but, fearing reprisal, seldom complained of ill treatment. In spite of many laws to the contrary, police brutality was common and prison conditions notoriously bad. Their political role varied with the government in power. Especially under Machado and Batista, they were used as terrorist units and for assassination of political opponents. As one consequence, the police were among the earliest victims of public vengeance in the revolutions ending these two regimes.

Under Batista the National Police was a thoroughly military organization consisting of seven divisions, one in each of the six provinces with an additional central division for the city of Havana. About half of the total force was stationed in and around Havana. The greater part of the police force was under the direction of the minister of defense and in times of political stress was used in close cooperation with the army. The army chief of staff at all times had operational control of the Rural Guard, a separate branch of the police which was stationed throughout rural areas. Other police forces included the Judicial Police, which performed investigative services for the courts under the authority of the Department of Justice, and the National Secret Police, which carried out criminal and political investigations under the Ministry of Interior.

Patronage

The merit system was introduced into the government service in 1909—earlier than in any other country of Latin America—under a law passed during the second United States occupation. The resulting Civil Service Commission recruited personnel and supervised examinations for public service appointments and promotion but never became independent of political control. Its provisions were flagrantly evaded by the designation of thousands of government jobs as confidential or political. Article 107 of the 1940 Constitution limited the positions that might be treated as political or confidential to ministers, assistant secretaries, directors-general of government departments; ambassadors and other top diplomatic posts; provincial governors and mayors; and officers and employees appointed for periods of less than one year as a charge on contingent allotments. All other positions were to be filled only through examinations. The Board of Public Offices, intended to enforce this, was never established. Statistics on government employment are extremely scanty and conflicting, but the 1953 census placed total government employment at 173,188.

The government was the largest employer in the country, especially of educated persons. Civil service salaries were often inadequate, and many persons either kept other jobs or profited extralegally from their government positions. Holders of *botellas* (sinecures) generally appeared only to receive their paychecks. The excessive number of government employees was an accepted part of the social and political system. According to the 1950 IBRD mission:

> . . . approximately 80 percent of the budgetary expenditures are salary payments, while the rest consist mainly of purchases of material, pensions (about 8 percent), and debt payments (about 3 percent). . . . The situation reflects political patronage and the fact that during the last twenty-five years there has been chronic unemployment in Cuba and a lack of alternative jobs. Government employment has thus become a form of social assistance, and the Cuban government the biggest 'industry' and employer in the country except for sugar.

Some patronage was legislated and some was contrary to the law at least to the extent that the procedures used led to graft. In addition to providing jobs or income, patronage also provided means of influencing important groups within the society thus placed in obligation. Examples of specific forms of patronage could be seen in the functions of the Ministry of Public Works and the government-managed pension funds, as described in the IBRD report, as well as in the national lottery—the oldest, most popular, and often the most graft-ridden patronage structure. The lottery was established in colonial times, abolished during the United States occupation, and restored in 1909 by the Gómez administration in response to popular demand. A law in 1912 gave the president power to distribute the tickets and control the sale with immunity from auditors. Each week 25,000 lottery *billetes* containing 100 tickets were printed and assigned in collectorships to various individuals, chiefly congressmen, who then sold them to others.

From time to time the legal provisions governing lottery operations were changed, but each individual involved in the distribution process derived a profit. The director-general of the lottery, in theory subordinate to the Minister of the Treasury, was usually a close friend of the president.

Patronage practices in the Ministry of Public Works contributed greatly to central government control over local governments. Governments measured their success partly in terms of the public works projects launched. Expenditure on public works in election years was often double the normal rate, and, as a result, according to the IBRD mission, "Cuba is littered with unfinished public works projects." In addition:

> Congressional representatives control appointments—absentee or otherwise—even of manual workers employed by the district offices of the Public Works Ministry. In distributing public works projects, therefore, the central government has powerful ways to control local politics and to strangle local initiative.

In addition to maintaining pension funds for government employees, the government managed pension funds subsidized either by specific taxes or from general government funds for a large number of private organizations. Regarding the pensions of government employees, the IBRD mission reported:

> Of recent years benefits have been paid to many ex-employees or their dependents who do not meet the [legal] requirements. For instance, former policemen and members of the armed forces who are far below retirement age have received benefits since their discharge for political reasons. . . . The official Cuban survey [by the Junta Nacional de Economia] in September 1950 brought out the startling fact that the number of pensions and retirement benefits paid during 1949 amounted to more than 25 percent of the number of regular government employees.

In describing the professional funds, the IBRD mission reported:

> Of these, the following may be listed: medical personnel, mercantile registrars, registrars of property, barbers and hairdressers, pharmacists, veterinarians, lawyers, attorneys, substitute judges, notaries, customs brokers, and architects.
>
> In nearly all these cases, part of the funds' income is derived from taxes, fees, and other charges arbitrarily imposed on the general public. . . .

Architects, for instance, are favored in this way. Building costs all over Cuba are increased by a tax on cement of ten cents per ton, which is devoted to the architects' retirement fund. . . .

Almost one-half of the income of the Cuban journalists' pension fund is paid by the Cuban people, by means of a budgeted government subsidy. . . .

It is less easy to discern any reasons for a special subsidy to the pension fund of the barbers and hairdressers. It can only be conjectured that during the period of record government revenues, from 1945 to 1948, this profession rendered exceptional services to the Cuban people of a political rather than tonsorial nature.

Local Government

With but minor changes, the present territorial-administrative division dates from the colonial era. The six provinces are divided into 126 *municipios*, very roughly equivalent to counties in the United States. In theory, the *municipio* has the powers usually associated with local government and is the smallest area exercising governmental functions. *Municipios* vary greatly in size, ranging in population from about 6,000 to the *municipio* of Havana which has 787,000. *Municipios* in turn are divided into *barrios*, the typical *barrio* having a population of from 2,000 to 10,000.

The major function of the provincial government, as defined in the 1940 Constitution, was to provide means for cooperation among the *municipios* within its boundaries. The provincial council was composed of the elected mayors of the *municipios* and was required to meet at least every two months. Its stated functions were to draw up a regular budget and determine the quota to be paid by each municipality in proportion to its revenues; render public services and execute works of provincial interest, especially in the areas of health and social welfare, education, and communications; and to appoint and remove provincial employees. The council might also pass on loans for public works, or economic or social projects, with the prior approval of the Tribunal of Accounts. In general the provinces were units for central administration rather than local action.

The constitution was much more explicit in providing for municipal government and guaranteeing its autonomy than in providing for provincial government. Historically, the preservation of the right of the *municipios* to handle local matters has been viewed as the primary means of protection against central government despotism. The municipality was declared autonomous, but also "an auxiliary body of the central power which the nation exercises throughout all of the national territory." Powers not expressly delegated were reserved to the central government. A municipality could choose among three forms of government— commission, municipal and manager, or mayor and municipal council. The system actually in use throughout the country was that of mayor and council, both elected by direct vote for four-year terms. In practice, the municipalities did not achieve the autonomy guaranteed by the constitution. Mayors and councilmen were elected and employees hired, but they performed few of their designated functions because of lack of funds and the assumption of their functions by the central government.

POLITICAL DYNAMICS TO 1958

NEARLY EVERY KNOWN MECHANISM for the transfer of power has been utilized at one time or another during Cuba's sixty years of independence, but whether change was peaceful or violent, the resulting government was soon faced with a new opposition. Twice, in 1933 and in 1958, the opposition was of revolutionary proportions. Both explosions came after periods of dictatorship in which the regime increasingly relied on police suppression.

In each case, the original leadership emerged from a new generation of young intellectuals of middle- and upper-class backgrounds who found no place in the existing system as they saw it. Their programs incorporated a variety of the tenets of political liberalism, radicalism, extreme nationalism, and socialism, but their major bond was reaction against despotism rather than agreement on future programs. On each occasion they acted in the name of, and with some support from, population groups previously omitted from major participation in the formation of national policies.

In politics the effect of *personalismo* was that such designations as Zayistas, Machadistas, Batistianos, and Fidelistas have often been more accurately descriptive of political groupings than the names of the political parties led by these men. A man with such a following is a *caudillo*, a leader, and if he is the chief of state, as was Batista, he may be described as the *jefe supremo*. The ideal chief of state is expected to show qualities which inevitably conflict with his prescribed constitutional role. The characteristics most important for political success are skills in political negotiation and manipulation of influential groups, and the ability to appeal directly to "the people." Presentation of the leader as the personal embodiment of national aspirations who would carry out the national will has been the most successful technique for gaining popular support—whether confirmation of this support came through election or by some other means.

The *jefe supremo* was not all-powerful—absolute dictatorship was rare and brief—but he was expected to be the final arbiter of all major questions and to maintain a balance of power among rival political interests. Requiring the support of the army, but not able to rely on military power alone, he was compelled to take into consideration organized labor, political parties, university students, professional associations, major business interests, and, to a lesser extent, the Catholic Church, all striving to protect or augment their role in the society and their political power. The United States also was influential because of the substantial United States private investment in Cuba, the number of United States citizens resident there, the large volume of United States-Cuban trade, and, until 1934, its special status under the Platt Amendment.

The network of personal relationships, extending from the presidential palace, through Congress and government departments, throughout all society, appeared to provide a means of balancing the demands of various population groups and interests. Although one man held the balance at the top, power was diffused downward through political parties and the relations of the administrative structure with other social institutions. The executive was expected to be responsive to public pressures, and at some point in the complicated hierarchy many if not most Cubans had a spokesman or a patron—even if he were only a minor functionary, the local union leader, or the local politician to whom they had given or sold their votes.

During the period from 1933 to 1958 four major groups prominent after the 1933 revolution competed for power: the Auténtico party under Ramón Grau San Martín; Batista, whose strongest support was the army led by men he promoted from sergeant to officer status in 1933; conservative groups; and the Popular Socialist party (Communist). The sharpest rivalry was between the two most successful *caudillos*, Batista and Grau San Martín. Conservatives, divided into factions and lacking a popular spokesman, often allied with Batista rather than support programs inimical to their interests. Some, however, allied at times with the Auténticos, and many conservatives could find no party reflecting their point of view. The Communists, although even they sponsored a presidential candidate chosen for his *caudillo* qualities, had the smallest numerical support during most of the period.

Neither Batista nor Grau San Martín had all the qualities of the ideal leader. Batista lacked higher education and other cultural credentials signifying a man above the common run. Grau lacked the administrative competence necessary to perpetuate his power. They relied for primary support on different forms of appeal. Grau San Martín, the leader of the most popular political party to emerge after 1933, could rely considerably on party organization but as a result was subject to strong party patronage pressures. Batista, although he created a party coalition of supporters, drew his main support from the army and business and was freer of party demands. Each in turn was supported by organized labor. Both, however, eventually succumbed to the basic weakness of *caudillismo*: their inability to fulfill promises produced public disillusionment equal in strength to former hopes, and the disillusionment extended to parties and supporters.

Along with pressures for establishment of "real" democracy after 1933, there were strong reactions against democracy. Many of those dissatisfied with the government process condemned democracy as a system giving power to the rich and riches to the powerful and advocated increasing the power of the central government in order to achieve large-scale socioeconomic reforms impossible under a government based on a tenuous balance of interests. Radicals of either the right or the left usually justified their preference for revolutionary change with the argument that concentration of political power was the essential precondition for creating a social and economic structure in which democracy eventually could function adequately. They frequently made little reference to specific programs or labels but identified themselves with the idea of direct action and the historical tradition of individual heroism and martyrdom for liberty.

Promising utopian solutions, radicals sought support among the underprivileged in opposing the upper economic and social strata. The two most extreme solutions offered were Communist, emphasizing the achievement of a classless society through destruction of the upper and middle classes; and corporative, the realization of social harmony by giving the government absolute authority to control the interest groups for the benefit of all. Individuals seeking such total solutions could be found in the Popular Socialist party, among those partially sympathetic to Communism, and in groups favoring the Spanish Falangist movement or "social justice" programs similar to that of Juan Perón. Some of the radical left supported the Auténticos, some of the radical right supported Batista; their common premise that the need for government-imposed order justified a disregard of constitutional procedures and the use of violence in the struggle for power also enabled individuals to traverse rapidly political dividing lines between left and right.

Elections and Major Political Parties

Elections were conducted under a series of electoral laws, each more specific than its predecessor in detailing legal procedures designed to prevent and punish abuses. A new electoral code was enacted in 1943, and elections held under it from 1944 through 1950 were considered to conform more closely to the law than previous ones. Batista's *coup d'état* precluded elections in 1952. The national and municipal elections held in 1954, under a new code adopted in late 1953, were generally considered rigged. The only elections after this were held on November 3, 1958, less than a month before the victory of the Castro forces; constitutional guarantees were suspended at the time, and elections aroused little popular interest.

The electoral law required all political parties to conform to a specified structure designed to insure internal democratic procedures. In general, the parties followed the required procedures, but political realities, such as *personalismo,* the use of force, and more subtle means of pressure, frequently made possible controlled elections and contrived conventions. Campaigning, unless the election was considered contrived, was intense. Candidates toured their constituencies extensively, held large rallies, and organized demonstrations. Slogans were coined and posters exhibited everywhere. The candidate was presented as a hero, his opponent as a villain. Little attention was given to the issues dividing parties. Large sums of money were spent, the provisions of the electoral law requiring financial disclosure being apparently among the least enforced.

No election was free from such abuses as vote buying, use of government patronage, bargains with supporting groups and individuals, or from undoubtedly exaggerated charges of these abuses by each group. Little information is available concerning the mobilization of votes at the local level, but such techniques as purchasing votes, promising jobs, or threatening their loss appear to have been common. The incumbent government had a definite advantage over the opposition in the use of these techniques, but the charge of government-rigged election, or *imposición*, generally was saved for extreme cases, such as the elections held under Batista in 1954 and 1958. In such cases most opposition groups, assuming that the government would control the elections, withdrew rather than cooperate in what they considered the government's attempt to legitimize itself by fraud.

Several national parties had a more or less continuous existence from 1933 to 1958. In addition to the national parties, many others functioned only at the municipal level; almost no information is available about them or their relationships with the national parties. Six parties contested the national elections of 1948. The relative strength of the pre-Batista parties is indicated by their registration figures in 1948 (see Table 8).

The Democratic, Republican, and Liberal parties, led by men prominent since the 1930's, divided the conservative field in 1944 and 1948. Their programs differed little and together they had the support of most of the upper class. Campaign slogans stressed democratic, constitutional, and honest government; supported private enterprise with some government regulation for the purposes of economic development and public welfare; and opposed Communism as destructive to social order. In general, the tone of conservative spokesmen was one of regret: regret that leftwing threats had weakened conservatism's former control as they had weakened religion and morality; and regret that conservatives had reacted to the challenge by withdrawing or dividing rather than by uniting in common action. The Liberal and Democratic parties were part of the Batista coalition in the 1940 elections, and together supported the candidacies of Carlos Saladrigas in 1944 and Ricardo Núñez Portuondo in 1948. Much weakened after two terms out of office, they supported Auténtico candidate Carlos Hevia in 1952 and entered the Batista coalition once more in 1954, although factions split off in opposition. The Republican party came into existence as a factional split from the Democratic party during the 1944 campaign; it therefore allied with the Auténticos in the 1948 elections.

The Party of the Cuban Revolution (Auténtico) was organized in 1934 under the leadership of Dr. Ramón Grau San Martín, prominent physician and professor at the University of Havana. During most of the 1930's it was denied, or did not desire, participation in legal political activity, and operated as an underground organization under the name of Organización Auténtico. The Auténtico party first participated in electoral politics in 1939 when it won a strong position in the Constituent Assembly; its general program was reflected in the social and economic provisions of the 1940 Constitution. It was the leading government party from 1944 to 1952.

The Auténtico was considered one of several Aprista parties of Latin America; the latter name is taken from the prototype, the Alianza Popular Revolucionaria Americana (APRA), formally organized in 1924 as an inter-American party by Peruvian exiles in Mexico. Characteristics common to all of the Aprista parties included a Marxist approach to social and economic problems, without the acceptance of modern Soviet doctrine, and a commitment to political democracy—in practice sometimes modified by recourse to direct action. The Auténtico platform consistently stressed prolabor policies, social security, agrarian reform, industrialization, expansion of public health and education facilities, and government regulation of the economy in the interests of public welfare and a more equitable distribution of income.

The nationalism of the Auténticos was expressed most strongly during the 1930's when Yankee imperialism was a major target, but softened by the time the party came to power. Grau San Martín used the term *Cubanidad* to describe his party's nationalistic stance. The "50 percent law" of 1933, required all business firms to hire at least 50 percent Cuban-born labor, was a major legacy of *Cubanidad*. Nationalism continued to be expressed in the party's emphasis on the need to regulate foreign companies.

Like all other governments, the Auténtico government was dependent on coalition support. It governed in coalition with the conservative Republican party which had little sympathy for the Auténtico platform. Grau San Martín's problem, on becoming president in 1944 without majority support in the legislature, was particularly illustrative of the problem of a Cuban chief of state and head of a party. In order to obtain a majority he accepted support from the Communists at the price of ignoring their dominance in the labor movement. This antagonized Auténtico labor leaders who had counted on government support to restore their control. Only after winning congressional majorities in 1946 did he turn against the Communist labor leaders and restore unity within his own party.

Grau faced a similar problem with terrorist groups—a legacy of the Auténticos' revolutionary past—several of which were linked to figures in the Auténtico party. Their demands increased the already tremendous pressure for patronage distribution, and the gangsterism in which they participated led to criticism of the government for its failure to keep order. When, after his term as president, Grau was charged in the Havana *audiencia* with misappropriation of government funds, a band of gunmen stole the dossier, and the case was never brought to trial. Prío Socarrás, Grau's chosen successor in 1948, came under increasing criticism because of activities of terrorist groups, and in preparation for the 1952 elections his government began to take police action against them. The Auténticos had come to power after an era of Batista-dominated government, and much hope had been vested in them. The Grau and Prío governments enacted some needed legislation, particularly laws setting up institutions called for in the constitution, but Cubans judged them harshly for their failure to achieve promised reforms in the political system. In the struggle to balance interests, prevent the development of large-scale opposition, and preserve the dominant political party, they pursued essentially the same policies as other governments. Labor was favored, business was placated, the press subsidized, and professional groups encouraged with jobs for individuals and pensions for all. Disillusionment found an outlet in the hope offered by a new leader with a new party.

The Ortodoxo party (Party of the Cuban People) was founded in 1946 by Eduardo Chibás, a follower of the Auténtico party since its beginning. The Ortodoxo program differed little from that of the Auténticos. In fact, the Ortodoxos claimed to be orthodox Auténticos. Chibás' personal popularity stemmed primarily from his weekly radio broadcast in which he spared no one implicated in graft and venality. Disillusioned with the Grau government Chibás turned his ire on the Auténtico party. Although many classed Chibás as a "professional agitator," his attempt to arouse or create political conscience drew rapid popular support and attracted a number of very competent political leaders. In the 1948 campaign the Ortodoxos, using a broom as their electoral symbol and with no other party in coalition, polled about 16 percent of the popular vote—nearly twice their registration figure.

In 1951 Chibás committed suicide at the end of a broadcast, his desperate act apparently prompted by frustration and by his inability to obtain proof substantiating a particular public accusation. His martyrdom, popularly accepted as such, drew further support to the party, and the expectation that the Ortodoxo candidate for the presidency in 1952, Roberto Agramonte, would win precipitated the Batista *coup d'état*.

Both Auténticos and Ortodoxos were thrown into confusion after the *coup d'état*, and many leaders fled into exile to escape prosecution or persecution. When parties were allowed to become active again in preparation for the 1954 elections, both parties were divided into factions, some favoring opposition through violence, others passive resistance, and still others participation in the elections. Small factions of each party did participate in the 1954 and 1958 elections, but the majority chose other means to oppose the Batista regime.

The Partido Comunista de Cuba (Communist Party of Cuba), founded in 1925, was an important force from the early 1930's when Communists became powerful in the labor movement and participated in the overthrow of Machado. Under the capable leadership of Blas Roca (pseudonym for Francisco Calderio), secretary-general since 1934, the party survived the shifts and reversals of policy dictated by the changing requirements of Soviet foreign policy. After 1934 it presented a fairly consistent domestic program supporting democratic government, honesty in government, extension of social services, and the economic advancement of urban and rural workers. The Communists' fortunes shifted mainly according to their relations with the government in power. During most of the period after 1933 the party's main antagonist was the Auténtico party.

President Machado declared the Communist party illegal in 1925 and deported the first secretary-general, Juan Antonio Mella. Mella was killed in Mexico in 1929; some say by Machado agents, some say by the Communists. Within Cuba the first major Communist success came in 1929, when César Vilar, a Stalinist, became the second secretary-general of the Confederación Nacional Obrera de Cuba (CNOC), formed under anarcho-syndicalist leadership in 1924. A Trotskyite faction under Sandolio Junco subsequently left the party and helped organize the new Auténtico party's labor group.

The Communists participated in the initiation of the general strike that precipitated the downfall of Machado, and later claimed full credit for its success. Their opponents claimed, however, that the Communists subsequently tried to call off the strike either because Machado offered them a deal or because they realized that much of the credit would go to other groups. In 1933 the Communists, following a proletarian revolutionary policy, would not cooperate with other leftwing groups. During Grau San Martín's 1933-1934 government, they fomented labor unrest and public disturbance, formed rural "soviets" and kept up a barrage of antigovernment propaganda. Grau San Martín was the main target, but nearly as much venom was directed at Antonio Guiteras, the most radical member of Grau's cabinet and often referred to in non-Communist writings as a Communist.

After the Comintern adopted a new popular front policy beginning in 1934, the Cuban party, like many others, apologized for having pursued an incorrect course:

> The basic error of the party consisted in mechanically setting the class interests of the proletariat against the interests of the national liberation struggle, the aims of the bourgeois democratic, agrarian, and anti-imperialist revolution in Cuba. . . . This . . . position . . . objectively facilitated the coming into power of the present reactionary government.

The Communists then attempted to form an alliance with Grau San Martín against the Batista-supported conservative government, but the overtures were rejected.

Subsequently they sought and obtained legality by supporting Batista in his efforts to obtain popular support. A Partido Unión Revolucionaria (PUR), composed of Communists and Socialists was allowed to organize in late 1937. Juan Marinello, one of the island's most distinguished essayists and critics, was its president, Blas Roca its secretary-general. In 1938 the PUR published a newspaper, *Noticias de Hoy,* and supported Batista, maintaining that it was pressing him toward "yet more democratic positions." In September Batista announced that the Communist party could operate openly because it had renounced violence in favor of peaceful tactics.

In January 1939 a new labor federation, the Confederation of Cuban Workers (Confederación de Trabajadores de Cuba—CTC), was organized under Communist leadership. During the next few years Communist labor officials were favored by the government and by late 1939, when elections for the Constituent Assembly were held, the PUR and the Communist party had been merged into the Partido Unión Revolucionaria Comunista (PURC). The shifts in Soviet policy during World War II put a strain on the Cuban party, but had little effect on its relationship with the government. Two Communist leaders, Juan Marinello and Carlos Rafael Rodriguez, served as ministers without portfolio. After the signing of the Nazi-Soviet pact the party directed propaganda against the Allies and assisted in the dissemination of Nazi propaganda; this policy led the socialist group within the PURC, headed by Juan Arévalo, to found an independent Socialist party. When Germany invaded Russia in 1941, the Communists shifted their position, and throughout the war they pursued the popular front program, avoided all talk of violence, and even refrained from criticizing the United States. In 1942 Cuba, for the first time, recognized the Soviet Union and established diplomatic relations.

The party again changed its name, in preparation for the 1944 elections, to the Partido Socialista Popular (PSP). It supported Batista's candidate, Carlos Saladrigas, who lost to Grau San Martín. Although defeat of the PSP-supported candidate threatened their dominance in the CTC, the Communists were able to maintain their position temporarily by shifting support to Grau in Congress. In 1946 and 1947 Grau and Prío Socarrás, then minister of labor, began to attack them; the labor confederation was split and gradually came under Auténtico domination.

From 1947 until 1952 the PSP steadily lost strength. In the 1948 elections it was unable to form a coalition with either government or opposition parties. Although the party's registration was the highest yet achieved—158,000 voters—it received fewer votes than in 1944 and 1946. The administration of Prío Socarrás took stronger action against the PSP than had Grau. By 1950 few unions remained under Communist control, and in the congressional elections of that year the PSP registered only 55,000 voters. Although the core of the organization was never broken, the PSP remained isolated through 1952. The most prominent leaders of the Communists from 1933 to 1958 were Blas Roca, secretary-general from 1934 and an extremely able organizer, Juan Marinello, well-known intellectual and titular head (president) of the party, and Lázaro Peña, Blas Roca's opposite number in the labor movement. Blas Roca was quick to sense and adopt changes in the international Communist line, and only in 1946 did he lag long enough to have to issue public recantation. Lázaro Peña, leader of the tobacco workers in the 1930's, became secretary-general of the CTC when it was formed in 1939 and held this position until forced out by the government in 1947; after that he remained the leader of the rump Communist labor groups. Juan Marinello, playing the leading role in public life, led the Communist delegation in the 1940 Constituent Assembly, served in the Cabinet under Batista, spent several years in the Senate, serving briefly as vice-president of that body, and was his party's candidate for the presidency in 1944 and 1948.

The Cuban party, like others in Latin America, has drawn its support and its leadership almost entirely from young intellectuals, including university and secondary-school students, and organized labor, most notably when the party was favored by the government. The majority of the persons voting for the party apparently were drawn to its program stressing democratic reform and progress. In 1958, for example, the published platform of the PSP was a relatively mild statement demanding the recognition of fundamental political rights and economic and social reform. The hard-core support, a fraction of the voting support, probably was drawn from among those who supported the general program, but who, in addition, were drawn to the authoritarian structure and hoped to gain status as functionaries. A party spokesman claimed 37,000 dues-paying members in 1946, when the PSP was at its height of popularity. The party appears to have maintained a dual structure during the period of legal activity, keeping an underground organization intact for use in insurrectionary activity or for infiltrating legal organizations in case the party's legal status were withdrawn.

The specific relationship of the Cuban party with parties in other countries has been only sporadically documented. Cuban representatives attended most of the major Communist international congresses held after the early 1930's, and some party leaders spent several years in Communist countries. An East European, Fabio Grobart, was reported to be the main liaison for the Cuban party. Communist labor leaders in the 1920's and 1930's appeared to have contact with Mexican groups led by Vicente Lombardo Toledano.

During the popular front era (1935-1946) the Cubans had frequent contact with the United States party. During and immediately after World War II, the Soviet Union maintained a large embassy in Havana, its staff numbering over fifty in 1946; Havana probably was a center for directing the other parties in the Caribbean region. Several Cuban Communists were in frequent contact with Guatemalan Communists during the Arbenz regime, and a Cuban,

Severo Aguirre, adjudicated an internal dispute in the Guatemalan party during that period. No information is available concerning contacts after the Cuban party was declared illegal in 1953.

The Batista Coalition

The care with which Batista created a Progressive Action Coalition that would elect him to the presidency—two years after he had become president by illegal means—was indicative of the importance attached to popular election as the only truly safe means of proving a mandate, the absence of which justified dangerous criticism from the opposition. Although substantial numbers of politicians from conservative parties supported him, segments of the parties broke off in protest.

Batista's successful *cuartelazo* (barracks *coup*) on March 10, 1952 depended mainly on adequate military support, which he had obtained during his earlier tenure, and the element of surprise, which he achieved by taking over Camp Columbia at 2:43 A.M. Consolidating his position required consummate political skills. He capitalized on President Prío's indecisiveness. Prío resigned and left the country as ordered, making no effort to arouse his followers. In his first statements, Batista appealed to the discontent of many prominent persons with the widespread gangsterism and graft. Promising order and honest administration until such time as elections could be held, his immediate justification for the *coup* was his charge that the Prío government planned to perpetuate itself by illegal means. He temporarily suspended constitutional guarantees, dissolved all political parties, prohibited strikes, dissolved the Congress while keeping the Congressmen on salary, and raised the pay of the army.

The most threatening move against Batista was made by Auténtico labor leader Eusebio Mujal, who called a general strike, but Prío had already fled, and labor did not strike. Within a few days, Batista and Mujal had reached an agreement of mutual support. A number of prominent government administrators resigned in protest, and opposition parties entered a plea in the courts protesting the unconstitutionality of the *coup*, but the protest went unheeded in the rush to develop new avenues of power and patronage.

Batista already had a nucleus of party support in the Party of Unitary Action which he had formed after his return to Cuba in 1948 and which alone had supported his candidacy in 1952. It was dissolved after the coup and then reconstituted as the Progressive Action Coalition in preparation for the 1954 elections. Its leadership was composed largely of persons who had supported Batista between 1934 and 1944, many of them sometime members of the regular conservative parties, particularly the Liberal. The Progressive Action party, the strongest within the coalition, was joined by the Democratic and Liberal parties and the Liberal leader, Rafael Guas Inclan, became the coalition's vice-presidential candidate. In 1955 Batista's brother assumed leadership of the Democratic party. The Progressive Action Coalition placed greater emphasis on economic and social development than did the Democratic or Liberal parties. In addition, Batista had the support of a Radical Union party which, while espousing radical social policies and appealing to anti-American sentiment, supported Batista as the restorer of order and unity. One of its leaders, Rolando Masferrer, later became particularly prominent as the head of a terrorist organization, the Movimiento Socialista Revolucionario, which aided the government against Castroist opposition in Oriente province. Although a former Communist and for a time a senator supporting Prío Socarrás, Masferrer lent his strong-man capabilities so thoroughly to the Batista government that his name became symbolic of everything hated in the regime.

The PSP was publicly critical of the *coup d'état* but proceeded to seek means of adjustment. Within a month of the *coup*, however, two Soviet diplomats arriving in Cuba were subjected to regular customs procedures; the Soviet Union broke diplomatic relations with Cuba. During 1952 and 1953 Batista gradually moved against the PSP and on October 21, 1953 the party was declared illegal. Batista created a Bureau for the Suppression of Communist Activities within the government, and most of the top PSP leaders were arrested or went into exile. Although he was accused of using some of the less prominent Communists to organize his own labor support, Batista relied heavily on his action to suppress Communism as a justification for his regime.

During the first few years of the Batista government, the Communists were engaged primarily in consolidating their underground organization. From 1956 on, the PSP actively sought allies among anti-Batista groups, but continued to suffer from the long-standing hostility of much of the leftwing. As late as July 1958, when most of the major anti-Batista groups signed an agreement under the leadership of Fidel Castro, the Communists were omitted, but shortly after that they allied with Castro.

Batista's coalition won the 1954 elections easily after many of the opposition leaders withdrew or fled into exile. Assured that he could now function as a constitutional president, Batista granted amnesty to political offenders in 1955. As time progressed, however, his support narrowed until eventually he was compelled to rely for positive support almost entirely on the army and police bolstered by the acquiesence of business and organized labor.

Major Interest Groups

Organized interest groups exerted pressure on the government partially through lobby activities but more often through personal relationships with government officials and, if the interest group was a major source of power, through the public issuance of position statements. The first adjustment to a change in government by an association or other interest group was to replace its leadership—either voluntarily or under government encouragement or coercion—with one agreeable to the new regime. In the army, for example, senior army commands were reshuffled and officers considered too closely tied to the former government were retired. In the labor unions, coercion might be applied more subtly or bargains struck. In a private business, there might be a quiet shift at the executive level to bring to the fore men having the best connections with the new government.

Interest groups were seldom linked more than tangentially to political parties. The majority of men in the professions were sympathetic to the Auténticos or the Ortodoxos, the majority of businessmen to conservative parties, and large numbers of students to radicalism, but political parties seldom provided adequate means of reflecting their interests. In addition to the major interest groups of the army, labor, and the professions, there were a large number of less influential organizations such as associations of landowners growing various crops, chambers of commerce, manufacturers associations, etc. Negro societies were grouped into a national federation to improve the position of Negroes. Spanish regional societies functioned largely as social clubs and medical benefit societies but occasionally as pressure groups. There were many civic and educational associations, which, in the absence of adequate local government, often took responsibility for whatever improvements were made in local affairs. Each of these groups had its own functions and interests, and each required some degree of government support, ranging from tolerance to positive aid.

The political role of such organizations varied tremendously according to size, importance, and the nature of the leadership. Many of the associations were composed largely of individuals from the upper and upper-middle classes whose scorn of the corruption of party politics kept them from participating actively. When such groups needed government action, they usually relied upon members who were politically active and had contacts.

On occasion, the interest groups dealt with issues unrelated to their specific purposes. In the late 1930's, for example, the Centro Gallego (largest of the Spanish regional societies) came into brief political prominence because it was headed by Pepín Rivero, editor of *Diario de la Marina* and at that time a leader of Falangist organization in Cuba. Similarly, in 1947, Raúl Roa, later foreign minister in the Castro government and then dean of the Faculty of Social Studies at Havana University, conducted a university council meeting which protested a clause in a sugar quota law enacted by the United States Congress. Batista's *coup d'état* was followed by declarations of acceptance or support from a number of associations, beginning with the Association of Cane Planters and soon followed by the banks and the labor confederation.

The army has never fought outside the island but has been used frequently to preserve order and quell rebellion. Until the Machado dictatorship (1924-33) the army was a weaker political force than were the veterans of the wars of independence. Machado, however, vastly increased the size of the standing army as armed opposition led to armed suppression, and from 1930 on, the army was the latent, if not the active, factor controlling political life.

Batista's "sergeants' revolt" consisted initially of replacing several hundred officers who served under Machado by former noncommissioned officers. As chief of staff from 1933 to 1939, Batista kept the army large, improved its organization, training, and equipment, and raised its pay; officers owed their positions to his appointment. He used it to break up the attempted general strike of early 1935. After he was elected to the presidency in 1940, however, he reduced overt military participation in government.

Batista's reliance upon the army made it a power that no one could seriously threaten. Presidents Grau San Martín and Prío Socarrás each altered the personnel of the high command to promote men more sympathetic to themselves, but no serious effort was made to reduce the size of the establishment or the funds, usually 20 percent of the budget, absorbed by the military.

A reserve of loyalty to Batista within the army and widespread military concern over the prevalence of violence during the Prío administration greatly facilitated Batista's appeal in 1952. Although dissatisfaction with Batista's regime later developed within the army—among young officers actively opposing him and others seeking a nonpolitical role for the army—the majority remained loyal until Batista's increasing reliance on repressive force and his appointment of officers willing to use extreme brutality brought about a gradual loss of military as well as civilian support.

Organized labor was second only to the army as a controlling political force. The leaders who had emerged in the early 1930's, divided among Auténtico, Socialist, and Communist loyalties, remained dominant until 1958.

As in the case of the army, the powerful position of labor was in part the result of Batista's political requirements in the late 1930's. At lower levels, union members were interested primarily in material improvements, which could be obtained only when labor leadership had a successful working relationship with the government. At most times, therefore, labor confederation leadership changed when the government changed; sometimes the change was made with difficulty or, as in 1947, with violence.

The collective interests of various specific groups were represented to the government both informally and through a structure established by statute. The Cuban Sugar Stabilization Institute, for example, was a semiautonomous government agency composed largely of representatives from the Association of Mill Owners and the Association of Cane Planters. These associations obtained their operating funds from special sugar taxes. Usually they limited their interests to matters directly affecting sugar. Private business interests were among the major sources of financial support in political campaigns, mostly of the conservative parties. Many of the top members of the business community, however, avoided political participation beyond their immediate needs and companies usually conducted their business with the government through reliable personal contacts. The widespread corruption in such matters as tax payments was initiated as much by the government as by the companies, and businesses often found it necessary to provide jobs for needy friends of politicians, or, as in the case of the Cuban Telephone Company, to provide its services to the government without charge.

Students both at the secondary-school level and in the universities were extremely active in political life at all times. A history of student martyrdom goes back to the colonial era (a monument in Havana commemorates the eight medical school students shot by the Spanish Volunteers in 1871). Most student attempts at violence have been badly organized and suicidal, but students also formed the nucleus of the successful revolutionary efforts of 1933 and 1958.

Students organized both to demand a part in school administration and for purposes of general political activity. The autonomy of the University of Havana was a prized right, considered to have been violated on the occasions when police were sent into the University to make arrests. In 1923 the students, in reaction against the many professors who never met their classes, drove out the faculty by armed force and obtained from the government the dismissal of over one hundred of them and the right of the student federation to participate in selecting the University president.

While students tended to unite on questions concerning their rights within the University, they were divided on national politics, usually along political party lines. Political activity was greatest in the law school. The focal point for student political activity was the Federation of University Students (FEU), many of whose officers went on immediately into professional political activity. Two successive presidents of the FEU were killed during anti-Batista moves in late 1956 and early 1957. From 1930 to 1933, under Machado, and from 1956 until 1958, under Batista, when the government could no longer tolerate the opposition organized from within the University it was closed.

A number of *colegios* (professional associations), in which membership was required of all practitioners, brought together doctors, lawyers, teachers, journalists, architects, and other groups. The government was the major employer of teachers and lawyers, and they were directly dependent upon political patronage. The government also administered the pension funds of many of the associations, often dishonestly. Journalists usually were directly involved in political life since most newspapers were published by political leaders and depended upon government subsidy. The leadership of all these groups generally divided along political party lines and, especially among the journalists, shifted rapidly with a change of government.

Generally, the Catholic Church was apolitical from the time of independence, the Church refraining from involvement in politics, and the government from interference in the Church. In the view of a great many of the country's intellectuals, however, the Church remained a conservative force; this was reinforced by the fact that only the most conservative political parties mentioned "Christian principles" in their official programs. Although the leftwing accused the Church of Falangism, the Church held relatively little property and was too weak a political force to provide an important target. After women obtained the vote in 1936, however, all parties made use of religious appeals in their slogans and posters aimed at the women's vote.

The Church hierarchy seldom spoke on purely political questions except to stress the incompatibility of Catholicism and Communism. During the 1940's and 1950's, however, Catholic Action groups became numerous and, reflecting moderate reformist views, influenced political opinion particularly within the schools and universities. During the years after 1954, when constitutional guarantees were suspended more often than not and police brutality was commonplace, the Church hierarchy began to assume publicly positions critical of Batista. In an unprecedented move in 1955, for example, Cardinal Manuel Arteaga, Archbishop of Havana, openly criticized the repressive actions of the government and called on Batista to negotiate with the opposition.

LABOR CONDITIONS AND ORGANIZATION

ALTHOUGH NO CENSUS HAS BEEN TAKEN since 1953, the composition of the labor force has probably changed little. In that year it comprised nearly 54 percent of the population fourteen years of age and over, more than half of whom were concentrated in the two provinces of La Habana (31 percent) and Oriente (26 percent). The labor force is very young; in 1953 roughly half were between fifteen and thirty-four years of age, and during the 1960's pressure on the labor market from the younger age groups was expected to increase because of the sharp upswing in the birth rate after World War II.

Employment throughout the economy reaches a height during the *zafra*. During the seven months of the dead season about 20 percent of the labor force is unemployed and even during the *zafra* unemployment reaches an estimated 8 percent. At the same time, the demand for labor for the sugar harvest is so concentrated that localized labor shortages are always possible. Workers in general have feared any threat, real or apparent, to their livelihood from technical innovations or other efforts to increase efficiency and productivity. Demands for a rigid guarantee of jobs and attempts to stretch work have arisen, in part as a consequence of a marked lack of confidence in the economic future—justified by the many failures of the government and private enterprise to diversify and expand the economy. Efforts to overcome the threat of unemployment have usually relied upon political influence and legal measures rather than economic expansion. An outstanding example is the highly nationalistic 1933 law, reaffirmed by the 1959 Fundamental Law, requiring that at least 50 percent of all workers in every industry and business be native-born Cubans, and that they receive at least 50 percent of all wages paid. As the law was interpreted to mean 50 percent of the workers in each department or occupation within an enterprise, and as Cubans were given priority in filling vacancies and were the last to be fired, over the years the entire payroll tended to become Cuban. No exception was made for foreigners who had long been resident in the island, although technical positions for which there were no "academically qualified" Cubans and representatives and attorneys-in-fact of the employer were excepted. Spaniards were especially affected and were forced into domestic service and self-employed occupations not covered by the law. On the other hand, the great demand for labor during the *zafra* led for many years to the importation of Jamaican and Haitian laborers who were required to leave after the harvest. After the 1959 revolution, many technicians, Cuban and foreign, left the island, and the government was forced to hire a large number of new technical experts, mostly from Communist bloc countries, to assist with industrial and agricultural development programs.

In general, the Castro government was as committed as its predecessors to forbidding dismissals and stretching work to provide a livelihood for the unemployed and underemployed. Since the new government assumed control over most production facilities and all capital investment opportunities, it was able, directly or indirectly, to control the labor force. The immediate effect of the revolution was to increase unemployment, particularly among construction workers in Havana, dock workers in Santiago de Cuba, and employees of some nationalized businesses. Nevertheless, government estimates released at the end of 1959 did not recognize any sudden increase in unemployment; only at the end of 1960 did the government admit that unemployment had increased to an estimated 550,000. At the same time, anti-Castro forces in the United States estimated that 700,000 workers were unemployed, but the government continued to claim that they had provided more urban jobs, and predicted the creation of some 200,000 additional jobs by the end of 1961. While it was not possible to evaluate the prediction, it appeared unlikely that the new regime had greatly reduced either chronic urban unemployment or unemployment resulting from the revolution. Nor did official figures indicate that the regime had reduced seasonal unemployment in the sugar industry in spite of the government's claim that during the 1960-1961 *zafra* there was a shortage of sugar workers for the first time in history, because sugar workers had found more satisfactory employment elsewhere. Nongovernment sources attributed the shortage to the mobilization of the militia in January 1961. Aside from their function as indoctrination centers, the militia and the youth corps proved useful in providing work for young Cubans who would otherwise drift into the ranks of the unemployed and underemployed.

The enthusiasm created by the revolution modified some of the old attitudes toward work and productivity that had led the tobacco workers, for example, to resist mechanization and had discouraged university students from taking lowly manual or agricultural jobs. The government fostered this change by a continuous emphasis on greater productivity and the promise of increased employment opportunities for displaced workers. But any basic changes in the distribution and traditional attitudes of the Cuban labor force must rest upon long-term efforts by the government to train its agricultural labor force to grow food crops and to provide increased industrial employment for the urban work force.

The 1959 revolution may have produced some changes in occupational distribution—for example, the number of domestic servants has probably fallen and many technicians have left the island—but as a general rule, the pattern indicated in the 1953 census has probably changed little. Most of those employed worked for wages in private concerns or for the government; only a quarter were self-employed and about 4 percent were unpaid family workers. Unlike rural workers and peasants in many other Latin American countries, rural workers in Cuba are accustomed to working for wages.

In 1953, some 42 percent of the labor force worked in agriculture, forestry, and fishing; over half in the sugar industry. Of the approximately 17 percent engaged in various types of manufacturing about one-third were employed in sugar mills. Of those engaged in commerce, approximately 12 percent, nearly all were in retail trade. The number of workers in services included 96,073 government employees (apparently civil service employees). In 1960, the number of government employees was reported to have increased to 238,000, indicating the growth of government administrative responsibilities under the Castro regime.

In 1953, 22 percent of the workers, or about 450,000, were classified as skilled (see Table 9). Of these, approximately 52,000 were truck and bus drivers, 75,000 were skilled construction workers—carpenters, woodworkers, masons, and tilesetters—most of whom were concentrated in La Habana province. While the number of skilled workers and technicians was sufficient to meet the demands of industry in 1953, it is doubtful whether that supply can meet new demands arising from the industrialization program projected by the Castro regime. Even before Castro a lack of vocational training and apprenticeship plus resistance to mechanization led to a shortage of certain skills. Employers tended to draw skilled workers from those already employed elsewhere, particuarly in the sugar industry. After some experience in shop work, mill workers were often hired to work in other industries or in railroad centers like Camagüey.

Perhaps the greatest shortage of skilled workers existed at the managerial and foreman level—a shortage intensified after the 1959 revolution. Moreover, the 1953 census showed only 309 mechanical, industrial, and mining engineers, and 294 agricultural engineers; all engineers represented only 8 percent of the professionally trained group, while teachers represented almost 50 percent. The Castro regime had great difficulty in finding managers for the many nationalized industries or for the projected industrialization program. The exodus of American personnel after nationalization was followed by that of Cuban skilled technicians and professional men. At the end of 1960 the government banned the emigration, without special permission, of engineers, petroleum specialists, government employees, and Cuban executives of nationalized businesses and urged those who had left to return. The incentives offered, however, were offset by the hostility and distrust of the regime toward professional men as members of the upper class.

Although only 17 percent of the labor force were women, they formed an important part of the urban skilled labor force. They have long worked in the tobacco industry, where they outnumber men; it has been held that the selection and stripping of tobacco leaves requires the touch of a woman. Over a fourth of female wage earners worked as domestic servants, particularly in Havana, where wages were highest and the wealthy congregated. Women are important in the professional group, particularly as teachers in the lower grades. They also dominate the field of pharmacy. In the countryside, it was felt that women should not engage in heavy agricultural tasks, although they might do other work, particularly during the *zafra*. The appeal to the women to help harvest cane during the 1960-1961 *zafra* warranted a near-apology from a govern-

7. Labor Conditions and Organization

ment official: "Of course, women are not supposed to cut sugar cane."

More than 60 percent of the agricultural labor force worked for wages. This proportion was probably even greater in the sugar industry, where almost all rural wage workers were concentrated and were they greatly outnumbered the *colonos*. Most agricultural laborers were completely landless or could not derive a sufficient income from their small properties; very few had permanent work all year long. The rest lived for much of the year on credit or on *malanga*, a tough vegetable root which is the symbol of poverty. Forming the bulk of the unemployed, they competed for off-season work or for a job on some politically inspired public works program. The rural reform program may in time improve these conditions, but it is only in its initial stage.

The characteristics of the agricultural labor force as revealed in the 1946 agricultural census were probably little changed by 1958. Workers were employed by all classes of tenants, even squatters if the land they occupied was large enough to require outside help, but most worked on rented farms. A small number of large farms hired most of the labor.

Sugar workers were drawn from many sources. In the smaller Cuban mills and larger *colonias*, where most of the cane was grown, some workers came from families who had lived there for generations. Many temporary as well as permanent field and mill workers lived the year round within the *bateyes* (urban concentrations around the sugar mill) or in communities located near the "administration cane" fields and *colonias*. Sugar workers for the big eastern mills had many advantages in terms of housing, medical care, and education that the migrant field hands, housed in barracks, lacked. A small number of workers were assured of some permanent employment during the dead season as guards or in mill and railroad maintenance, and some were provided with land by the mill. They formed, along with the mill office workers and technicians, the core of the sugar workers' union. Workers were also drawn from the *bohíos* and small settlements adjacent to the mills and fields, connected with the mill by a network of railroad lines. A third source was migrant labor from nearby districts or the adjacent province. Many migrant laborers returned year after year to the same *colonia* or mill, often moving from one province to the next following the harvest. A few workers lived in the city and moved to the interior during the harvest.

Of the remaining 40 percent of the agricultural labor force, most were small, self-employed cultivators producing for the market. This group included sharecroppers in tobacco, small-scale *colonos* linked to the sugar mills, and farmers suplying the cities with truck-garden crops and dairy products.

Among all urban wage earners, the goal was and is to become permanently employed through the law that prohibits the dismissal of workers after six months' employment. Thus the unskilled *jornalero* (day laborer) strives to establish a record of employment with a particular employer. Before the revolution, the mass of unskilled casual workers lived in the poor sections of the city, in slum communities on the outskirts of Havana, or on vacant lots next to residences of the wealthy for whom they performed services. Many did odd jobs, dividing the city into territories where they parked and washed cars; the better established among them commanded the profitable downtown blocks. They also sought jobs as vendors of lottery tickets. At the very bottom of the urban occupational scale were the beggars; begging was unlawful, but in 1958 there were some 5,000 of them.

Permanently employed skilled and semiskilled workers tended to develop into exclusive, privileged, and conservative groups with a stake in the existing political and economic order. Even those not organized into unions had their interests carefully protected by labor laws. Although they themselves might be denied opportunities for upward social mobility, skilled workers and those at the foreman level were in a position to provide their sons with an education that would enable them to move ahead. The middle-class character of these groups, especially in the Havana unions, and their exclusive concern with their own interests and habit of achieving their ends through political contacts and compromise, disqualified them in the eyes of the Castro regime for leadership of the labor movement as a whole. Extreme examples were the electrical workers, who were singled out for criticism by the government, and the restaurant workers, who by the end of the Batista regime were sufficiently wealthy to own part of the luxurious Havana Hilton hotel. In striving to protect their position, permanent workers went so far as to oppose formal apprenticeship and vocational training. One of the few ways to obtain a permanent job in the city was through the sponsorship of a relative or patron; employment exchanges run by the Ministry of Labor were apparently rarely used. Under these circumstances it was difficult to operate a business impersonally, even if the employer wished to do so. Among the few roads to economic and social advancement based on merit was employment in certain large foreign corporations; but in these too the unions influenced hiring and firing.

Union leaders stressed measures to assure employment and tenure, even through the creation of unnecessary work. Featherbedding, make-work, and rigid tenure were permitted by law. Many unions opposed mechanization, and when machinery was finally installed much of the advantage was lost because of restrictions on its operations. Such restrictions, however, usually did not extend to new industries. The Castro regime made an effort to change union attitudes, emphasizing increased productivity and the elimination of privilege. Production norms were established in various industries. In its efforts the government relied increasingly on its control over union organization.

The urban occupations included a number of small entrepreneurs, such as taxicab drivers, shopkeepers, prostitutes, street vendors, and gamblers. Weak and underprivileged, usually without political influence of any kind, they were reportedly forced under Batista to pay tribute to a "collector" in order to stay in business. Voluntary donations to pay for arms after the 1959 revolution probably provided the same protective service to the small entrepreneur unsure of his status under the new regime.

The tobacco industry is one of Cuba's oldest, and its workers, numbering some 33,000 in 1953, were among the most politically alert. Traditionally, they formed a workingman's intelligentsia, a reputation based on their practice of hiring persons to read to them during working hours. The industry is considered the cradle of the labor movement and known for the financial support it gave to the war for independence.

The hand-rolling of cigars required considerable skill, and systems of strict apprenticeship and rank were established; the "master" was proud of his work and actively hostile to efforts to modernize the industry. Resistance to mechanization, however, led to a decline in the competitive position of the cigar industry by keeping production costs high, even for cigars of mediocre quality. The cigarette industry, on the other hand, has long been mechanized. According to the new regime, wages have been raised, markets expanded, and workers no longer fear mechanization because they trust the government to provide alternative employment.

Port labor, much of it unskilled and uneducated, formed one of the most protected working groups, numbering about 11,000 in 1953. Faced with severe unemployment between October and January, and assured of only irregular employment during the rest of the year, stevedores and port workers were able to obtain passage of laws that raised daily wages, stretched work, and guaranteed that certain products would be moved by boat. The net effect of these measures was to attract more workers to these already overcrowded occupations. In some cases, the laws enabled workers to earn incomes far out of proportion to those earned in other industries for similar work; costs to shippers and producers were almost prohibitive. The demand for stevedores dropped sharply, however, with the 1959 revolution and the subsequent decline in foreign trade with the United States.

Construction is one of the principal urban occupations, providing jobs not only for large numbers of casual workers, but also for the skilled trades. It is difficult to estimate, from the 1953 census, the number of workers engaged in construction. Between 1953 and 1959, however, their number increased rapidly in response to the great building boom in Havana and its outlying communities. After the revolution, the building industry collapsed and most of the workers were thrown out of work. Eventually many probably found work in public housing and works programs.

White-collar workers shared many of the general characteristics of permanent industrial workers; they faced job insecurity and underemployment, and relied on political and personal ties for placement and promotion. Their social aspirations, however, led to an even greater desire for a secure and adequate income, which they sought through political avenues, with the result that they often appeared to be engaged less in the practice of their profession than in that of politics. There were few well-paying jobs in the private sector available to young university-trained men and women, most of whom scorned manual work and sought employment in the government. In this already overcrowded occupation, however, salary scales were generally low, and as a result many government employees and minor officials found part-time employment in addition to their government jobs. Government payrolls also included officials and teachers who reported only to collect their pay. This practice was in part a method of rewarding political loyalty, but it also reflected the fact that there was too little work to go around.

Between 1933 and 1940 a large number of measures were enacted, the basic principles of which were later incorporated into the

1940 Constitution and the Fundamental Law of 1959. Altogether, they constitute a body of advanced labor legislation. In addition, a number of special laws, applicable to particular industries or groups of workers, were passed. Minimum wages were established for various occupations, and when industries such as tobacco and sugar were mechanized, compensation to displaced workers was made mandatory.

Before 1959, labor laws were usually enforced when attention was called to abuses. Enforcement was stringent in large, foreign-owned enterprises and sectors where the workers were well-organized, negligent elsewhere. When a law was vague, or called for a decision by government officials, employers often resorted to bribery, while the shortage of inspectors meant that there was little enforcement in smaller, semiclandestine establishments, particularly of regulations pertaining to wages, safety, and health.

The extent to which labor laws enacted by previous regimes were superseded by the Castro regime is not known. Theoretically, the laws were still on the books. Some, notably social security, were put into effect for the first time in 1959 and 1960. There were, however, specific instances in which the new regime disregarded the law. Some violations meant little to the workers because the law had not been enforced before. In other instances, evasion meant a real sacrifice, as in the case of the electrical workers, who were pressed into working 9 hours for 8 hours' pay, or workers in rice cooperatives, who were not permitted to accrue paid annual leave.

The regular working day is 8 hours (6 hours for workers between 14 and 18 years of age), and a 48-hour week for which the worker receives 48 hours' pay—a change from the 1940 Constitution, which established a maximum 44-hour week for 48 hours' pay. An exception is made for industries like sugar which, for a certain period of the year, must operate for more than 48 hours a week. Most large companies paid their workers time-and-a-half for overtime.

A special summer working period (*jornado de verano*) is in effect during June, July, and August. After 1952, establishments not normally closed Saturdays and Sundays were required to give their workers a second day off in addition to Sunday, and to rotate the work among their employees or to hire substitutes if they wished to remain open. Some businesses apparently chose a five-day week. In 1960, the Castro government went a step further and required commercial businesses to stay open the sixth day and to increase their personnel by 20 percent so that employees could continue to have the additional free day a week. The government hoped thereby to provide employment for 25,000 workers.

Workers are guaranteed a one-month paid vacation every eleven months; in 1942, this provision was extended to agricultural workers. As in the *jornado de verano* laws, one purpose of this law was to increase employment during the summer months. The employer was not permitted to increase the workload of the remaining workers or to close down during the vacation period. It was customary to grant workers paid leave for Good Friday, May Day, Christmas, and New Year's Day in addition to national holidays. A Christmas bonus of one month's pay was customarily given to many urban workers. In 1960 the Castro government wrote this bonus custom into law but did not make it equivalent to a full month's pay. Work and apprenticeship by minors under fourteen years of age was prohibited. Laws restricted the employment of women in dangerous occupations and in night work. Pregnant women received six weeks' compulsory paid leave before and after childbirth, and could not be discharged during pregnancy or maternity leave. The laws also included various health and welfare provisions, among them workmen's compensation.

A decree of 1938 prohibited an employer from dismissing a worker except through procedures and for causes stipulated in the law; among those excepted from the law were domestic servants, agricultural workers, and workers whose contract was for less than six months' duration. This protection was embodied in the 1940 Constitution and the 1959 Fundamental Law. The inability to fire workers, even for cause, was perhaps the most acute problem faced by employers and came to be described as *inamovilidad* (immobility). It was commonly said that it was more difficult to fire a worker than to divorce a wife (although it was often easier to find a new wife than a new job). In 1959, the Castro regime went even further by prohibiting all dismissals, freezing workers in their jobs, and threatening to "intervene," or take over, enterprises that expected to reduce or end operations. Later, however, in nationalized and intervened enterprises, the government as employer showed a readiness to fire workers and cut wages for economic reasons until checked by the severe unemployment problem.

Like the 1940 Constitution, the Fundamental Law guarantees workers a minimum wage, to be determined by regional conditions and needs of the worker. Minimum wages are to be established periodically by commissions composed of employers and workers in each industry. The law also guarantees equal pay for equal work and stipulates that wages must be paid in legal tender, not in tokens, merchandise notes, or other means. This latter provision was often disregarded and payment by voucher occurred before and after 1959. Between 1946 and 1955 wages and salaries in the private sector showed an over-all increase of 46 percent.

National minimum wages were last fixed in April 1958, the first change since 1944 and one that had little economic impact, because most large industries had already met or exceeded the new levels and other establishments evaded them. Even several thousand government employees were paid less than the new level. The wages were set at $85 a month in the Havana area and $80 and $75 a month in semiurban and rural areas respectively. Between 1937 and 1947, wages for sugar workers were fixed in relation to the price of sugar but thereafter raised by a series of decrees that extended to agricultural labor, at least in law, many of the benefits enjoyed by industrial labor. Although the minimum wage rose from $0.80 a day in 1938 to $2.88 in 1948, the usual wage for unskilled sugar workers was in practice about $1.50 a day.

Wage rates were high in relation to other countries with similar economic conditions, but long periods of unemployment largely negated any benefit. Considerable disparity existed between the rates received by workers in similar occupations but employed by different firms, and more skilled workers did not necessarily receive higher wages. To what extent price changes offset wage increases during the 1940's and 1950's was a matter of controversy because the indices differed. However, by mid-1950 the number and variety of goods available to consumers and the increase in spending on nonessential goods indicated that purchasing power had grown. Moreover, the public works programs in this period offset somewhat the seasonal decline in incomes during the dead season.

Before 1959 an estimated 800,000 to 1,500,000 workers, of a total labor force of two million, belonged to labor organizations. Although the higher estimate was probably inflated, the labor movement was strong and since 1933 had exercised great influence in political and economic life. After 1959 the number of labor organizations and the size of the membership increased as the Castro regime moved rapidly to draw all workers into the tasks of the revolution and mobilize mass support. By early 1961 the national labor confederation claimed a membership of two million workers, of an estimated labor force of 2.4 million. During 1960 it became more and more apparent that the political functions of the labor unions were overshadowing their role as representatives of their members' economic interests.

The connection between labor organizations and political activity has always been close. Sympathy for and encouragement of the labor movement came not only from politicians genuinely concerned over labor problems but also from those who saw in the emerging unions a valuable source of political support. Strikes paralyzing important sectors of the economy often heralded political change. The government in power usually sought to control or restrict unions while seeking their political support through financial contributions and favorable decisions in labor disputes. This mutual dependence operated apart from the ideologies and principles of the labor and government leaders involved. Thus, the Communist party controlled organized labor from 1933 to 1948 with the benevolent support of Batista, himself a defender of private business interests. The Castro government came to power without the support of organized labor and, like preceding governments, undertook to acquire it.

The right of workers to form unions (or syndicates, as they are called in Cuba) and to strike, as well as the corresponding right of employers to form associations and engage in lockouts, were guaranteed in the 1959 Fundamental Law as in the 1940 Constitution. Many of the earlier basic decrees and laws governing labor organization and activities also remained in effect after the Castro revolution, but there has always been a considerable discrepancy between law and practice. Membership in official associations (*colegios*) is mandatory in professions requiring a university degree and for certain other occupations licensed by the state; members must be Cuban-born citizens or naturalized citizens with five years of residence. The *colegio* may bar a member permanently or temporarily from the practice of his profession. In 1954 there were 203 *colegios* covering lawyers, doctors, architects, teachers, journalists, pharmacists, chemists, veterinarians, and notaries. Although theoretically the associations served as a means by which the government could supervise professional standards, the *colegios*, since 1959, have enabled it to ensure the loyalty of the professional classes.

Before 1959 there were a number of compulsory "producers' associations" such as the Sugar Mill Owners' Association, the Sugar

Cane Growers' Association, the Union of Tobacco Manufacturers, and the National Association of Cigar Manufacturers. Most of these organizations, representing the concentrated wealth of Cuba, were dissolved with the nationalization of the sugar and tobacco industries. The functions of the Sugar Mill Owners' Association were transferred to the Sugar Stabilization Institute. The Sugar Cane Growers' Association was dissolved in late 1960 and replaced by an Association of Small Farmers, composed of *colonos* with five *caballerías* (33.16 acres) or less of land.

Most unions are organized according to industry rather than trade and cover all employees, laborers, and office workers in each establishment. Since Castro, the ideological principle of erasing all social privilege has led to the inclusion of superintendents and other members of the managerial staff in the same unions with workers and employees. Before 1959 there was typically a wide gap between the union leadership and the rank and file. Membership was frequently nominal, dues rarely paid, and little active, informed participation in union affairs existed even at the shop or factory level. Attendance at meetings, congresses, and demonstrations often indicated only that trucks had been provided to transport union members to the gatherings.

Although the unions were confined legally to social-economic activity, they found it virtually impossible to obtain improved conditions without participating in politics. Labor unions, in turn, were often used as a means of entry into the political arena by ambitious men who sought to advance their personal fortunes or promote some political doctrine or party. Although this was in part the result of the workers' failure to demand responsible leadership, it also reflected an important function of the labor unions, which was to provide an outlet for leadership and opportunity for advancement to men otherwise barred by their social status from political and economic influence. Negroes, for example, were active in agricultural and industrial unions; Lázaro Peña, a powerful leader of the national labor confederation, is a Negro, and until 1960 most union federations had special committees to deal with Negro problems.

The unions with the most active membership and with leaders most responsive to their followers were made up of those who, by the nature of their occupation or skill, were literate and better educated, such as the telephone and telegraph workers, the bank clerks, and some cigar workers. Their bargaining power in the labor market was greater than that of unions comprised of unskilled or semiskilled manual workers, and their leaders depended less on political connections and support in bargaining with employers. On the other hand, these same workers, by virtue of their social background, tended to be deeply involved in political activity and were often found in the forefront of political strikes.

Local unions were linked into nationwide federations, a few of which contained provincial federations that in the sugar industry, for example, exercised great influence on, or even dictated, the policies of the national federation in Havana. Generally, however, authority was centered in national headquarters. In 1960 there were thirty-three such federations claiming a membership of 1.2 million workers. The nationwide federations are affiliated with the Confederation of Cuban Workers (Confederación de Trabajadores de Cuba, or CTC) which also has provincial federations, acting as branch offices, to which its local affiliates belong (see Table 10). Before and after 1959 the CTC exercised considerable control over most of its affiliates, a situation arising from the support of the government at the top and the absence of a strong democratic base. The CTC frequently intervened through the Ministry of Labor in the administration of some of its affiliates, particularly small unions, when they disregarded CTC policy and directives.

The major federations and some local unions in Havana were influential within the CTC, and most of the important CTC leaders were officers in the major federations. The most influential were the National Federation of Sugar Workers (Federación Nacional de Trabajadores Azucareros—FNTA), which claimed nearly half the entire membership of the CTC; the construction workers; tobacco workers; electrical workers; and transport workers. The CTC was very active in the international field. Before 1959, when it was affiliated with the non-Communist International Confederation of Free Trade Unions and its regional organization, the Inter-American Regional Organization of Workers (ORIT), the CTC regularly paid its dues and sent full-strength delegations to international congresses and meetings. The CTC withdrew from these organizations after 1959 and turned its attention to the formation of a Latin American confederation to rival ORIT. It took the initiative in establishing a rival organization of plantation workers and called a conference in Havana in March 1961 for this purpose.

Modern personnel practices were rare in both foreign and Cuban-managed firms, although in a few instances the employer or his representative undertook to acquaint himself with the day-to-day problems of the workers. As a general rule Cuban managers seemed to be more successful in dealing with labor difficulties than foreigners, who were invariably faced with union antagonism. The bitter struggle for labor rights before 1933 and the recollection of past abuses under the Machado dictatorship provided a basis for hostile attitudes toward management. Labor leaders frequently viewed management-labor relations in terms of the "class struggle," and employers often refused to deal with unions except through their lawyers. Moreover, before the union movement could develop enough independent strength, prestige, and tradition to cooperate voluntarily with management at the shop or industry level, the pattern of state intervention had been firmly set. These attitudes, however, could be mitigated by the development over several years of a personal relationship between the employer and his workers or their union representative. In the case of a subsidiary of a large American company in Havana, for example, cordial and cooperative relations gradually replaced earlier labor difficulties. On the other hand, the Compañía Cubana de Electricidad, another American-owned company, was beset with labor problems and aggressive union demands from the time the union of electrical workers was established in 1933 until 1959.

Paternalistic labor relations were sometimes found in the smaller Cuban-owned mills and the larger *colonias* where the supervisory staff and the field workers were drawn from families that had lived on the old estates for many generations and had developed a certain loyalty to the mill or the *colono*, supported by the proprietor's benevolent interest in them and their families. Under these circumstances, the management was able to evade the minimum wage law but at the same time the workers were always sure they could petition for help in emergencies. Although the large corporate-owned mills did not lend themselves so easily to such relationships and their workers were more highly organized, the labor laws governed the employee's working hours in a manner approaching paternalism; and in all other aspects of his daily life, such as consumer buying, housing, and care in time of illness, he was inevitably dependent upon his employer. Unionization did not necessarily protect the urban worker from exploitation. Union leaders supporting the government were allowed wide latitude in the exercise of responsibility to union members, and in the numerous small urban commercial and service enterprises labor laws were frequently evaded. As in the smaller sugar mills, the loyalty of the workers, even if they were members of a union, enabled the owner-operator to disregard legal requirements.

The desirability of collective bargaining and the peaceful settlement of disputes was recognized by appropriate provisions in the constitution, although again there was a considerable discrepancy between the law and actual practice. This gap has been somewhat bridged since 1959 by a frank recognition of the dominant role of the government. Before 1959 the law required an employer to enter into contract discussions under the auspices of the Ministry of Labor if a majority of his employees so desired; if no agreement was reached, the Ministry was authorized to establish a contract by decree. Contracts for a limited period could be modified only with the consent of both parties, but contracts that ran indefinitely could be amended by order of the Ministry if the parties failed to reach an agreement through the collective bargaining machinery. In such cases both sides had the right to appeal to the Supreme Court.

Although collective bargaining methods were, in theory, widely used, negotiations were undermined, first, by the large role the government assumed in determining the labor contract and, second, by a lack of confidence between workers and employers. Issues, including those concerning wages, often were referred to the government and settled by administrative order. Similarly, the machinery provided by law for the settlement of disputes often failed to function. There was no effective civil service system to promote the development of a body of trained conciliators in the Ministry of Labor, and since most officials were political appointees, both labor leaders and employers distrusted their impartiality. During the 1940's the strongest unions were able to pack the Ministry of Labor with friendly officials.

From the point of view of the employer, the application of the laws appeared invariably to benefit workers. Although an impartial decision might eventually be obtained from the courts, it was a lengthy and costly process and both labor leaders and employers resorted to political and personal influence or bribery. Thus, labor-management relations were always affected by political currents, and influence in Havana was often more important than economic bargaining power. The issues that most concerned management and to which unions were quick to react were precisely those most closely regulated by law, such as rigid job tenure, rigid seniority requirements by the union, make-work rules, and restrictions on mechanization. Laws and decrees governing conditions of work were numerous and complex, and discussions tended to become debates. On the other hand, no one had precise information on even the most elementary facts, such as unemployment in the industry, or the relation between wage rates and the cost of living, that were relevant to a fair settlement. Only rarely did genuine collective bargaining and negotiation take place.

Because communication between employers and workers was usually poor, troubles broke out with little warning. There were, however, relatively few strikes, and those were of short duration. Government, interested in maintaining labor peace, quickly intervened and the dispute was settled by mediation, extralegal methods, or official decree. Open government interference in the area of industrial relations through suspension of the right to strike and intervention of private enterprises occurred during periods of national emergency or political insecurity. The use of such drastic measures indicated complete collapse of the behind-the-scenes political arrangements.

Before 1959 intervention was used mainly when employers found it impossible to comply with the rulings of the Ministry of Labor and still stay in business. During the inflationary period of the 1940's, when the government ordered wage increases and employers said they were unable to comply, the government occasionally intervened the enterprises. The Batista regime of 1952, less prolabor than preceding governments and coming to power during a period of relative prosperity, opposed intervention. Toward the end of 1958, however, it was forced to curb the economic freedom of both labor and the employer. The right to strike was suspended and requests from business to close down were largely ignored.

EDUCATION AND WELFARE

EDUCATIONAL AND WELFARE SERVICES and the general health of the population during the first half of the century compared favorably with those of other Caribbean countries, partly because of the relatively high per capita income. The statistical averages were deceptive, however; urban and rural conditions differed considerably and a still wider gap was apparent between the standards applying to the upper and lower classes. For most people, the available facilities fell far short of both what they needed and what politicians promised.

The school system, the medical services, and to a smaller extent the social insurance programs all suffered the excessively centralized control of bureaucracies in Havana and all were important centers of graft and channels of patronage. In general the best services in each field were provided by private and cooperative agencies, including religious organizations. Some of these agencies were also channels of patronage, either on a small, personal scale or in the wider context of class relationships.

Public school programs were particularly susceptible to political manipulation because an education was the inescapable minimum qualification for advancement from lower-class status. Education for all was one of the slogans of the victors of the war of independence in 1898 and was restated after subsequent upheavals, but in each case the egalitarian concern of the leaders for the underprivileged scarcely outlasted the success of the revolution. For their own children the educated resorted to private schools, often at considerable expense. Their lack of interest in public schooling lowered its quality, increasing the incentive for those with means to go elsewhere and accentuating the cultural disparity between the social classes.

Throughout the colonial period nearly all educated Cubans came from the upper class. Members of prosperous families attended secondary schools and universities in Spain, North America, or Mexico, or were privately educated in Cuba. Such education as was available locally was provided and controlled by the Catholic Church. At the end of the eighteenth century, however, the growing nationalist movement attacked the Catholic monopoly of education as part of its general attack on the comprehensive Spanish monopoly of authority, profit, and opportunity. Secular education was promoted as a means to the creation of a base of popular support for the cause of independence.

Following a survey in 1793 by the Sociedad Económica de Amigos del País, this liberal intellectual organization established two free secular schools in Havana. Despite opposition from the clergy the Sociedad Económica was instrumental in the establishment of many other schools throughout the island which in several cases offered free elementary instruction to poor children, Negro as well as white, and attracted some of the foremost educators of the day, who instilled liberal ideals and an intense nationalist spirit in two generations of Cuban students. Among their students were José Martí and other leading revolutionary figures of the nineteenth century.

The nationalists were concerned not only with the expansion of the secular education system but with modernization of the curriculum. By 1825, through their influence, courses in anatomy and political economy had been added at the university in Havana and the teaching of law had been framed in a more modern spirit. In 1842, with assistance from the United States, the university was reorganized and secularized as the University of Havana. In this same year legal provision was made for free and compulsory education for children between seven and ten years of age. The burden for providing this schooling was placed on the local governing councils. Several hundred public schools were established in various parts of the island in the remaining decades of the colonial period.

The principle of free and compulsory schooling was established in the Constitution of 1901 and elaborated in the basic school law of 1909, whcih required attendance for all children of primary school age at public or approved private schools. The state-controlled education system had the help of the United States military authorities during the occupation. Over-all responsibility was given to a Commissioner of Public Instruction and six provincial superintendents. Popularly elected local boards of education, exercising a considerable degree of autonomy, actually performed most of the administrative functions. United States missionaries were also active in education; of the ninety-eight Protestant *colegios* (secondary schools) in 1956—with an enrollment of 14,000—90 percent had been founded between 1898 and 1901.

The system was organized into pre-elementary, elementary, secondary, and university levels. Each stage led directly to the next, except for vocational schools at the secondary level. The elementary stage lasted six years, the secondary stage four years. Toward the end of the Machado administration a new type of school, known as an upper primary school, was added which gave a three-year course paralleling that of the first three years of secondary school. It was not, however, an integral step in the ordinary pattern of progression from one stage of schooling to another.

The University of Havana was the only university during this period and, as such, became the focus of the cultural and intellectual life of the period. Students actively participated in national political affairs as well. National, cultural, and welfare societies operated schools, as did various religious groups. Catholic education, after a setback in the initial period of independence, had by the early 1930's regained its pre-eminent role in private education.

For all the apparent effort to extend education, however, only moderate progress was achieved in this period and the shortage of schools continued. The percentage of persons aged ten or older who were able to read and write was 43 in 1899, 56 in 1907, 61 in 1919, and 71 in 1931. The percentage of children of school age in school was 63 percent in 1925-26 for the country as a whole, and it was much lower than this in rural areas. In 1929-30, the last year of normal operation in this period, about 12,000 students were enrolled in secondary schools, nearly all of which were located in urban areas. Slightly over 5,500 students were enrolled at the University.

In 1933, when former sergeant Batista became the nation's most powerful figure, educational reform was widely regarded as the country's most pressing need. The strongest advocates of this and other reforms were the students and intellectuals who followed Ramón Grau San Martín, a professor of the University. Batista attempted to attract wide popular support by advocating a better school system but at the same time took steps to break the political power of the University group. A prominent part of the Batista program was the use of the army to extend education to rural areas. In line with the proposal that the army construct schools, rural teachers were given the rank of sergeant. When a sergeant-teacher reported for duty, however, he was likely to find that his new school lacked furniture and that he would have to appeal, as before, to the local estate manager to make good the deficiency.

Although there were improvements here and there, the general level of education declined during the 1930's, a trend related to the social and political unrest and the severe economic depression of the period. Between 1931 and 1943 there was virtually no increase in literacy for the population as a whole. Only among the Negroes, who were moving to the cities in increasing numbers, did the relatively rapid progress of the preceding three decades continue.

In the Constitution of 1940 the earlier stipulations regarding free and compulsory primary education were reiterated. Secondary education was to be free except in schools that prepared students for university training. Article 52, attesting to the importance attached to popular education, declared that the budget of the Ministry of Education should be no less than the ordinary budget of any other ministry, except in case of national emergency, and that a teacher's monthly salary should not be less than one-millionth of the annual national budget.

Despite the new constitution, education levels showed no appreciable progress during the 1940's. The generous financial provisions for education in the constitution made the Ministry of Education a center of wholesale graft which, by 1948, had become a national scandal. The sale of teaching appointments was a common practice; teachers were civil servants who had life tenure and were paid whether they taught or not. Appointments were made with exceptional generosity just before national elections and the Minister of Education himself made a fortune of several millions. Although some progress was recorded during the early 1950's, there was no indication that by 1958 there had been much improvement in the situation summarized in 1950 by the IBRD:

> The typical citizen is one whose children, if he lives in town, go to school two hours a day 120 days a year for the first few grades only. If he lives in the rural district, his children are more likely to be out of school than in school, and, for the short time that they

do attend, their instruction is received in a one-room schoolhouse where the teacher has all six grades, is probably inadequately trained, and works without adequate books and supplies.

The education system in this period was strongly nationalistic and highly centralized. The local boards of the earlier period ceased to be popularly elected and lost most of their authority. The Minister of Education, a Cabinet member, established educational policy and had final jurisdiction in matters of school administration, curriculum, teaching methods, textbooks, and examinations. The only schools not under his immediate direction were those operated by the Ministry of Agriculture and the private schools which, however, could operate only in conformity with the same regulations as applied to public schools. New types of schools were developed for rural areas and a wider variety of vocational training was offered.

Lower primary schools far outnumbered all other types combined. In the early 1950's their enrollment represented about five-sixths of the total school population. In 1953-54 there were only 188 advanced primary schools as compared with 6,423 at the lower stage. They covered two years' work, although the system theoretically provided for three. Most were located in urban districts and were inaccessible to rural children who could not meet transportation costs. An exception was the small number of rural children accepted at special advanced primary schools with boarding facilities where the focus was on practical training in agriculture. General academic training was supplemented by practical work in fields, gardens, and workshops.

The level of secondary education during the early 1950's showed some improvement over that of the early 1930's. Schooling beyond the elementary level was offered in three types of institution: general secondary, normal, and vocational training schools. To enter, students were generally expected to have finished upper primary school, although this requirement was not always enforced in the vocational schools. A few vocational schools selected students through competitive entrance examinations. Although the number of general secondary schools more than tripled between 1930 and 1950, there were still disproportionately few both in relation to the number of lower primary schools and to the number of school-age children in the country. The problem was primarily a rural one since the majority of general secondary schools were located in urban areas.

The excessive specialization of the curriculum presented another serious problem. General secondary schools concentrated exclusively on the preparation of students for university admission although the majority did not continue their education beyond the secondary level. The five-year course included four years of general academic work and one devoted to the student's intended area of specialization at the university, either letters or science. Nearly four-fifths of the class hours were devoted to routine academic work; the remainder to so-called practical work in workshop or gymnasium. Students who completed the program were awarded a *bachillerato* certificate.

Public normal schools provided secondary education for many students who otherwise, because of the shortage of secondary schools, would have had none. But candidates for admission were inadequately screened and, as there were few summer refresher courses, many teachers were very poorly trained.

The relatively few public vocational schools in Cuba in the early 1930's had developed, by mid-century, into a multiplicity of such institutions offering courses of varied duration and quality. They included schools of commerce, schools of arts and crafts, polytechnic schools, and schools of journalism, fine arts, and surveying. As a rule standards in the schools of arts and crafts were not high. Most such schools suffered from mediocre instruction and a shortage of equipment; some from inadequate financial support.

The polytechnic schools were of much more importance than the schools of arts and crafts—both in terms of the number of pupils receiving training and the number of courses offered. They supplied food, lodging, tuition, and sometimes clothing to the pupils free of charge. Several of these institutions had been set up essentially as welfare institutions to provide for orphans. But, in at least one case, most of the students had been admitted because their parents, eager to have them supported and educated for three years at government expense, had appealed to political patrons.

One of the best polytechnic schools, in Ceiba del Agua, had various dormitories, workshops, a power plant, dining hall, laundry, and a motion-picture theater. Although it had a relatively large operating budget—one million dollars yearly in 1950—the school was still short of funds and some facilities were falling into disrepair through lack of maintenance. The program lasted three years and led to a certificate in the principal field of study. Specialization was by aptitude and choice, a condition with unfortunate results in terms of national economic needs. The best students tended to go into industrial trades; the poorest into agriculture.

In 1950 there were six secondary-level agricultural schools, one in each province. Like the polytechnic schools, they had boarding facilities; tuition, board, room, and clothing were furnished free. Admission was by competitive examination, but apparently only boys who were from farm families and who had finished at least five years of primary school were considered. The three-year program, consisting of academic work and practical farming, led to a certificate as Master Farmer. Few of the graduates actually became farmers afterwards, however, preferring to engage in some type of agricultural advisory work. On the whole the schools provided relatively good training. Each had its own land and livestock and was adequately, if not generously, equipped. Shortages of operational funds were the chief difficulty. The problem lay not so much in the caliber of the schools, but in the fact that there were only six in all.

There were three state-controlled universities. Largest, and by far the most influential, was the University of Havana, in existence since the eighteenth century. New universities were founded in Santiago de Cuba in 1949 and in Santa Clara in 1952. Total enrollment in these institutions was nearly 20,000 in 1953-54 with most students enrolled at the university of Havana; total faculty members numbered 628.

Admission to the University of Havana was generally open only to students who had earned a *bachillerato* certificate. There were thirteen faculties of the University of Havana: philosophy and letters, education, science, engineering, agriculture, architecture, medicine, pharmacy, dentistry, veterinary science, law, social science and public law, and commerce. The faculties of medicine, law, commerce, and education were the most popular. In 1951-52, for example, students in these faculties represented about two-thirds of the total enrollment. Few students, by contrast, elected social science and public law, pure science, veterinary medicine, or agricultural programs. The distribution of students among various faculties reflected both social attitudes and economic realities. Students with degrees in medicine enjoyed the best employment opportunities as well as the most respect from less well-educated Cubans. Their degree gave them the choice of practicing a profession or obtaining a government bureaucratic post, the latter being offered on the theory that, since such degrees took longest to earn (five years as compared with the usual four), those who held them were the best equipped educationally. Since the content of education was largely theoretical, the question of the applicability of their particular field of knowledge to the given job was not considered highly relevant. In 1956 the University of Havana had about 450 professors, many of whom practiced a profession, held an outside job, or did freelance writing in addition to teaching. Most professors failed to keep up with developments in their fields.

Because of the declining caliber of public education, there was a significant increase in private school enrollments in the 1940's. By 1953-54 the country had nearly 900 officially recognized private schools with a total enrollment of slightly over 100,000 pupils. Of the country's 129 general secondary schools, 108 were privately operated. Some students attended on scholarship, but most were drawn from the relatively wealthy middle- and upper-income groups.

The only university outside state control was the Catholic University of Saint Thomas of Villanueva in Havana, founded by Augustinian Fathers from the United States in 1947. There were schools of arts and sciences, economics and business administration, commerce, law, pedagogy, philosophy and letters, chemical engineering, pharmacy, diplomatic law, and psychology, as well as an institute of languages. In the early 1950's students at the University numbered about 500, the faculty 83.

In 1953-54 there were about 25,000 teachers in the public school system, over three-fourths of whom were women. In addition there were some 3,500 teachers in private elementary schools and over 800 in private secondary schools. Teaching methods were to a large extent mechanical and the emphasis was on extensive memorization and drill work. Both public and private schools tended to follow a formal and bookish curriculum.

Overtaxed facilities and a dearth of equipment and supplies were serious drawbacks. Despite the vast sums allocated to the Ministry of Education, only a few of the school buildings were actually owned by the state. At one time during the 1940's, the state owned 450 schools, rented three times that number, and used 4,400 privately owned buildings lent free of charge by their owners.

Textbooks, paper, and pencils were usually scarce. Teachers and the local citizens interested in education frequently found it necessary to pay out of their own pockets to maintain the schools or to buy supplies.

General Health

In the mid-1950's Cubans seem to have had enough to eat in that their daily per capita caloric intake (2,740 calories) was higher than their estimated requirements (2,460). The occasional general or local famines that plague some Latin American countries were unknown, and most Cubans ate two meals a day. The typical diet is, however, high in carbohydrates, particularly starches, and low in proteins, minerals, and vitamins. According to the 1950 IBRD Mission, an estimated 30 to 40 percent of the urban population and 60 percent of the rural population suffered from serious nutritional deficiencies, manifested in small bone structure, overweight, general physical weakness, anemia, and low resistance to disease.

Low income encourages the persistence of the starch-oriented diet. The farmer will sell in town readily available items like eggs rather than consume them at home, for with the price brought by eggs a farmer can feed his whole family on a more filling diet of carbohydrates. Without rice and beans (or some substitute such as peas) a Cuban does not feel he has really eaten. Substantial amounts of sugar are consumed and there is a large proportion of fat in the diet. Meats often are fried, and deep-frying is the customary way of preparing most starchy foods, which would otherwise be unpalatable.

Cubans eat insufficient amounts of meat, poultry, fish, eggs, and dairy products. Pork is the most commonly eaten and preferred meat. So basic is pork to the diet that almost every farmer raises a few pigs. Chicken is a relished luxury.

Green vegetables play a minor role in the diet. The people have not developed a taste for them and have a positive dislike for some green vegetables such as lettuce. Even though many varieties of fruit such as oranges, guavas, and bananas are readily available, little fruit is eaten. Except for an occasional glass of lemonade or limeade, or an orange eaten between meals by children, the chief use of citrus fruits is for seasoning.

The availability of foods is not an important factor in the nutritional imbalance of the diet. Even increasing wealth does not bring major shifts away from carbohydrates, although upper-income families consume more meat, fowl, dairy products, and canned goods. Cubans like meat, and meat consumption rises with sugar prices. But the popular saying is that to go to heaven one needs rice and beans.

Apart from economic considerations, Cubans love to eat. This is reflected in such popular sayings as *barriga llena, corazón contento* (full stomach, contented heart) and *el amor empieza por la cocina* (love enters through the kitchen). Standards of masculine and feminine beauty encourage the consumption of weight-producing foods. Plump women are more highly appreciated and sought after than slender ones, and the North American emphasis upon dieting and the maintenance of a slim silhouette has no place in Cuba.

The level of sanitation during the 1950's showed marked improvement over conditions existing at the beginning of the century. Nevertheless it continued to fall far short of making any truly positive contribution to the well-being and strength of the country. In 1950, the IBRD Mission noted the "often almost complete lack of . . . municipal services, such as water supplies, sewers, and paved streets." According to the 1953 census, 23 percent of all houses were without toilet facilities of any kind; 43 percent had no running water; and more than 55 percent had no shower or bath. Nearly 31 percent of all houses had dirt floors; almost all were overcrowded.

Sanitary conditions were worst in the province of Pinar del Río, followed by Oriente and Las Villas provinces. The better conditions prevailing in La Habana and Camagüey reflected the urbanization of those provinces and the fact that sanitary conditions generally are better in the urban areas than in the countryside. Whereas 50 percent of all urban dwellings had bath or shower facilities, only 9 percent of rural dwellings had them. Five percent of the urban homes had no toilet facilities, but half the rural dwellings were without them.

In rural Cuba, people generally do not have a safe water supply, most sources being exposed to contamination and pollution. Under these conditions, the drinking of water without first boiling it holds the same serious risks of infection as the custom of river-bathing. In addition, garbage is left exposed and fields and roadsides are often used as latrines without thought for problems of drainage and fly-control. Government controls and programs for environmental sanitation have not been vigorously applied in the rural zone, with the result that there is continued infestation of rural people, especially children, with parasites.

But compared with other Central American countries, Cuba could claim a relatively favorable state of health. World Health Organization statistics for the period 1950-1955 gave Cuba an estimated annual death rate for all ages of 15 per 1,000 persons, and an annual infant mortality rate of 125 per 1,000 live births. Life expectancy at birth was an estimated fifty years. Only Costa Rica, Jamaica, and Puerto Rico enjoyed a higher level of health than Cuba; Mexico was about on a par with Cuba. Thanks to the efforts of men like Carlos Finlay, the Cuban doctor who identified the domestic mosquito as the transmitter of yellow fever, and William Gorgas, the American chief of Havana's Department of Sanitation during United States occupation in the first years of this century, Cuba in the 1950's was relatively disease-free for a tropical country. Malarial infection, for example, had fallen to 2.1 cases per 100,000 population. Cuba did not escape the influenza epidemic during World War I, but there has not been an epidemic since the 1920's.

The chief communicable diseases in 1956 were syphilis, with a reported case rate of 61.9 per 100,000, tuberculosis with a rate of 31 per 100,000; and typhoid fever with a rate of 16.5. It was estimated in 1950 that 80 to 90 percent of rural children were infested with intestinal parasites. Parasitical infection among adults was also common. Nutritional anemia and gastrointestinal disorders were commonplace, and the latter accounted for most cases of infant mortality.

Many Cubans, both in the cities and the countryside, hold a wide variety of traditional, nonscientific beliefs concerning the causes and cures of ill health. Most common are those with a religious base—the attribution of accidents and illness to the wrath of offended God or of a saint, to a spell or the evil eye of some malevolent spirit or person, or to the "possession" of the body by a spirit. Another belief, common in many areas of Latin America, is that objects and foods are intrinsically "hot" or "cold" and that imprudent contact of a "hot" patient with "cold" objects or foods and vice versa disturbs the healthy equilibrium of the body. Knowledge of folk medicine is widely prevalent, particularly among older rural people, and there is a tendency to depend upon home remedies, but faith in modern medicine is firmly established, and people look to the physician for injections and penicillin, which are popularly believed to cure all but the most minor ailments.

Mid-century Cuba, with about one physician for every 1,000 inhabitants and about one dentist for every 3,000 inhabitants, had a higher proportion of doctors and dentists than any other Caribbean country, the commonwealth of Puerto Rico included. There was about one graduate nurse for every 2,200 inhabitants, a ratio surpassed only by Costa Rica and Jamaica. Moreover, Cuba had a higher percentage of hospital beds, about one for every 300 inhabitants, than any other country in the region, with the exception of Costa Rica and the Bahamas. Some Cuban doctors were among the world's best but not necessarily because of the training available in Cuba. The medical school of the University of Havana had neither a full-time faculty nor modern equipment and training facilities.

The distribution of the ample health services heavily favored urban areas, in particular the city of Havana. Although nearly half the population lived in the countryside, most doctors worked in the cities, where other medical services also were concentrated. Although the 1953-1954 national budget allocated some 23 million, or 7.5 percent of all expenditures, to health and welfare, the provision of these services, like that of public works, was accompanied by graft and waste. In private practice, it has been the long-established custom for small groups of physicians to join together as associates and form clinics that offer medical plans through which the public can receive care and medication in return for fixed monthly membership payments. Similar programs were sponsored by the various Spanish *centros* (see below). Physicians associated with a clinic or medical plan also maintained their own individual private offices; members or nonmembers who wanted the services of a particular doctor or immediate or special attention could go for private consultation and be charged accordingly.

In 1956 the central government supervised and controlled the practice of medicine and auxiliary professions in Cuba and had direct supervisory control over the district health services in each of the island's 126 municipal districts. Administration of government activities was centered in the Ministry of Health and Social Welfare with special areas of responsibility assigned to eight directorates-general.

The provision of health services has been the vehicle for political publicity, patronage, and graft. At the beginning of this century, for example, the program for the extermination of mosquitoes became the object of intense political exploitation. Although malaria had been largely brought under control by 1909, the number of government jobs on antimalaria teams continued to expand for many years after. Everyone wanted to get on a spray team and go *matando la culebra* (slaying the serpent) although, according to a popular poem, "all we succeed in doing is to increase the bloodsuckers."

The construction of hospitals and other public health facilities by the Ministry of Public Works was most often the result of political rather than technical decisions. The Ministry was one of the major vehicles for the distribution of patronage. According to the IBRD Mission:

> . . . in Santiago de Cuba, there is the concrete skeleton of a hospital building, in front of which stands a huge placard advertising the government which started it. And, only about twenty yards from this rejected "ruin" there is another hospital under construction financed by the Workers' Maternity Fund. . . . Such projects, while they remain unfinished, not only represent a waste of capital and labor, but also suggest that their sponsors may have been more interested in making a show of giving work to the people than in furthering economic and social progress.

Often, access to a clinic or a hospital bed could be obtained only through the political organization of the town. Services were channeled to the rural population through leaders of the party in power. Those using the health services and facilities were strongly reminded of the source of the benefits, and many were required to vote accordingly. Public health positions, like other government jobs, also were subject to the patronage system.

Welfare Services

Before the establishment of the republic in 1902 almost all welfare activities were channeled through the Roman Catholic Church. Religious orders and lay groups operated the schools, hospitals, orphanages, and homes for the aged. After independence the government assumed control of most hospitals and schools but other institutions remained largely under clerical administration. The Little Sisters of the Helpless Aged, a Spanish order, ran homes for old people that were noted for their pleasant surroundings and their air of friendliness and general well-being. The many orphanages maintained by the Catholic orders were said to give good care, although lack of teachers and other staff members was a serious problem and the need to provide for large numbers of children tended to make for regimentation. Also there was usually no provision for separate care for sick or mentally defective children. One of the outstanding orphanages in the country was the Casa de Beneficiencía y Maternidad in Havana which at one time boarded seven hundred boys and girls. In the cities lay members of religious orders, such as the Society of St. Vincent and St. Paul, distributed medicines, visited the sick, and sponsored homes for the blind.

Secular welfare activity proliferated in the nineteenth century as small groups of wealthy Spanish expatriates formed charitable organizations to extend assistance to newcomers so that they should not become public charges or succumb to disease and other hardships. Each organization concerned itself with immigrants from a particular region of Spain. The oldest was the Sociedad de Beneficiencía de Naturales de Galicia, founded in 1871, but twelve other such associations remained active in the capital alone as late as 1960.

Huge *centros* (clubs) were cooperatively organized for mutual aid and social purposes. Like the charity-dispensing groups, they were mostly associations of persons from particular regions and provinces of Spain. The Asociación de Dependientes del Comercio, however, was originally intended chiefly for a particular occupational group; another *centro* was exclusively for women. The membership of the *centros* ranged from about ten thousand to ninety thousand. The largest *centros* also maintained schools, homes for the aged, mausoleums, and some of the finest hospitals and clinics in the country. An outstanding example was the Covadonga Hospital, run by the Centro Asturiano. The *centros* were also medical insurance cooperatives. For a fee of $3 per month a member was entitled to not only the use of the *centro's* educational and recreational facilities but also free medical treatment for himself and his family. Most members were interested chiefly in the medical privileges.

Many other secular organizations sponsored welfare services. Upper-class women in Havana were particularly active, but their gift-giving, prompted by a recognition of social and religious obligation but also an important means of expressing social status, was done conspicuously, focusing attention on the social distinction between those giving and those receiving aid. The wife of the

President distributed gifts to the poor at Christmas time in front of the palace. The Lyceum y Lawn Tennis Club carried on recreational and playground work and supported children's libraries and adult education. The Patronato Nacional de Colonias Infantiles, a small group of women in the capital, was interested particularly in child welfare and sponsored a colony for children at the seashore.

Before 1959 the government operated various health and welfare institutions, including hospitals, dental and maternity clinics, and detention homes for juveniles. The level of care in these institutions appears to have been fairly good, although many apparently suffered from poor administration and lack of operating funds. Responsibility for administration lay with the Ministry of Health and Welfare.

While still fighting in the hills, the Castro forces shared the medical resources of the rebel army with civilians in the rural countryside. After reaching power, the new government stated its intention to distribute health services more equitably between rural and urban areas; amounts allocated to the health ministry grew steadily between 1959 and 1961. But far more important was the attack on the sources of the problems of poverty, illiteracy, and disease, through the institution of such basic programs as those for agrarian and urban reform. In contrast to the earlier system, the needy themselves were made to help in their own rehabilitation. Responsibility was centralized in a new Ministry of Social Welfare.

The government organized health brigades to extend health services into remote rural areas, and other services to benefit workers and students; in late 1959, for example, the government announced the opening of a free dental clinic in the Student City of 26 de Julio of Santiago de Cuba. In order to fill the ranks of the health brigades, a law was passed making it obligatory for each new graduating class of the medical school at the University of Havana to serve two years in the health brigades. Pressure was brought to bear on practicing physicians to volunteer their services enabling the financially embarrassed government to get professional personnel to work for little or nothing. Intensive mobilization of the medical profession occurred during the first major invasion scare, January 1-19, 1960.

A few private clinics were taken over by the regime, but the government retreated from the course of rapid socialization of medicine and turned to less direct methods of controlling the private clinics, using informers and agitators. To protect them-

millions of pesos from these trusts without even publicly acknow-
ledging the fact or, much less, getting the agreement of fund
administrators. The Prío government, which came to power in
October 1948, made an attempt to right this unfortunate situation,
but it also was short of funds, and by mid-1950 the indebtedness
still amounted to about $50 million. Another financial drain was
the payment of benefits to many persons who were not actually
entitled to them. In the early 1950's it was estimated that millions
were being distributed in fraudulent payments each month.

Permanently employed persons in industry, commerce, government, and agriculture, who were injured on the job or contracted
an occupational disease, were entitled to benefits financed entirely
by the employer under the Workmen's Compensation Act, a program introduced by the government in 1916 and enlarged in 1933.
Even as amended, however, the plan failed to provide for domestic
servants in private homes or family and casual workers. A law enacted in 1934 provided for maternity insurance supported by
contributions from the insured and the employer.

Under the Castro regime, the government for the first time took
steps to develop a comprehensive social security system. A Social
Security Bank was established in early 1959 and its administrators
were made responsible for developing an acceptable and coordinated social security program. The bank was also to serve as
a central depository for all reserve funds. In January 1960 the
coverage of old age and disability insurance was extended to all
wage and salary earners in the country. Whether it was further
extended in July of that year, as scheduled, to include persons
working for themselves was not known. The funds already in
existence before the revolution appeared to have been still operating
as separate entities within the framework of the new system.

FOREIGN TRADE AND
UNITED STATES INFLUENCE

Cuba will probably always have an export economy and therefore foreign economic relations will probably always have central
importance. But until 1960, the country maintained almost exclusive ties with the United States as a market and as a source of
imports, and the economy depended on the export of one crop,
sugar. Although closeness to the eastern markets of continental
United States helped explain this trading relationship, it was often
criticized as making the island overly dependent on the United
States. The close relationship was supported by a series of commercial treaties giving preference to United States businessmen.
The firm and advantageous United States market for sugar, obtained under a special quota arrangement, brought obvious material
prosperity, especially during periods of war, but it meant a sacrifice
of economic independence. In times of economic distress, Cubans
tended to blame the United States for their difficulties.

Large American investments were also regarded as evidence
of American economic imperialism. As early as 1896, United States
investment amounted to between $30 million and $50 million.
Between 1920 and 1945, United States and other foreign interests
dominated the economy, wielding almost exclusive control over
the sugar industry and the banking system. Former governments,
although nationalistic and aware of this economic influence, did
not attempt any confiscatory policies; in fact, such an approach, the
bane of foreign investors in other areas, was largely avoided.

Castro's revolutionary program in 1959 was in part a reaction
against long dependence on the United States. His attacks on the

9. Foreign Trade and United States Influence

United States frequently identified American business and trade, sometimes justifiably, with the corruption prevalent in previous governments. Relations between the two countries steadily worsened. In July 1960, the United States cut off Cuba's sugar quota. By the end of 1960 Castro had nationalized all American business, valued at about $1 billion.

Before 1950 the outstanding features of the international balance of payments had been the trade surplus and the favorable current account balances. Trade surpluses normally offset losses in services, freight, insurance, tourist expenditures, and remitted profits on investments (see Table 11). Insurance and other services handled by United States and Canadian firms caused a heavy outflow of capital. The income from foreign tourists, a potentially large source of earnings, was offset by the amount of money Cubans spent abroad. The largest debit item was usually profit remittances on foreign investments in sugar and other enterprises, averaging over $65 million a year between 1946 and 1954. These were, however, more than balanced by high earnings, chiefly from sugar. There was an unfavorable balance of trade in only one year, 1921, when the drastic drop in sugar prices gave the economy little time to adjust to the sudden decrease in export earnings.

Partly responsible for this favorable balance of payments was the remarkable flexibility in adjusting imports to export receipts, a characteristic which emerged after the signing of the 1903 reciprocity treaty with the United States. The adjustment was almost automatic and was quickly effected, since importers cut orders whenever sugar sales abroad slackened, knowing that incomes would fall. Outpayments for freight and insurance and the reparation of earnings by foreign sugar planters all fell with lowered sugar exports; even tourist expenditures made by Cubans abroad fell.

In the absence of acute balance of payments difficulties before 1958, the government employed no import or exchange controls except those imposed during the World War II emergency. No import permits were required except for a few items—rice, flour, potatoes, beans, butter, canned milk, tires, and tubes—whose domestic production the government apparently hoped to encourage, although there were many customs taxes, fees, and levies to burden the importer and dissuade the exporter.

After 1950, on the other hand, although sugar earnings remained high, sugar exports fluctuated and did not cover expenses in foreign transactions as in the past. Unfavorable current account balances occurred in every year from 1950 to 1959, except in 1953. In 1958, for the first time in over three decades, export earnings did not cover import expenditures. The responsiveness of imports to exports similarly declined as the result of two factors: the opposition of organized labor, including the sugar workers, to wage reductions during periods of low sugar prices; and the compensatory spending policies of the Batista regime. Both helped maintain a high level of domestic economic activity during the slump in sugar prices after the Korean war. By the end of 1958 the increasing strain on the balance of payments led the government to require exporters to turn in a large percentage of their foreign exchange receipts for Cuban pesos.

Since the end of World War II exports have represented about one-third of the gross national product and 40 percent of the national income. Sugar has accounted for over 80 percent of export earnings, sometimes reaching 90 percent. Other exports are far behind, with tobacco, minerals, and food products the principal items (see Table 12). Under these circumstances, a drop of even a fraction of a cent in the price of sugar has a marked effect on the entire economy.

Before 1959, diversification had consisted of replacing imports rather than developing new exports. While the exact plans of the Castro regime were not known, it appeared that increasing attention was given to developing new export industries. The chief expansion in nonsugar exports occurred in minerals during World War II, but there was a significant retraction in this sector after the crisis. According to the recommendations made by the International Bank for Reconstruction and Development, Cuba stands to gain most by developing exports of minerals, fruits and vegetables, and sugar by-products.

The market for sugar has reached a saturation point, and any further increase in Cuba's sugar production for export would, over the long run, merely compound an already existing marketing problem. It has been amply demonstrated since 1930 that complete dependence on a single export had been the source of serious instability because of quotas, wars, business cycles, tariff revisions, and changes in human tastes over which Cuba has no control.

The ratio of imports to national income, one of the highest in the world, was made possible up to 1959 by the sizable quantities of foreign exchange provided by sugar exports. Imports include a great variety of items (see Table 13). Foodstuffs make up the single most important group, but they are gradually being reduced as domestic production of foodstuffs increases. During the last years of the Batista regime and especially under the Castro regime more attention has been given to domestic production of most food requirements.

Domestic industry depends greatly on imports for raw materials, capital goods, and equipment. Illustrating this dependence was the fall in production in late 1960 after trade with the United States, the normal supplier of industrial goods, stopped. As the Castro regime's industrialization plan proceeds, dependence on import of capital goods will increase.

From 1902 until the end of World War II, about 80 percent of all exports went to the United States. Between the end of the war and 1959 the figure declined to about 60 percent as sugar exports to European markets increased. There was, however, no comparable decline in imports from the United States. The United States furnished about 66 percent of imports from 1911 to 1940, 80 percent from 1946 to 1950, and 75 percent from 1950 to 1956. On balance, therefore, Cuba ran trade deficits on its current account with the United States. Between 1949 and 1958, trade with most of the western hemisphere also showed a deficit. Trade with Europe, on the other hand, generally showed a large surplus.

In trade with East Europe a significant feature was the sudden surge of exports to the USSR after 1953. Between 1949 and 1952 exports to the Soviet Union amounted to $4,000, against approximately equivalent imports. Between 1953 and 1958, exports to the Soviet Union amounted to $108,258,174.

United States businessmen dominated the field of foreign investment although other foreign investors were represented. Before the Castro regime, over 90 percent of the telephone and electric services, one-half of the public service railways, one-fourth of all bank deposits, about 40 percent of sugar production and much of the mining, oil production and cattle ranching was in the hands of United States business. The major American companies were closely knit, both by interlocking directorates and by common interest; business was conducted and decisions made with reference to their mutual interest. American business naturally promoted ventures which promised dollar profits, and American-controlled banks concentrated on the financing of the sugar industry and foreign trade.

United States sugar interests and, to a lesser extent, tobacco, coffee, cocoa, cattle, and mining interests were active in Cuba from the Spanish colonial period, but a phenomenal increase in American investments took place between 1900 and 1925, especially after World War I. During this period such large enterprises as the Bethlehem Steel Corporation, the United Fruit Company, the American Tobacco Company, the Cuban Telephone Company, the Cuba Railroad, National City Bank of New York, the Cía. Cubana de Electricidad (a subsidiary of the American and Foreign Power Company), the First National Bank of Boston, the Chase National Bank, the Cuban-American Sugar Company and the Cuba Cane Sugar Corporation were established.

In 1914 European capital still predominated, but, as a result of the war, American capital supplanted it. Between 1913 and 1928 United States investment increased about 540 percent. The war had inflated sugar prices, bringing in a large amount of United States capital. Large sugar producers bought out smaller companies; many companies went heavily into debt in order to increase production.

The drop of sugar prices after 1920—from an all time high of 22.5 cents in 1922 to 1.6 cents a year later—and the consequent bankruptcy of many sugar mills, led American banks, which held many of the defaulted loans, to enter the sugar industry on a major scale. The National City Bank of New York, for example, organized the General Sugar Company, absorbed a number of mills, and became heavily involved in sugar production. United States capital became the driving force in efforts to modernize the sugar industry and also invested considerable sums in public utilities and transportation. By 1929, just before the Wall Street crash, American investments totalled about one billion.

American investments dropped sharply after 1929 and during the ensuing world-wide depression, mainly because of a revaluation of assets and a contraction of corporate activities in the sugar industry. Bankrupt sugar mills were increasingly taken over by the banks. American investments in manufacturing also dropped drastically, especially in the tobacco industry.

Not until after World War II did United States investments again begin to show a rise, but the pace was slow and in no way comparable to the surge of the 1920's. Investments in the sugar industry increased only slightly, reaching a total of $285 million by 1956. More of the increase was in reinvestment of earnings than new capitalization. Manufacturing industries received more attention from United States investors. Direct investment was made in several important new industries, such as detergents, vegetable shortening, and rubber goods. An increase in public utility investments improved the power supply by the Cía. Cubana de Electricidad.

The trend toward increased American investments in manufacturing and mining industries continued during the 1950's up to the time of the Castro revolution. In an effort to stimulate and diversify the economy the Batista regime removed some of the impediments to foreign investment. New industries received preferential tax treatment and lower tariffs on imported raw materials. Thus encouraged, several large American enterprises had projects under construction or in the planning stage when Castro came to power.

One of the largest projects, involving investment by the United States government, was the Nicaro nickel plant in Oriente province. Expansion in the late 1950's put the total value of the United States government's investment in this plant at $90 million. Esso Standard Oil Company and the Texas Company were among the important American private investors after a 1954 law favorable to oil refining provided the necessary incentive.

In contrast to United States investments, other foreign investments have been small. The British, particularly active early in the century and before World War I, owned part of the railway network and several sugar mills. Canadians were active in banking and insurance. French, Belgian, Dutch, and Spanish concerns were involved in sugar mills and other private ventures. By 1955 the British had liquidated most of their assets; the United Railways of Havana, Ltd. had been sold to the Cuban government, and total investments which in 1950 had been between sixty and seventy million, had declined to only one million. The Cía. Petrolera Shell de Cuba, however, whose distributive facilities represented most of Britain's remaining investment, was building a refinery in the late 1950's at a projected cost of twenty million.

Except for one French sugar mill, all non-American foreign-owned mills had been sold to Cubans by 1956. Direct Spanish investments have been negligible since the 1930's, consisting chiefly of reinvested earnings of local enterprises.

Because of the importance of foreign trade to the economy, commercial policy, concerned chiefly with selling sugar, has been of central importance in foreign economic relations. Before 1959 good public relations with the United States were fostered not only by the government but by private groups, including the Confederation of Cuban Workers (CTC). Under the Castro regime, key economic officials undertook missions to Communist bloc countries for the purpose of selling sugar.

Until 1948 commercial policy centered primarily around a series of bilateral trade agreements with the United States, beginning with the reciprocity treaty of 1903 according to which Cuban sugar entering the United States was given a 20 percent preferential tariff reduction, and United States products received 20 to 40 percent reductions in the Cuban tariff. The treaty, initiated by the United States, aroused much disagreement between American businessmen looking for markets in Latin America and domestic sugar producers seeking to keep out Cuban sugar. Its ratification gave the United States a virtual monopoly of the Cuban market, and in exchange Cuba was permitted higher sugar sales to the United States.

The next phase of tariff negotiations began in 1927 when the problem of inadequate markets for sugar was aggravated by the increase in sugar production. Seeking diversification of the economy, the tariffs of 1927, 1930, 1931 and 1932 were designed to protect and promote domestic agriculture and industry. Under the new tariffs, which in some cases were as high as 100 percent of the import value, domestic industries developed at a much more rapid pace, especially the production of foodstuffs. The preferential system with the United States nevertheless was maintained.

The Reciprocal Trade Agreement of 1934, conceived by the Roosevelt administration as a means of developing America's markets abroad, lowered duties on numerous United States' exports to Cuba in return for a substantial lowering of United States sugar import duties. Equally important was the Jones-Costigan Act of 1934 which established the sugar quota system. The act empowered the secretary of agriculture to estimate the annual sugar consumption level in the United States and allot a share of the total to each sugar producing area. The quota varied from year to year. These two important acts ushered in the age of managed sugar markets and controlled competition. Henceforward, the United States government, rather than private interests, determined Cuba's share of the American market.

Another important development was the establishment of the second Export-Import Bank in March 1934 for the express purpose of lending money to Cuba, thereby promoting American exports to that area. These agreements remained in effect during World War II except for certain measures taken by the Cuban government to meet the emergency.

The prewar pattern of commercial relations with the United States required serious modification after World War II. On the one hand, industry, which had developed quite rapidly during the war, sought added protection from American imports in the form of higher tariffs. On the other hand, sugar growers were eager to maintain the preferential system with the United States. Both policies came into direct conflict with the General Agreement on Tariffs and Trade (GATT), negotiated in 1948 by 23 countries, which sought to remove world-wide obstacles to trade by discouraging bilateral trade agreements and by removing quotas and tariffs. Cuba, whose favored trade position vis-à-vis the United States was directly threatened, only signed the agreement after negotiating a separate agreement with the United States preserving in its essentials the preferential system. Protective tariffs for developing industry were increased in return for tariff concessions to United States exporters.

After a period of suspension between 1942 and 1947 sugar quotas were revised under the United States Sugar Act of 1948. The new system allotted fixed quotas to United States beet sugar producers and to Hawaii, Puerto Rico, the Virgin Islands, and the Philippines; Cuba and several other countries were allotted percentages of United States consumption requirements not filled by the fixed quotas. Cuba's percentage of this remainder was 98.6, but in no case was Cuba to receive less than 28.6 percent of total United States requirements. The United States Congress renewed this legislation in 1952 and 1956.

In 1956 the tariff arrangement was classified under six headings— a maximum general tariff, an intermediate tariff, a minimum tariff, a United States preferential tariff, a GATT minimum tariff, and a GATT United States preferential tariff. Generally, the stiffest tariffs were placed on goods from countries which made few Cuban purchases. The United States-Cuban preferential tariff, separately negotiated within the GATT agreement, gave the United States a 20 to 90 percent reduction of tariffs applying to other countries. During the late 1950's important tariff concessions to new industries were granted by decree.

In March 1958 a new tariff system was established, affecting only countries that did not have trade agreements with Cuba. Changes in the preferential United States and most-favored-nation rates awaited new negotiations. Preparations for a renegotiation of these rates were cut off by the revolution. Thus, the most critical issue in commercial relations—whether Cuba could maintain her preferential position with the United States and still increase tariff duties on imports from the United States—never came to a test.

The commercial policy in effect until the Castro regime, designed primarily to favor the United States in return for advantageous sugar sales, had two unfortunate effects. The tariff discriminated unnecessarily against exporters in countries other than the United States, including those countries with which Cuba had a large export surplus. Moreover, the close trade ties with the United States reduced Cuba's economic independence and, in effect, forced Cuba to forego tariff protection for nascent domestic industry. Although diversification of domestic production was concentrated in import-substituting products, producers found it difficult to compete with American manufactures because of the strong influence exerted by sugar and importing interests over economic policy. In addition the proximity of the United States and Cuba's large dollar reserves made the importation of goods attractive, and the government feared that Cuba might lose its special advantages in the United States market, on which it greatly depended.

Besides the special arrangements with the United States, public and private interests attempted market controls to promote sugar sales and determine prices. The Cuban Sugar Stabilization Institute, established in 1931, controlled domestic production of sugar and exercised an important function in negotiating trade agreements abroad. After 1951, bilateral trade agreements with several nations were concluded; the main feature of each was a lower tariff in exchange for purchases of Cuban sugar, although the special preferential rates allowed to the United States were not affected. Cuba signed the 1954 International Sugar Agreement, renewed in 1958, providing for reduction of export quotas whenever world sugar prices fell below 3.15 cents a pound. Quota restrictions could be removed if world prices exceeded 3.75 cents a pound. These, like earlier measures, failed to solve chronic marketing problems, although they often eased the situation.

BANKING AND FINANCE

UNTIL 1959 PUBLIC AND PRIVATE FINANCIAL RESOURCES were sufficient to have made economic development a reality, but instead public finances were exhausted through wasteful expenditure, and a large proportion of private funds were left idle. Castro inherited a depleted treasury and low foreign exchange reserves; although he succeeded temporarily in accumulating sizable revenues through tax increases and drawing on private savings, they were inadequate to finance the many projects planned and the responsibilities assumed by nationalization. The basic weakness of the public financial system before Castro was explained in 1950 by the IBRD:

> On the one hand, there is criticism of wasteful expenditures, resentment against the complexity of the tax system, and general suspicion of those in charge of public funds. On the other hand, the same groups exert pressure on the politicians to secure benefits for themselves by diverting as much public revenue as possible in their own direction. Under the impact of such pressures, long-term needs have repeatedly been sacrificed to short-term political expediency.

In most respects, this problem continued to exist until the Batista regime was overthrown.

The tax system, originating in the Spanish colonial system of indirect and regressive taxation, continued to favor the wealthy and powerful. Although, in theory, allowance was made for local and provincial financial responsibilities and independence, in fact the central government was responsible for virtually all services from education to sanitation and absorbed almost all tax revenues. Mismanagement made any full and precise audit impossible; the status of government finances at any particular time could not be determined.

The underlying concept of the tax system was expressed by one official to the IBRD as "the government takes the money wherever it finds it." Some two hundred levies and taxes, many of them of a nuisance nature, were established without any consideration of their economic and social effects and without regard to the possibility of effective enforcement. Every time a new project was proposed, a new tax was levied. A favorite target for taxation was the sugar industry. The changing yields of such special taxes, however, often had no relation to the purpose for which they were imposed, and the taxes remained in effect after the original need had been met.

The suspicion and distrust with which Cubans viewed government officials and the financial system led to widespread tax evasion which was facilitated by the many loopholes in the tax system and by inadequate enforcement. Penalties for evasion were mild, usually only a small fine. Typically, an individual would say that he paid his taxes regularly and promptly, but would add that he knew nobody else did. Most revenue, therefore, came from taxes easy to collect—those on consumer necessities and on imports.

If the tax system was complex, budgetary operations constituted a virtual labyrinth. The budget was divided into three parts—the ordinary budget, the extraordinary budget, and the so-called extrabudgetary account which included the receipts and expenditures of special funds, retirement funds, autonomous agencies, provinces, and municipalities. The 1940 Constitution called for a General Accounting Office (*Tribunal de Cuentas*) to audit all government accounts. Finally established in 1950, in the ensuing years it was never able to prepare a complete statement of the government's financial transactions. By the end of the Batista regime, for example, extrabudgetary expenditures had become so large as to threaten seriously the financial solvency of the government.

Budget policies were little used to promote development or to offset cyclical changes in the economy, partly because of the lack of a simplified and flexible tax system. In prosperous times the tax structure yielded more than enough funds with which development programs or later counterdeflationary deficit spending could have been attempted, but modern fiscal manipulation of this kind was not undertaken, and budget and tax policies played a neutral and conservative role in the economy. The deficit-spending, pump-priming operation of public works undertaken by the Batista regime in 1953 succeeded in increasing economic activity at least in Havana, but the plan was undertaken outside the budget, and tax policies continued to play a passive role. It was a departure from earlier conservative policies only in that it led to a new record in the size of the public debt.

A rapid increase in revenues between 1940 and 1952 was based on war and postwar prosperity and on increasing use of direct taxation. Revenues fell between 1952 and 1954 because of declining sugar prices, but rose after that until the collapse of the Batista regime (see Table 14). Most revenues were obtained from taxes; only small amounts being provided by various fees, the postal service, telecommunications, and the national lottery. Over half of the tax yield came from import and consumption duties, and, until 1940, direct taxes on income and profits accounted for only 6 percent of all tax receipts; after 1941 direct taxes became increasingly important, and by 1950 they yielded 21 percent of all tax receipts.

Although some import duties were levied to protect domestic industry, most notably on textiles, import duties generally were moderate and were collected to raise revenue. Imported goods were subject to many other levies, however, such as consular fees for invoices and certain customs surcharges for specific purposes which added greatly to their price. Sales and other internal taxes on imports were also collected by customs; these included the sales tax, stamp taxes on textiles, and luxury taxes up to 20 percent. Sales taxes of 10 percent were levied on imports, but the levy was reduced on some consumer staples. A general sales tax of 8 percent was levied on goods produced in Cuba.

Taxes on personal income and profits were modest compared with those in the United States. Profits were subject to progressive taxes on successive increments, the rates depending on the general type of business. In no case did taxes exceed 36 percent. The failure of direct taxes to yield amounts reflecting the wealth in Cuba also resulted from a provision in the tax laws dealing with excess profits and declared capital. Declared capital was subject to an annual tax of $5 for every $1,000 of capital. The tax on excess profits was 25 percent of all profits over 10 percent of the declared capital. The taxpayer could, however, declare any capital he desired, and could change the amount from year to year whether or not there had been any actual change in value. Thus, to escape the excess profits tax, a business could declare a capital value at least ten times greater than its anticipated profits.

The only formal export tax was one of 2 percent levied on the export of money or its equivalent in goods. The assessment of this tax was so complicated and collection was so difficult to enforce that it was widely evaded. Sugar taxes were also in effect an export tax, since most sugar was exported. Some of the many taxes on sugar and molasses were merged in 1954, but because they were levied at a flat rate the taxes did not yield a greater revenue when sugar prices were high. Taxes on urban and rural real estate and on vacant land yielded very little revenue. The taxes were collected by municipalities, except for those on sugar estates which were paid directly to the central government.

Laws enacted in 1953 and 1954 to encourage new domestic investment granted exemptions from import and consumption taxes and taxes on the export of money and lowered tax rates on profits and excess profits. The term "new industries" was broadly defined to include additions to existing industries. Businesses and corporations, particularly in the sugar industry, continued, however, to be burdened with a variety of petty levies that had no reference to ability to pay. There were, for example, stamp taxes for documents, invoices, and contracts.

The 1940 Constitution authorized the division of the ordinary budget into two parts: a "fixed" budget covering service on the public debt and funds for the legislature and judiciary; and an "annual" budget covering all other receipts and expenditures except those for the "development of the national wealth."

In addition to the ordinary budget, there was an "extraordinary" budget—the indirect effect of three constitutional provisions. These unusual provisions stipulated that the ordinary budget of the Ministry of Education should not be less than the ordinary budget of any other ministry; that the monthly salary of a primary school teacher should not be less than one-millionth of the total budget; and that, if the University of Havana was unable to meet its expenses, it should receive 2.5 percent of the total budget less service charges on the public debt. Because of the great increase in government revenues during the 1940's, these requirements meant that, in theory, teachers should receive salaries far greater than those of other government employees and that the University should receive subsidies far in excess of its actual needs. By 1948 the Ministry of Education naturally had become the principal focus of graft and patronage, and the minister a millionaire.

In 1949 a courageous Minister of Education undertook to correct the problem by skirting the constitutional requirements. The Ministry's budget was reduced by cutting the size of the ordinary budget and placing additional funds in an "extraordinary" budget. The legal basis for creating the extraordinary budget was found in emergency wartime legislation. In order to maintain this system the government retained the legal state of war with the Axis powers until 1959. In practice, the two budgets were treated as one.

The budget was less significant in many respects than the extrabudgetary accounts. As a general rule, the ordinary and extraordinary budgets did not show the actual extent of government spending. Budgeted expenditures, for example, indicated that between 1946 and 1950 there should have been a surplus of $59 million. Yet a report prepared by a group of financial experts revealed an accumulated deficit of $104.6 million. This deficit had apparently resulted from spending outside the budget—through extrabudgetary accounts which amounted to about one-third of all government receipts and expenditures.

The same authority that enabled the government to create an extraordinary budget also empowered the executive to draw on surpluses by decree and to carry on all kinds of transactions outside the budget. Extrabudgetary appropriations matched those in the budget in importance if not in size. Most public works programs, for example, were financed outside the budget. The government was responsible for no less than 243 extrabudgetary accounts. It was the great sum of money spent through these accounts that produced the rapid expansion of the public debt to over $1 billion at the end of 1958—nearly five times the figure for 1952. Taken together, expenditures through the budget and the extrabudgetary accounts indicated one of the most important functions of the central government—the provision of social assistance to the middle sector of the society. In the budget alone, personnel payments, together with pension and retirement payments, accounted for over two-thirds of all expenditures. In 1955 the government payroll was second only to that of the sugar industry. Public works spending followed a cycle determined by political expediency. Around the middle of its term, a government would suddenly become concerned with its political prospects and, in a burst of activity, would

188

undertake a number of public works projects. At the end of its term, the work stopped, completed or not. Between 1949 and 1952 some of the most notorious excesses were reduced, but after 1952 they were resumed as a regular feature of government operations.

A characteristic of government expenditure was its concentration in the Havana area. In part justifiable because almost a quarter of the national population lived there, the spending of so much of the public works funds in urban areas—benefiting urban workers, urban contractors, urban merchants, and urban industrialists—widened the gap between such areas and the countryside, where the need for off-season work was greatest. Government spending benefited not only those of the middle-income group whose livelihood virtually depended on government favor, but also industrialists, landowners, and businessmen. For example, between mid-1952 and mid-1957, the period of the Batista regime's development program, savings and fixed-term deposits in banks jumped from $140 million to $358.5 million, indicating that a considerable share of the cash benefits derived from the public works and development spending was absorbed by the upper income group, the principal savers.

Historically, the government was viewed as the benevolent provider of all social services, a tradition that, coupled with the central government's search for tools to control local politics, led to the centralization of local finances and local patronage. The result was that only a few communities outside Havana maintained even a modest standard of municipal services, although the 1940 Constitution assigned to municipalities the responsibilities customarily assumed by local governments in the United States.

The tax system, moreover, did not give local governments adequate incomes. Only the municipalities were empowered to collect taxes, principally from the declared value of urban and rural real estate, and the provinces obtained funds through surcharges on municipal taxes. Municipalities were also empowered to borrow money for public works, subject to the approval of the General Accounting Office; as this office was not set up until 1950, no money could be borrowed until then.

In some municipalities, such as Santiago de Cuba, able and orderly local governments assisted by local interest and determination were able to overcome some of these difficulties. In other communities, civic associations such as Los Mil and Acción Cívica assumed duties that municipal governments had failed to carry out. But, as a general rule, local communities lived hand-to-mouth and there continued to be either noticeable deficiencies in, or a complete absence of, such services as sewers, paved roads, and water supplies.

At the end of 1951, shortly before Batista assumed leadership, the over-all public debt stood at only $218 million. By the end of 1958 it was an estimated $1,280 million. The estimated floating debt was about $100 million in 1955, composed largely of long-standing claims against the government; some of these claims antedated 1940, and all but $10 million antedated 1952. The government had a poor domestic credit standing; unpaid telephone and electricity bills were always large.

Only a small percentage of the public debt was in foreign obligations. Since the Cuban record of servicing its foreign debt was good by Latin American standards, and spotless from 1938 to 1958, Cubans found holding the government debt in foreign currencies attractive, and most of this debt was in Cuban hands, as were internal bonds issued in dollars. In both cases, purchase of these bonds enabled Cubans to hold assets in foreign currencies without paying taxes on them.

The government did not undertake to float internal bond issues on a large scale until 1950. Between 1950 and 1955, however, through several devices, the government borrowed in the internal market almost twice as much as it had borrowed during the half century between 1900 and 1950; between 1955 and 1958, the amount doubled again. The main cause for the increase was the financing of development and public works costs after 1952. The Economic and Social Development Plan called for the expenditure of $350 million over a four-year period from 1954 to 1958. The first $100 million of bonds were issued in 1954, the second $100 million in 1955; the remaining $150 million was authorized for allocation during the fiscal year 1956-57. Official investment credit banks also floated their own bonds to finance the program, and the government was ultimately responsible for this indebtedness also.

In the report of the 1950 Mission the IBRD concluded that it would be inadvisable for the government, together with official investment credit banks, to issue more than $25-$30 million worth of bonds each year. It also suggested that during periods of inflation the government sell such bonds mainly to private nonbank investors and to the general public, rather than to commercial banks. It warned, moreover, that the open market operations of the national bank should be limited to transactions to preserve "orderly conditions." It concluded on the optimistic note that:

> Should inflationary measures become increasingly strong, every effort should be made to finance the government's public works and other developmental activities out of current revenues. This is probably more feasible in Cuba than in most other countries because a tightening in tax administration can give surprisingly good results. . . . There are also ample opportunities to restrict expenditures in other directions by improving general administrative efficiency and honesty.

These warnings apparently failed to impress the government and the public debt continued to mount. By 1957 virtually the only purchasers of the bonds were the commercial banks and the national bank whose holdings of public securities rose from $148 million at the end of 1957 to $211 million toward the end of 1958. By the end of 1958, however, these purchases failed to absorb all the bonds being offered for sale, even at 10 to 15 percent below par. In spite of the generous 1958 reserve requirements, which permitted private banks to hold as much as 40 percent of their minimum reserves in securities, the effort to encourage commercial banks to increase their holdings met with little success. Other purchasers were pension funds, insurance companies, and capital formation banks; at the end of 1958, a government decree forced the professional and labor retirement funds to put much of their non-working capital reserves into government securities.

In contrast with the ambiguous attitudes Cubans held toward budgetary and tax practices, their attitude toward money and its value was highly conservative. By 1950 the economy rested on a sound monetary basis. The currency was among the hardest in the world, in part because of the enormous gold and foreign exchange holdings of the government and its close link with the United States dollar, but also because of decisions made by private individuals: money was left idle instead of contributing to rising prices, and bank credit was almost matched by savings deposits. One of the few elements of stability in the economy, this advantageous position probably encouraged much of the foreign and domestic investment that took place. On the other hand, it led to excessive concern over the level of the nation's gold and exchange reserves.

By the end of 1951, two important institutional changes had

taken place in the monetary system. The first was the creation of the National Bank of Cuba, legally authorized in 1948 and in operation by mid-1950. The second was the recognition, with a few exceptions, in mid-1951, of the Cuban peso as the sole legal tender. The changes were received with some skepticism by Cubans, who habitually lacked confidence in their government's financial operations. In 1950 the IBRD summarized these fears:

> Indeed, if Cuba's switch to an independent monetary system and the creation of a national bank are to imply merely the underwriting—by means of unlimited Central Bank credit—of government expenditures which do nothing to stimulate the growth of the economy, then, sooner or later, Cuba will be forced to sacrifice exchange and price stability without having made any progress. The fears of those who do not believe that Cubans can develop the sense of responsibility and practical wisdom that have to go hand-in-hand with monetary independence would have proved well founded.

By the end of 1958 the fears had been more than justified. The money supply swelled, and that inflation was not as bad as it might have been was the result not of government policy, but of the growth of idle savings deposits. Almost the entire banking system had been transformed into a tool, not to maintain long-term monetary and exchange stability, but to finance the government's extravagant spending and to channel funds to certain groups.

In the early years after its establishment, the National Bank of Cuba had been a very influential economic institution, its outstanding research department filled a long-standing need, and for a time the Bank commanded great respect both within the government and on the outside. Its powers and functions were those ordinarily associated with modern central banks: it was the fiscal agent of the government and the bankers' bank; it could make advances to the government, limited to 8 percent of the average revenues over the previous five years and payable within the fiscal year; and it could rediscount short-term paper for commercial banks. The National Bank could also buy long-term government securities in the open market if the securities had been in circulation at least a year, and it was the sole bank of issue, holding the legal reserves of member banks.

Because of the doubt with which Cubans had viewed the formation of a central bank, the operations of the National Bank had been hedged with restrictions to insure conservative and cautious policies. After 1952, however, its policies and those of the official credit institutions over which it exercised control were changed to meet the need of the government for cash and increased spending, and its executives were replaced. Between 1950 and 1952 National Bank and commercial bank credit to the public sector had been relatively unimportant, but between mid-1952 and mid-1957, credits granted to the government and official bodies increased almost fourfold, from $125.3 to $483.2 million, an increase that was in large part responsible for the monetary expansion in those years. While the increase in bank credit for government projects occurred during a slump period and therefore helped stimulate economic activity, it did not encourage long-term economic growth; credit expansion apparently continued even after signs of inflation became obvious. At the same time, moreover, the country's foreign reserves were being depleted, and exchange stability was undermined. The extent to which public confidence in the government's monetary policy had been shaken was revealed by a rumor in April 1958 that the government was about to seize private assets, a belief that led to a temporary run on the banks.

The Cuban monetary unit is the peso of 100 centavos (cents); nominally it is freely exchangeable, one for one, with the United States dollar. Until 1914, the dollar was used for most official and foreign trade transactions, while the French luis (louis: 20 francs) and Spanish centén (25 pesetas) were used in local trade. Between 1914 and 1932 the dollar became almost the only medium of exchange, even though the first Cuban pesos were issued in 1914. Thereafter, the dollar and the peso were both used. By 1950, however, the peso had become virtually the only currency used in domestic transactions, and the dollar had largely disappeared from circulation, although it was estimated that some 250 million U.S. dollars were still in Cuban hands as precautionary reserves. By 1956, this amount had fallen to an estimated $100 million.

Most of the peso stock in circulation was in the form of paper banknotes, very little in silver pesos. The money supply in circulation—currency in the hands of the public, together with deposits—rose between 1950 and the end of 1958 by over $200 million (see Table 15). The volume of money in circulation (including bank deposits, checks paid, bank clearings, and bank loans) fluctuated semiannually, along with trade and wages paid, according to the sugar seasons. The effects of the *zafra* and the *tiempo muerto* were less marked during the 1950's than during the 1930's because of the government's spending policies and the post-World War II prosperity.

The money supply was larger than necessary, the excess being held idle, in the form of savings or bank balances; commercial banks themselves were very liquid, carrying reserves at a very high proportion of their liabilities. This excess constituted a threat to monetary stability since if drawn into circulation, it would heighten inflationary pressures; and if moved abroad when a change in exchange rates occurred, it would diminish the country's international exchange reserves.

Responsibility for maintaining a stable exchange rate was entrusted to the Cuban Currency Stabilization Fund, originally established in 1939 and, after 1948, integrated with the National Bank. The Fund was empowered to exchange for pesos up to 100 percent of the foreign exchange earned by exporters and could also make recommendations for the regulation of transactions involving foreign exchange in order to protect its reserves and the balance of payments and to effect economic and social development.

The National Bank was required to maintain a minimum reserve backing—in gold, dollars, and short-term foreign securities—of 25 percent of its peso note issue and some of its other liabilities. In 1951 gold and foreign exchange reserves amounted to $534 million, or 90 percent of the National Bank's liabilities. In 1956, reserves totaled $521 million, but because liabilities had increased, the percentage had fallen to 73 percent. As government spending and imports mounted, international reserves fell dangerously. By the end of 1958, they had fallen to $373 million; of this amount, $262 million were pledged with foreign banks against credits and loans, leaving a net reserve well below the required legal minimum. Despite the fall in reserves after 1955, the government imposed no exchange licensing or import controls, aside from the 2 percent tax on the export of money. It was not until the very end of 1958, and only a week before Batista fled Cuba, that the percentage of foreign exchange proceeds exporters were required to turn into the government was raised from the customary 30 percent to 75 percent.

Until 1945, foreign institutions dominated the banking system in Cuba, holding over 80 percent of all deposits. After 1945, however, Cuban banks gradually recovered the position they had held before the disastrous crash of 1920-21 and by 1955 held 60 percent of all deposits. The recovery was greatly assisted by the spectacular postwar prosperity, by the formation of the National Bank, and by recognition of the peso as sole legal tender. It was also encouraged by the diversification of bank functions and by the willingness of Cuban banks to take somewhat greater risks than foreign banks.

In 1956 there were 49 commercial banks with 204 branch offices throughout the island, the 15 principal banks being centered in Havana. Six of them were foreign-owned—the National City Bank of New York, the Chase National Bank (later the Chase Manhattan Bank), the First National Bank of Boston, the Royal Bank of Canada, the Bank of Nova Scotia, and the Bank of China. The nine principal Cuban banks, together with the foreign banks, furnished most of the sugar and commercial loans and accounted for almost all the total bank assets. The many smaller Cuban banks catered to some of the local needs of professional people, small merchants and manufacturers, and storekeepers.

The substantial cash reserves of private commercial banks, averaging between 30 and 50 percent of all deposit liabilities, and the large amount of idle savings were indicative of the conservative attitudes of those who had funds to invest. A high proportion of bank loans were short-term, again reflecting the desire for liquidity, and the overwhelming proportion were made to the sugar sector (to sugar mills and large *colonos*) and to commerce (urban export-import merchants, retailers, and wholesalers). Some cattle ranchers, rice-growers, and prosperous industrial entrepreneurs were granted loans, but businessmen and farmers generally had their credit needs satisfied outside the banking system. They were at the end of a chain of credit beginning with the banks and ending with commercial retailers. Small *colonos* usually obtained credit from the mills, as a general rule, at high interest rates that often involved the borrower in a lifetime cycle of indebtedness.

Savings and fixed-term deposits were high, especially during periods of prosperity. Institutional savings and deposits, moreover, constituted only a portion of all gross savings by Cubans. In 1950 only 20 percent of total gross savings and 50 percent of individual savings were held by institutions. Savings inside and outside savings institutions were concentrated in the hands of a relatively small group of people and represented liquid earnings retained by private business and unspent incomes of the very wealthy. These groups had proportionately the lowest propensity to consume and found few domestic outlets attractive for investment.

The inactive balances or hoards often were considered by their owners as precautionary reserves against some future calamity and were exported in the form of dollars or other foreign currencies to foreign bank deposits, invested in foreign securities, or used to speculate in foreign real estate ventures, especially in Florida. A large amount went into urban real estate in Cuba, especially during the building boom beginning in 1950; this investment had the triple attraction of visibility, high speculative return, and ready cash value. It was also fairly common to finance the purchase of a house through a capitalization company. Members of these companies paid a fixed monthly fee; in return they were entitled, after two or three years, to borrow against their investment and were guaranteed the return of a larger sum than they had paid into the fund. A member could buy a company-built house in part with his accumulated savings and in part with company mortgages. Between 1945 and 1950 building construction absorbed at least one-fifth of individual and business savings and represented between one-quarter and one-half of all gross capital formation. It is likely that these proportions were maintained, if not increased, during the mid-1950's. New construction, however, did little to relieve the deterioration and congestion of low-income housing.

Although gross capital formation by foreign firms was substantial, until 1955 much of it consisted of replacement and maintenance, financed out of reinvested profits. There was no large capital market; trading on the Havana Stock Exchange was mainly in public bonds.

In an effort to provide medium- and long-term funds for diversified investment in industry and agriculture, and to provide the small farmer with credit at reasonable interest rates, the government founded in 1950 the first official credit bank, the Agricultural and Industrial Development Bank—BANFAIC (Banco de Fomento Agrícola é Industrial de Cuba). In 1953, 1954, and 1955 four other official banks were established—the National Finance Agency (Financiera Nacional de Cuba) for financing self-liquidating or revenue-producing public works projects; the Cuban Bank of Foreign Trade (Banco Cubano de Comercio Exterior) to assist exporters, especially those dealing with soft currency countries; the Mortgage Insurance Institute (FHA, Fomento de Hipotecas Aseguradas) to insure commercial bank loans for private construction, particularly for low-cost housing; and the Economic and Social Development Bank (BANDES, Banco de Desarollo Económico y Social), with virtually unlimited credit facilities, which administered the Economic and Social Development Plan begun in 1954. Majority control over all the institutions was held by the National Bank.

One source of funds for some of the banks was the rediscounting of paper by the National Bank, but each institution was also empowered to issue bonds. Originally the bond issues were modest, floated with the realistic understanding that the market for the bonds would be limited. After 1952, however, public confidence in the bonds, which had been painstakingly built up in the early stages, was progressively destroyed. The amounts issued far exceeded the limits suggested by the IBRD in 1950; the market became saturated, and the government virtually forced institutions to buy bonds.

By the end of 1958 the debt of the official banks reached an estimated $480 million; of this amount, over half was charged to BANDES, $135 million to the National Finance Agency, $75 million to FHA, and only $20 million to BANFAIC. The banks also made foreign short- and medium-term loans to finance some of the foreign exchange requirements of the development plan. Between mid-1954 and mid-1957 these obligations rose from $35 million to $172 million and were guaranteed by the banks' international reserves.

The public works program and the extension of credit facilities by the banks stimulated some private investment, although by the end of 1957, only a very small proportion of the total credits issued through the banks, including part of the financing of projects carried out under the Social and Economic Development Plan and channeled through BANDES, had gone into agriculture, and only about 29 percent to industry. The remainder, together with government spending not channeled through the official banks, went into public works and basic social services. By the end of 1958 this picture had not changed.

THE DEBATE BETWEEN CATHOLICISM AND RATIONALISM

ESTIMATING THE RELATIVE INFLUENCE of various forms of belief is rendered almost impossible by overlapping, syncretism, and socially created barriers against the transmission of information. In the 1950's approximately 85 percent of the people were nominally members of the Roman Catholic Church. Catholic clergy estimated, however, that only about 10 percent were active and informed members; at least 25 percent were in practice agnostics. Church and state have been constitutionally separate only from the beginning of the twentieth century, but the Church has never been as powerful in national life in Cuba as in other countries of Latin America. Nevertheless, since most of the people have at least some Spanish ancestry and since Spanish Catholic cultural influences have dominated the life of the island since the sixteenth century, Cuban attitudes and values, expressed in innumerable details of thought and observance, are those of a Catholic country.

The Church's poor following was partly attributable to a reputation for corruption and antipopular policies acquired during the nineteenth century. Leaders of the principal revolutionary movements in Cuban history have made the Church one of their major targets, associating the Church, whose strongest supporters have always come from the upper class, with the governing circles and with imperialism. Competing moral systems are offered by the rationalism of many middle-class intellectuals, Protestant missionaries, and the African traditions brought in by slaves. Rationalism, in the form of Freemasonry in the nineteenth century and neo-Marxism in the twentieth, has challenged Catholicism through parallel institutions—especially those devoted to the dissemination of propaganda in the urban lower class—in a dialogue intimately related to the political and social history of Cuba since the late eighteenth century.

Catholicism, rationalism, and Protestantism are principally concerns of the middle and upper classes. Possibly half of the people participate only rarely in any kind of organized religious exercises. In the rural areas, churches are few, those to be found often having been built by a local patron in the community economically dependent on him. This situation strengthened the Church's reputation as a nonpopular institution and meant that churches, like schools but unlike social clubs, were not important as centers of neighborhood groups and focal points of social intercourse. However, the poverty and isolation of rural families inhibited the development of non-Catholic congregations as well.

The Spanish colonial empire in the Americas was carefully regulated to create societies subservient to the Spanish crown and free of subversive and corrupting elements. The moral and spiritual guidance of the people, particularly of the indigenous Indians, was entrusted to the Church; the clergy themselves were subject to imperial control. The king of Spain was empowered by the pope, under the *patronato real* (papal grant of royal patronage), to appoint clergy to their benefices and to exercise other ecclesiastical prerogatives, including the collection of tithes. In the Americas these privileges were delegated to the viceroys and governors-general.

The resultant close relation of church and state was particularly evident in Cuba. The large Indian communities that provided an economic and social base for the Church in Mexico and the Andean countries were lacking; Negro slaves did not form communities of their own but lived under the direct control of their owners. The Church remained dependent on a share of tax revenues and, although there were frequent conflicts between clergy and government, the Church in general did not exceed its original function, which was to advise and assist the governor.

Comparatively few churches were built and few formal public schools were founded until the late eighteenth century, when the Church was already experiencing the opposition of rationalist and secularist thinking. *Criollo* nationalists adopted the libertarian philosophy of the French Revolution—deist and anticlerical, rationalist and antiauthoritarian. Opposition to the Church and the government was chiefly centered in the Freemasonry movement.

11. *The Debate between Catholicism and Rationalism*

Freemasonry was introduced during the British occupation of Havana in 1763 but expanded and acquired its specific political orientation under the French influence. It was outlawed in the Spanish empire in 1751 but tolerated by the Cuban authorities until 1811, when membership was declared a crime against the state. Thereafter, it existed clandestinely, and was subject to attack by the Holy Inquisition in the 1820's.

Masonic doctrine asserted the existence of universal moral truths which were accessible to the individual intellect without the intervention of ecclesiastical tradition. The initiation procedures of Freemasonry, the lodge structure, and the custom of secrecy provided ready-made facilities for subversive intrigue. Until 1891 there were a few lodges professing loyalty to the Spanish government and to the Masonic hierarchy in Madrid, but most others were centers of revolutionary sentiment. Some lodges even included in their oaths of initiation a pledge to fight for independence. From the first, Cuban Freemasonry was linked with lodges in Philadelphia and elsewhere in the United States which gave moral support and on occasion money to help the anticolonialist cause.

Most of the leading revolutionaries, including José Martí, were Masons. In his writings Martí thus summarized the anticlerical doctrine: "Christianity has died at the hands of Catholicism. . . . There is no better religious rite than the free exercise of human reason." Freemasonry also provided much of the symbolism of the nationalist movement, including the national republican flag designed in 1849.

During the first half of the nineteenth century, the Church itself was strongly influenced by the fashionable rationalism of the period. The Jansenist emphasis on inner faith rather than on outward observances induced the leading Cuban bishop of the time to discourage many features of traditional piety, "even removing altars and images from the churches," according to a Catholic historian, and thereby allying the Church with the tastes and interests of the governing elite. Disregarding papal reproofs, this bishop also permitted marriage to the clergy.

As the nineteenth century progressed and the conflict between the *criollo* nationalists and the Spanish authorities grew sharper, propaganda competition between the rationalists and the Church intensified. Both sides, directing their appeal chiefly to the educated minority, set up libraries and schools and published journals and pamphlets.

The assertion that the Church was opposed to the independence movement is dismissed by Cuban Catholics as a slander, but in fact the Church was never able to break its dependence on the governing class. There were, however, a few conspicuous examples of priests who supported the nationalist cause, and a persistent tension between the *criollo* minority and the Spanish majority sharply divided the clergy on occasion.

The success of the independence movement in the struggle with Spain in 1898 also represented the triumph of the rationalist interpretation of morality. The separation of church and state required by the constitution adopted in 1901 was intended to deprive the Catholic Church of its tax revenues, the political support of the government, and its voice in the direction of official policy. Civil marriage was permitted to all citizens, although the controversy surrounding this question made the situation uncertain until civil marriage was made compulsory in 1918. The rationalist viewpoint in education was upheld by the constitutional provision that education was to be compulsory, free, and secular. Foreigners were forbidden to teach Cuban history, literature, geography, or civics in private schools. Religious instruction in public schools was forbidden.

The economic position of the Church, never strong, was weakened by the termination of state subsidies. In addition, proposals were made to deny the Church compensation for properties seized by the colonial government for its own uses. General Wood and later Governor Magoon arranged for the Cuban government to buy these properties, thus angering some extreme secularists who accused Magoon of complicity to defraud the Republic.

The longstanding association between Cuban and American Masons was strengthened during the United States administration and the early years of the Republic. High-ranking officers of the military government were admitted to the Grand Lodge of Cuba, and an English-speaking lodge was founded in Havana. Freemasonry, while nominally retaining its political ideals, lost its revolutionary purpose and became increasingly conservative. It still claimed credit, however, for its revolutionary antecedents; Masons continued to denounce the Church as a suppressor of liberty. The lodges remained influential but only as one of the most prominent among the many middle-class associations used by their members to establish personal connections and influence opinion.

11. *The Debate between Catholicism and Rationalism*

Under the Republic the Church began a slow recovery. Despite the establishment and growth of a number of Protestant missions from the United States, Catholicism was still the dominant religious influence in the island. A new conservative moral synthesis emerged which united once again the Church, the upper class, and the conservative press. The corresponding insurgent opposition which developed after the economic crisis of the 1920's was collectivist and atheist rather than libertarian and deist in the nineteenth-century manner; its leading doctrines were Marxist and syndicalist, and one of its component organizations was the Communist party (legally forbidden until 1938 and again after 1953). The propaganda battle was waged as before in newspapers and pamphlets, but in the educational field it shifted to the universities.

In colonial Cuba the Church had been the principal public welfare agency, the channel through which much of the charitable contribution of the wealthy was dispensed. Under the Republic, the Church's place in this field, although still important, was subordinated to that of the government, especially in the matter of hospitals and of subsidized education. President Batista in particular made the most of state charity as a means of attracting popular support. The Church did not get much of the credit it should have had for providing needed services and was the more readily attacked as parasitic by its opponents.

The principal expansion of Catholic activity occurred in the 1930's, and during this period the number of Catholic schools rose to 180. Most of the teaching was done by religious orders, and the majority of pupils came from middle-class families. In 1946 the University of St. Thomas of Villanueva was founded in Havana and was the only nongovernment institution offering instruction at the university level. The Knights of Columbus organization was introduced, and the Asociación de Caballeros de Cuba (Association of Cuban Gentlemen), founded in 1929, later became the men's branch of Catholic Action, the principal lay organization. Catholic Action founded schools and libraries and established social clubs and clinics in the usual manner of Cuban middle-class associations. It also endowed scholarships, organized more direct forms of propaganda such as mass meetings and demonstrations, and served as a coordinating body for laymen's organizations.

Efforts were also made to demonstrate the relevance of the Church to the life of all the population, particularly the urban lower class, and to introduce the Catholic voice into the forum of political and social debate. The Christian Social Democracy movement, founded in 1942, provided speakers for meetings called by Catholic Action and other mass-membership groups. The social objectives sponsored by the movement—limitation of excess profits, abolition of large estates, extension of workers' benefits—were essentially those of the 1940 constitution and in no sense controversial. The program was strongly supported by *Diario de la Marina*, the leading conservative newspaper.

Church authorities did not endorse any particular candidates for political office and deliberately abstained from party politics, except to warn Catholics not to vote for the Popular Socialist (Communist) Party, and, during the 1950's, to make specific denunciations of Communism. As the opposition to the Batista regime grew more radical, however, the Church was forced into a more restricted political posture. On the one hand, the rationalist insurgents, whose appeal for popular support was based increasingly on the proclamation of nationalist ideals and *criollo* virtues, denounced the Church and the government as allies in the service of foreign interests. Attention was drawn to the predominance of Spanish citizens among the clergy and to the longstanding association of several prominent members of Catholic Action with the Spanish Falange.

On the other hand, as popular confidence in the Batista regime waned, conservatively inclined people looked more and more to the Church for leadership and in so doing forced a political role upon it. *Diario de la Marina*, in a series of editorials in 1957 defining its position in the face of the deepening national crisis, implied that the radical movement was Communist-inspired and that the growth of uncertainty and violence was attributable to the weakening of the upper class and of Catholic morality in public life. "The failure of religious conviction in general and in the abandonment of Catholic principles in politics, economics, and conduct, determines the underlying cause of the crisis." The spread of "discord and indiscipline" was attributed to the frequency of divorce.

This sense of national crisis, created by the growing violence of the Batista regime against the radical opposition, prompted so many upper- and middle-class people to demonstrate their loyalty to the Church that during the middle 1950's observers spoke of a national religious revival. Young people and students in particular, who five years before were inclined to be scornful and critical of the Church, began to attend services and join laymen's organizations in substantial numbers. Increasing official concern with problems of social justice was apparent not only in the programs of Catholic Action but in direct appeals by the archbishops to President Batista to make concessions to the opposition.

There were in 1959 two hundred parishes served by seven hundred priests, most of whom were Spanish. Cuban nationals numbered only about one-fifth of the total, but all but one of the highest officials were Cuban. In addition to the secular clergy, in 1959 there were 1,000 men and 2,400 women in religious orders, most of these also Spanish.

Despite the belated vigor of Catholic Action, the effort to associate the Church with the life and interests of the lower class showed few results by 1959. While funds and personnel were short, in the opinion of many Catholic observers the Church showed too little initiative. Churches continued to be found almost exclusively in urban areas. In the countryside, the formal religious life of peasants was usually limited to the occasional visit of a priest to perform baptisms.

Church congregations were made up largely of women from the middle class. The general male attitude was that religion was women's business and that the woman of the house was sufficient representative for the whole family. Only in wealthier areas, such as the Miramar suburb of Havana, did entire families regularly attend church services together. Most Cubans who entered holy orders also came from the upper class.

Periodic festivals—primarily secular holidays of religious origin—are celebrated by a majority of the people, at least in urban areas, with little difference among the classes. Christmas is the most popular holiday, but before and after Lent are also occasions for popular celebration.

The most numerous festivals, both national and local, are those of patron saints. The benefits sought from a saint—the protection of his name, defense from unforeseeable evils and deliberate malice, special help in particular fields of human activity, and intercession with higher authority—are essentially similar to those expected of a worldly patron. Educated, wealthy people might profess to despise the popular attitude and yet show great respect for the traditional powers of particular saints.

The rationalist opponents of Catholicism deliberately created their own heroes to challenge those of Catholic tradition. Settlements were named after heroes of the struggle for independence such as José Martí and Máximo Gómez. Independence Day celebrated not only the historical event but the moral virtues independence had made supreme. As the republic matured and its divisions healed, the growing cult of José Martí—excommunicated by the Church—symbolized the new moral synthesis uniting the nation, including the Church. Statues of Martí were seen in public places and his picture in private homes. Rationalists referred to him simply as El Apóstol (the apostle).

Protestantism

Protestantism in general remained outside the political and social debate dominated by Catholicism and rationalism—both of which Protestantism opposed. Although first introduced in a tobacco factory in 1884 by a Cuban Presbyterian convert, Protestantism remained insignificant until the United States occupation in 1898. Thereafter, about forty Protestant denominations from the United States established missions varying widely in size and importance as well as clinics, hospitals, and schools. Nearly all of them depended heavily on their parent organizations for money and staff, but by the 1950's the leading groups—Southern Baptist, Methodist, Presbyterian, and Episcopal—were described by Catholics as well-established and financially sound.

Foreign support enabled Protestantism to demand less from its congregations for the material support of its clergy and the upkeep of its buildings. Whereas Catholic clergy usually made a charge for the performance of marriages and baptisms, for example, the Protestant offer of "free religion" assisted the missions in winning converts. Most of the missionary effort was directed toward the lower- and middle-income groups, chiefly in urban areas. In rural areas the poverty of the majority was such that even the Protestants could not afford to establish churches. A further difficulty in rural areas was popular resentment at the contrast between peasant living standards and even the humblest standard acceptable to a missionary accustomed to life in the United States. In the 1950's, however, the missions made rapid progress in recruiting Cuban personnel.

With the puritan cast of its values, the austerity of its rituals, and its limited emphasis on intercession as a means to salvation, Protestantism conflicted in many ways with the fundamental trends of Cuban culture. Its recent introduction, furthermore, meant that although it offered educational opportunities it did not open avenues into the upper class. But in spite of their multiple ties with the United States, Protestant organizations were not accused by nationalists of serving the interests of imperialism. In general, the Protestant clergy were more sympathetic than Catholics to the aims of Fidel Castro.

Afro-Cuban Religions

Estimates of the influence of African religions in Cuban life are rendered difficult by the impossibility of distinguishing them from Catholicism in lower-class practice. In the lower class, especially among colored people, cults of African origin have survived in an alien environment despite sporadic persecution by the authorities. They are strongest in towns where the Negro population is relatively stronger and the standard of living higher. Full-time priests are supported by the cult groups. With few exceptions, however, educated Cubans have regarded the cults as barbaric relics, doomed to disappear with the progress of civilization. As a result, very little is known about them, although it has become apparent that with increasing prosperity in the cities they are becoming more and not less popular. Catholic estimates of cult membership are extremely low—less than 1 percent—but the same estimates recognize the existence of a large body of popular belief described as "superstition" which is in fact drawn largely from African tradition.

Particular Afro-Cuban religions are associated with specific ethnic groups and African homelands, but their observances have been shrouded in the secrecy appropriate to sacred mysteries, intensified by the need to avoid police persecution. Some of the festivals are celebrated publicly and involve participants from many *cabildos;* hundreds of people appear in the streets of Havana with music and costumed dancers, yet the upper-class Cuban has no idea what the significance of the occasion is, who the participants are, or even whether the holiday is religious or secular.

Santeria

The Santería comprise a number of closely related cults varying according to the ethnic backgrounds of the participants. Most important is that of the Lucumí, the most numerous and influential Negro group; the language of this branch of the Santería is Yoruba (Lucumí) with some Spanish added. Next in importance are the cults of the Arará, who in Africa are Dahomeyan neighbors of the Yoruba; Arará rituals employ the Fon (Arará) language and Spanish. Closely related is vodun, the dominant popular religion of Haiti. Vodun is the Haitian development of Arará belief, employing the French and Fon languages; it is practiced in Cuba by immigrants from Haiti and their descendants.

All of these versions of Santería have incorporated items of Catholic ritual and mythology. Their devotees regard themselves as Catholics and believe that the names of the Catholc saints are translations into Spanish of the Nigerian names of African gods. Catholicism is viewed as the Spanish tribal version of Santería; the alternative loyalty to Santería thus is not Catholicism but Protestantism.

The association between Catholic and African belief is based largely on the superficial similarity between the Yoruba pantheon and the Catholic saints, particularly in the emblems pictured with each saint or spirit as an indication of the particular field in which he has power. The spirits are called indifferently *santos* (Spanish, saints) or *orishas* (Yoruba); an alternative term for Santería is Regla de Orisha (rule or religion of the *orishas*). The parallels between saint and spirit ignore differences of sex—some Yoruba spirits are bisexual, and many Catholic saints are shown wearing apparently feminine robes. Thus St. Barbara is equated with Shango, god of war; the two are in fact regarded as the same deity, addressed in Spanish or in Yoruba according to the ritual context. (In different parts of the island, however, the same *orisha* may be linked with two different saints, especially if the *orisha* is a minor one). Cheap colored prints displayed on the walls of lower-class homes, perhaps with candles burning in front of them, represent the saint-*orishas*; plaster statuettes serve the same purpose. On occasion an unmistakable Catholic Madonna is shown with tribal identification scars.

The *orishas* are the spirits of important men now dead, most of whom were kings and founders of tribes. In part, the Regla de Orisha is thus a cult of the dead. The equivalent of Almighty God—the Creator and therefore not himself an *orisha*—is Olofin. He is so remote from this world that he has no cult and no particular attributes. It is the *orisha* whose will is effective in mundane affairs and whose intercession must be sought.

Another independent spirit is Orunmila, Destiny, whose voice is Ifa, identified in Cuba with St. Francis of Assisi. The priests of

11. *The Debate between Catholicism and Rationalism*

Orunmila, the *babalaos*, of whom there were said to be two hundred in the city of Havana in the 1940's, are the most influential of the *santeros* (Spanish, priests; Yoruba, *babalorisha*). They alone may conduct the Ifa divination procedure, in which the *babalao*, in the interests of a client, casts sixteen palm nuts in a prescribed manner to obtain one of more than four thousand possible combinations. The *babalao* has memorized a recitation appropriate to each combination, indicating the proper course for the client to take to solve his problem. Usually the client is advised to make an offering to a certain *orisha*, and in addition he must pay the *babalao* a fee.

Ifa divination is relatively expensive and its details are kept secret. Cheaper, better known, and adequate for ordinary purposes is Elegua divination. The link between Ifa and Elegua is obscure; sometimes Elegua is described as the servant of Ifa, sometimes as Destiny in its malicious, capricious aspect. The priests of Elegua are of lower rank than those of Ifa.

Divination procedures resemble the casting of an astrological horoscope. They determine which spirit is influencing the affairs of the client and the direction from which the influence comes. There are four principal directions, corresponding to the points of the compass, and many intermediate ones. Each spirit may appear from any direction and has a number of different aspects or characters, each of which has its own name and distinctive attributes. The resulting multiplicity of possible spiritual influences accounts for discrepancies in Lucumí belief, since it is pointed out that no *santero* could be familiar with them all. The Santería thus easily accommodate new beliefs, Catholic or African, and the question of heresy does not arise.

It is the power of destiny working through the divination procedure which determines the direction of spiritual influences, and therefore Elegua is called the Master of the Paths, or Directions (el Dueño de los Caminos). He is identified with St. Peter, who opens the gate of Heaven, but also, because of his intermediary position between the worshiper and the orishas, with the souls in Purgatory, to whom the devout may burn candles for immediate help. Elegua in a capricious mood, or as the *santeros* put it, in the *camino* of Eshu, is the Lucumí equivalent for the Devil. Offerings to Elegua are placed at crossroads, in open spaces, and behind the front doors of homes.

The most important of the *orishas* is Obatala, whose female aspect is Odudua, sometimes described as the wife and sometimes as a *camino* of Obatala. Obatala was given the task of completing the work of creation begun by Olofin; he is more directly concerned with the world's affairs than the Creator but more aloof than the ordinary *orishas*. He is identified with Christ Crucified and, in various *caminos*, with the Holy Sacrament, Our Lady of Charity, St. Manuel, and others. His color is white and alcohol is abhorrent to him. Odudua is god of the dead, the underworld, and darkness, identified with the Virgen del Carmen, the Immaculate Conception, the Holy Ghost. White chickens are sacrificed to her every month.

Subordinate *orishas* and the mythology linking them and describing their origins and characters recall the Olympian cults of ancient Greece. The most important *orishas* are offspring of Obatala. One is Yemaya, who lives in the sea and is goddess of fresh waters and patroness of sailors; she is identified with the Virgin of Regla and her colors are blue and white. Ogun, identified with St. John the Baptist, is a wild man and a drunkard, patron of blacksmiths, hunters, and soldiers. Another is Oshun, the Aphrodite of Lucumí belief, famous for her beauty and love affairs. Her color is yellow; in Nigeria her followers wear brass beads, and in Cuba her shrine in the mining town of El Cobre (copper) houses the miraculous statue of the mestizo Virgin of Charity, to whom childless women burn candles.

Each worshiper has his own patron saint, chosen by divination or to suit his personality or because his family regards a particular *orisha* as its ancestor and guardian. As a "son" of the *orisha* he belongs to a cult-group or congregation (sometimes called a *cabildo*) which holds regular meetings. An important feature of these meetings is the music, consisting chiefly of songs and drumming. The songs are hymns and prayers in the Yoruba language. The drumming, which serves to raise the emotional tension of the proceedings, is done according to fixed patterns which are themselves hymns and prayers, employing the rising and falling tones of the Yoruba language to convey actual meanings.

The ritual of the Santería varies according to the inclination of the *santero* from an imitation of Catholic ritual, complete with candles, the Lord's Prayer, Hail Mary, and appropriate ritual gestures, to the deliberate creation of a hysterical atmosphere in which the *santero* and other persons present are "possessed" by the spirits. When "possessed," the worshipers put on the clothes and adopt the character of particular *orishas*, who are at once recognized by the congregation. While in this state of trance the worshipers speak with the voice of the god, who in this manner offers advice to his followers. The procedure lends itself to manipulation by the *santero*, but probably most of the trances are genuine.

The power of the *orishas* is held to reside not only in the sacred stones but in the earth, thought of as the Mother of Creation, and in trees and mountains, which are emblems of the earth. The royal palm and the ceiba (a species of acacia), both conspicuous trees in the Cuban landscape, have special religious significance. The ceiba, the Tree of the Gods, is reputed to be the only tree never uprooted by hurricanes; it is said to be the home of Shango, god of storms, and also of the *orishas* and the souls of the dead in general. Ceiba trees mark the traditional sites of the principal events in Cuban history.

Santeros of non-Lucumí versions of Santería regard the Lucumí priests as colleagues and may speak Yoruba as well as Fon. Expert drummers also often know more than one African language. The vodun term corresponding to *orisha* is *loa*. Ordinary Lucumís, however, are inclined to believe hair-raising stories about vodun; Haitians are believed to command zombis to pursue chosen victims "at all hours, with a burning candle in hand."

Abakua

The most famous of the legendary secret religions, Ñáñiguismo, was rediscovered in the 1950's by the Cuban Negro scholar and writer Lydia Cabrera. Ñáñigos are members of the Abakuá secret society believed by most Cubans to have been extinct since the early twentieth century but notorious in the nineteenth century for its reputed practices of child sacrifice. The Abakuá originated among the Efik of eastern Nigeria. Cabrera speaks of thousands of adepts, Negro, white, and mestizo, in the cities of Havana and Matanzas, but no more accurate estimate of the modern strength of the Abakuá is available.

An important feature of Abakuá rites is the oath of secrecy required of initiates. The beliefs of the cult emphasize the dangerous influences that threaten people, particularly those of African descent, for whom Cuba is full of "evil shadows." Membership in the Abakuá, however, confers protection in this world and the next: "God will accept a brother of the religion" and "To say Ñáñigo is to say brave man."

The Abakuá deities, spirits of the dead whom it is necessary to placate, are represented by masked dancers, the *irimé* (Spanish, *diablitos*), who at one time appeared in public on saints' days and carnival occasions but are now only evident in the self-conscious folk revivals of the Cuban theater. Syncretism of Catholic ritual comparable to that of the Santería has taken place but on a much smaller scale. As in the Santería, drums are given ritual significance as the voices of the spirits, but it is believed that "possession" is not a feature of Abakuá ritual.

Minor Cults

Some Afro-Cuban cults—such as Mayombería, Regla de Palo, Regla Conga—are known by name only. These names may indicate the existence of active modern cults or may refer only to extinct cults. They are also used in a general sense to describe unfamiliar superstitions or suspected sorcery.

In addition to cults of ethnic origin, various cults of a more artificial character have arisen from time to time. Spiritualism in various forms is perennially popular, usually with a strong emphasis on hysterical experience and miraculous cures. Procedures borrowed from Santería, particularly music, dancing, and "possession" by spirits, are commonly combined with more pretentious spiritualist and necromantic doctrines of European origin.

Cubans are disposed to regard all unknown beliefs as sorcery or witchcraft (Spanish, *brujería*). Brujería is the usual upper-class term used indifferently to denote African cults and all practices dismissed as superstitious. It is also used by devotees of African cults to denote black magic—the deliberate misuse of legitimate religious techniques for malicious ends. Thus all *santeros* are supposed to be capable of black magic, but nobody admits to practicing it. The rituals of all unfamiliar cults are believed to consist exclusively of black magic. The smallest and least-known religious and ethnic groups are credited with the most dangerous powers.

In middle-class families stories of the fearsome techniques and mysteries of these groups may be told only to frighten children. "The Ñáñigos come for bad little white boys." In lower-class families, however, they may be given serious credence, partly because there is some knowledge of the actual existence of such groups.

INTELLECTUALS AND ARTISTS

THE INTELLECTUAL IS POTENTIALLY A HERO in Cuban culture. Typically, he is a poet and orator exhorting and inspiring a mass audience, not a scientist manipulating mathematical concepts. His subject matter is the potential greatness of the Cuban people, his inspiration strongest when political and social conditions apparently conspire against the fulfillment of his vision. The greatest intellectual achievements have usually been associated with insurgent political movements, beginning with the first articulation of a national consciousness toward the close of the eighteenth century.

Spain devoted little of its resources to Cuba and life in the Spanish colony was hard. Intellectual and artistic life during the first 260 years mirrored that of Spain to the best of the abilities of the small group of educated colonists. Tales of chivalry, heroic adventures, and historic ballads (Spanish *romances*), the popular *décimas*, as well as the works of Lope de Vega and Cervantes, representative of Spain's Golden Age, dominated their cultural life and reflected their Spanish orientation. The course of study at Cuba's first university, founded in 1721 for those training for the priesthood, closely followed that of the medieval Spanish universities, including Thomist theology, law, Aristotelian philosophy, and languages. The wealthier colonists sent their children to Spain to be educated.

It was through the returning students, whose number increased as the colony grew and prospered, that the colonists became aware of the liberalizing influence of eighteenth-century philosophy and natural science. Finally, in 1790, a living contact with this new atmosphere was established with the arrival of don Luis de las Casas as governor and captain-general. One of his first acts was to found *Papel Periódico,* Cuba's first newspaper, which provided a forum for the young intellectuals. Three years later Cuba's first public library was opened with the proceeds from the newspaper. And in 1795 las Casas presided at the founding of the Sociedad Económica de Amigos del País, which quickly became the focal point of political and economic liberalism in the colony and, throughout the nineteenth century, the intellectual center of the independence movement.

The initiation of the development of an indigenous intellectual and literary life, which can be dated from the time of las Casas, is credited to the teacher-essayist-political activist trio comprising Father Félix Varela, José Antonio Saco, and José de la Luz. These men were Cuba's *pensadores* in the tradition of the eighteenth-century *philosophes.* As William Rex Crawford, in *A Century of Latin American Thought,* observes:

> The term *pensadores* includes men who have tried to interpret the whole social reality that lay about them, seeking its roots in the past and looking with grave concern for their country and for America into an unknown future. They are moralists, critics, publicists, political scentists, and sociologists—rarely philosophers . . . Many of the *pensadores* were poets first, and nearly all wrote poetry.

The figure most closely associated with don Luis de las Casas was Father Félix Varela y Morales (1787-1853), eulogized as "the man who taught Cubans how to think." As professor of philosophy he trained two generations of students to think in political terms and to turn their attention to social problems, stressing justice, freedom, and the dignity of man as described in the Scriptures. He wished to see these principles applied to Cuba, although not necessarily to the slaves, and pressed for reform of the Church.

As Cuba's delegate to the Spanish Cortes in the early 1820's Varela favored a semiautonomous Cuba linked to Spain, but later he became an ardent advocate of independence. His activities to further the cause of independence soon earned him the enmity of Ferdinand VII, and he was forced to spend the last half of his life in the United States where he edited several reviews and wrote a prodigious number of essays collected in *Cartas a Elpidio* (1835-38).

Varela was the teacher and inspirer of José Antonio Saco y López (1797-1879), who also held the position of professor of philosophy. Saco, primarily a journalist and sociologist, became editor of the influential journal *Revista Bimestre Cubana*. He wrote extensively on economics and cultural subjects and, like other intellectuals of the period, pressed for political and economic reform. Saco also sought a compromise with Spain and opposed the abolition of slavery on the grounds that a repetition in Cuba of the Haitian revolution would result. He gradually changed his position and later wrote a monumental six-volume *History of Slavery*. Because of his political activities for abolition and independence, Saco was forced to join Varela in exile in the United States.

His chair at the university was taken by José de la Luz y Caballero (1800-1862) who taught for twelve years, passing on the ideals of freedom, independence, and social justice. One of Luz's pupils, the poet, journalist, and teacher Rafael Mendive (1821-86), was also caught up in the independence movement and forced to spend the last years of his life in exile. Mendive was the personal tutor of José Martí, giving him a foundation in the classics and encouraging him to participate in the movement for independence.

The poets of the period wrote passionately of their love for Cuba, creating an important body of literature for succeeding generations. Characteristic of this as well as the poetry of later periods was the identification of the poet's personal well-being with the welfare of his homeland. Much of it, written from exile, had a quality of unreality and sang of a country only dimly remembered, a country whose unity was idealized.

One of the most quoted, and the last to write in the neoclassical style, was José María Heredia (1803-39). Exiled from Cuba in 1823, Heredia wrote in Mexico and published most of his work in the United States. Others included Gabriel de la Concepción Valdés, known as Plácido (1809-44), and Gertrudis Gómez de Avellandeda (1814-73).

Rationalism and Romanticism

Following their break with Thomistic philosophy and medieval scholasticism in the latter part of the eighteenth century, Cuban intellectuals turned to eighteenth-century French rationalism as a means to technical progress and independence. In their search for a philosophical base for the new Cuba which was to emerge with independence, they were attracted to Rousseau's view of man before his fall from the "natural state," finding easy analogues to his concept in the Spaniards' treatment of the Ciboney Indians and Negroes. Like the Encyclopedists, many of Cuba's revolutionaries were Freemasons, and Rousseau's concept of man's "natural state" of goodness permitted them to retain what they felt to be the principles of Christianity and yet reject the Church, which had allied itself with the Spanish oppressor.

Romanticism provided a visionary dream of the Cuba after independence. It was to be a free Cuba ("Cuba Libre"), in the words of Martí, ". . . restoring to men their personalities which have been trampled under foot or ignored."

José Martí (1853-1895) was the personification of revolutionary romanticism. As one of his numerous biographers remarked: ". . . the most extraordinary work which Martí left was not books, but his own life." His essays, poems, plays, and children's stories were often written hurriedly, between speaking engagements and in the midst of organizational activities, but he could fire a public that did not even understand his classical allusions or philosophical references. One of the many anecdotes told about him is the adulation accorded him by a poor tobacco worker, "I didn't understand much of what he said, but I felt like crying."

Martí was born of poor Spanish immigrants. His father came to Cuba as first sergeant in the Spanish forces assigned to Havana. Martí received an education largely because his godfather paid the tuition for his early schooling and then passed him on to his own kinsman, the revolutionary poet and teacher, Rafael María Mendive. Mendive had been appointed director of one of the three free secular primary schools established by the Havana district in 1864, during a brief interlude of relatively liberal reform. Mendive also paid Martí's tuition to the private secondary school, the Havana Institute. The reform period ended with the beginning of the Ten Years' War in 1868 but Martí, then fifteen, had written an article full of revolutionary enthusiasm. In 1870 the Spanish authorities sentenced Martí to hard labor for six years. Thanks to the police connections of his father, Martí served only a short term before he was released into the protective custody of his father's friend. In January 1871 he was permitted to go into exile to Spain.

In Spain Martí found other Cuban and Spanish liberals who sympathized with the independence movement. He attended the universities of Madrid and Saragossa and received degrees in law, philosophy, and letters. Four years later he returned to Cuba via Paris, Mexico, and New York, but finding it impossible to work there returned with his family to Mexico.

Martí came back to Cuba with his wife in 1878 when the

Spaniards granted a general amnesty after the Pact of Zanjón. Promised reforms were short-lived, however, and in 1879 Martí was again exiled by the Spanish authorities. In 1880 he reached New York where he supported himself by working as art critic for the *New York Sun* and serving as North American correspondent for a string of South American newspapers.

Much of his time was spent trying to bring together the many diverse and squabbling exile groups, a task not accomplished until 1892 when the Cuban Revolutionary Party was formed with Martí as delegate and coordinator. Martí's martyrdom in the revolutionary cause took place three years later on May 19, 1895.

After his death his stature as national hero grew slowly but was fostered with increasing zeal from the 1920's onward by nationalists and revolutionaries anxious to present their own struggles as the continuation of the unfinished battle for independence. In modern Cuba he is known simply as El Apóstol (the apostle), from whose voluminous gospels the spokesmen of contending factions quote moral judgments of uncertain context and doubtful interpretation in support of their arguments. Martí wrote seventeen volumes on life in the United States, several volumes of poems, and many political essays. Although he wrote with pleasure of the air of freedom he found, his most often quoted remark concerning the United States is, "I know the monster, I have lived in its entrails."

Martí reserved his poetry for the expression of his inmost thoughts, his love life, and his increasing preoccupation with death. Other forms of literature, according to Martí, should carry social and ethical messages. Like most Cuban intellectuals, Martí favored universal education, for "what can an ignorant man in government be but the natural prey of those who know his defects and play upon them?" He argued for diversification of the economy, so as to avoid colonial status, and desired that all citizens receive a scientific and moral education.

Martí was one among many intellectuals who wrote on all aspects of art, jurisprudence, sociology, literature, biography, and history. Their writings appeared in the short-lived revolutionary newspapers. After the Ten Years' War three newspapers were founded which eventually came to represent the greatest literary outpouring of the period: *Revista de Cuba* (1877-84) to which Varona and others contributed; *Revista Cubana* (1885-95), organized and directed by Varona and boasting Martí as contributor; and *Hojas Literarias* (1893-94).

Because magazines and books were subject to strict censorship, many revolutionary themes had to be disguised. One school of writers, the *costumbristas*, wrote rich, descriptive, often satirical accounts both in long novels and short sketches of everyday life in the early nineteenth century. The best-known writers were Cirilo Villaverde (1812-1894), Ramón Palma (1812-1860), and José Antonio Echeverría (1815-1855). In 1960, the Castro government republished several *costumbrista* works, particularly those of Ramón Meza, which were critical of upper-class Spanish life.

Another group turned to Cuba's aboriginal inhabitants and to the slaves. The major writer on the slave theme was Anselmo Suárez y Romero (1818-1878), whose *Francisco* was calculated to raise emotions akin to those produced by Harriet Beecher Stowe's *Uncle Tom's Cabin*. Another theme was *ciboneyismo*, contrasting the presumably happy, sin-free life of the Ciboney Indians before the conquest with their destruction and slavery under the Spaniards. The foremost contributor to this school was the poet José Fornaris (1827-1890).

Modernism was widely popular in Latin America. Imitating luxurious verbal textures of contemporary "decadent" poets in Europe and the United States, nonpolitical, introspective, fond of the exotic in verse form and subject matter, the modernists sought to develop a distinctive, regional Latin American style. The precursor of this trend in Cuba was the poet Julián del Casal (1863-1893), whose verse, affected by his timidity and ill-health, was increasingly concerned with death. He wrote three books, *Hojas al viento* (1890), *Nieve* (1892), and *Bustos y rimas*. The principal exponent of the related symbolist school was Federico Urbach (1873-1932).

The Twentieth Century

With the success of the independence movement, literary effort lost its chief inspiration. The first two decades of the Republic were prosperous years in which a new upper class consolidated its hold on the wealth and power formerly in the hands of the Spaniards. The revolutionary intellectuals hoped to create a society in which individual reason and emotion would be the source of authority, restricted only by the principles of scientific method and a regard for what was felt to be "natural" truth.

Enrique José Varona (1849-1933), Cuba's outstanding philosopher, spanned the revolutionary years and more than three decades of independence. An early proponent of autonomy, Varona eventually joined Martí in New York and worked for independence. Returning to Cuba after the war of independence, he reorganized the secondary and university level educational systems and in 1913 served a term as vice-president.

Influenced by Spencer, Tarde, Comte, and Durkheim, Varona looked to science for an ethical system, in the same manner that Martí considered economics to be a branch of ethics. He is credited with the introduction of French positivism and English empiricism to Cuba. His name rests on his three-volume *Conferencias filosóficas* (1880-82), in which he expounded the principles of experimental and antimetaphysical scientific positivism. In addition, Varona was a poet and in numerous essays, critiques, and philosophical studies dissected Cuban character.

Varona exemplifies much of the best of the Cuban intellectual tradition and many of its weaknesses. Politically active, he was at the same time at home in a number of scholarly fields, displaying wide-ranging erudition and keen awareness of contemporary trends. But despite his personal abilities and the wide respect accorded him, Varona and his group were unable to bring into being the ideal Cuba. Varona could, like Martí, speak with passionate intensity of the high destiny of his countrymen:

> We Cubans are few in number, but we are all illustrious. Our history is not just history, it is an epic. Nothing that we do is a mere fact, it is a doughty deed, a fiery feat. Except for our stature, everything about us is great and admirable.

But he had little faith in institutions alone: "It is useless to change the form of institutions if men's hearts are not changed. Equality, before being written on the statute books, should be written on the heart." He urged his disciples to examine their society under the "illusion of liberty" so that once given the economic, social, and political freedom to act, they could set themselves free and embark upon the road to national greatness. But Varona suffered the disillusion of the postrevolutionary years and critically attacked his own class for succumbing to a love of ostentation and the unprincipled pursuit of quick profits.

The influence of Varona could be traced in the preoccupation of the new generation of intellectuals with social studies but, whereas Varona had pressed for an empirical orientation in the school system, the manipulation of abstract concepts rather than laboratory experiment and practical application continued to characterize thought and education. The low level of Cuban achievement in the physical sciences excited little academic interest. It seemed logical that the naturalistic studies of French-educated Felipe Poey (1799-1891) formed the basis for any study of Cuba's native fauna and flora. Cubans pointed with pride to Carlos Finlay (1833-1915), the discoverer of the mosquito vector of yellow fever, claiming as their own a man who spent his early life in France and who received his medical education at Jefferson College in Philadelphia. Similarly, the members of the Sociedad Económica, to whom zeal for progress no longer seemed necessary, remained content with the economics of the early nineteenth century.

According to one scholar of the Latin American scene, J. P. Gillin:

> The word is valued more highly than the thing. The manipulation of symbols . . . is more cultivated than the manipulation of natural forces and objects. Patterns of medieval and sixteenth-century mysticism are strong . . . and these patterns show no inconsistency with those of argumentation, for, as with the medieval scholastics, the worth of the logic lies in the manipulation of concepts not in the empirical investigation of premises.

Social studies absorbed much of the imagination and energy that had formerly gone into literary activity and philosophical speculation. What little new poetry there was tended to be frankly nonpolitical and often morbidly introspective. More than ever, intellectuals regarded themselves as a social and political elite. Their studies confirmed this estimate by demonstrating the applicability to Cuba of neo-Darwinian theories of social evolution in which the elimination of the unfit resulted in the steady march of the best elements of society toward perfection. Negroes were used to illustrate failure in the evolutionary competition—not, as in the nineteenth century, to portray idealistic primitive happiness. Even the languages of Cuban Negroes, which lacked the suffixes of European languages, were treated as examples of evolutionary failure, *darwinianamente hablando*, because they had "no grammar." Until after 1940, however, no effort was made to find out what these languages were or how widely they were spoken. The problem of the integration of Negroes into the new social order provoked on the one hand the Negro risings of 1906 and other years, and on the other hand an active interest among intellectuals in "criminal anthropology," by which they sought to demonstrate that the social characteristics of Negroes followed inevitably from their biological characteristics.

Under the general heading, "The Cuban Underworld," Fernando Ortiz (1881-   ) published the two best-known studies of the history and culture of Negroes in Cuba, *Los negros brujos* (1906) and *Los negros esclavos* (1916). Ortiz studied law in Barcelona and Madrid and, after serving as chancellor of the Cuban consulate in Genoa, returned in 1906 to Havana and secured a post as assistant prosecutor in the Audiencia of Havana. Three years later he was appointed professor of public law at the University. From 1910 on he edited the *Revista Bimestre Cubana*, organ of the Sociedad Económica. At the 1914 meeting of the association he told the members to follow the examples of nineteenth-century thinkers who "by establishing magazines, newspapers, schools, universities, museums, and botanic gardens; financing scholarships; importing professors; and publishing books and reports on all Cuban problems, showed us how the work of a group of men with faith can carve a people and a nationality out of an exploited colony."

In succeeding years Ortiz produced works on Cuban history, ethnography, linguistics, archaeology, law, and political affairs. He is most widely known outside of Cuba for his study, *Contrapunto Cubano del tabaco y del azúcar* (Cuban Counterpoint: Tobacco and Sugar). In 1923 he established the Sociedad del Folklore Cubana and in 1926, with Nicolás Guillén, the Sociedad de Estudios Afrocubanos (Society for Afro-Cuban Studies). As the leading and almost the only permanent member of the Society for Afro-Cuban Studies, Ortiz became known as an authority on Negro culture. His studies were concerned almost exclusively, however, with nineteenth-century historical records.

From 1916 to 1926 Ortiz held a congressional seat but after his withdrawal in the 1930's from active politics concerned himself increasingly with the artistic aspects of Negro culture, writing essays on music and dancing which abandoned the evolutionary approach. Following the revolution of 1958 he wrote several articles guardedly favoring the regime and in 1960 gave his entire library to the nation.

From about 1925, when the expected democratic and libertarian society failed to develop and the collapse of the sugar market made existing injustices more obvious, growing discontent among middle-class intellectuals was accompanied by an increased literary output, much of it concerned with themes deliberately revived from the colonial period. The philosophy employed to rationalize the new discontent was neither the anarchic liberalism of Martí nor the complacent neo-Darwinian natural science of the early republican days but a Marxist historical and economic determinism conveniently adapted to place the blame for Cuba's troubles on the forces of capitalism and imperialism and to sanction revolutionary efforts.

Poets and essayists abandoned both romanticism and introspection in favor of social themes. Presaging the emergence in the 1930's of a self-consciously proletarian literature was "La Zafra," a poem written in 1926 by Agustín Acosta (b. 1877) which depicted the life of the sugar worker. In 1927 Jorge Mañach founded a literary magazine, *Avance,* which articulated the concern of the new generation of poet-politicians. Mañach, born in 1898, received a degree in science at Harvard in 1920 and took other degrees in law, philosophy, and letters at Havana University. His career, like that of many other middle-class Cubans, showed a shift from radical leftist beginnings toward conservatism, corresponding to his steady advance upward in the social scale. At the end of the Machado dictatorship he was active in the ABC revolutionary movement and in later years was minister of education (1934), senator (1940-44), and editor of the conservative daily, *Diario de la Marina* (1945). He left Cuba in 1960.

Mañach's biography of José Martí, written in 1933, was one of several contributing to the Martí legend that grew with the revived nationalism of the 1930's. Other conscious attempts to reassert the validity of the antiauthoritarian tradition included a renewed interest in the culture of the Negro and the Indian. Much of this interest was expressed only in such bookish fantasies as tracing contemporary Cuban folklore to the aboriginal Ciboneys or back through West Africa to Egypt, but a few articles and lectures gave evidence of first-hand observation. The department of social science at the University of Havana was dominated by lawyers prompted by chronic underemployment and political frustration to study society but not equipped by their antiempirical training to be effective. One such was Raúl Roa, sometime head of the department, later minister of foreign affairs in the Castro government.

Demagogic politicians, anxious to seize power from the self-consciously white upper class, appealed to the masses by glorifying Cuban culture as the distinct achievement of a mestizo race, drawing on the best in all the contributing races. Factual studies of Afro-Cuban culture and compilation of the history of Negroes in Cuba had to wait, however, until Negroes and mestizos themselves turned their attention to these matters.

Many Negroes, possibly encouraged by the color prejudices of Cuban society, became thoroughgoing Marxists. Nicolás Guillén, credited with originating the *negrismo* school in poetry, used Afro-Cuban forms and settings to write strongly political proletarian literature which portrayed the bitter life of the lower classes, both Negro and white, and their exploitation by those in authority. Such poems of Guillén's as "West Indies Ltd." (1937) and "Sones para turistas y cantos para soldados" (1937) are typical of the *negrismo* school as is the work of Regino Pedroso, a Havana factory worker.

In his "Motivos de son" (1930) Guillén translated the musical form of the *son* dance rhythm into a literary form. In this and later poems he imitated African drums, using repetition and alliteration in a style reminiscent of the American poet, Vachel Lindsay. Juan Marinello, later leader of the Popular Socialist Party, was another poet of *negrismo*. Alejo Carpentier used the *negrismo* style for his novel, *Ecue Yamba-O*. Lino Novás Calvo, another *negrismo* writer, is also one of the few Cubans to make use of the sea in his stories.

Not all the literary effort of this period was preoccupied with nationalism and politics. Alejo Carpentier created a wide audience in the United States and Latin America in 1953 with his romantic, fantastic novel, *Los pasos perdidos* (The Lost Steps), which is set in a semimythical jungle country. Eugenio Florit (b. 1903 in Madrid and for the past twenty years or so on the faculty of Columbia University) wrote fastidious, contemplative verse, collected in *Poema mío* (1947) and *Antología poética* (1956). Guillén became head of the cultural department of the ministry of education under Castro.

The Press

In the period from 1935 to 1958 the government maintained firm, if not absolute, control over the nation's newspapers through an intricate system of official bribery. Of the fifty-eight daily newspapers in circulation in 1956 probably no more than six or seven were meeting their entire costs from subscription fees and advertising revenue. An article published in a government newspaper early in the Castro period revealed that Batista had been distributing a total of $217,300 monthly to various newspapers in allotments ranging from $500 to $16,000, as well as about $22,000 monthly to individual journalists. A newspaper dependent on government money was hesitant about pointing up weaknesses in the regime.

But apart from this more or less open bribery Cuban journalism in the 1940's and early 1950's had high standards in comparison with the Latin American press as a whole. All newsmen had to be graduates of the excellent four-year course in journalism provided by the ministry of education at about half a dozen secondary schools and to belong to the Newspapermen's Association, which exercised disciplinary powers over the profession. Cuba ranked fourth in 1956 among the nations of the western hemisphere in the ratio of newspaper circulation to total population, being exceeded only by the United States, Canada, and Brazil. This circulation was largely urban, given the low literacy level in the rural areas, but Havana in 1956 had only two fewer newspapers than London, a city nine times its size.

Music

The synthesis of Spanish, African, French, and North American musical traditions to create uniquely Cuban music represents a definite contribution to world culture. Classification of the music of Cuba according to foreign musical influences becomes blurred as the purity of adopted forms and expressions gives way in most cases to varying combinations of these influences in a Cuban idiom, but useful divisions are possible between Euro-Cuban, Afro-Cuban, popular or mulatto, and concert music utilizing classical, neo-classical, and modern forms.

Euro-Cuban and Afro-Cuban music developed somewhat separately until the twentieth century. Euro-Cuban music, confined largely to white groups in the countryside and the upper class in the cities, was based on Spanish forms and melodies scored for the small guitar, occasionally the violin, and the human voice.

"Warmed by the tropical climate and humanity," to quote Fernando Ortiz, the Spanish forms underwent modification: the tempo was slowed, the beat shifted until new rhythms emerged—the *punto*, the *guajira*, and the *zapateo*. The Spanish bolero also was changed from 3-4 time to 2-4 and became the Cuban bolero. Perhaps the best known of the Cuban-developed rhythms is the *habanera*, although it is a more stately dance than is suggested by

Bizet's use of it in *Carmen*. The *guaracha* is the favored song form
for serenades. The ability to sing and accompany oneself on the
guitar (usually a *tiple*, the small Spanish guitar) is a manly attribute
possessed by many Cubans. The guitarist will often be accompanied
by someone playing the *claves* (two hardwood sticks which make a
clacking sound) and the *maracas* (gourds filled with seed or metal
shot). His personal popularity depends to a large extent on his
skill at improvisation.

While the stately *habanera* was being danced at the elaborate
formal balls of the white upper class, the lower class, almost entirely
Negro, was enjoying and elaborating on its own varied African
musical heritage, primarily religious in origin, to the beat of the
drum and other percussion instruments.

Drumming and Yoruba songs are an integral part of the Santería
Lucumí, the widespread ritual of the Lucumí (Cuban descendants
of the Nigerian Yoruba). The Yoruba drum (*batá*) is hour-glass
shaped and is held across the knees while the player hits both ends.
The drum body is made from a tree trunk hollowed by fire, and the
skins are permanently attached so that tension or pitch is not
adjustable. Usually, three drums of differing sizes, producing three
different pitches, are used, which approximate the meaningful tones
of the language so that the drums are said to "speak a language."
It is believed that the voices of the spirits speak through the drums,
and therefore much of the knowledge of drum playing is esoteric
and not to be taught to nonmembers of the cults.

Early in the nineteenth century a secular Afro-Cuban music
developed which gradually came to the attention of the white
population. Lower-class benefit societies (largely Negro) began
to appear in public to drum, sing, and dance in masks and costumes
on such feast days as Epiphany (El Día de Reyes), and many of
these societies came to have their own distinctive songs, dances,
and costumes.

Spanish melodies were superimposed on the secular Afro-Cuban
music, and the guitar was added to the drums, producing, in the
words of Ortiz, "love affairs of the Spanish guitar with the African
drum." The dances and rhythms that resulted from this mingling—
the rumba, conga, *son*, and bolero—spread to much of the world.
Perhaps the oldest of these blends is the *son*, which is thought
to have come originally from Haiti. Its name probably derives from
the French, *le son* (the sound). The rumba known outside of Cuba

actually is more closely related to the *son* and the Cuban bolero than to the native rumba, which is a much faster, more dramatic dance, usually confined to exhibition dancing.

The development of popular or mulatto music came somewhat later. Increasingly, after independence, Negroes moved to the major urban centers, and their music was taken up by professional musicians, composers, and poets. It was scored for additional instruments—pianos, trumpets, and trombones—and the resulting popular or mulatto music came to override completely the Euro-Cuban forms which had flourished previously. Many of the more stately dances of the rural and urban upper class are now found only among poorer groups in the countryside.

A list of Cuban popular songs created in this century reads like a North American hit parade: *Malagueña, Siboney, Siempre en mi Corazón*, all composed by Ernesto Lecuona, who also devoted himself to more serious works. To these must be added such dance forms as the *mambo* and more recently, the *pachanga*, which closely resembles the conga in rhythm and form and allows for the interpolation of verses on current political and social events. Many popular songs circulate with lyrics lauding or deriding the regime.

Cuban concert music has not developed the distinctive character recognizable in other types of Cuban music. Formal compositions antedating independence either remained within the Euro-Cuban tradition or generated too little musical interest to inspire an indigenous development.

Between 1898 and 1930 Cuban composers, like poets and writers, went through a cosmopolitan period, writing in styles derivative of Debussy, Stravinsky, Schoenberg, and other modern composers. The Castro regime has singled out two composers from this period: Amadeo Roldán (1900-1939), composer, violinist, and for a while director of the Havana Philharmonic; and Alejandro García Caturla (1906-1940), composer and municipal judge, whose murder by a convicted criminal awaiting sentencing forms part of the growing Caturla legend. Both composers were admirers of Nicolás Guillén, the *negrismo* poet, and took part in the rediscovery of Afro-Cuban music. Roldán, also influenced by the Mexican composer Silvestre Revueltas, consciously wove African rhythms into his music. Caturla, after a period of experimentation in Afro-Cuban forms, turned for inspiration to the Euro-Cuban *danzas* and Spanish *romances* of the colonial era, thus following in the footsteps of his immediate predecessors Joaquín Nin (1879-1944) and the famous *habanera* composer Eduardo Sánchez de Fuentes (1874-1944).

By 1932 the Renovation Group, led by José Ardévol (b. 1911), was spearheading a movement away from both cosmopolitanism and Afro-Cubanism and back to the rigidity of classical and neo-classical forms. Besides Ardévol, son of the director of the Barcelona Musical Institute, composers in the group included Julián Orbón (b. 1925), Harold Gramatges (b. 1918), Eduardo Martín (b. 1915), and Argeliers León (b. 1918, and in early 1961 director of the department of music of the National Library). There was a new emphasis on gigues, gavottes, fugues, canons, and pieces in sonata form, with little if any attempt to draw upon the Cuban idiom. The group began to disperse in 1945 as many composers, and eventually Ardévol himself, returned to Cuban sources for inspiration. Ardévol was still musically active in early 1961 and was on the governing board of the National Symphony.

Before 1959 the audience for the composer of concert music was very small and confined to Havana. There were a number of small amateur groups that periodically performed Cuban compositions before the Lyceum y Lawn Tennis Club of Havana and the Sociedad Pro Arte Musical. The former organization also brought international artists to Havana. The sole orchestra, the Philharmonic Orchestra of Havana, did not tour the country. According to the 1953 census, there were only 2,929 "musicians and professors of music" in the country.

In early 1961 three orchestras were performing—the National Symphony Orchestra, the National Chamber Orchestra, and the Symphony Orchestra of the National Theater of Cuba. The National Symphony was created in 1960 (Laws 590 and 813) to "offer concerts for all the people and work assiduously to educate our people in the love of music." Articles on the symphony appeared widely in newspapers and magazines, charging that in the past the Havana Philharmonic had benefited only guest artists, particularly from the United States, and had played for the elite who attended more to dress up than to hear the music.

In 1961 the National Symphony was directed by Cuban-born González Mantici (b. 1912) who received his musical education at the Tschaikowsky Conservatory in Moscow and is considered a protégé of Kleiber. Government sources said the orchestra had an annual budget of $600,000, and its musical staff of more than a hundred was guaranteed work over the entire year with a minimum monthly salary of $300. Following its debut in November 1960, the orchestra toured most of the country giving free public concerts of music by the major Cuban, European, and North and South American composers. In addition to their own musical activities, Havana and the provinces were visited by the Peking Opera and the Khachaturian Orchestra of the Soviet Union.

Dance, Theater, and Plastic Arts

Cuba has a national ballet company, the Ballet de Cuba, whose prima ballerina is the internationally famous, Havana-born Alicia Alonso. The national ballet is built upon the Academia Nacional de Ballet formed by Alonso in 1948. After Castro came to power, Alicia Alonso, who has danced with her own company as well as with the Ballet Theater in the United States, was invited to help form the national ballet, and her husband, Fernando Alonso, was named director. Dancers in the company come from all over Latin America and the United States. Like the National Symphony, the Ballet de Cuba toured the provinces and in October 1960, with Leon Fokine as ballet master, went on tour in Europe and the Soviet Union.

The Castro regime also supports a modern dance company as a department of the National Theater. The troupe is headed by Havana-born Ramiro Guerra, who serves as director and choreographer. Guerra, who studied with the Russian Ballet as well as with such leading American dancers as Martha Graham, Doris Humphrey, and Charles Weidman, has choreographed and presented several works which draw heavily upon Cuban materials. His ballet, *Yoruba,* for example, deals with the cult surrounding the *Virgen de Regla,* and his *Mambí* portrays the struggle for independence. Another work, *Auto Sacramental,* is set in the Middle Ages. The group has toured extensively and has recevied very favorable notices and good audiences. In addition to the Cuban companies, Bhaskar, India's Hindu ballet, and the Georgian Dancers from the Soviet Union have played in Havana and the provinces.

Cuba has a very weak theatrical tradition. Only 288 persons described themselves as actors, actresses, and entertainers in the 1953 census. During the colonial period some religious and imported Spanish plays were put on in the Teatro Principal in Havana. The legitimate theater received official attention when Governor Miguel

Tacón in 1834 imposed a tax on every slave imported into Cuba and used part of the fund to build the Teatro Tacón, completed in 1838. The most noted Cuban dramatist at the time, Francisco Covarrubias (1774-1850), wrote many plays for this theater, most of which were imitative of popular Spanish plays of the period, particularly the comedies and operettas of Ramón de la Cruz.

After independence, plays continued to be written on Spanish models but revealed the growing influence of a mélange of European techniques and conventions. Since 1959 the government has supported the National Theater of Cuba and awarded scholarships and prizes to playwrights. It has mounted plays by young authors such as Virgilio Piñera, Carlos Felipe, Matias Montes Hidobro, and Manolo Reguera Saumell, all of whom also hold minor positions with the government or official publications. But attendance has been negligible at such performances, even though there is no charge. The press has severely criticized new plays on artistic grounds, including plays with obviously "correct" contemporary revolutionary themes and one awarded first prize in a competition sponsored by the municipal government of Havana.

The government has also sponsored a number of foreign plays in Havana and the provinces, including plays by Federico García Lorca, Bertolt Brecht, Anton Chekhov, and Tennessee Williams.

Architecture, sculpture, drawing, and painting lagged behind the other arts up to this century, but according to contemporary Cuban critics, drawing and painting are moving toward development of a unique Cuban style and great popular appeal. Architecture during the colonial period generally imitated Andalusian and Castillian forms, but Cuba, having been a backwater after the first thirty years of the Spanish conquest, lacks the magnificent churches and public buildings to be found in other areas of Latin America. After independence, architecture became one of the more popular courses of study at the University of Havana as it led to lucrative positions with and contracts from the ministry of public works. Modern Cuban architects tend to use functional monolithic concrete or marble forms, ill-adapted to the subtropical setting, but several schools and playgrounds built since 1959 show considerable ingenuity and lightness and much of the extensive new housing is extremely attractive.

Cuban sculpture also had a late beginning. The major modern movement dates from 1927 when José Gómez-Sicre, Cuba's most renowned sculptor, returned to the country after many years of study in Europe, became professor of fine arts at the government-supported National School of Fine Arts, and introduced European forms, largely French neoclassical. His best pupils are the contemporary sculptors Alfredo Lozano, Roberto Estopiñán, and Agustín Cárdenas. Another great influence on Cuban sculptors was Bernard Reder, a Czech who came to Cuba during World War II and is now residing in the United States.

Estopiñán makes great use of the intricate patterns of Cuba's tropical vegetation while Cárdenas' work is more simplified, tending toward elongated shapes. Sculpture too has its exponents of Afro-Cuban themes, the most representative of which is Teodoro Romas Blanco.

The first art academy, the San Alejandro Academy, was established in 1818 as the successor of a painting school organized by the French painter Jean Baptiste Vermay. Until the 1920's, however, painters were largely trained in the academic school and followed Spanish and eighteenth-century French models. After Cuba gained independence its artists turned away from Spanish and colonial culture, and many sought to absorb the latest European developments. In the 1920's Leopoldo Romanach, who finally broke with the academic tradition, headed the Academy (later to become the National School of Fine Arts). Many students returning from Paris joined him, and the result was a rapid blossoming of a vibrant, rhythmic, and colorful art movement.

Cuban artists, then as now, drew upon all schools for their technique and method of handling color, but in terms of subject matter could be divided into two schools: a *criollo* group which drew upon the vestiges of colonial life with the natural landscape and people; and an Afro-Cuban group which used material drawn from Negro life, particularly magic and religion.

The most noted exponent of the *criollo* group today is Amelia Peláez, who studied with Picasso and Braque. Her work, which has been widely exhibited, is cubist in form and uses elements of Cuba's vegetation and its colonial architecture. The *criollo* painters referred chiefly to a Spanish and upper-class culture increasingly irrelevant to modern Cuba, refreshed erratically by modern Spanish, French, and Mexican art. Its uncertain inspiration is evident, for example, in the work of Mario Carreño, who held his first one-man show in Havana in 1930. Thereafter Carreño lived in France, Italy, Mexico, and the United States, returning to Cuba only for short visits and in 1946 taking up permanent residence in the United

States. His work directly reveals the influence of the various schools with which he has been in contact, leading the sculptor Sicre to comment, "We have no way of foretelling what new surprise may be in store for us."

In contrast, the work of the best-known painter of the Afro-Cuban school, Wilfredo Lam, shows the steady development of a highly personal idiom. Lam, born in 1902 of Chinese and Negro parents, studied in Madrid and Paris, returning to Cuba during World War II. The influence of Picasso and other modern as well as classical Europeans is evident, but in all except his early paintings any foreign influence is subordinated to the artist's own experience and there is an unmistakable regional inspiration in Lam's work, with popular Afro-Cuban rituals and costumes contributing strongly to his symbolism.

Cuban engravings in wood, metal and linoleum are of excellent quality and show imaginative and full use of their respective materials. At the end of 1960 four exhibitions of Cuban engravings were on tour in Latin America.

GENESIS OF A REVOLUTION

THE LEADERS OF THE TWENTY SIXTH OF JULY MOVEMENT trace the history of the revolution to the attack on the Moncada barracks at Santiago de Cuba by Castro and about 170 followers on July 26, 1953. At the time, the men involved were unknown recent graduates or students of the university, most of them politically active, articulate, and impatient young men who had been drawn to radical movements or to the ardently reformist Ortodoxo Party of Eduardo Chibás.

Neither the type of action chosen nor the nature of the participants was regarded as very unusual, the attack being dismissed by most influential, established political leaders as but one more incident in the tradition of direct action, rarely successful, but always present in political life. Public sympathy was subsequently drawn to the rebels, however, by police brutality in the roundup of suspects and by Batista's reaction in suspending constitutional guarantees throughout the island and issuing a restrictive law of public order, and Castro began to emerge as a hero squarely in the Cuban revolutionary tradition.

The plan for the attack on Moncada had evolved from meetings in Havana in the months after the Batista *coup d'état* of March 10, 1952. The rebels had collected arms at a chicken farm outside Santiago and at dawn on July 26, divided into attack groups, each with a specific objective: a small military post at Bayamo, the Moncada fortress, a nearby civilian hospital, and a radio station. After taking these vantage points they planned to broadcast two radio addresses, one a recording of Eduardo Chibás' final program, the other a statement of their own purpose.

In this statement they were to announce a revolution based on

"criollo values," led by "new men . . . free of all obstacles with
foreign nations and . . . of appetites of politicians." They promised
welfare and economic prosperity, social justice, respect for other
nations, and respect for the constitution. They professed loyalty
to the ideals of José Martí, the platform of the Partido Revolucionario Cubano (Auténtico), the Manifesto of Montecristi, and the
revolutionary program of Young Cuba, the ABC radicals, and the
Partido del Pueblo Cubana (Ortodoxo), which together formed
the heritage of Cuban political utopianism. But the rebels failed to
reach any of the main targets. Some were killed, most were
captured.

Although the attack ended disastrously, the movement had a
new beginning in Castro's defense plea before the Urgency Court
of Santiago de Cuba on October 16, 1953. During the earlier trials
of his co-defendants, Castro had served at first as counsel for
defense. When he used this position to the embarrassment of the
Batista regime, the government prevented his attending the court
under the pretext that he was ill. His own trial was later carried
out in secret in the nurses' lounge of a hospital. His five-hour speech
in his own defense, concluding, "Sentence me. It doesn't matter.
History will absolve me," became the testament of the revolution
when later published and publicized by the revolutionary movement.

Like most of his later public speeches, Castro's address to the
court was both highly discursive and carefully wrought. In it were
interspersed precise statements of legal rights reflecting his education in law, emotional appeals for justice, and an outline of his own
program for Cuba together with long supporting quotations from
the works of José Martí.

The prosecution's case rested on Article 148 of the Code of
Social Defense:

A penalty of imprisonment of from three to ten years shall be imposed upon the perpetrator of any act aimed at bringing about
an armed uprising against the constitutional powers of the state.
The penalty shall be imprisonment for from five to twenty years, in
case the insurrection actually be carried into effect.

In defense Castro maintained that the uprising had favored,
rather than opposed, the constitution, because Batista's power
derived solely from violation of the constitution. He addressed the
court at length on the right of the individual to rebel against
tyranny, guaranteed by Article 40, "It is legitimate to use adequate

resistance to protect previously granted individual rights," and supported by political philosophers from the ancient Chinese to the authors of the United States Declaration of Independence and the French Declaration of the Rights of Man. He went on to review the circumstances surrounding his trial, pointing out in detail the several ways in which his treatment had been contrary to provisions of the law and chiding the judges for submitting to the insolence shown them and due process of law by the military.

In presenting his program for the country, Castro reflected the many ideas and approaches to Cuban problems—some of them incompatible—familiar to those who lived with the realities of Cuban politics and debated solutions. On the one hand he expressed his loyalty to goals of political democracy—specifically to representative government and respect for civil rights—and called for the restoration of the 1940 Constitution. On the other hand he recognized that the 1940 Constitution had not been sufficient to ensure the effective guarantee of those rights for the poor and the powerless, a recognition that led to an attack on all vested interests and to promises of the transformation of society through revolution and centralization of power.

The Moncada speech could appeal to individuals who sought a return to constitutional government, to others who advocated large-scale, government-directed social and economic change, and to all whose point of view was between those extremes. Conflicts between them and problems of ends and means did not become crucial issues until after the success of the revolution, when men representing these divergent attitudes found themselves uneasily allied within the new government.

Castro repeated his belief that if only his followers had been able to make contact with the people through the radio, the people would have risen to the call. He went on to define the people and their needs in the manner of all Cuban radicals convinced that government had served only the wealthy and the politicians:

> When we speak of the people we do not mean the comfortable ones, the conservative elements of the nation, who welcome any regime of oppression . . . the people means the vast unredeemed masses, to whom all make promises and whom all deceive . . . who long for great and wise changes in all aspects of their life; people, who, to attain these changes, are ready to give even the very last breath of their lives . . . when they believe in something or in someone, especially when they believe in themselves.

He then outlined the five revolutionary laws that would have been announced if the Moncada attack had been successful. These remained the essentials of his program; similar measures were among the first acts of the new government in 1959.

The First Revolutionary Law would have returned power to the people and proclaimed the Constitution of 1940 the supreme law of the land, until such time as the people should decide to modify or change it. And, in order to effect its implementation and punish those who had violated it—there being no organization for holding elections to accomplish this—the revolutionary movement, as the momentous incarnation of this sovereignty, the only source of power, would have assumed all the faculties inherent to it, except that of modifying the constitution itself: In other words it would have assumed the legislative, executive, and judicial powers. . . .

The other revolutionary laws would have redistributed agricultural land with government indemnity to former owners, granted employees the right to share 30 percent of business profits, redistributed the sugar production quotas in favor of small producers, and ordered the confiscation of property of persons who committed fraud during previous regimes. More fundamental laws of agrarian reform, educational reform, nationalization of public utilities, and collection of evaded taxes would follow. These measures would be drawn up to implement articles in the Constitution of 1940 calling for a maximum limit on land ownership and making the government responsible for providing full employment and a decent livelihood.

The problems concerning land, the problem of industrialization, the problem of housing, the problem of unemployment, the problem of education, and the problem of the health of the people; these are the six problems we would take immediate steps to resolve, together with the restoration of public liberties and political democracy.

Implicit in Castro's socioeconomic program was the assumption that the economy must come under more thorough government control because the profit motive of individuals had been gratified at the expense of the common good:

Everybody agrees that the need to industrialize the country is urgent . . . but the capitalists insist that the workers remain under a Claudian yoke.

If the State proposes lowering rents, landlords threaten to freeze all construction; if the State does not interfere, construction goes on so long as the landlords get high rents, otherwise, they would not lay a single brick even though the rest of the population should have to live exposed to the elements. The utilities monopoly is no better: they extend lines as far as it is profitable, and beyond that point, they don't care if the people have to live in darkness for the rest of their lives.

Public hospitals which are always full, accept only patients recommended to them by some powerful politician who, in turn, demands the electoral votes of the unfortunate one and his family so that Cuba may continue forever the same or worse.

The future of the country and the solution of its problems cannot continue to depend on the selfish interests of a dozen financiers or on the cold calculations of profits that ten or twelve magnates draw up in their air-conditioned offices.

The specific solutions he proposed seemed designed to provide a wider distribution of wealth. Land was to be distributed among the landless; the government would provide cooperatives in farming and cattle raising. Rents would be cut in half and new construction financed by the government "with the criterion that, just as each rural family should possess its own tract of land, each city family should own its own home or apartment." He maintained that the amount of money ordinarily disappearing in graft alone would be sufficient to finance such projects.

Castro was sentenced to fifteen years in prison and together with the other convicted rebels spent the period from October 1953 until May 1955, when they were released in a general political amnesty, in the military prison on the Isle of Pines. Although they formed the nucleus of a new movement already known by the date of their action, 26th of July, they gradually emerged as an independent organization as Castro became embittered with, and eventually disassociated himself from the Ortodoxo party.

At the trial of the Moncada group, the government had attempted unsuccessfuly to show proof of a link between the defendants and both the Communists and the Ortodoxo party. Leaders of those parties and the defendants denied any connection, although Castro defined the composition of his following by saying that the majority of them "militated" in the Ortodoxo party.

Factional disputes within the major political parties arose immediately after Batista's *coup d'état* in 1952 and were intensified

by the elections held in November 1954. Many of the Auténtico and
Ortodoxo leaders had gone into exile immediately after the *coup*
and did not return until the 1955 amnesty. Auténtico leaders Carlos
Hevia and Antonio de Varona had organized a meeting in Montreal
in 1953 to try to find a formula for united opposition. According to
Castro's analysis when he broke with them, three Ortodoxo factions
emerged.

The "electoralists" were dismissed by the rest because they
advocated participation in elections held by the Batista government. The independents, loyal to the Ortodoxo tenet of non-alliance
with other parties, refused to cooperate. The Montrealists, who
sought agreement with the Auténticos and of whom a faction led
by José Pardo Llada proposed a common front of all opposition
groups including the Communists, were unable to work out an
acceptable alliance. These divisions continued through the 1954
elections when small factions of the Auténticos and Ortodoxos
began to participate; they withdrew their presidential candidates
before election day in protest against government harassment,
but the withdrawal did not restore unity.

The elections, however, served their purpose of legitimizing
Batista. He was assured a four-year term as president, the 1940
Constitution was restored, and Congress was convened. To still
the continued criticism of his regime, he inaugurated a Civic
Dialogue composed of representatives of many political and other
organizations to seek a formula for restoring political peace. In
May he bowed to domestic and international pressure and approved
an amnesty law under which hundreds of political prisoners, among
them the Moncada group, were released.

On May 15, Castro and his followers were freed; the next morning
they were met in Havana by enthusiastic crowds. Castro, declaring
his continued adherence to the Ortodoxo party, remained in Cuba
for two months, but the government prevented him from speaking
over the radio, and he apparently failed to obtain the position of
Ortodoxo leadership that he wanted. In July he chose to continue
revolutionary activity from Mexico, according to plans made while
on the Isle of Pines.

While in Mexico, Castro became increasingly bitter about the
vacillating position of the Ortodoxo leaders, who did not give
him full support. In March 1956 he denounced the party leadership, appealing to the party "militants" to support him rather than
the politicians.

When Castro arrived in Mexico, his brother Raúl and a few other members of the movement were already there. Raúl Castro had become acquainted with Ernesto (Ché) Guevara, a young Argentine doctor who had taken part in anti-Peronist activities and radical movements in several countries. The three were joined quickly by many of the Moncada survivors and by some others who had been in exile. Castro obtained the services of Alberto Bayo, a veteran commander of the Spanish loyalists, to train the men in guerrilla warfare. They rented houses in Mexico City and an estate in the country for training. Although they were hampered on a few occasions by the Mexican police, under prodding from the Cuban Embassy, they completed a course of training by late 1956.

In seeking support, Castro turned to the exiles living in the United States. During the fall of 1955 he made a trip to the United States and raised money among the exiles in Florida and New York City. In September 1956, when his men had nearly completed their training, Castro made a brief trip across the border into Texas where he conferred with Prío Socarrás, who apparently provided the funds with which the rebels bought an old yacht, the *Gramma*, to take them to Cuba. Eighty-two men left for Cuba on the *Gramma* on November 25. Their transit was delayed, and when they reached the shore of Oriente province on the morning of December 2 they were immediately spotted by the military. During the next days they tried to reach the hills in small groups, but most were killed and some captured. Twelve men survived to reach the Sierra Maestra.

The landing had been timed for November 30; on that day a group in Santiago attacked the Moncada barracks, without success, and there was a student strike at Havana University. Batista closed the University (it remained closed until 1959) and suspended constitutional guarantees in most of the island. The failure of the rebels to reach Cuba until December 2, their decimation by government forces, and government announcements that they had been annihilated, were followed by a period of silence and confusion rather than by the general uprising the Castro forces had hoped to spark by their arrival. In January Castro sent one of his men, Faustino Perez, to Havana, to arrange publicity. Perez made contacts resulting in the visit of *New York Times* correspondent Herbert Matthews to the Sierra Maestra; Matthews' articles in February were the first convincing evidence that Castro was still alive.

The heroic life of Castro and his small band in the Sierra Maestra was successful in providing the focus and symbols around which revolutionary activities in cities throughout the country were organized. Although thousands of Cubans participated actively in the movements against Batista before his final flight, Castro had been the first, the most publicized, and the most individualistic. By 1958 he had emerged from his former position as a young hero of a kind familiar in Cuba to assume the symbolic role of national leader, vacant since the death of José Martí. Within the rebel army, power was vested in Castro and the two men whom he had come to trust most completely, his brother Raúl and the Argentine, Ché Guevara.

In 1956 the Castro brothers were thirty and twenty-five years old, men whose lives from adolescence had revolved around the intricacies of Cuban radical politics. They were of a prosperous family, but one known for the mutual hostility of its members. Their father was a sugar planter in Oriente province, a Gallego immigrant whose rise to success had also earned him a reputation for lack of scruple. Their mother, Lina Ruz Gonzales, was a servant in the Castro household whom Angel Castro married after the death of his first wife. In addition to Fidel, Raúl, and two daughters, there was another son, Ramón, who took over the family farm in the early 1950's and from it organized much of the supply system to the rebels in the mountains. There were also two children of the first marriage, from whom the others seem to have remained aloof.

Fidel Castro was born August 13, 1926, and attended schools run by the Christian Brothers and the Jesuits in Santiago de Cuba; he received his secondary education at the highly reputed Colegio Belén in Havana where he had a good scholastic record and was active in athletics. Castro's active political life began with his entrance into the University; much of this activity later became a matter of sharp dispute between his supporters and his opponents. At the University his close friends included men of political leanings from conservative to extreme radical. He quickly earned a reputation for personal ambition, forcefulness, and volubility, but his efforts to obtain leadership in student associations were only partially successful. He had some association at different times with two terrorist groups operating in the University. Cuban police files implicated him in the murder of a rival student leader, but nothing was proved. On at least two occasions charges against him were dropped because of insufficient evidence. In Cuba this might mean that there was insufficient evidence, that the accusation was fabricated, or that friends intervened to prevent prosecution; Cubans later presented arguments supporting each of these interpretations.

In the political turbulence of the late 1940's there were many roads open to young radicals; Castro attached himself to a number of organizations. He left the University for a time in 1947 to take part in the Cayo Confites expedition against the Trujillo dictatorship. In April 1948 he was one of a large number of Latin American youths who gathered in Bogotá for an anti-imperialist meeting timed to coincide with the meeting of the Ninth Inter-American Conference. Castro's role in the rioting in Bogotá was a subject of particularly sharp dispute after his rise to fame. Communists and Peronists competed for leadership in efforts to exploit anti-American sentiment and disrupt the conference. The Cuban students distributed propaganda leaflets of anti-imperialist content; Colombian authorities, considering them suspect, assigned a detective to search their hotel rooms and detained them for questioning. The students were caught up in the rioting that followed the assassination of the Colombian liberal leader Jorge Eliécer Gaitán on April 9, but their role in the next days is not known. Colombian police planned to question them again, but the Cubans took refuge in their embassy, from which they were flown home.

The same year, 1948, Castro married Mirtha Díaz Balart, daughter of a prominent conservative family. Her brother, a university friend of Castro's, subsequently became the head of the youth section of Batista's party, and the family tried to steer Castro into a more conservative political career. Castro, however, appears to have linked himself more and more closely to the Ortodoxos, further identifying himself with the "militants" in the party. After graduating in 1950 he opened a law office in Havana and devoted himself to rising within the Ortodoxo party; he became a member of the party's national assembly and was a congressional candidate in 1952. His turn to conspiracy and violence after the Batista *coup d'état* apparently caused the final break in his marriage; he was divorced in 1955.

There were as many conflicting impressions of Castro's character as of his politics. Cubans who knew him in his youth agreed mainly on two traits: his insatiable appetite for conversation, which often became monologue, and his tendency toward self-dramatization. His sisters wrote, for example, that as he read a book he would rip out the pages to demonstrate his powers of memory.

At the University, Castro adopted a bohemian appearance not consonant with the usual Cuban attention to niceties of dress. His height, close to six feet, gave him a commanding physical appearance, later accentuated by the strength that a beard lent his face. Stories of his physical prowess circulated widely—to escape arrest when the Cayo Confites expedition was prevented, he swam shark-filled waters with a machine-gun on his back. From the mountains came stories of his humanitarian concern for the people, his reaction to the sight of an undernourished child, or his decision to try, and execute, a rural guard who terrorized the local people. Whether these traits were appealing or not depended largely on the viewpoint of the observer. Castro obviously reacted violently to the caste-like manners of the upper class. Some saw this as a necessary symbol of his social revolution; others dismissed him as one who failed to wash, or traced his behavior to early family hostilities and psychic peculiarities. The incident of the execution of the rural guard was mentioned by some to support the thesis that Castro was the "Robin Hood of the Sierra Maestra," by others to indicate Castro's readiness to kill to gain a desired effect. Stories of his physical prowess and courage were countered by critical reports that at Moncada, and throughout his days of guerrilla life, he protected himself from the dangers to which he willingly exposed his followers.

Raúl Castro followed his brother into the University and radical politics about 1950. Very little is certain about his activities. He was, according to his own and Castro's statements, the more radical of the two. He apparently did not complete any university course. While at the University he was associated with the Socialist Youth—the youth branch of the Communist party—and was a delegate to a world youth conference in Prague in 1953, after which he traveled in East Europe. He returned to Cuba in June 1953, carrying Communist propaganda, which was promptly seized by police. He took part in the Moncada attack and in all subsequent activities of his brother. After his release from the Isle of Pines in 1955 he preceded Castro to Mexico.

Raúl Castro, though he remained very much in the background of public life, seemed to have aroused less divided reactions than had Castro. Unlike his brother, he was taciturn and therefore an enigma. Many more Cubans suspected and feared his radicalism than hesitated to support Fidel Castro. In addition Raúl was slightly effeminate in appearance and had obtained a reputation for brutality. Although he appeared to lack the popularity of his brother, he instilled a great loyalty to himself in the men he commanded in the rebel army. After the rebels came to power, certain individuals with the government were identified as "Raúl's protégés." His wife, Vilma Espín, had been an active agent of the 26th of July Movement and, after their marriage in 1959, lent her abilities to organizing women's groups in support of the government.

Ernesto "Ché" Guevara's background in Argentina was similar to that of the Castros. The son of an architect, he was born in 1928 and trained in medicine at the University of Buenos Aires. He engaged in anti-Peronist activities at home and, later in exile, in anti-dictatorial conspiracies in other countries of Latin America. In 1954 he held a minor post in the Arbenz government of Guatemala; his antagonism toward the United States, already well developed, was reportedly cemented by United States support to the movement against Arbenz. Guevara went to Mexico after the fall of Arbenz and there met Raúl and Fidel Castro. Colonel Bayo rated Guevara first among the men he trained, and after the landing in Cuba Guevara gradually become the major strategist of the revolutionaries.

Of the three who led the revolution, Guevara appears to have had the most carefully formulated program. He could deal with details for which Castro had no patience and could argue cogently when Castro was carried away in vague disgressions. As an Argentine he remained suspect to many Cubans, but, like Raúl Castro, Guevara left public leadership to Castro himself. He was more willing than Castro to identify himself by political labels, describing his position as Marxist, but non-Communist. During and after the guerrilla struggle he wrote an analysis of guerrilla warfare tactics used by the rebels; printed in 1959, it was distributed widely in Latin America by the Castro government.

For most of the two-year period that Castro spent in guerrilla warfare, the rebels were on the defensive in the mountains. Instead of the mass popular uprising against Batista which Castro apparently expected to spark, there developed four types of organized opposition to the increasingly dictatorical government.

The rebels in the mountains, who numbered fewer than 1,000 in mid-1958, alternated attacks on police posts and army patrols sent against them with flights from major engagements in which they had no chance of success. They remained in the Sierra Maestra, winning good will and some recruits from the local peasantry and relying on supplies channeled through their underground organizations.

A much larger urban resistance movement harassed the army and police in the cities; later estimates of fatalities in the struggle against Batista totaled about 1,000 in the mountains, 19,000 in the cities. Throughout the island, underground cells of the 26th of July organization and of the closely allied Civic Resistance Movement conducted terrorist activity, distributed propaganda, and brought thousands of persons into participation in the opposition. Eventually an allied labor organization established cells in some unions, and student groups joined the alliance.

A third focus of opposition was formed by the several existing political parties and factions in open opposition to Batista; many of their leaders were in exile. Despite their earlier reluctance to support Castro, many of the prominent Ortodoxo leaders during 1957 and 1958 became active members and leaders within the 26th of July Movement or the Civic Resistance Movement. Castro himself first indicated his desire for alliance with other groups in a statement issued in July 1957, but the mutual suspicions that beset the political organizations prevented agreement until July 1958.

As important as the active opposition in the downfall of Batista was the gradual withdrawal of support by the permanently organized institutions on whose acquiescence any government depended. According to their individual character and their relationship to specific political groups, professional, business, and church organizations had increased the pressure for moderate changes in government by pressing for negotiation with the opposition or for new and honest elections. When the Batista government adopted instead a policy of suppressing all opposition by means of increasingly brutal police terrorism, they gradually withdrew support. The failure of Batista's army to fight during the last months of 1958 was the final and indisputable blow.

Through the organizations engaged in active or passive opposition, many individuals representing the strongest groups in Cuban society had given support to Castro. Money and arms came from a variety of sources among the exile community, and from other Latin American countries. Some of the largest sugar and manufacturing interests gave financial aid, and much of the urban resistance operated in and through small business establishments where clandestine meetings might be held, contacts made, and literature printed. There were many instances of interlocking membership in several organizations. An individual's allegiance to a particular group was often circumstantial. Most of the activists were young men of no long-standing identification with any particular party.

A few incidents were particularly important in marking either the progress of the active opposition or the withdrawal of support from Batista of influential individuals and groups. In April 1956, an unsuccessful *coup d'état* was organized by a Montecristi Group, composed primarily of business and professional men, with army support. Justo Carrillo headed the civilian organization, Colonel Ramón Barquin, the army officers.

In March 1957, students of the Federation of University Students attacked the palace in an attempt to assassinate Batista. They seized the CMQ radio station briefly, but failed at the palace. Apparently because the police believed the group to have Ortodoxo support, the president of the Ortodoxo party, Dr. Pelayo Cuervo, was murdered the next day. One of the incidents that aroused much public reaction, this also led other Ortodoxos to seek reconciliation with Castro.

On May 11, 1957, Dr. Manuel Urrutia, presiding over Urgency Court proceedings against rebels, including captured members of the *Gramma* expedition, declared that the defendants were within their rights in rebelling against dictatorship, and left for exile.

In June 1957, the Joint Body of Civic Institutions, a loose federation of professional and civic associations issued a public statement calling on the government to negotiate with opposition groups for a peaceful solution to the national crisis.

On July 12, Castro issued a statement, the first to indicate a desire for alliance with other opposition organizations and the first to stress a political rather than a socioeconomic program. He outlined a political program on which unity might be achieved among the opposition political parties, the civic institutions, and the revolutionaries, and he proposed the formation of a Civilian Revolutionary Front. The civic institutions should select the Front's presiding officer in whose favor Batista would be forced to resign. No military junta would be permitted to assume control, even temporarily. No foreign mediation or intervention would be accepted. The program of the provisional government would be to restore all constitutional freedoms, reform the administration, and adopt economic policies aimed at monetary stability, industrialization, and full employment. Elections for all offices would be held one year after the provisional government took over.

On September 5 a naval revolt at Cienfuegos failed. Timed to coincide with uprisings elsewhere, the revolt apparently was postponed at the last minute, but word failed to reach the Cienfuegos group. Antonio de Varona, chief aide to Prío Socarrás, was arrested, but was allowed to go into exile. Escaping participants fled to the Escambray where they became the nucleus of the Second Front of the Escambray.

In October seven opposition groups, including the 26th of July Movement, signed and published a Document of Unity in Miami. Castro subsequently denounced the agreement, stating that the representatives of his movement had not been authorized to make such a commitment and criticizing the politicians in exile who sought to determine policy while others carried on the real work of revolution. In February 1958 the Castro forces began regular broadcasts over Radio Rebelde from the Sierra Maestra. A group from the Directorio Revolucionario led by Fauré Chomón, a participant in the March 13 attack on the palace, began guerrilla operations in the mountains of Las Villas.

Carrying out a decision made on March 4, the Joint Body of Civic Institutions, led by the head of the National Medical College, Raúl de Valasco, and the Dean of the Bar Association, Miró Cardona, issued a long statement on March 15: "Until now, the Joint Committee has proposed formulas of compromise and civilized understanding . . . it now calmly demands that the present regime shall cease to hold power. . . ." After issuing a personal statement of his reasons for this move, Miró Cardona went into exile.

In an announcement drafted March 12, Castro issued a manifesto declaring total war on the dictatorship. The strategy of the final stage was announced to be a general strike supported by military action. The strike was to be led by the National Labor Front, the Civic Resistance Movement, and the National Students' Front, the military action by the 26th of July Movement militia with "all revolutionary organizations which back the Movement." April 5 was given as the date beginning the final stage. He also declared that as of April 1, the payment of taxes to the government and, as of April 5, the holding of any executive or judicial office in the government or service in the army, would be regarded as illegal acts by the future provisional government.

On March 14 the United States Department of State placed an embargo on the shipment of arms to Batista. Castro forces, recently strengthened by the receipt of a large arms shipment from Mexico, began to move from Sierra Maestra on April 1. Raúl Castro led a group to establish the Frank País Second Front in the Sierra del Cristal of eastern Oriente.

The general strike was called for 11 A.M., April 9, and was successful in many cities but failed in Havana, apparently because instructions were given only at the last minute and did not reach many of the participants. The Communist party newspaper, *Carta Semanal*, published a statement pointing out that a general strike would not be successful unless the Communists were included in its direction.

Seven revolutionary organizations at last achieved a superficial unity in the Caracas Pact of July 20, of which the final draft was dictated by Castro. The Civilian Revolutionary Front was created with Miró Cardona as coordinating secretary-general. The three bases of agreement were a strategy of armed insurrection accompanied by a civilian general strike, the brief institution of a provisional government to restore constitutional and democratic procedures, and a governmental program to punish the guilty and to ensure workers' rights, public order, freedom, and progress. The statement further asked the United States government to cease giving aid to Batista and urged all Cubans to join the united effort.

Official Communist party contact with the 26th of July Movement was made by Carlos Rafael Rodriguez, central committee member and later editor of the party newspaper, *Hoy*, who went to the Sierra Maestra in early summer, 1958. Despite their efforts the Communists were not included in the Civilian Revolutionary Front. During the fall, however, the party appeared to have ordered its members to give full support to the movement through joining the guerrilla forces and urban terrorist activity.

During August and September, Guevara led a column into Las Villas province where he reached agreement on common action with forces already active there, the Second Front of the Escambray and the Revolutionary Directorate. On October 10, Castro issued two laws: one was an agrarian reform law; the second declared guilty of treason, punishable by sentences including death, any candidate for elective office in the elections scheduled by Batista for November 3. When the elections took place, Batista's candidate, Andrés Rivero Aguero, was elected president of Cuba.

13. *Genesis of a Revolution*

On November 5, Castro began to move from the Sierra Maestra in a military operation calling for his and Raúl Castro's troops to converge on Santiago de Cuba. The forces in Las Villas province began operations to converge on Santa Clara. In December top military officials of the Batista government sought to arrange for a government to replace Batista. Batista retired or arrested many officers. On December 31, when Santa Clara, capital of Las Villas, was surrendered to the rebels led by Guevara, Batista, his family, and most of his Cabinet fled to the Dominican Republic. Although he designated a temporary head of government, underground groups loyal to Castro took over Havana. Other major cities were surrendered immediately, and the rebel group began their march to the capital.

VICTORY AND THE
CONSOLIDATION OF POWER

CASTRO'S FORCES WERE UNPREPARED for Batista's flight. Their only substantial military victories had occurred in December, culminating in the seizure of Santa Clara on December 31. Fearing that the vacuum in Havana caused by Batista's departure would be filled by some new government established by *coup d'état,* Castro issued orders for an immediate attack on Santiago, and over the radio called for a general strike until such time as revolutionary victory was achieved; this time the PSP cooperated. In Havana, however, Carlos Piedra made little attempt to form a government; Colonel Ramón Barquín was released from prison on the Isle of Pines and placed in command of the army, but he made it clear that he considered his position an interim one.

January 1, 1959 was a day of public celebration marked by widespread looting and many vengeance killings until the 26th of July and Civic Resistance underground groups emerged to take over police stations and restore order. The rapidity and firmness with which they took command and the discipline and politeness of the first guerrilla troops who arrived from Las Villas the next day prevented the widely expected days of anarchy.

Tension among the victors developed when, on Castro's orders, Guevara and Camilo Cienfuegos led their troops into Havana to occupy La Habana Fortress and Camp Columbia. The Directorio Revolucionario, occupying the presidential palace and Havana University, refused to turn over command to Guevara. The Second Front of the Escambray similarly appeared fearful for its future role and resisted giving up its independent command. Castro and presidential-designee Urrutia were in Santiago de Cuba; Urrutia reached Havana on January 5.

Castro's forces made a triumphal march across the island, with Castro making speeches lasting hours in each of the major cities, and arrived in Havana on January 8. During this period President Urrutia selected his Cabinet and named Castro the commander-in-chief of the army. By January 10 an agreement had been reached with the dissident groups in the capital, and the Cabinet and rebel army were in control.

The Cabinet reflected the composition of the opposition to Batista, but the older and more experienced leaders, rather than the youthful *barbudos,* predominated. Miró Cardona became prime minister as agreed by the Civilian Revolutionary Front; Roberto Agramonte, head of the Ortodoxos, became foreign minister. Luis M. Buch, secretary of the Cabinet, Manuel Ray Rivero, minister of public works, and Rufo Lopez-Fresquet, minister of treasury, had been leaders of the Civic Resistance Movement. Several Cabinet members were appointed from Castro's staff. Luis Orlando Rodríguez, minister of interior, had joined Castro after his newspaper, *La Calle,* was closed by Batista in 1955. Faustino Perez, one of the twelve who survived the *Gramma* landing and who subsequently organized the Castro underground in Havana and many of its contacts with other groups, was made minister for the recovery of misappropriated assets. Armando Hart, minister of education, had been a Havana underground leader with Castro since the Moncada attack; Humberto Sori Marín, minister of agriculture, had been Castro's judge advocate general.

Tension between the Cabinet and the rebel army appeared immediately as the largely civilian Cabinet formulated policy while the rebel army replaced the regular army and much of the police. Twenty-Sixth of July Movement officers were in positions of command in the provinces. The Cabinet itself was divided in opinion over the extent of change needed. At the same time, Castro alone was the national hero, and on television he frequently announced government policies of which the Cabinet had no prior information. On February 13, Miró Cardona resigned the premiership in favor of Castro to bring the government into line with the situation.

In the first months, marked by tremendous public enthusiasm for Castro, for liberation from fear, and for the future of Cuba, the Castro government operated on *ad hoc* procedures. Rapid changes of government personnel, though temporarily stopped in February because of administrative chaos, gave to the whole structure an atmosphere of youth, energy, purpose. Castro spoke constantly on television, and his words were absorbed by the nation.

The principles of the new government as first enunciated were politically moderate and socially reformist. Cuba would respect its international obligations and pursue national policies toward economic development and political freedom. Civil liberties were restored; exiles returned; newspapers and magazines had free access to information sources and might publish what they pleased. The many organizations of Cuban society were free to operate, although government intervenors replaced the former leaders, which in most cases had been pro-Batista.

The first measures of the new Cabinet, most of them in fulfillment of specific promises made by Castro or projects long considered vital by various Cabinet members, were intended to consolidate the power of the new government, to reform previous procedures conducive to corruption, or to provide an immediate improvement in the standard of living. Such policies required little change in the structure of government. Most of the ministries of former governments were retained: State (foreign affairs), Government (interior), Defense, Justice, Education, Health, Labor, Finance, Agriculture, Commerce, Public Works, Communication and Transportation. New ministries were created for Social Welfare, Economy, the Recovery of Misappropriated Assets (to administer properties confiscated from officials of the Batista government) and the Study of Revolutionary Laws. The administrative agencies of government remained much as before, although committees were appointed to study means of making the government's role, particularly in economic activity, more rational and more effective. Within government ministries large numbers of personnel were dismissed or replaced, tenure laws having been suspended. The standards of government morality were high; while much of the turnover was intended to replace Batistianos with persons who had supported the revolution, the ministries also eliminated thousands of *botellas* (sinecures) and for the first time in many years the government appeared to give higher priority to investment in new construction and facilities than to meeting patronage requirements.

The most controversial actions of the government were those designed to punish the officials and supporters of the Batista government. From January to May 1959 revolutionary tribunals, hastily set up during the first weeks of January and staffed by 26th of July Movement officers, tried former army and civil officials. The trials were widely publicized and some were televised. The accused were tried under the laws issued by the rebels in the Sierra Maestra in early 1958 and confirmed in February by the Fundamental Law. Although the outcome of the trials was predetermined and the sentence of execution carried out quickly, criticism of procedures infuriated Castro and other government leaders, who considered their methods a vast improvement over those of Batista. For the new government the trials provided at once a means of publicizing the most brutal aspects of the Batista regime and of channeling popular vengeance into demonstrations of support for the Fidelistas. Mounting criticism of the tribunals led to their dissolution in May 1959.

Cubans were more critical of the government's actions against persons whose relationship with the Batista government had been tenuous or whose fault had been failure to support the 26th of July Movement. Property of persons convicted in the trials and of the Batistianos who fled Cuba was immediately confiscated. In late February and early March the definition of collaborators with the regime was extended to include all persons who had held elective or top-level appointive jobs in the government after March 1952 and all candidates for electoral office during Batista's tenure, whether they supported or opposed his coalition. Another measure, invalidating the degrees of students completing their education in private universities during the period when Havana University was closed, was subsequently modified to the extent that the degrees might be validated individually.

The Fundamental Law issued by the Council of Ministers on February 8, 1959, was a modified version of the 1940 Constitution. Since the 1940 Constitution was a social blueprint as well as an outline of governmental procedure, large sections concerned with the family and culture, labor and property, suffrage rights, the organization of the judiciary, the responsibilities of provincial and municipal governments, and the national economy were incorporated with almost no changes. The framers, however, rewrote clauses concerning powers of government so as to vest all powers in the Council of Ministers. The Council might amend the law by a two-thirds vote.

Certain articles were changed to facilitate personnel changes already in progress and to legitimize the revolutionary tribunals. The right of habeas corpus was suspended in cases before them.

New provisions made possible the trial of persons who had committed crimes "in the service of the tyranny," the imposition of the death sentence for such crimes, and the confiscation of the property of the convicted. Laws and administrative decisions of the rebel army command before December 31, 1958 were declared in effect throughout the country.

In January 1959, five major types of organization had potential political influence as a result of their roles in destroying the Batista government. The rebel army itself was one, intensely loyal to Castro and to some extent divided in secondary loyalty to individual subordinate commanders. A second was the conglomerate urban resistance made up of the 26th of July Movement in the cities and the Civic Resistance Movement. The remnants of the old political parties constituted a third; their leaders had returned from exile, but, after six years of dissent and relative inactivity, they had little organization in the island. The fourth was made up of organized groups, representing labor, students, and business and professional associations, which were accustomed to making their influence felt through pressure on the government and to receiving benefits from it. The fifth was the PSP which, despite the vicissitudes of underground existence since 1953, remained remarkably well organized. In the new government the many points of view represented in the victorious forces came into conflict.

In the first weeks of his victory, Castro sought to define his program in various ways, usually as "humanism." He consistently refused to place any of the standard political labels on his views or his government. For several years he had talked of a program for an ideal, a utopian Cuba. He described this as a land of equal opportunity in which people were well fed, well housed, provided with education, medical care, and the means of earning an adequate living, and free from police repression. He maintained that the revolution was the necessary result of historical forces and that his own role was imposed upon him by the nature of revolution rather than sought by him for purposes of holding power. He believed that most men were dominated entirely by their economic status. If wealthy, they sought to exploit. If poor, they sought justice. He proposed to make them equal. By identifying himself with the "people," the "vast unredeemed masses" of his Moncada speech, by preserving the image of the beard, the fatigues, the spartan and sacrificial life, he maintained both roles—the impersonal fulfiller of historical necessity and the extremely personal redeemer of the people.

Both the programs he espoused and the image he created aroused opposition among the groups which had given him strongest support. Many of his supporters had intended exactly what Castro accused them of intending, a political revolution to restore civil liberties, elections, constitutional government, and an economic and social system little different from that prevailing in 1952. Many others, including the "moderates" in the first Cabinet, defined national needs in terms of honest public administration, a new and rational tax structure, planned government expenditure in public works and social services, encouragement of private investment, and a return to the free exercise of political rights. The more radical proposals of Castro, reinforced by his appearance and techniques of public appeal, to them appeared dangerous. When, however, they sought to limit the revolution to accord with their several ideas of its purpose, they were attacked and eventually dismissed.

Attitudes toward the future of the revolution were dominated by the controversy over Castro's role. His conflicting statements on policy had led to widely diverse interpretations of his intentions. Many reached the conclusion that he had no coherent program. By mid-1959 it was clear that Castro had become the most sucessful *caudillo* that Cuba had yet seen. Within his government many of his most loyal supporters became convinced that his dominant characteristics were extreme susceptibility to flattery and violent reaction to criticism or to disagreement which he chose to regard as criticism. His hours-long televised speeches, his public addresses to thousands of assembled admirers, his unexpected visits across the island to schools or army camps or new cooperatives created a daily schedule few could keep up with and a system of personalist government no one could challenge.

To give the people the things he had promised them, Castro required their cooperative effort and their unanimous support. Many of his speeches, though marked by frequent digressions and highly emotional appeals for loyalty and enthusiasm, were masterly expositions of the nature and purpose of government actions or of the need for some desired popular response. The same technique was used to obtain mass support for a major policy such as agrarian reform or to obtain mass acquiescence in the denunciation of a formerly popular figure who had left or had been dismissed from the government. To achieve the revolution the government imposed an economic and social equality on the people; the only discrimination permitted was one based on loyalty to the revolution. To criticize the government, to voice protest on considerations of legality, to raise the spectre of Communism, all were threats to the ideal society Castro had promised and of which he was the embodiment; all were therefore counterrevolutionary.

Although Castro had appeared hopeful of retaining the support of a Communist-liberal alliance, the liberals—unequal partners because they lacked cohesive organization—objected to that alliance. In return for its increasing power, achieved as moderates left or were forced out of government, the PSP supplied Castro with three essentials in the order in which he found them necessary: a rationale and organized support for his own position as *líder máximo;* a coherent program that appeared similar to his own and that reinforced with doctrine his preconceptions concerning the nature of capitalism and Yankee imperialism; and a structure capable, with his sanction, of organizing the population into a new political system for defense against his enemies. Most of the leaders of the opposition to Batista hoped to reduce personalism in government and feared the substitution of one dictator for another; they sought to limit Castro's sphere of individual control while, in contrast, the PSP gave him full and effective support.

Although some of Castro's early supporters had previously been active in the Communist youth organization, Juventad Socialista, the party had refrained from giving official support to Castro until the summer of 1958. The Communist version of the revolution, as described in *Pravda* on January 3, 1959, was that while the revolution was not Communist it offered an opportunity for the development of a "real popular liberation movement."

> The Cuban working class raised the banner of struggle against the hateful tyranny by organizing a series of large-scale strikes. The peasantry, a large part of the intelligentsia, and representatives of business circles joined in this struggle. Armed resistance to the dictatorship regime came from the rebel movement headed by a leader of Cuban young people, Fidel Castro, who is now making decisive gains. . . . The resistance movement is being actively supported by the Popular Socialist Party of Cuba—the advance detachment of the Cuban working class. It sees the rebels first of all as patriots who have set as their goal the revival of democratic freedoms in the country, the transformation of its backward economy, the implementation of land reform and the liquidation of illiteracy.

14. *Victory and the Consolidation of Power*

The Popular Socialist Party of Cuba is fighting stanchly for the unity and solidarity of all patriotic forces and for a real popular liberation movement.

The Process of Radicalization

In the progressive radicalization of government three processes occurred simultaneously—the totalitarian development of the government; the gradual shift by Castro from reliance on the 26th of July Movement to reliance on the Popular Socialist (Communist) Party (PSP) with an accompanying change in official ideology; and the parallel shift in foreign policy from an acceptance of close relations with the United States to the cultivation of close relations with the Communist bloc. A step in one of these processes often created the rationale for a step in another. In the sequence of events that led to the declaration of a "socialist Cuba" on May Day 1961, the threat of counterrevolution, at first largely imaginary and later quite real, was consistently used by the government to justify radicalization.

In the spring of 1959 the first major political crisis arose. The government had implemented many of the plans it had announced and on which the Council of Ministers could agree. Further plans divided the Cabinet as Castro, backed by radical pressures, sought to continue a revolution that moderates considered virtually complete.

The first major issue of public discussion was the role of the PSP, whose attempt to take over labor union leadership became particularly apparent, ending in some instances in armed conflict. Another issue was the government's economic policies, particularly its proposals for major agrarian reform. Foreign policy became an issue as Castro's statements increasingly criticized the United States and as he discussed the need for similar revolutions throughout Latin America. The degree of persecution deserved by Batistianos and persons who had not supported Castro was still another issue; government leaders divided over the extent purging of government personnel was necessary.

The pressures on Castro from the moderates, who felt the government should plan elections and return to normal procedures, and from the radical left led by the Communists, were apparent in the conflicting statements he made during the spring of 1959. On April 2, 1959, when asked in a television interview to comment on the concern about Communism being expressed in Cuba at the time, Castro identified anti-Communism with counterrevolution in the manner that later became official government policy.

In mid-May, however, he made a speech, which was to be widely quoted, indicating his dissociation from Communism:

> The tremendous problem faced by the world is that it has been placed in a position where it must choose between capitalism, which starves people, and Communism, which resolves economic problems, but suppresses the liberties so greatly cherished by men. . . . Our idea of freedom is different from that of the reactionaries who talk of elections but not of social justice. Without social justice, democracy is not possible, for without it men would be slaves of poverty. That is why we have said that we are one step ahead of the right and of the left, and that this is a humanistic revolution. Capitalism sacrifices man; the Communist state, by its totalitarian concept, sacrifices the rights of man. That is why we do not agree with any of them. Each people must develop its own political organization, out of its own needs, not forced upon them or copied.

Evidence that Castro was seeking to retain moderate support was seen in many of the statements he made during his visit to the United States in April and in the decision in May to dissolve the revolutionary tribunals. This impression was strengthened by Castro's reported opposition to Guevara's suggestion that a civilian militia be formed and by his decision, apparently made after a speech by Guevara in favor of radical economic policies, to send Guevara on a long trip to the Middle and Far East in early June.

Castro, however, refused to consider proposals for establishing more regular procedures of government or for planning elections and was determined to press through the Agrarian Reform Law over the moderates' opposition. To do so and to gain a commanding position in the government he called on the true revolutionaries to support him and to join him in denouncing the moderates.

Although the major argument concerned the means chosen, all opposition was interpreted as opposition to agrarian reform. Later, observers tended to point back to May 1959 and to apply to that period such descriptive terms as "the turning point," "the moment of truth" or, according to the PSP executive secretary, "the time when the true revolution was defined."

The Agrarian Reform Law, drawn up in May and enacted by the Cabinet on June 2, 1959, led to the resignation on June 17 of Luis

14. *Victory and the Consolidation of Power*

Orlando Rodríguez, Roberto Agramonte, Humberto Sori Marín, Julio Martínez Paez, and Elena Menderes; it was the first major step in the process referred to by Castro and his critics as the "radicalization" of the government. The essential issue resolved by the new law was the extent to which the government would intervene to direct the national economy, an extent never envisaged by most of Castro's supporters. The revolution was to be a restructuring of the economic system rather than a reform of the political system, and opposition to the program was equivalent to disloyalty to Castro and the revolution.

On July 17, the initial step in radicalization was completed by Castro's resignation from the premiership and his appeal to the people to force the resignation of President Manuel Urrutia, who had expressed concern about Communist influence. In a long television speech Castro reproached Urrutia for placing obstacles in the path of the revolution and for refusing to accept personally the morality of the revolution, symbolized by acceptance of a lower salary than had previously been paid the national president. Urrutia resigned, Castro again became prime minister, and Osvaldo Dorticós Torrado became president.

Major Communist influence was first apparent in the rebel army and in labor unions. During the first months of the new government revolutionary indoctrination became a regular feature of army training. According to Guevara's book on guerrilla warfare, indoctrination should be considered the most important element in training new recruits who usually did not have a clear conception of why they came and should therefore be taught history, economics, and "a correct analysis of the domestic situation." This had been a feature of guerrilla life for the men under Raúl Castro and Guevara in the mountains and was continued in the army, at least in areas under their commands. The first use of known Communists in the government was as lecturers on the revolution in army camps. By June, the role of the PSP had become a public issue of considerable importance; the chief of the air force, Pedro Díaz Lanz, resigned in protest against Communist influence in the military forces.

The army was the principal means used to make the first transfer of political power from the moderates to the radical left, which would support Castro's program. Publicity statements constantly stressed the army's role as the repository of revolutionary zeal and its new function in society—to aid in construction rather than to repress the people—and strove to perpetuate the image of the *barbudos* as national heroes. Outside observers were led to speculate on the apparent rivalry in 1959 between the men of the mountains and the men of the plains as the role of the army was continually enhanced while the civilian and urban apparatus of the 26th of July Movement was bypassed and allowed to disintegrate. By bringing the army into government, and particularly into the National Agrarian Reform Institute (INRA), which came to be staffed primarily by army officers, the *barbudo* image was transferred to the civil government as radicalization progressed.

In the labor unions the PSP relied at first on its own efforts rather than on government sponsorship. Most unions had been under Batistiano leadership in 1958; the Castro government appointed new leaders loyal to the 26th of July Movement until an elected leadership could be chosen. David Salvador, leader of the labor group that supported Castro, headed the Confederation of Cuban Workers (CTC). The PSP renewed its efforts in the labor unions, but had relatively little success in the first six months. Efforts to coerce acceptance of its candidates for union office led to open fighting in some instances; the army was used to guard the offices of the PSP newspaper *Noticias de Hoy* in May when anti-Communist union members had threatened direct action against it. In the many union elections in June the PSP lost in most cases to 26th of July Movement candidates.

Between July and November 1959 Castro made changes at the top level of government which vested nearly all government power in the radical left. The key issues were government economic policy and the threat of organized opposition. Men in key economic positions favored a cautious policy, which threatened to slow down projects favored by Castro, including the forming of agricultural cooperatives and arms purchases. Labor demands for wages and benefits created an additional drain on funds. Castro feared the development of organized opposition from exiles whose property had been confiscated; from the United States which, he assumed, would oppose the trend of his government; and from within Cuba itself, where increased criticism was expressed in the press and by political leaders who formerly had supported him. Mild reproaches and counsels of caution from these sources were denounced as counterrevolutionary.

Castro's reaction was to turn again to those whom he trusted and who assured him that ways could be found to carry out the revolution. The five Cabinet members who resigned in June were replaced by men more radical in outlook or whose personal loyalty to Castro was unquestioning. The most prominent was Raúl Roa who replaced Roberto Agramonte as foreign minister. Roa, a former professor at the University of Havana, traced his political loyalty to the revolutionary tradition rather than to any particular party, but, like many Cubans of radical persuasion, he had been in and out of the PSP. Antonio Núñez Jiménez, formerly professor of geography at the University of Santa Clara and previously active in the PSP, was named director of INRA. The new president, Osvaldo Dorticós was a lawyer who had served as minister for the study of revolutionary laws from January to July; in earlier years he had been active in the PSP and reportedly had been secretary to PSP president Juan Marinello.

In October and November, Raúl Castro and Guevara were given Cabinet-level positions. On October 17 Raúl Castro became minister of the armed forces. In the next few weeks the revolutionary tribunals were re-established on a permanent basis and the government began the organization of the civilian militia as a means of augmenting military strength, providing a new channel for revolutionary indoctrination and strengthening internal security. At the same time the former minister of defense, Augusto Martínez Sánchez, became minister of labor.

In November, when the Confederation of Cuban Workers (CTC) held a convention to elect national officers (and at which David Salvador and his slate of 26th of July Movement candidates had majority support), Castro personally intervened to urge the selection of a "unity slate" giving the PSP candidates greater power. Subsequently this group, led by CTC organization-secretary, Jesus Soto, and supported by the Ministry of Labor, gained control of the CTC and directed the removal of many lower union officials opposed to them.

Guevara, after his return from a trip in the summer of 1959, was made director of the Department of Industrialization within INRA and began to assume direction of economic planning despite the existence of more formal planning groups elsewhere in the government. On November 26, he was appointed to succeed Felipe Pazos as president of the National Bank. According to his own statement, he received this appointment, not because he was an economist (he was not), but because Castro trusted him. Other economic posts were similarly filled. Two of the top 26th of July Movement leaders were replaced: Public Works Minister Manual Ray by Osmani Cienfuegos; and Minister for the Recovery of Misappropriated Assets Faustino Pérez by Rolando Díaz Aztarain.

Although there were some Cabinet changes after November 1959, the inner council of the government was already firmly established. A year later President Dorticós, in an interview with a *New York Times* correspondent, summed up the workings of government. He said that the actual business of government was conducted by a small junta of the nation's leaders who met weekly and were formally entrusted with economic coordination. Informal consultations of virtually the same leaders also played a large role in policy formulation. The Council of Ministers, the president explained, was convened primarily when decisions needed the form of law. The key figures, members of the Central Planning Council, included Castro, Minister of Armed Forces Raúl Castro, National Bank President Guevara (who was also advisor to *Prensa Latina* and head of the Department of Instruction of the Armed Forces Ministry), Minister of Finance Rolando Díaz Aztarain (whose wife was the sister of Raúl Castro's wife), and Antonio Núñez Jiménez, director of INRA.

With this group in command the government embarked on rapid reorganization by taking over most economic enterprises and public information media, by reorganizing the school system and, in foreign policy, by cultivating close ties with the Communist-bloc countries from which economic assistance was expected.

The government's interpretation of its political position during this period was that it had none. Although from the beginning government leaders had used the technique of personifying the revolution in order to explain policies (as when Raúl Castro declared in May 1959 that "the Revolution knows what it is doing"), after November 1959 this became the constant theme. The revolution was autonomous and Cuban; each step was declared to fulfill revolutionary necessity. In Castro's speeches no more was heard of humanism, and the official doctrine became the revolution, otherwise undefined. Government spokesmen maintained that the revolution was far more radical than the position of the PSP, which was allegedly hesitant to espouse a truly radical program, and pointed out to foreign visitors that the Chinese in Latin America did not even bother with the local Communists but went "straight to the leftwing." At the same time Communist definitions of social classes and class interests became standard in government speeches and exhortations. Formerly Castro liked to speak in vague terms of the humble and their struggle against exploitation; now he began to speak of the peasants and workers and their struggle against capitalist exploiters and the bourgeoisie. The "peasant" character of the rebel army was stressed. Opposition to the government was attributed to the bourgeoisie if not capitalistic exploiters.

The political result was the demise of the 26th of July Movement as an organization. The explanation of its disappearance was summarized by Simone de Beauvoir after a visit in March 1960. Having seen a crowd disperse quickly after attending a rally at which Castro spoke, she noted that in China the audience would have remained longer, organized in groups, to demonstrate their support. Concluding that the Cuban revolution must lack cadres, she asked why:

> The replies varied a little, but all of them were in the same general vein. The 26th of July Movement, from which the revolution sprang, had an organization, but it was a petty bourgeois organization which was incapable of keeping up with the revolution in the radicalization phase it has been going through since the seizure of power; it was incapable of espousing the march toward agrarian reform. And so it was dropped.

The close of this period was marked by the dismissal from the Cabinet of the last of the moderates, Rufo Lopez-Fresquet, who was replaced as minister of finance by Rolando Díaz Aztarain.

By mid-1960 the lines of conflict were tightly drawn. Opposition within Cuba had lost all means of expression beyond the occasional private gesture of dissent, usually followed by taking asylum. The exiles were actively planning invasion and had obtained United States government support. Within Cuba clandestine groups were active and appeared to have considerable support among the remaining professional men, small businessmen, students and among the membership of labor unions not yet brought under Communist leadership.

From July onward the PSP appeared to have a free hand to take charge of all organizations and thus to supply the cadres which the government found more necessary in the face of increased opposition. At a meeting of the plenary session of the PSP during the first week of July the major decisions reported were to increase revolutionary awareness and mobilization of armed defense and to work toward the unity of all revolutionary forces. During the next week the ambassador to Moscow, Fauré Chomón, was reported to have announced that all revolutionary groups would unite into a single revolutionary party which already in effect ruled Cuba. As usual, the revolutionary groups were defined as the "active members" of the 26th of July Movement, the PSP, the Revolutionary Directorate and "other groups."

During July, and continuing during the next months, the increased power of the PSP was seen in the purges of virtually all professional associations and of the University of Havana and in the creation of new unitary associations of youth, women, and civic groups.

Of the three nominally active organizations remaining from the revolutionary alliance of 1958—the 26th of July Movement, the PSP and the Revolutionary Directorate—only the PSP, called "el Partido," retained an effective organization. The most prominent leaders were: Carlos Rafael Rodriguez, editor of the PSP daily newspaper *Noticias de Hoy,* and Communist liaison to the Castro forces in late 1958; Aníbal Escalante, executive secretary of the PSP Central Committee; and Jesus Soto, organization secretary of the CTC. As the party gained power during 1960 the "official" party leaders, including the older ones who formerly remained in the background— Blas Roca, Juan Marinello and Lázaro Peña—were much more active publicly, appearing on the rostrum at public events and speaking frequently over the radio.

Party strategy appeared to be exactly what party leaders said it was, to support Castro and the revolution. Raúl Castro and Guevara relied on PSP support apparently from the beginning; the party through them, and by other means, made itself indispensable to Castro. Party leaders were particularly conscious of the Guatemalan experience of 1954 and frequently mentioned the importance of avoiding the mistakes made there, such as the failure to ensure the revolutionary loyalty of the army. While their primary access to power was through the alliance with the three top government leaders, the PSP also relied on the usual tactics of selective denunciation, the organization of rallies and demonstrations in support of government policy or against opposition, infiltration, and harassment of persons opposed to them.

One of the clearest statements of the process of transition was given by Castro in an interview with the Italian Communist newspaper *Unita* on February 1, 1961; the analysis was subsequently repeated by Castro and by other government leaders. Although denying that he considered himself or the revolution Communist, Castro gave credit to the PSP as the only party consistently dedi-

cated to the radical reorganization of society and described the
meeting of minds that had brought him into alliance with it:

> At any rate, you wish to write that this is a socialist revolution,
> right? And write it, then. . . . Yes, not only did we destroy a tyran-
> nical system. We also destroyed the philoimperialistic bourgeois
> state apparatus, the bureaucracy, the police, and the mercenary
> army. We abolished privilege, annihilated the great landowners,
> threw out foreign monopolies for good, nationalized almost every
> industry, and collectivized the land. We are fighting now to liquidate
> once and for all the exploitation of man over man, and to build a
> completely new society, with a new class content. The Americans
> and the priests say that this is Communism. We know very well that
> it is not. At any rate the word does not frighten us. . . . Yet, if such
> a great welfare conquest—which can be seen by my own eyes—is
> Communism, then you can even call me a Communist. . . . It
> [the Popular Socialist Party] is the only Cuban party which has
> consistently called for a radical change of social structures and
> relations. It is true that at the beginning the Communists distrusted
> me and us rebels. Their distrust was justified, their position was
> abolutely correct, both ideologically and politically. They were
> right in being distrustful because we of the Sierra who were con-
> ducting the guerrilla war were still full of petit-bourgeois prejudices
> and defects, in spite of our Marxist readings. Our ideas were not
> clear, although we wished to destroy tyranny and privileges with
> all our strength. Then, we met with each other, we understood
> one another, and started to work together. The Communists have
> shed much blood and heroism for the Cuban cause. At present, we
> continue to work together in a loyal and brotherly way.

In the development of a common program, both Castro and the
PSP leadership recognized errors of the past. The PSP acknowledged its error in regarding Castro as a "bourgeois putschist."

The Opposition

The means of expressing political opposition shifted as the government became totalitarian. At first there was dissent within the
government; in late 1959 it became increasingly apparent that
this means was ineffective and dangerous only to the dissenters.
The second major vehicle of expression, public opinion media, came
under government control by the spring of 1960.

Opposition then was expressed through university organizations,
the business and professional associations and, finally, the Church—

much as in the last years of the Batista regime. Castro, however, by undermining, suppressing, or allowing the PSP to take over such organizations, succeeded in silencing the voices of dissent. Men who earlier had left the government but had remained in Cuba, exercising a private profession such as teaching, increasingly came under attack and sought asylum abroad. Strife between rival leadership groups broke out among university students until the government intervened in support of its dependents. A pastoral letter warning of the dangers of Communism was issued by Cuban bishops in early April and was answered by the first major government attacks on the Church. At first such attacks were carefully phrased to refer only to "fascist" priests whom the government claimed represented a minority view within the Church; at the same time the government sought to identify the revolution with the true teachings of Jesus.

Because of the nature of the Castro dictatorship, opposition within the island was more difficult to organize than in earlier eras of crisis and participation in it more dangerous. The government's intelligence service appeared to be highly effective; estimates of the number of political prisoners on the island in early 1961 ranged from 15,000 to 35,000. Persons caught in overt opposition activities were usually given summary trials and shot. Several hundred persons were in asylum in various embassies. The government's system of informers provided an additional bulwark against subversion.

Despite this network there were many groups in active opposition. Most of them could not be linked definitely to any of the major organized groups outside of Cuba. Guerrilla groups were reported at various times, invariably identified by the government as followers of Rolando Masferrer, symbol of Batista repression. In reality they appeared to represent several different opposition groups with and without ties to movements organized outside Cuba.

The strongest guerrilla activity, beginning in the fall of 1960, was in the Escambray where many men from the Second Front of the Escambray of 1958 appeared to be involved. Unlike Batista's army, however, Castro's army was trained for guerrilla fighting; by the spring of 1961 the Escambray group had been decimated. Smaller groups were active in the mountains of Oriente and Pinar del Río provinces in the spring of 1961.

Urban terrorism was sporadic during the second half of 1960 and showed a marked increase in early December and again in early

April when it was coordinated with preparations for landings of troops by the exile organizations. Sabotage, carried out by electrical workers in Havana in December, was the immediate cause of the government's much-publicized purge of the electrical workers' union, one of the last to maintain some independence of leadership. During the next few months there were almost daily incidents.

Publicly advertised opposition centered in the United States, since that within Cuba survived only by preserving anonymity. By January 1961 there were about 100,000 exiles in the United States, and more in various countries of Latin America. Their efforts to organize effective action were hampered by rivalries among themselves in choosing leadership and in the search for outside support and by the presence of Castro agents among them. The methods appeared to have changed little from the 1930's when, according to former Ambassador Guggenheim:

> Traditionally the Cuban inaugurates his propaganda campaign in the United States by establishing there a junta, or revolutionary committee. There are, as a rule, three points of concentration for the junta; one in New York, where financial aid is solicited and filibustering expeditions are organized; one in Washington, where political aid is sought; and one in Miami, where the rank and file of emigrés and followers of the junta concentrate, since they can live more easily in Florida's sunshine.

Cuban exiles usually divided the dozens of organizations competing for their loyalty into three general categories based on the nature of leadership and the date of their departure from Cuba. The first exiles, categorically defined by the others as Batistianos, formed groups of their own; one of the earliest was the White Rose of Rafael Díaz Balart, named for Castro's former brother-in-law. These exiles were concentrated in the Miami area and in Guatemala and Nicaragua. Other opposition groups sought to avoid collaboration with them.

A second type of opposition group, formed somewhat later, centered around men previously well known in politics and associated with the Auténtico political party or with Catholic Action. They had been active in the opposition to Batista; many had been prominent in business and professional groups, and some had been in government employment in the first months of the Castro government.

A third group centered around some of Castro's most prominent early supporters and former Ortodoxo leaders, who left the government during 1959 and 1960; they disassociated themselves from the second category primarily in desiring to effect a greater degree of social and economic reform than was espoused by the others.

The Democratic Revolutionary Front (DRF), a coalition formed in June 1960 by five smaller anti-Castro groups, was the first major step toward unity among the opposition forces. In its initial manifesto, the DRF, which soon became the dominant exile organization, stressed the Castro government's suppression of civil liberties, economic destruction, and reliance on Communism. The signers promised to restore full national sovereignty, civil rights and government under the 1940 Constitution. They appealed for the support of all Cubans except those affiliated with the Batista government. The DRF leaders had all been active in the opposition to Batista.

Manuel Antonio de Varona, one of Cuba's more highly respected politicians, was named coordinator-general of the DRF. He had been premier and then president of the Senate in the Prío Socarrás government and was considered the titular head of the moribund Auténtico party. A lawyer whose record of revolutionary activity went back to his secondary-school days, he had participated in the opposition to Machado from 1930 to 1933, in the general strike of 1935, and in the anti-Batista movements, and he had spent considerable time in exile. Varona had been a signer of the Caracas Pact by which the anti-Batista forces achieved a measure of unity in July 1959. He was an early critic of Castro in 1959 and subsequently was one of the first to seek effective opposition unity. Although his organization appeared to exist largely in exile, his name was expected to attract considerable support to the DRF.

One of Cuba's leading economists, Justo Carrillo Hernández had been president of a government bank during the first months of the Castro government. José Ignacio Rasco Bermudez, a professor at Villanueva University, had formed the Christian Democratic Movement in an effort to unite democratic pressures within Cuba in a political party to oppose the growth of Communist power. The movement's manifesto, published on April 13, 1960 in the newspaper *Diario de la Marina* (which shortly afterward was seized by the government), protested the government's economic policies (particularly the role of INRA), the growth of Communism, and Castro's failure to provide for elections. The movement appeared to be linked to Catholic lay organizations active at that time.

14. *Victory and the Consolidation of Power*

The Movement for Revolutionary Recovery (MRR) was the only organization during the first half of 1960 reported to have an effective activist organization within Cuba. The MRR issued a clandestine proclamation during the first week of April 1960 calling upon Cubans to fight for the return of democracy and the rescue of Cuba from totalitarianism and Communism. The leaders stressed their total disaffiliation from Batista supporters and their desire to preserve the social reforms achieved during the first months of the Castro government. Leadership of the MRR appeared to come from young officers of Castro's army. Manuel Artime Buesco, who left Cuba for the United States in the spring of 1960, became the MRR representative and the military commander of the DRF. Previously he had been active in university politics as a representative of Catholic student groups, had served in the revolutionary army, and then had been an administrator in INRA.

The DRF maintained a labor affiliate, the Cuban Revolutionary Democratic Labor Front, and a students' organization, the Revolutionary Students Directorate, and committees for propaganda, finance, agriculture, commerce, industry, public relations, and planning. It opened offices in big cities in the United States and in most Latin American capitals. Although it sought to unite all Cubans in a single movement, there was internal dissension on several points including: choice of leadership; program and tactics, particularly on the degree to which changes in Cuba such as nationalization and agrarian reform should be retained and in what manner; and whether, in excluding support from Batistianos, that category should include only persons actively allied with the Batista regime or also those who failed to oppose it actively.

The major group not included in the DRF was the Revolutionary Movement of the People (Movimiento Revolucionario de Pueblo— MRP). Organized inside Cuba during 1960, it received little publicity outside the country until fall when it reportedly had the most effective opposition movement on the island. The leaders made known were among the most prominent of Castro's earlier supporters and had served in the government during 1959. Manuel Ray Rivero, an engineer, had been the leader of the Civic Resistance Movement in 1958 and was minister of public works from January to November 1959. Felipe Pazos was president of the National Bank from January to November 1959 when he was succeeded by Guevara. Raúl Chibas, former president of the Ortodoxo party and brother of the party's founder, was in 1958 treasurer of the

26th of July Movement and commissioner of railroads in the Castro government. Colonel Ramón Barquin, military leader of the Montecristi Group's attempt to overthrow Batista in 1956, had served in the army in 1959 until he tangled with Raúl Castro in May and was sent on a mission to Europe. Apparently operating much like the Civic Resistance Movement of 1958, the organization had a cell organization, largely urban, and relied mainly on sabotage operations. It claimed a labor affiliate. The MRP appeared to direct the greater part of the activist opposition within Cuba during the winter and spring of 1960-61. The MRP was suspect among the more conservative of Cuban exiles for its program, which someone labeled "Fidelismo without Fidel." MRP leaders claimed that the DRF was accepting support too easily from persons who wanted mainly to get their property back. They maintained that some of the DRF leaders had been too long away from Cuba, failed to understand the immense popularity of many of the early reforms of the revolution, and were too tied to traditional Cuban politics to arouse strong support. In matters of tactics the MRP insisted that the war against Castro must be achieved within Cuba by organizing effective and coordinated sabotage and guerrilla operations.

The Invasion and Its Aftermath

Although discussions regarding the amalgamation of the MRP and the DRF began in late 1960, agreement was not reached until March 21, 1960 when the two groups, under pressure from the United States government, submerged their differences and announced the formation of the Cuban Revolutionary Council. The Council was to lead a united opposition to Castro and set up a provisional government to assume power as Cuba was liberated. It remained, in effect, a loose alliance of the DRF and the MRP. Since there was also mutual suspicion among groups within the DRF, the Council reflected only a superficial unity, similar to that which characterized the Civilian Revolutionary Front of July 20, 1958. A few of the leaders were the same as in 1958. José Miró Cardona was named coordinator-general; other members were Manuel Antonio de Varona, Manuel Ray, Antonio Maceo, Justo Carrillo Hernández, Carlos Hevia, and Manuel Artime.

The minimum program on which the DRF and the MRP announced their agreement included the acceptance of José Miró Cardona as provisional president; he had been premier for six weeks in early 1959, was then made ambassador to Spain, and had been designated ambassador to the United States when he defected in July 1960. The Council promised a return to constitutional government and national elections within eighteen months of victory. Confiscated property would be either returned to former owners or nationalized under constitutional procedures with compensation to former owners. Agrarian reform would be carried out with former owners compensated in bonds. Private ownership of property would be guaranteed, union rights restored to workers. The two groups agreed to differ on two points of the MRP program not adopted by the DRF: the nationalization of major public utilities with compensation and government action to prevent the concentration of economic power in a few banks. The groups agreed to outlaw the PSP and to restore Cuban foreign policies in the interests of hemisphere security.

On April 8 the Council issued a call to Cubans to support a new revolution against Castro:

> We are not, nor could be counterrevolutionaries. . . . We are revolutionists against the tyrant who betrayed a whole nation, which aspired and still aspires to better living conditions, but which has been led by Castro Communism into the depths of poverty and misery.

At the same time the Council announced its plan of operations. Arguments concerning tactics had centered around two plans: one to launch a single invasion at some point and there to establish a beachhead of liberated territory in which a provisional government could be installed; the other to land small groups of guerrillas at many points to coordinate with internal sabotage operations. The Council announced its acceptance of the second plan which appeared to be the one strongly supported by the MRP.

The army which was to carry out the military operations of the Council had been formed long before the Council, and the Council as a whole apparently had no control over it. Under United States government authority Cuban recruits were trained in camps in Florida, Louisiana, and Guatemala; most of the training was apparently given during the second half of 1960. Liaison with Cuban opposition groups was effected mainly through Manuel Artime. Although the MRP in particular was critical of the failure to screen recruits to prevent the inclusion of men who had served in Batista's army, training was completed by early 1961. Despite the reported decision of the Council to launch small forces at several points on the island, the strategy chosen for the action on April 17 was the spearhead invasion.

An estimated 1,500 troops were landed at the Bahía de Cochinos in southern Matanzas province on April 17. The leaders of the Council, with the exception of Manuel Artime who commanded the landing operation, were held in Miami pending a military success which would permit their landing in Cuba to declare the establishment of a provisional government. The landing force, however, failed to gain a hold over any territory and failed also to coordinate the operation with organized resistance on the island. Within a few days the Castro government claimed 1,200 captives.

In the welter of accusations and recriminations exchanged as a result of the invasion failure only fragments of the story became public. Most of the recriminations, given much airing on the Cuban radio as members of the government interviewed the prisoners, were directed at Cuban exile leaders and United States officials who had led the men to believe that a mass uprising was certain to be sparked by their arrival. Cuban and United States officials responsible for the expedition variously attributed the failure to faulty intelligence, which underestimated Cuban military force and internal security network, and to failure to coordinate the landing with the existing underground opposition in Cuba. The latter charge was voiced principally by the MRP which had most strongly insisted on the alternate plan. On May 23 Manuel Ray announced the withdrawal of the MRP from the Revolutionary Council.

In the aftermath of invasion the Castro government showed renewed confidence. The radio for ten days before May 1 featured discussion of the invasion and interviews with prisoners. Those who had served in Batista's army, whose families had owned large tracts of land, who had been educated in private schools or were in any way linked to the "old regime" were identified. May 1, heralded by a much-publicized announcement that the government would declare a state of socialism, was an occasion for national celebration of the victory with military parades and addresses by major government and PSP leaders. In the triumphant atmosphere of this climax, the next steps in the revolution could be announced.

While the crowds, brought together to hear May Day speeches, were guided into shouting such slogans as "we are with you, Fidel and Khrushchev," and "long live our socialist revolution," Castro limited his Havana May Day speech to a rather vague declaration of socialism and announcements of new government policies which were in line with the trends of the previous year: a new Socialist constitution would be drawn up to replace the outmoded 1940 Constitution; foreign priests would be expelled; private schools would be nationalized. Raúl Castro in Santiago de Cuba spoke of vesting power in the peasants and workers. Guevara spoke of the "first socialist revolution of Latin America" and outlined national economic needs and plans, pointing out the similarity between economic organization in Cuba and in socialist countries and the important assistance being given Cuba by Communist-bloc technicians in planning and effecting industrialization.

The declaration of socialism brought little actual change in policy. It made clear the regime's dependence on Communist-bloc economic assistance and its reliance on Communist models for economic structure and control of the population. The identification of the invasion with United States imperialism and of the invading troops as Batistianos served to consolidate support among Cubans fearing foreign intervention or the loss of privileges they had gained by supporting the government. Beyond this it was a means of obscuring still further the fine line between the government's and the party's verbal presentation of revolutionary doctrine.

An explicitly Communist analysis of Cuban socialism was presented by PSP executive secretary Aníbal Escalante, differing from that of others primarily in the more precise use of terms. According to Escalante, the revolution had completed the national liberation stage "defined" in May 1959 and, in May 1961 was entering the socialist stage as a decisive step on the road to Communism. The socialist stage was marked by the collective ownership of the instruments and fruits of production, a planned economy and the motto, "from each according to his ability, and to each according to his work." This was an essential transitional stage before the promise of Communism, "from each according to his ability, and to each according to his need," might be fulfilled. Maintaining that in Cuba it was outdated to espouse socialism without admitting that socialism is but a stage toward Communism, he concluded that the people now had a clear choice, and that choice lay between imperialism and Communism.

Government statements during May also indicated concern for the future. Delays in harvesting sugar cane continued to be a problem, and government leaders continually exhorted the people to increase productivity in all areas, to identify themselves more strongly with the government, and to renew revolutionary enthusiasm and vigilance. They reminded the people that additional sacrifice might be required of them, warning of continued imperialist conspiracy and of possible rationing of some consumer goods and attributing the second possibility to the first. A major campaign to expand the network of vigilance committees was begun, and official forms were announced to be available for the denunciation of counterrevolutionaries.

THE NEW SOCIETY

THE REGIME SOUGHT TO CONSOLIDATE popular support behind it by identifying the revolution of 1959 as closely as possible with the nineteenth-century nationalist movement. The Cuban people consider the decades immediately preceding the winning of their independence from Spain as the most glorious in their history and regard the philosophers and patriot-heroes of this period as the noblest men the country has produced. Revolutionary spokesmen therefore depicted their program of economic and social reform as the culmination of an idealistic tradition which dates back to José Martí and the War of Independence. Premier Castro himself regularly and freely drew on Martí's writings for his public addresses and, when he posed for photographs, there was often a picture or statue of Martí somewhere in the background.

The assertion that the revolution is building a new and different society was constantly affirmed. In this new society, it was said, economic and social reform would bring about a more equitable distribution of material goods, and the array of goods itself would be larger than ever before. Society would be imbued with a new and different morality, involving greater and deeper respect for the rights of the individual. All persons were to be enabled, not only to meet their material needs, but also to develop culturally and intellectually. "The day when the oligarchy of Cuban society was a cage of wild beasts fighting to divide the wealth of the people is gone" said a high government official early in 1961.

Cubans who attended public gatherings and listened to government radio broadcasts found themselves constantly urged toward work and sacrifice for the revolution. Its goals, they heard, could only be achieved by heroic labor. To a group of secondary schoolteachers, meeting in Havana in February 1961, Armando Hart, minister of education, said: "What we are founding here is a society in which we cooperate and unite to solve everybody's problems . . . all prejudices will be liquidated." President Dorticós told the same audience that "heroic labor can be performed in many ways—a life may be offered, blood may be shed freely, but lacking an opportunity to offer these sacrifices there are many other opportunities . . . of complying with your responsibilities and your work."

By early 1961, the government had nationalized the functions of the upper class. In the name of the people, it became the greatest *latifundista* ever known in Cuba. Most of the traditional, distinguishing marks of the old upper class were abolished. Manual labor was made respectable, and Cabinet ministers publicly indulged in it. Salaries were reduced, profits nationalized, and dividends confiscated; the possession of enough wealth for even a modest display of domestic luxury became grounds for impeachment. Even enemies of the regime admitted its honesty, although there was evidence that on the lower level officials used their positions to their own advantage in the traditional manner.

Many members of the middle class had been early supporters of Castro; but there was a growing disillusionment among them as it became apparent that they thought of the revolution as something less radical than he intended. As Castro said, in January 1961, "Those who wished to rebuild on the old foundations are desolate at the destruction we are causing." They expected that the basic social structure of the old regime would remain and that they as members of the socially-defined upper class, *hombres responsables,* would continue in their traditional paternalist role, running the country in the interests of the people but without direct popular participation. But in Castro's view, "revolution means the destruction of all privileges, it means profound and basic changes in society, or it would not be truly revolution . . . revolution is the power of the people, not of a privileged caste." After the forced resignation of President Urrutia (July 1959), Castro began to insist more and more on the need for the re-education of the older generation and the upper class to the new social morality of the revolution.

The merchants and small businessmen were seriously hurt by many of the economic measures of the regime, and as a new autocracy built a social order increasingly incompatible with their ideals, the middle class as a whole gradually turned against the revolution and sought refuge abroad. By December 1960 there were more than 30,000 refugees, largely from the upper and middle class, in Miami alone; 69 percent of the refugees were white-collar workers and professional people, although these groups amounted to only about 16 percent of the total labor force.

Organized labor, already well off under Batista, had little to gain from the revolution; but its leaders found themselves free to support only the views propounded by the regime. Their leadership also was challenged by self-appointed works committee representatives and those who, obtaining the support of the Ministry of Labor, had advanced themselves to managerial roles in intervened enterprises. The very poor, however, were promised immediate benefits in such matters as housing, social amenities, conditions of work, and above all were made to feel that their opinions and interests were of prime importance to the new regime. Progress in the fulfillment of these promises was more evident in rural than in urban districts. The construction of schools, new agricultural undertakings, roads, housing projects, and social centers did much to integrate rural communities into the national society. Crops were diversified to provide a better diet and employment all year round.

There seemed little likelihood that the material benefits to the lower class would ever be matched by the political benefits also promised. The increasing reliance of the regime on the slogans of class war and socialist unity was apparently intended to conceal the concentration of power in the hands of a small group of typical middle-sector politicians, including lawyers, university students, and labor leaders. The opportunities for political dissent and competition which had formerly existed were eliminated and competing middle-sector groups were forced into exile or compliance. After the initial period of chaotic change, in which a wide range of people had been able to advance themselves to higher social status, such mobility was increasingly limited to people prepared to accept Castro's leadership.

The new government patronage system extended to virtually the entire society. Competing personal loyalties were absorbed into a single loyalty to Fidel Castro. *Personalismo,* in the guise of Fidelismo, was explicitly proclaimed in 1960 as a more important justification of conduct than those embodied in the law, the constitution, or even in the early speeches of Fidel himself. Jealousy and antagonism toward competing groups were taken to extremes in the expulsion from their privileges as citizens of thousands who had failed to attach themselves to the new hierarchy of privilege; in the execution or imprisonment of hundreds who had openly expressed opposition; and in the violence of the government's renunciation of its ties with the western hemisphere.

The identification of the government with the interests of the lower classes presented a few problems to government theorists. The failure of much of urban and rural labor to aid the anti-Batista movement was attributed to ignorance of historical necessity and to false leaders who were traitors to their class. In any event the fulfillment of their historic roles by the revolutionary classes of peasants and workers, alternatively known as "the people," came in the "real" revolution which only began in 1959. Later expressions of opposition to the regime by persons who by definition were of the revolutionary classes, such as sabotage by men indisputably members of the electrical workers' union, caused the regime more serious ideological embarrassment; it could attribute them only to agents in the pay of fascists and imperialists.

The initial changes in administration were intended primarily to place persons who had taken part in the overthrow of Batista in positions of trust. Officers of the rebel army were given the key commands in the army, the police, and the provincial and municipal administration. With the abolition of all elective offices, political administration was centralized completely under the Cabinet and was carried out through provincial and municipal commissioners, the representatives of government ministries, the police and the army. As the positions of the less radical members of the Cabinet and their supporters became more and more precarious, the replacement of personnel continued and the division between the military and the civil government became increasingly obscure. The government, always highly personal, became still more so since each person placed in a post of authority brought with him his own lieutenants.

Although all ministries had been purged in the first months of the regime, subsequent purges were carried out in either preface or response to the adoption of new policies or the appointment of a new minister. Government officials who refrained from showing the proper degree of radicalism might be ignored, if their position was not one of particular importance, or they might hear their resignations, on grounds of health or other pressing responsibilities, announced over the radio, or they might receive a threatening phone call from the local militia. Individual journalists and radio commentators occasionally bragged that they had been the "first" to denounce some official subsequently dismissed by the government or frightened into exile.

Among the most important new structures within the government were those created to reorganize the national economy under government control. The Agrarian Reform Law, as implemented, created a new system of government for the rural population. The prohibition of large estates, contained in the 1940 Constitution, was renewed, but although some land was to be distributed to individuals in private title, sixty percent of all land was vested in the National Agrarian Reform Institute (INRA) to be administered through "cooperatives." Private owners could not transfer land without the consent of INRA and were expected to follow INRA exploitation policies; none could retain more than about 1,000 acres.

In the cities the chief problems were the economic strength of the upper class and the disparity between upper- and lower-class standards of living. Solutions for both were seen in the wholesale appropriation by the government of all major income-producing capital investments and the removal of the upper class from managerial responsibility.

The urban housing situation was critical. Housing construction had always been one of the most vigorous industries, but the upper class was the principal beneficiary; some wealthy families owned 2,000 or more houses. Much urban housing was in very bad condition, slums grew rapidly, and the supply of new housing was not nearly adequate to meet the growth of the urban population. In 1959, rents were reduced by 50 percent and for the first time a public housing program was set up. The National Institute of Savings and Loans (INAV), financed by government bond issues and the national lottery, was given responsibility for the development of urban housing. Mass production of simple modern units was begun. Payments were collected from the new tenants in place of rent and were applied toward the purchase price. New construction under the government's programs partly made up for the end of all private building. But even the rapid progress achieved by the end of 1960 was not adequate; an estimated 15,000 new houses yearly were needed to keep up with the anticipated urban growth. A margin of more than 5,000 new units a year was needed to replace substandard housing.

The Urban Reform Law, enacted in October 1960, was a far

more drastic measure. Under the slogan "every tenant an owner," the government proposed to make it possible for every family to live in a house or apartment that was in acceptable condition and to own the premises within twenty years; during that time the state would be, in effect, the nation's landlord. All tenants were to pay to the INAV a monthly sum equivalent to their former rent. After a number of years—from five to twenty depending on the age of the house—they would receive title to the property. A house built in 1946, for example, would be considered paid for in eight years. In compensation, the original owner of the house was to receive a monthly check from the state for the same amount as the tenant was contributing and for as long as these payments continued. But, under the arrangement, no one could collect a total of more than $600 monthly. After the payments had stopped, the state would pay pensions—again not more than $600—to people without other income. The law also decreed that the state would become the outright owner of tenement buildings, whose owners would receive no compensation. In government propaganda, landlords were represented as rejoicing at being relieved of taxes and upkeep expenses.

Still more effective in giving the government control over social as well as economic processes was the policy of intervention, which under Castro became the inevitable formula for the incorporation of every major undertaking into the nationalized economy. In late 1960, it was estimated that 80 percent of the labor force was employed directly or indirectly by the government. The upper class thus lost most of its entrepreneurial function. Intervention enlarged the role of INRA. The Department of Industrialization, headed by Guevara until he became president of the National Bank in November 1959, ran many of the enterprises taken over by the government and supervised the Petroleum Institute and the Institute of Mining. In early 1961, a government reorganization created new ministries which absorbed departments formerly within INRA. At the apex of economic control remained the Central Planning Council, a Cabinet committee established in February 1960 to coordinate the national economy; it was composed of the prime minister, the ministers of defense, finance, commerce, public works and economy, the president of the National Bank and the chief of INRA. The secretariat of the committee was responsible for economic planning, drawing up the national budget, and collecting statistics. INRA remained, but industrial administration was transferred to a new Ministry of Industry headed by Guevara. A new Ministry of Foreign Trade assumed control of all foreign trade. The Ministry of Commerce was abolished and a new Ministry of Internal Trade created to supervise all matters of internal distribution of goods and to manage state enterprises. Laws vesting in the Ministry of Labor control over the hiring or dismissal of workers completed the government machinery for control of the production and distribution of goods.

The police, although temporarily in a semichaotic state because of the nearly complete turnover in personnel, quickly developed into a reliable arm of government control. Although there was superficial reorganization, the structure remained much as it had been under Batista. The rural guard, the branch of police stationed in rural areas under army command, was dissolved and replaced by the "revolutionary rural police" under army command. New organizations within the police and the army were similarly formed to replace the military intelligence and secret police units dissolved in January 1959. The most powerful of the new groups was the Directorio de Investigaciones del Ejercito Rebelde—DIER—(the Department of Investigation of the Rebel Army).

New laws gradually legitimized the arbitrary exercise of police powers and subordinated the judiciary to political control. The revolutionary tribunals dissolved in May 1959 were reinstituted by constitutional amendment on October 28, 1959, after which they had permanent jurisdiction in any case in which the accused was considered counterrevolutionary. Crimes of counterrevolution, for which the death penalty might be imposed, were extended to include acts contributing to internal subversion or damaging to the national economy. Judicial reorganization had been carried out immediately after January 1959 when the Cabinet appointed a new Supreme Court. In a second reorganization in late 1960 most Supreme Court justices were dismissed, and their number was reduced from thirty-two to fifteen.

In the spring of 1959 the army was considered the only area of government in which PSP influence was significant. The theme of the revolutionary role of the army was stressed and the use of army personnel in government was encouraged, particularly in INRA. After November 1959 members of the Cabinet and officials of the CTC usually appeared in uniform. During 1960, however, the army was transformed into a more regular force. This appeared to be a reaction in part to loyalty problems; the resignation in October 1959 of Major Huber Matos, one of the most popular of the senior officers, and of several of his subordinates in Camagüey province, was considered so threatening that Castro denounced him at length on television, and he was tried and convicted of conspiracy. In July 1960, the soldiers were ordered to shave their beards as an indication of the transfer from "revolution" to "administration." It appeared that a strong political role for the army was no longer desired and that the much larger civilian militia, in which Communist personnel figured prominently through their demonstration of superior enthusiasm, was to be relied upon for preserving militant revolutionary zeal.

Although a few newspapers and radio stations had closed or had been confiscated with other property of Batistianos, the majority were taken over between October 1959 and July 1960, because they became insolvent, having lost advertising revenues; because they published something "which might tend to impair the independence of the nation or provoke the non-observance of the laws in force," a crime since July 1959; or because the workers of a particular institution chose to denounce the management. Typographers in several instances added their own editorial footnotes. An editorial in *Diario de la Marina* in January 1960, for example, carried a postscript saying that "the contents do not conform to the truth, nor to the most elemental journalistic ethics." All information media subsequently came under the direct control of the Ministry of the Treasury or the Ministry of Labor, or were sponsored by the labor federation, the Popular Socialist Party or the 26th of July Movement, and acted primarily as channels by which government policies could be explained fully to the people. The government supported the only domestic news agency, operated the radio and television networks, and was the sole important domestic producer of films and books. At the same time it exercised rigorous censorship over foreign information media and controlled the importation of books and periodicals.

As Castro said at a banquet honoring Carlos Franquí, editor-in-chief of *Revolución*:

> Newspapermen have a great task ahead . . . [they] must coordinate the news among all papers and orient public opinion jointly . . . always remember that the revolution comes before the newspaper . . . the campaign for its success depends on our effort. The reasons, the justice, the cause of the revolution must be printed. The formidable press service must form a strong revolutionary conscience.

In February 1961, only six general newspapers were being published daily in Havana, as compared with sixteen on January 1, 1959. Of these *Revolución, La Calle, El Combate, El Mundo,* and *Prensa Libre* were semiofficial newspapers. The sixth, *Noticias de Hoy,* organ of the PSP edited by Carlos Rafael Rodriguez, was second in circulation to *Revolución,* organ of the 26th of July Movement.

The government also encouraged a news agency, *Prensa Latina,* which began operations in May 1959. Organized by an Argentinian friend of Ché Guevara, Jorgé Ricardo Masetti, a veteran of Agencia Latina (Juan Peron's press agency from 1952 to 1954), *Prensa Latina* claimed to provide objectivity in a news world dominated by imperialistic interpretations. Its extensive activities in offices and radio outlets throughout Latin America suggested that the agency was subsidized by the Cuban government; although it claimed financial independence, it installed costly equipment in many bureaus and served clients whether or not they paid.

All associations rooted in the upper and middle class disappeared or, as in the case of the representative professional groups, were placed under government control. Well-educated and technically trained people were badly needed by the new regime but became increasingly scarce as doctors and lawyers fled to Miami and New York. Those who remained were organized to make declarations of support for Castro and to disqualify from professional practice persons guilty of counterrevolutionary activity (including emigration). It was at the professional level that the revolution clearly showed its debt to the younger generation, most of whom had been university students during the last years of Batista and had not had time to develop vested interests in the old order. With the nationalization of nearly all large enterprises, business associations faded into non-existence.

PSP domination of the CTC, obtained with government aid beginning in November 1959, gave the party a key weapon in urging or compelling action in the process of intervention and nationalization and gave the government assurance of labor peace. Union members could then be used in organizing the mass rallies and demonstrations of support for government policies desired by Castro as proof of his popular democracy or to demand some further action. A second transformation of the CTC occurred in early 1961 when it lost the function of representing labor.

In October 1959, the students' organization, the Federation of University Students (FEU), at the University of Havana was placed under two government-appointed leaders, Angel Quevedo and Rolando Cubela, army officers who organized student pressure on the government and represented government policy among the students. Between April and June 1960, there was public controversy within the University as student opposition to Communist influence was expressed by such means as a petition supporting a radio commentator under attack. Much of the opposition was led by students associated with Catholic Action groups. During May, controversy became heated over the appointment of PSP leader Carlos Rafael Rodríguez to the University faculty. In June and July 1960, the FEU forced the reorganization of the University governing council in one of the first major moves toward giving the PSP control of intellectual and professional associations. Late in June, FEU withdrew its representation from the University council in protest against the conservatism of the faculty members of the body. Then it demanded the resignation of the council. In July, a new "superior government junta" was appointed with full governing power within the University. This was followed by purges and new appointments within all faculties.

Purges of professional associations (*colegios*) also began early in July 1960 and continued through the year with announcements that various members had been dishonorably expelled; some of the expelled were already in exile. The usual technique was an accusation of some sort followed by the appointment of a new board of directors; often the board acted "in the capacity of a revolutionary tribunal." The "revolutionary board" of the Havana association of lawyers had expelled about sixty members by mid-July. With the backing of the regime, a medical Revolutionary party was organized within the central College of Medicine; once its candidates were placed on the National Executive Board they suspended the annual conventions of the medical profession and dissolved all other parties within the profession "for the sake of unity." Similar events occurred within the associations for journalists, radio announcers, public accountants, theater artists, and engineers.

The benefit societies had not been nationalized in late 1960, chiefly because the facilities they provided were entirely consistent with the needs of the regime and because they were not useful in the organization of opinion and morale. Their governing boards, however, were generally taken over by Castro followers. The Spanish element, with its nostalgic interest in the European homeland and its professional preoccupation with commerce and real

estate, suffered a setback in the general outburst of *criollo* sentiment and the program of nationalization.

Two types of new associations appeared. Ostensibly non-govern-
mental associations, known as the popular organizations, were the
remains of revolutionary groups and the transformed associations,
together sometimes referred to as the Union of Civil and Revolutionary Organizations. The government directly organized the
civilian militia and "committees for the defense of the revolution"
to guard the country against subversion. The popular organizations
usually listed as demonstrating their support for government
policies, cheering foreign delegations, or pressuring the government
to take further revolutionary action were: the PSP; the CTC, which
appeared to have little other function left; the 26th of July Movement and the Revolutionary Directorate, both of which appeared
to be defunct except for the name and a few leaders to represent
them; the Federation of Cuban Women, formed in August 1960,
from several existing women's organizations, by the wives of Raúl
Castro, Núñez Jiménez, and Guevara; the National Front of Professional Men and Technicians, formed of the reorganized *colegios*
and similar organizations; and the Association of Young Rebels.
This paramilitary organization, formed in October 1960 of the
youth of the 26th of July Movement and the PSP Socialist Youth,
was open to all young people from the ages of fourteen to
twenty-five. A Union of Rebel Pioneers, for children seven to fourteen was also created to prepare for later membership in the
Young Rebels.

Most of the characteristic Cuban enthusiasm for joining associations was absorbed by the militia, with its schedule of weekend
and evening training. The militia, created in late 1959 and expanded
to 200,000 members during 1960, became the backbone of the new
social order as well as of the nation's military strength; through it
popular support for the regime was organized and popular education furthered. Peasants in rural districts, wearing as part of their
uniform the *guajiro's* straw hat, and workers from industrial plants
were formed into militia companies trained under the supervision of
Ernesto Guevara, chief economic and social planner of the regime
and head of the Department of Instruction of the Armed Forces
Ministry. Professional and trade associations formed support units,
such as the medical corps, which were gradually integrated with the
regular militia. In this way every important occupational group
was reconstituted as a branch of an armed Fidelista movement. By

joining the militia, men and women who had not fought in the revolution itself ("in the mountains") could actively associate themselves with the revolution's symbolic figure, an armed peasant or factory worker defending his right to build a better future. People who were unable to fill prestigious roles in the old order, including a noticeably high proportion of both Negroes and middle-aged women, could see themselves as members of a new elite.

Linked to the popular organizations (which were urged to cooperate with them) and to the civilian militia (with which they worked in each locality) were "defense committees" or "vigilance committees" organized for the specific purpose of ferreting out counterrevolutionaries. They apparently were first organized in the fall of 1960 after a speech in which Castro threatened that, if necessary, there would be spies in every block. They were organized within factories, cooperatives, schools and residential areas. At the time of the invasion of April 16, 1961, the lists of suspects turned in by defense committees appeared to be the basis on which an estimated 20,000 persons in Havana and at least 100,000 persons throughout the island were immediately imprisoned; the government subsequently lauded the work of the committees and announced their expansion.

Before 1959, various political leaders gained electoral support by promising to uphold Negro rights but subsequently failed to carry out these promises. The legislative initiative gradually fell to the Communists and to the Frente Civico contra la Discriminación Racial, sponsored by the CTC and incorporated in Batista's patronage system. Many Negroes resented leftwing efforts to capitalize on the issue, and pointed to progress made by the United States in racial matters as a commendable example. Others saw signs of a deliberate imperialist effort to weaken Cuba by depriving it of part of the resources of its population.

Castro asserted that freedom was native to Cuba and that American Negroes could see there an example of just social treatment. In the larger cities conspicuous desegregation was accomplished although the familiar patterns were to be observed in provincial towns in 1961. Increasing popular dissatisfaction with Castro included a measure of disillusionment on the part of Negroes. The intervention procedure, drawing Negro societies into the nexus of power, took away their right to express any corporate opinion except wholehearted approval of the regime. According to official propaganda, the revolution superseded the Negro societies, which were encouraged to wither away by administrative actions depriving them of their income and office space. At the same time the regime gave maximum publicity to the role of Juan Almeida, army chief of staff, as a Negro in the highest councils of government. But Almeida was widely regarded as a stooge and was in any case a mulatto. Blas Roca and some other leading Communists were also mulattos, separated by a certain traditional social distance from Negroes, but could hardly be regarded as stooges.

When Castro's rebellion was still confined to the mountains of Oriente province a number of clergy, Catholic and Protestant, were sufficiently in sympathy with his cause to serve as chaplains to his troops. When the revolution was won Church leaders were prepared to accept the initial reform program, whose main features were matters of long-standing general agreement. Nationalist resentment against the Church was modified by the knowledge of assistance given to Fidel personally by Archbishop Pérez Serantes of Santiago de Cuba.

The Roman Catholic Church

Official Catholic denunciation of Communism was renewed in 1959, however, when the Communists became the only political party allowed to operate by the new regime. Such denunciation rapidly came to be considered by the regime the equivalent of counterrevolutionary activity, and the Church found itself the center of the growing urban opposition to the new regime's policies. Government propaganda indiscriminately labeled Catholics and former followers of Batista as reactionaries. Past histories of alleged ecclesiastical tyranny in Cuba and elsewhere were revived; the existence of a conspiracy between the Catholic Church and the interests of imperialism and colonialism was reasserted. Even the question of Church properties was brought up; in 1961, as in 1902, it was proposed to deprive the Church of its valuable income-producing cemeteries in the cities.

Because of the age and infirmity of Cardinal Arteaga, Archbishop of Havana and Metropolitan of Cuba, the chief public spokesmen for the Church's views became Archbishop Pérez Serantes and Mgr. Boza Masvidal, head of Villanueva University. Since radio, television, and newspapers were controlled by the government, the pastoral letter was the principal means of expression used. (Catholic radio and television programs were closed in September

1960.) The reading of such letters in churches was a frequent occasion of demonstrations and the singing of revolutionary songs in the churches and outside. At the end of 1960 a few small Catholic periodicals such as *La Quincena* were still being published; *La Quincena* gave generous space to articles on unsatisfactory conditions inside Russia, for example, and to statements of the Catholic position on social problems, but guardedly supported the basic principles of reform. It was suppressed in early 1961.

Government propaganda directed against the Church harped on the association of the Church in Spain with Franco; "Falangist priest" became a standard abusive phrase. Distinctions were made between the hierarchy, "under orders from Franco to refuse to cooperate with the Cuban people," and "true Christians," defined as those who supported Castro. The government position was supported by a laymen's organization, For Cross and Country, which demonstrated against the hierarchy and in favor of the regime, and by a number of Catholic clergy, said to be Basque refugees from Spain belonging to the Franciscan order, some of whom made public speeches in favor of Castro and of socialist policies.

The moral alternative explicitly offered by the government (in February 1961) was not Communism as such but a nationalist rationalism which echoed the utterances of José Martí. The accidental death of three militiamen, a Catholic, a Jew, and a Communist, provided Ernesto Guevara with an opportunity to point out that the three had sacrificed themselves to the ideals of a still higher morality. Martí himself was increasingly honored as a "patron saint" of true morality and of the best interests of the Cuban people, especially "humble" people. The dedication of cooperatives and other enterprises of the INRA to the memory of "martyrs" of the 1958 revolution drew a protest from a Catholic spokesman. Considerable attention was given to the creation of a legend of Camilo Cienfuegos, the highly popular Castro lieutenant who disappeared in mysterious circumstances in 1959. In 1960, on the anniversary of his death, flowers were cast into the sea (into which his plane was said to have crashed) and adulatory poems were featured prominently in the newspapers.

Much of the quasi-religious fervor attached to the revolution was spontaneous and not simply an invention of government propaganda. From an early date the resemblance of Castro and his bearded followers to Christ and the Apostles caught the popular imagination. Cheap colored prints of Fidel appeared beside those of the saints in humble homes; statuettes were hawked in the streets. Fidel was regarded as a patron, guardian, and guarantor of salvation in a sense that had both religious and secular overtones.

Christmas 1960 and New Year 1961 were special seasons of contrived moralistic outpourings in the Cuban press. Rationalist arguments appeared to the effect that Christmas was really a festival of rebirth far older than Christ and an appropriate time to celebrate the rebirth of Cuba. A nativity scene in Havana showed Fidel Castro, Guevara, and Almeida as the Three Wise Men; a popular song, "Todos Con Fidel" (Everybody with Fidel), was sung to the tune of "Jingle Bells."

By February 1961, government propaganda was ready to attribute every untoward event to a conspiracy between Catholics in Cuba and in the United States. When a volunteer teacher (a Negro) who had "dedicated himself to the priesthood of teaching" was executed by counterrevolutionaries, it was said that he had been killed by "cassocked thugs" with "money supplied by Uncle Sam with the blessing of Cardinal Spellman; for the fascist priests, to be a Negro is a crime and to be a teacher is to attack the basic precepts of the Church."

In a speech on May Day 1961, in which he announced for the first time the socialist character of his regime, Fidel Castro said that all foreign priests would be expelled, with the exception of those who had not displayed "an attitude opposed to the revolution."

Education and the Arts

In his many speeches before and after his rise to power, Castro followed the classical Cuban reformer's tradition of making educational reform a prerequisite of progress. But, whereas in 1898 and 1933 education was thought of as simply another benefit to be extended to the poor (along with an improved diet, better housing, and better working conditions), in 1959 Castro saw it primarily as the key to a complete reconstruction of society. In his view society had consisted, until 1958, of a privileged minority using education deliberately as a means of controlling the exploited masses. The rich relied chiefly on private schooling for their children and made certain that the few of the poor who received any education at all were taught to accept the existing state of society as right and just.

In the new Cuba the government assumed the role of re-educating a population. Almost every major effort of government was presented by Castro, expanded and interpreted by the supporting press and radio, and reduced to a slogan by which the people echoed in brief what they were told at length. The regime justified its every move, explaining any action expected to be popular as another step forward in the social revolution, presenting any action expected to arouse questioning as a reaction made necessary by counterrevolutionary conspiracy. Although the government sought to create a new system of national goals and values, its success in this could not be measured since only applause was allowed.

The educational tasks of the revolution, in addition to teaching children and illiterates to read and to be better farmers, mechanics, or accountants, were to teach history, economics, and politics to the younger generation so that they would understand their rightful place in a future Cuba and also to re-educate older people whose understanding had been distorted by the corrupt society in which they had lived. In January 1961, at the beginning of the Year of Education, Castro said:

> There are some men who are genuine sons of the past, products of the past . . . influenced by the privileged minority because the minority was educated, had political power, monopolized all means of culture, and propagated its own ideas. . . . Sometimes a large part of the mass does not understand the revolution, as for example, the case of the servant of an expropriated estate who demanded to know why his boss's land had been taken away even though he was a good man.

The regime's extreme emphasis on youth as the hope of Cuba was based on Castro's conviction that hardly anyone over the age of thirty-five could ever be re-educated to "understand the revolution."

Revolutionary education became a complex undertaking of which the school system was only a part. At the highest level Castro himself, President Osvaldo Dorticós, and, to a lesser extent, Raúl Castro, Ernesto Guevara, and others all became teachers, patiently expounding economics and history to mass audiences. At the opposite extreme thousands of scarcely literate secondary-school graduates were sent out to live with peasant families, to teach them to read, to help with the harvest, and to consolidate understanding of the revolution among the poorest and formerly least privileged of the people. In this process, however, the teacher was himself a pupil because his own bourgeois urban background was still only partially cleansed of social anachronisms and intellectual vices. "The peasants," said Castro in May 1961, "will teach you the why of the revolution better than any book."

According to press reports a complete reorganization of the administrative machinery of the Ministry of Education took place. It appeared that administration was completely centralized in Havana under a board of technical advisers which in turn received its instructions from the Cabinet. The board formulated daily lesson plans for use in public and private schools and made no provision for local administrators and teachers to express their views.

A new agency within the Ministry of Education, known as the National Council of Culture, was formed in early 1961 to plan, direct, and guide all activities of a cultural nature sponsored by local, provincial, or national authorities. Among those named to the Council were a number of prominent persons with Communist backgrounds, including Carlos Franqui, Nicolás Guillén, and Alfredo Guevara. The Minister of Education, Armando Hart, was a party to Castro's unsuccessful Moncada assault in 1953. In the early months of 1961, the Year of Education, Hart went to Moscow to study Soviet education methods, for which he expressed admiration. During his absence Castro assumed the responsibilities of minister of education. The director-general of primary education, as of mid-1960, was Dulce María Escalona Almeida, a member of the PSP.

A new emphasis on science and technology was evident in the many plans for new vocational schools, to which wide publicity was given. New technological schools were proposed or started in Pinar del Río, Las Villas, Camagüey, Bayamo, and other cities. In early 1961, it was announced that farm schools were planned for rural youth, in which children would be boarded and given practical agricultural training on the land. One thousand Soviet youths were to lend assistance in setting up the farms, and a similar number of Cuban youths were to travel to the Soviet Union to study methods in the agricultural cooperatives there.

The government also laid much stress on physical education and established a Ministry of Physical Education in early 1961. Work was started on an elaborate stadium in Pinar del Río which included baseball, softball and track fields, a basketball floor, medical department, X-ray section, and laboratories. Similar units were planned for other cities. Czechoslovakian gymnasts were invited to help in getting physical education and sports programs underway.

Extensive publicity was given to the conversion of some of the army camps of the Batista regime to school use and to the construction of new educational centers for primary school students. Moncada fortress, site of Castro's abortive first attack in July 1953, became the Centro Escolar 26 de Julio. Camp Columbia was partially converted into an educational center in early 1960 and renamed Camp Libertad. Another school center in operation by mid-1960 was the Camilo Cienfuegos School Center in Oriente province, conceived as a means of providing schooling for thousands of children who lived in scattered and remote parts of the Sierra Maestra.

Revolutionary ideology and nationalism were increasingly important influences on curriculum and teaching methods. Textbooks written abroad could no longer be used; new lesson plans and textbooks, written by revolutionary writers and educators, were prepared. For example, a new geography of Cuba by Antonio Núñez Jiménez, director of the National Agrarian Reform Institute and one of Castro's closest associates, was already in use in secondary schools in 1959. A new primer taught that "a" stands for agrarian reform, "c" for cooperatives for the peasants. A lesson plan on "Friends and Enemies" cited the Soviet Union, China, and Communist countries as Cuba's greatest friends, imperialism as its greatest enemy.

For 1961, the Year of Education, the government set itself an ambitious goal: to become the first nation in the world with a totally literate population. The plan called for the mobilization of roughly 100,000 *alfabetizadores* (teachers of illiterates), most of whom would work in villages and remote mountainous regions teaching the country's illiterates, numbering possibly two million, to read and write. Some of the volunteers for the rural program would be drawn from secondary schools and others from the ranks of professional teachers. The majority, however, would be young men and women recently graduated from normal school. Schools were to be closed for an eight-month period beginning in April 1961 to allow student volunteers to participate in the campaign. The most difficult work was to be tackled by a nucleus of young teachers who were expected, not only to teach the three R's, but to serve as agricultural experts and community organizers in some of the most backward and isolated regions. To prepare them for this undertaking they were given a three-month course at an encampment at San Lorenzo in the Sierra Maestra in the summer of 1960. Obligatory for all normal school students who expected to qualify for teaching certificates, the course included daily military drill with rifles, long hikes in the mountains and lectures on revolutionary doctrine.

In accordance with promises made by Castro, there was vigorous activity in school construction from 1959 on, particularly in rural areas where the number of new one-room school buildings multiplied rapidly. In late 1960 the government claimed that the number built already totaled 10,000 and would soon reach 16,000. Much of the $90 million education budget was earmarked for school construction.

In 1959 and 1960 Ministry of Education officials denied intending to nationalize private schools, although they expressed the view that the improved public schools would fulfill all educational needs. Private schools were subject to curriculum and other decisions by a Board of Technical Advisors and to classroom visits by government monitors—usually militiawomen—just as were public schools. Government regulations did not prohibit religious training, which is a right guaranteed in the Fundamental Law.

As the Catholic Church increasingly assumed the task of expressing opposition to the government's methods, denunciations of private schooling—most of which was given by Catholic organizations—were intensified. The "cassocked thugs," who were accused of fomenting armed counterrevolutionary activity, were also accused of poisoning the minds of a section of the country's youth in the interests of the expropriated and exiled upper class. The private schools, the Colegio Belén and the University of Villanueva, were in fact centers of counterrevolutionary feeling expressed in student strikes and other demonstrations. In his May Day speech in 1961 Castro announced that the private schools would be nationalized. He indicated that this would not apply to "a little school where one teacher gives classes, but private schools with several teachers." In the case of private schools that had not displayed counterrevolutionary conduct, he promised that the government would indemnify the owners or directors and invite the staff to participate in the national education campaign. On religious instruction Castro said, "The churches can remain open; religion can be taught there."

The regime spent large sums and considerable effort "to make Cuban culture the property of the people, rather than the possession of the few." In early 1961 it supported three orchestras, a national theater, and two dance troupes and had given numerous scholarships and grants to artists, composers, and writers. Until 1959, most intellectual and artistic activity was concentrated in Havana, but the Havana Symphony and other groups sponsored by the government toured the provinces. In addition, many attractions from the Sino-Soviet bloc, such as the Peking Opera and the Georgian Dancers, toured the country. The regime printed and distributed thousands of paperbound books that sold for 25 cents. Although many were propagandistic, the titles included Cuban classics and *Don Quixote, Robinson Crusoe, Marco Polo,* and biographies of Martí and Simón Bolívar. Sales of *The Tale of the Shark and the Sardines,* a political attack on the United States by Juan José Arevalo, former president of Guatemala, set a national record.

Until January 1, 1961, cultural activities were under the direction of the Marxist poet, Nicolás Guillén, who was head of the Cultural Department of the Ministry of Education. Early in 1961 the Department was enlarged to a four-member Council of Culture, including Guillén. The regime redefined the role of the intellectual. As before, intellectuals—professors, poets, painters, and government officials—were responsible for defining and describing the values of society with the clarity and profundity their talent made possible. Their audience, however, was no longer to be the privileged few, but the entire nation, including the lowliest peasant who, for the first time, would be able to read and write. The intellectual's function was to be not, as in former times, his privilege but his obligation to the common good. As before, but on an appropriately larger scale, the government would subsidize his work.

The compulsory identification of the intellectual's interests with those of the workers and peasants meant that he was no longer guaranteed membership in a social elite insulated by conscious cultural artificiality. For the first time a genuine pragmatism was upheld as the intellectual ideal, in conformity with Castro's assertion of the primacy of economic facts over philosophy. In the new scale of values proclaimed by the regime, economics, the physical sciences, industrial engineering, and community studies carried as much prestige as letters, law, architecture, and metaphysics.

Whether the new values would successfully replace the traditional ones remained undetermined. There was a marked shortage of intellectuals and even of educated persons, many thousands having emigrated since 1959. But the literacy campaign was being vigorously pressed, university courses were speeded up, and already, Castro reported, several peasants had written plays.

This means the peasants are no longer lagging behind. Satisfied in their basic aspirations, they are taking an interest in culture. This has encouraged the government to prepare to send out 3,000 music, drama, and dancing instructors to the cooperatives. In a couple of years, with the schools that will soon begin operating, we can send three instructors to every cooperative and people's farm; each can have its artistic group. The day will come when any city family can go to the interior on a Sunday and spend the day happily among the peasants, enjoying magnificent plays or dances. The peasant has a virgin mentality, free of a series of influences that have poisoned the intelligence of the people in the cities. The revolution is working with these fertile intelligences, as it works with the land.

NATIONALIZING THE ECONOMY

THE INTRODUCTION OF ECONOMIC AND SOCIAL REFORMS by the Castro regime led to dislocation amounting in some spheres to chaos. The chief social intention of the new program during the first two years was to remove every economic basis—in pay scales, housing, and what the regime comprehensively labeled "privilege"—for the class distinction between managers and manual workers. The only corporate economic interests implicitly recognized by the government were those of the "humble," meaning farmers and wage-workers, and of the "modest," meaning those who controlled a small capital investment but employed little or no wage labor. Larger enterprises, Cuban and foreign-owned, were nationalized, but the principle of private property was not itself attacked. To own one's own home and, if a farmer, one's own land, was upheld as an ideal of the new order. Small businessmen were repeatedly assured that nationalized undertakings were not to compete with them. In practice, however, it had become increasingly difficult even by 1960 for the independent businessman to continue operations.

Accompanying the elimination of privilege was the government's program for economic development. Far from depending upon individual initiative, the government assumed responsibility for all investment. The program required close central supervision of financial, monetary, and trading institutions in order to restore an economy crippled by the excesses of the Batista government as well as by subsequent nationalization of foreign firms and by the virtual end of trade relations with the United States. The government removed all private and independent influence on the economy and enforced an austerity program designed to counteract inflation and to husband the nation's limited capital resources. Businessmen could no longer obtain credit except for approved purposes; imports were severely restricted and exports were controlled by the government; labor demands were stifled and increased production constantly promoted.

The most important new structures within the government were those created to reorganize the national economy under government control. With the establishment of the National Agrarian Reform Institute (Instituto Nacional de Reforma Agraria—INRA), this body became responsible for the administration of most foreign and domestic enterprises as they were confiscated, intervened, or nationalized. Decisions regarding economic development were made within the Central Planning Council, in which the chief figure was Ernesto Guevara. Institutional changes culminated in a sweeping reorganization of ministries in early 1961. With tight central control, foreign aid from Communist-bloc countries, and the great productive potential of the economy, the government was able to avoid the economic collapse which was daily expected by its enemies.

By the end of 1960, trade with the United States had been very sharply reduced, but the dependence of the economy on foreign trade and its susceptibility to foreign influence were not ended, since the Communist-bloc assumed the role formerly played by the United States. As a market not only for sugar but for other exports developed by the expanding economy, the Communist-bloc did not offer the advantages available in the United States.

In July 1960, the United States eliminated the remainder of the Cuban sugar quota for that year and in October imposed an embargo on all exports to Cuba except unsubsidized foodstuffs, medicines, and medical supplies. The embargo virtually ended trade between the two countries, even in foodstuffs, since, in order to import unsubsidized foodstuffs, Cuba had to pay an additional amount representing the United States price support. Rice, wheat, soybeans, and maize could, under these circumstances, be bought more cheaply elsewhere. The elimination of the sugar quota, moreover, led to an acute shortage of dollars. The United States tightened controls even further in March 1961.

Trade with some European countries declined because of their reduced imports of sugar, but Cuba concluded trade agreements with Sweden, Denmark, Canada, Japan, and other non-Communist countries eager to expand their foreign trade. The government particularly encouraged trade with Canada. When foreign banks were nationalized at the end of 1960, only Canadian banks received some compensation. As Canadian officials pointed out, however, the predominance of trade with the Communist bloc would leave Cuba too short of dollars to allow financing of the quantities of Canadian imports planned.

Trade with the Communist bloc rose sharply as the government sought to fill the void left by the United States. It was estimated, for example, that about half of Cuba's trade in 1961 would be with the Soviet Union alone. In June 1960, discussions with China led to the purchase of 500,000 tons of the remainder of the 1960 sugar crop; because China was considered a new market, this sale was not included in Cuba's world sugar quota. The 700,000 tons rejected by the United States in July was purchased by the Soviet Union. The International Sugar Council at first maintained this amount would have to figure as part of Cuba's world market quota, but late in July it allowed Cuba this tonnage in addition to its world market quota and made it clear the council would not be too concerned should Cuba exceed its world quota in disposing of the sugar normally taken by the United States. A number of trade agreements were concluded with other Communist countries in the last half of 1960 and at the beginning of 1961.

Early in their relationship with the Communist bloc, officials encountered many difficulties, among them that of convincing the Communists of the need to raise the standard of living in Cuba. After a tour of the Communist bloc, undertaken to draw up trade agreements, Ernesto Guevara, chief economic figure of the regime, complained about a certain "lack of civilization" among his hosts, and the difficulty of convincing them of Cuba's need to manufacture toilets, ranked by the regime as "essential goods." It is doubtful whether the purchase of 3,000 artificial flies from Poland, 23,000 bamboo fishing poles from China, and 2,500 fiberglass fishing rods from East Germany for the newly established fishing cooperatives appeared to Cuba's new friends as essential for economic development.

In January 1961, the government announced that the Communist-bloc nations had agreed to a multilateral aid and trade program involving the purchase of four million tons of sugar and other goods in 1961 in return for assistance for the economic development program. Guided by political rather than economic considerations, the Communist nations could extend sizable credits and import larger quantities of sugar than nations whose criteria were more purely economic. Exports from non-Communist countries, therefore, were limited by the extent of the credit they were willing to offer.

The purchase of entire factories from the Communist bloc and the conversion of existing industry to spare parts and raw materials from Communist countries ensured a long period of dependence on these countries as a source of supply. It was questionable, however, whether the new trade arrangements would prove flexible enough to permit Cuba to widen markets for new non-sugar exports as economic development proceeded.

The shift in trade aggravated the balance of payments difficulties already conditioned by the excesses of the Batista regime and by low world prices for sugar. The worst year was 1959: the disruption caused by the revolution threatened sugar production, and exports were about 14 percent below the 1958 figure. A carry-over into 1960 of about 1.5 million metric tons forced the government to reduce its 1960 production. The customary inflow of foreign capital and tourist receipts declined, as did the reserves of disposable foreign exchange.

Despite the loss of the United States quota, sugar exports were larger in 1960 than in the previous year, mainly because of sales to China, the Soviet Union, and other Communist countries. However, the government still had a large sugar surplus, and revenues did not increase in proportion with exports because of the discrepancy between the high United States quota price and the world market price (although officials claimed that imports from the Communist bloc were much cheaper than from the United States and more than offset the lower sugar prices). Moreover, the growing practice of conducting foreign trade through barter, credit, and non-convertible currencies did not add substantially to the foreign exchange reserves. A fairly accurate guide to the difficulties encountered in disposing of the sugar crop is revealed in the proportion of alcohol made from molasses required by the government in domestic gasoline blends; the proportion rose from 18 to 20 percent in 1959 to 25 percent in December 1960.

The probable future market for sugar was not promising, but it appeared that the government was assured of an immediate market for most of its production. Communist-bloc countries agreed in 1961 to take four million tons at the high price of four cents a pound, the Soviet Union alone taking 2.7 million tons. In the world market, on the other hand, prices had fallen because of increased European sugar production, prospects that the Soviet Union might resell some of its sugar bought from Cuba, and higher production by countries anxious to take part of the United States quota lost by Cuba. Although the government could probably sell from 1.5 to 2 million tons on the world market, it could do so only by a sacrificial cut in price to 2.5 cents a pound, thereby undercutting marginal producers such as Brazil.

The balance of payments problems and the difficulties met in marketing sugar forced the government from the beginning to impose a series of controls over foreign transactions in order to preserve scarce exchange for import needs. Shortly after the government came into power, import licenses became mandatory for a long list of items, especially luxury goods. Exporters were obliged to turn in all dollar earnings to the National Bank in exchange for pesos, and American-owned sugar mills—until their nationalization following the 1960 harvest—were required to obtain credit abroad instead of from local banks. After December 1960, import licenses were issued only for essential items. Prohibitive tariffs were placed on luxury goods. The amount of foreign exchange tourists could take out of the country was reduced from $500 a year to $150. Family and business remittances abroad were first limited to $150 a month and then, in September 1960, to $100 a month.

These measures were supplemented by new government import policies. In late 1959, private trading in many food commodities was prohibited. Government agencies imported maize, chick peas, potatoes, eggs, and beans and sold them directly to state-owned People's Stores. The trend toward a virtual government monopoly over foreign trade reached a climax in April 1960 with the creation of the Bank for the Foreign Trade of Cuba. In July the Bank became virtually the sole importer and also handled important exports such as sugar, tobacco, and coffee. Private banks were deprived of decisions in transactions involving foreign exchange. In February 1961, the Bank was dissolved and its functions were transferred to a new Ministry of Foreign Trade, empowered to make commercial agreements, to control all exports and imports, and to manage all foreign exchange transactions and licensing formerly handled by the National Bank.

Agrarian Reform

The Agrarian Reform Act of May 17, 1959 contained the basic provisions of the government's agrarian program. The first and chief clause, the one most affecting the land system, declared that all large estates were to be abolished, that the maximum area of land in the possession of a natural or juridical person was to be thirty *caballerías* (995 acres), and that any land in excess of this amount was to be placed under cooperative management or distributed among landless peasants and agricultural workers. The significance of this measure may be judged by the fact that estates over 1,200 acres comprised about half of the total farm area. Exceptions were made for unusually active farms which, in production of sugar, livestock, rice, or other crops, met quotas established by INRA.

Sharecropping contracts were prohibited. Landowners were obliged to work their land, and absentee ownership was forbidden. All sugar plantations, after one year from the passage of the Act, were prohibited from operating as joint-stock companies unless the shares were registered, Cuban-owned, and held by persons not engaged in sugar manufacture. Rural property could be held only by Cuban citizens. Expropriated lands were to be distributed to peasants on the basis of a "vital minimum" of 66 acres per family of five. INRA could increase this amount according to such variable factors as fertility of the soil or need for irrigation.

Renters, subrenters, and sharecroppers were entitled to the land they previously cultivated provided it did not exceed the vital minimum. Owners of land below the vital minimum size were entitled to supplementary land. Awards of land were free, according to the following priority: peasants who had been evicted from the lands they cultivated; peasants, either landless or possessing land below the vital minimum, who resided in the district of an expropriated estate; agricultural workers working and living on the lands subject to expropriation; landless peasants of neighboring districts; agricultural workers of neighboring districts; others making an application for land. All owners of land in excess of the amount established by law were required to register their land with the INRA authorities or face expropriation without indemnification. For those who cooperated, indemnity, based on the assessed valuation of land and buildings, was to be paid in Cuban Republic Bonds bearing 4.5 percent interest and redeemable in twenty years.

To implement the law, agrarian development zones were established, each of which encompassed several *municipios*. The zones were to form the basis of regional agricultural development based on considerations of population, hydrology, soils, communications, and the like. Each zone was to have state aid centers with agricultural machinery, experimental stations, supply depots, and welfare establishments.

INRA was designated to carry out the reform program. Run largely by army personnel, it was headed by a chairman and an executive director appointed by the Council of Ministers; in 1960 these posts were held by Fidel Castro and Antonio Núñez Jiménez respectively. INRA's main functions, besides supervising all facets of agricultural production, were to determine tariff protection policies for agriculture, to supervise rural housing, health, and education, to direct distribution of land, to organize state aid stations, to compile administrative regulations for each agricultural zone, and to organize and supervise cooperatives. INRA established an agricultural production credit department and was responsible for drawing up its own budget.

By 1960 INRA had formed over 1,400 cooperatives, including 500 large state farms (granjas del pueblo). The state farms, using land taken over from large private estates, were mostly cattle-breeding enterprises; a few were devoted to breeding hogs, goats, chickens, and ducks. The land, equipment, and capital of the state farms were all state-owned, and all profits accrued to the government. Workers were furnished free housing and services and were paid a yearly wage.

Most of the large sugar estates had not been immediately intervened, in order to protect the 1960 harvest. By the end of the year, however, about 160 centrales had been nationalized and 600 sugarcane cooperatives formed. INRA worked toward preserving the sugar estates under cooperative enterprise rather than dividing them into small holdings, feeling that their productive capacity would be impaired if they were split into smaller units. In other sectors, however, small farming units were encouraged.

The creation of cooperatives (their exact number was not known even by the government) was perhaps the most successful phase of agrarian reform. Despite a great deal of administrative confusion, member workers and laborers were better paid and better housed, and agricultural production generally increased. Cooperatives, like the state farms, were managed by state-appointed managers who, so long as they followed INRA directives on acreages cultivated and types of crops planted, were allowed local organizational latitude. Almost all sugar cooperatives devoted part of their land to livestock and to supplementary crops. According to government statements, members of a typical cooperative received a daily wage of $2.50

plus a share of the profits. Day laborers hired by the cooperatives received only $2.67 daily. Members, previously landless and living in scattered *bohíos*, were aided by state funds and technicians in the construction of their own dwellings, schools, and community buildings.

Ownership of the land and capital of some cooperatives, like those in sugar, seemed to be vested in INRA. In some sectors, however, particularly tobacco, some farmers received individual title to their land and then banded together to form a cooperative. Generally the government did not encourage this type of association among small landowners, because, according to a statement of Castro in March 1961, it wanted to avoid the appearance of promoting cooperatives to the detriment of the small farmers. According to Castro "small farmers are allowed to join cooperatives only if they insist on it strongly and the entire group is willing."

The small landholder was encouraged to work his land independently. Within the limits imposed by the Agrarian Reform Law, he received title to the land he previously had worked and thus was relieved from paying rent. In May 1961, the government claimed to have distributed over 21,000 property titles to farmers. The new owners were subject to direction from INRA. State inspectors were sent to remote rural districts to assess credit needs of individual farmers. A National Association of Small Farmers, consisting of ranchers, coffee growers, sugar growers, and so forth, with five *caballerías* or less, was formed and endowed with a $35 million credit designed to aid 80,000 small farmers.

While the agrarian reform program initially caused inevitable dislocation in the economy, outside observers generally conceded that the over-all effect had been to increase production and improve the lot of many peasants. Production of paddy rice, a staple in the diet, increased about 30 percent; tobacco production increased about 15 percent; and beef a little less. Sugar production changed little because of the difficulty in securing sugar markets. In an attempt to lessen dependence on imports, priority status was given the cultivation of rice, corn, peanuts, cotton, and beans. By March 1960 newly cultivated land, much of which had been overgrown with *marabú*, amounted to 250,000 acres. Eventually, 13.25 million acres or 60 percent of the total farm land was to be redistributed under the Agrarian Reform Act.

Progress in agricultural production seemed inevitable, given any reasonable effort to improve it. Many economists had pointed to the

gross underproduction that had characterized the economy before
the revolution. It was difficult to judge the success of the agrarian
reform program in terms of statistics, many of which were unavailable to the government itself. The diversification program,
however, had made some progress despite administrative and
financial chaos and staff shortages.

Industry

There were many indications that industry suffered far more
disruption than agriculture. By the end of 1960, Castro had nationalized virtually all big business enterprises, sometimes retaining
the managers if they were willing to cooperate, but more often
replacing them by young, inexperienced militiamen. All foreign and
Cuban enterprises of any importance were nationalized by the
decrees of July and October 1960. Of the American companies,
194 subsidiaries and affiliates were placed under state control and
ownership: in August, the petroleum, sugar, telephone, and electric
companies; in September, United States banks; in October, the remaining United States enterprises as well as other foreign firms.
The seizures were not unexpected, since a number of enterprises
had already been taken over or intervened. The total value of the
American assets amounted to about $1 billion. Declaring itself
incapable of immediately compensating for the seizures, the government stated it would issue twenty-year bonds bearing 4.5 percent
interest. The bonds were to be based on the assessed valuation of
the properties as revealed on the tax rolls. As of 1961 the government had shown no indication of issuing any such bonds, even had
foreign businessmen been willing to accept them.

After the property seizures of 1959 the government declared that
70 to 75 percent of productive enterprises were owned by the state.
The numerous small industries remaining in private hands accounted for an extremely small share of industrial capacity. The
nationalization program, undertaken with rapidity and nationalistic
fervor, left little time for a gradual adjustment to new conditions.
Many technicians and managers fled during 1959 and 1960, and
the inexperience of personnel holding key positions proved one of
the government's major difficulties. Factories often had to close
because certain raw materials basic to the operations, even though
available, had not been ordered. The call for everyone to join the
militia further aggravated the shortage of industrial labor, and the

government was finally obliged to exempt key management and technical personnel from militia duty.

The United States embargo caused shortages of parts and supplies, such as pig iron, rolled steel, aluminum ingots, and sulfur, and stalled industrial production. Agreements to supply these items were concluded with the Soviet Union and other Communist countries but some items such as specialized chemicals were not available. Technical difficulties in adapting materials from the Communist countries to American machines often caused breakdowns. Soviet tin plate, for example, was found to jam in Cuban canning machinery. Although many of these difficulties could be solved in time, there remained the incontrovertible fact that industry, geared to American products and standards of operation, would encounter serious difficulties in the shift to Communist suppliers.

The mining industry suffered a critical setback, despite the provision of Soviet technicians. The lack of sufficient qualified personnel to run complex mining operations, the lack of domestic outlets for mining products, and the lack of foreign markets remained very serious obstacles which could not be solved by government decree. By the end of 1960, all mining operations had virtually ceased. The Nicaro plant was closed. The Moa Bay nickel plant, supplier to a processing plant in New Orleans, could not market its output. Soviet technicians declared the new plant useless because it was designed to produce a nickel extract adapted only to the plant in the United States. Most of the manganese mines were closed, as was the large Matahambre copper mine in Pinar del Río, which had exhausted its principal ore vein.

Manufacturing industries fared better than mining, but many consumer goods formerly supplied by Cuban factories were in short supply during the first years of the new regime. Nevertheless, the government announced it had invested $19 million in seventeen new industries during 1960. The factories included food processing plants for cocoa and rice, feed plants, textile mills, and plants for producing utensils, tools, and wire. Emphasis was placed on the production of items formerly imported from the United States.

In February 1961, the government reorganized its ministries in an effort to effect better control of the economy. Out of this reorganization came a new Ministry of Industry headed by Ernesto Guevara, director of the National Bank of Cuba and chief architect of trade agreements with the Soviet Union and its satellites. The Ministry included under its authority departments dealing with mining, petroleum, sugar milling, and others formerly under INRA (which remained in control of agriculture). The new Ministry of Industry was designated to carry out a five-year development plan with the help of Communist technicians and equipment. The Chinese People's Republic alone was to contribute, in exchange for sugar, twenty-four new plants.

Domestic Trade

The pattern of domestic trade and the distribution of income within the economy were severely affected by the government's program. Real estate fortunes declined rapidly after all rents were reduced and properties nationalized, but wages had increased 15 to 20 percent by early 1960, and purchasing power increased despite subsequent wage freezes, new income taxes, and wage deductions for social security and ostensibly voluntary contributions to the government's development program. As domestic industries were intervened and later nationalized under recalcitrant managers or inexperienced militiamen, they failed to keep pace with consumer demands. Major shortages of consumer goods occurred, especially after the United States embargo and the government's efforts to conserve foreign exchange. Soap, razor blades, electrical appliances, motor vehicle and machinery parts, beer, and other consumer goods gradually disappeared from stores. As stocks declined, retail prices of imported goods rose about 30 percent. Initially, the higher prices were offset by a 50 percent reduction in rents, cuts in telephone and electricity rates, and by wage increases. Although a black market reportedly existed in the urban areas where scarce imported and domestic goods sold for exorbitant prices, the government effectively policed price controls on a widening list of goods. Reports of the arrest and prosecution of violators of price law appeared in the press in 1960 and 1961 with increasing frequency.

Merchants, especially those dependent on supplies from the United States, suffered great hardships. Many of them were placed in desperate straits by import licensing, high sales and transportation taxes, exchange controls on imports of nonessential items, and government control of credit. According to official statements, the government did not wish to destroy the small merchant in the cities. Initially, only large commercial houses and department stores were intervened and nationalized. As the program gained momentum, however, the government intervened some smaller establishments and took over the business of owners who fled the country. The government promised to maintain the price levels of nationalized urban stores so as not to undersell small businessmen. Revenues from nationalized stores went into the government coffer.

The commercial policy in rural areas was quite different. Imputing that many farmers had been exploited by merchants charging exorbitant prices, the government established some 2,000 People's Stores to be run by INRA at a low profit. They took over retail trade previously handled by rural shops and the company stores of the sugar mills. Goods were sold, at prices lower than those obtaining in the city, in exchange for either pesos or *vales* (credit vouchers) issued to cooperative members in lieu of money wages. By early 1961, most of the purchases were made with *vales*. Although the government did not state that it intended to eliminate independent rural merchants, the lower prices at People's Stores threatened to put them out of business. Thousands of small merchants continued to do business, however, despite stiff controls on prices of clothing, food, and other items in daily use.

Domestic wholesale trade also came increasingly under government control. INRA supervised all cattle slaughter and meat distribution, took over the buying and selling of potatoes, rice, and eggs, and purchased all coffee. Railroads and shipping became a government monopoly. It appeared that private merchants obtained only what was left of domestic production after the People's Stores and the nationalized department stores had been stocked. Terms under which goods were distributed from the factory to the store shelf could not be determined, nor was it known whether all small independent farmers were obliged to sell farm produce (other than potatoes, rice, eggs, and coffee) to INRA or whether they were permitted to market their goods freely. In early 1961, the control of the state-owned retail stores and probably also the policing of price controls were transferred from INRA to the new Ministry of Internal Trade—a move which anticipated greater control.

Monetary and Financial Conditions

The Castro regime inherited a government with depleted funds and international reserves burdened by an immense debt. Considering the desperate financial situation in which it found itself early in 1959, and which it further aggravated by drastic economic changes, the government was very successful in avoiding the extremes of inflation. This success was achieved by imposing a program of austerity and exercising increasingly tight central control. Castro himself warned the population that they would have to learn to eat *malanga*, "bread of the poor."

Austerity and sacrifices, affecting to a greater or lesser degree all classes, were required not only to suppress inflationary pressure, but also to implement the regime's broad program for economic reform. The principal—and generally successful—methods were a direct tax program to foster public investment, and indoctrination of workers to promote production without higher wages. The development plans of the new regime were no longer limited by the complex of independent decisions by private individuals acting within a free enterprise system, which had slowed plans of previous governments. Taxes were collected efficiently, and dishonesty and graft were said to have been eliminated from government. Conservative banking policies of the earlier era were changed and various devices used to transfer savings into government hands. Lack of confidence in the future, which had so heavily influenced virtually all economic decisions, was remedied by making the government responsible for such decisions and enforcing them by every possible means.

But the plans set and the responsibilities assumed by the new regime were far greater than those of any previous government. Planned investment and the provision of social services such as programs for better housing, education, and health were much larger; through nationalization the government had become the largest employer but at the same time was compelled to stem unemployment through public spending; a sizable proportion of public revenues went to defend the regime against rebellion. The government did not have sufficient funds to meet these obligations. By the end of 1960 it was forced to rely on credit and on printing an increasing supply of money. Early in 1961 it undertook what appeared to be only the first of a series of radical, confiscatory measures to obtain private assets and savings. In spite of these measures, long-range plans for greater diversification and development of the economy remained largely on paper.

In 1959, the government collected a record $454 million in revenue. In 1960, the amount dropped to an estimated $400 million, but the need for revenues had increased as never before. In 1961, the government planned to spend more than $1 billion, half of which had to come from taxes or credit. Unlike previous governments, the new regime was manipulating the tax system and enforcing collections to cover planned spending. It appeared that, although credit continued to be necessary, a great effort was being made to draw out savings through tax increases.

The size of the revenues obtained in 1959 was derived partly from non-recurring items, such as the payment of back taxes and the seizure of assets of Batistianos, and partly from greater efficiency and honesty in the collection and payment of taxes. After 1959, when the prospect of a drop in funds arose, the tax system, originally revised in mid-1959, was changed and enlarged. The first reform in the tax code eliminated about 100 taxes and emphasized direct taxation. Enforcement was rigorous, and penalties for evasion were stiffened. Tax dodgers were required to pay past taxes.

Among the changes incorporated in the new tax code, put into effect in October 1959, was a straight 3 percent tax on all gross incomes, withheld by the employer every month without deductions of any kind; for the first time even the poor found themselves paying taxes. Personal income taxes were raised, although exemptions were almost doubled. Business profits taxes were raised, and the "guessed" taxes eliminated. Sales taxes were simplified.

The Agrarian Reform Laws obviated the need for a high tax on idle land. Before the law was put into effect, however, the government asked landowners to place a value on their land for tax purposes. Most owners, as in the past, placed a low valuation on their land; a high valuation would have been an admission of past tax evasion. As it turned out, compensation for expropriated land was based on the same low valuation.

The 1959 tax code was amended in August 1960. Among the new taxes were the "voluntary" contribution of 4 percent of wages designated for the industrialization fund, and the equivalent of a day's wage levied sporadically and set aside for the agrarian reform program or some other project. The employer was responsible for deducting these levies, along with the 3 percent tax, a 5 percent deduction for retirement pay, union dues, and the maternity tax; many employers complained about the additional paperwork required. After the first simplification, the tax system again tended to complexity. Tax rates on business earnings were increased, as were personal income taxes. Revenues from profits and income taxes had fallen—a result of nationalizing large private enterprises and lowering salaries of highly paid employees—and tax rates were raised to take a larger proportion of the yield of industrial, commercial, and distributive firms remaining in private hands. Most of these firms were small, however, and their profits relatively insignificant.

At the same time, the sales tax was abolished; later, in early 1961, customs duties and related taxes, many of which had been small and involved considerable paperwork, were annulled. These changes appeared to be merely the result of the centralization of imports and domestic trade under government control; since the government could set the prices, sales taxes were unnecessary. The government said it would not at present employ the Soviet practice of levying indirect taxes on products and increasing the tax yield by manipulating the price levels, but warned that it might eventually have to fall back on this method of raising revenues.

Non-tax revenues grew in importance. The yield from the lottery dropped because the government reduced the size of the prizes, earmarking most of the revenues for the construction of low-cost housing, and issued tickets in the form of "bonds." Other revenues, however, increased. The accumulated premiums exiles had paid into confiscated United States insurance companies were put, together with the assets of Batistianos, into the fund called the Recovery of Misappropriated Assets.

A major source of funds was the profit derived from nationalized firms (see Table 16). In some cases these companies had generous profit margins, estimated by the government to average 23 percent. The government hoped to increase this source of revenue by raising the efficiency of the companies; some factories were heavily overcapitalized and had operated below capacity because of labor costs or uncertain markets. On the other hand, such an increase in production, and in profits, would take a long time; meanwhile some companies were losing money and constituted a drain on government funds. The government also obtained revenue from urban land reform, rents, and agricultural enterprises. Revenues for 1961 were expected to reach a record high of over $1 billion. From the experience of the first two years, however, it was unlikely that this unrealistic estimate would be achieved.

In 1959, the regime spent $569 million and accumulated a deficit of $115 million. In 1960, expenditures amounted to an estimated $800 million—twice the revenues collected. The estimated budget for 1961 called for expenditures of a record $1.5 billion. Official commentators were quick to point out that administrative costs accounted for only 6 percent of the estimated 1961 budget, compared with 20 to 25 percent of the budgets before 1951. It was not clear how the administrative costs were defined. Although the sinecures which at one time were estimated at one-third of the payroll were abolished, the size of the payroll was subsequently enlarged.

There were some striking differences between the expenditure pattern of the new government and those of the previous regimes. Most apparent was the great sum, almost half the 1961 estimated budget, to be devoted to public investment (see Table 17). The second difference was in the size of the budget itself, which provided that almost twice as much was to be spent on education. Another difference was the low amount to be devoted to defense, which, according to the official estimate, averaged between $30 and $40 million pesos, compared with over $50 million in 1953-54. This low figure was effected partly by the use of the militia, partly by the exclusion of military spending from the budget.

Little was known of the government's developmental investment program. General plans called for an investment of 25 percent of the gross national product in 1961, compared with 12 percent in 1950, 15 percent in 1954, and 18.6 percent in 1957. The government announced a five-year economic development plan to begin in 1961, but the various aspects of the plan and the basis of allocating resources were not known. So numerous and varied were the tasks the new government set for itself that careful economic planning seemed disregarded as impossible or irrelevant. Earlier the government had concentrated on one-year crash programs—the Year of Agrarian Reform, the Year of Education. Industrialization was to begin in 1961; a considerable proportion of the new projects were to be financed through credit obtained from the Communist bloc.

The large deficits accumulated by the government, added to the enormous public debt and the obligations of the previous government, presented the regime with its most serious financial problem and threatened to slow some of its ambitious programs. The government seemed to be financing its large current deficits by encouraging the public to subscribe "voluntarily" to new bond issues; by obtaining credit from domestic sources and from the Communist bloc; and by increasing the money supply. The level of the public debt was not known.

During 1960 it became increasingly apparent that the government did not have the funds to honor its outstanding dollar obligations, including those inherited from the previous regime. The first defaulted were payments due in January 1961 for the interest and sinking fund on its dollar bonds. The government did not cancel the issues but refused to pay; the excuse given was that the United States bank acting as trustee had frozen the government's funds. The government did, however, begin in 1961 to redeem the peso bonds issued by previous governments.

Credits obtained from Communist-bloc countries amounted to some $245 million by May 1961, enough to constitute a sizable increase in the country's foreign debt. In addition, there were outstanding obligations, contracted by the government and by private traders, which the country could not honor from its very low holdings of dollars and gold.

By December 1959, the burden of the private commercial banks had become so great that many found themselves with reserves well below the legal requirements, a condition contrasting greatly with earlier years. Many had been forced to carry large sugar loans which were not liquidated because of reduced sugar exports; on top of these came new applications for the 1960 crop. Import regulations and the tightening of sales terms by foreign suppliers had further aggravated the banks' plight. Finally, there had been large withdrawals of private savings deposits, and the government, either to curb inflation or to discourage private capital investment, had raised the rediscount rate on all loans except those for production.

In September 1960, the government began the first seizures of private banks which culminated at the end of the year in the acquisition of the entire banking system. The first banks to be nationalized were the United States banks and the Bank of China. In October, all Cuban-owned banks were nationalized. In December, the last remaining banks, the Royal Bank of Canada and the Bank of Nova Scotia, were acquired by the government. These two foreign institutions escaped nationalization, and were apparently able to withdraw their capital stock. All nationalized banks became agencies of the National Bank which, in February 1961, was reorganized to assume responsibility for all financing of capital investment, for all long- and short-term credits, and for all international and domestic banking operations.

Nationalization of the banking system not only enabled the government to determine credit policies, but also placed the authorities in a position to obtain privately held dollar assets which the government badly needed. In early 1961, it ordered the confiscation of foreign currencies and securities held in safety deposit boxes and prohibited the use of these boxes after April 1961. The issue of new large-denomination peso notes invalidated the peso currency taken out of the country by exiles. The new moves hurt people, mainly of the middle-income group, who had over the years accumulated foreign assets as a safeguard against future emergencies.

Labor under Castro

The 1959 revolution gave the government effective control over the trade unions and made it the employer of an estimated 80 percent of the labor force. The government established the political and economic policies of the unions through the CTC and the Ministry of Labor; it exercised its role as employer mainly through INRA. Policy in the area of labor relations was designed to promote four goals: reduction of unemployment; increases in production, or at least maintenance of existing production levels; nationalization of private enterprises, largely through the process of intervention; and indoctrination of workers, through the unions, in the political, social, and economic goals of the revolution. Early in the revolution, it encouraged the correction of long-standing abuses, particularly in enterprises where labor had been weak. Later, it became increasingly concerned with production problems and inflation, and, through its control over unions, was able to stifle demands for higher wages and to obtain "voluntary" concessions from unions in the form of wage reductions, promises not to strike, and unpaid overtime.

The effect of intervention or nationalization on the workers' attitudes toward management varied. In some cases, the fact that workers were now employed by a government obviously committed to economic reform and progress erased their old attitudes toward management and led to a greater willingness to accept mechanization and other methods of increasing production. In other cases, nationalization produced disadvantages for workers, and they were unwilling to accept innovations that would destroy old privileges. The public transportation system in Havana, for example, had been operated by many owners, some of whom controlled only one route. Decentralized ownership had enabled the much better organized drivers and conductors to cheat their employers by pocketing part of the fares. The Castro regime nationalized the companies and merged them into one large enterprise. This action met with great hostility and during the Christmas season in 1960, the workers engaged in a slow-up; many called in sick, and bus service deteriorated.

It is not known to what extent the formation of sugar cooperatives altered the relationship between the mill management and the workers, or to what extent paternalism was replaced by worker initiative. Externally, the daily life of the sugar worker on the cooperative was as closely supervised as before. The "company store" was replaced by the "people's store"; payment of wages continued to be made in vouchers. The workers felt the influence of government policy through their union and the cooperative, and control was heightened by the grouping of workers into newly built communities.

Little was known of the means of settling workers' grievances at the shop or factory level and of the relationship between the union leader and the interventor or administrator of nationalized plants. Decrees governing the settlement of disputes followed one another with rapidity, and in the course of these changes, the activities of the union leader were limited to transmitting government propaganda. Grievances based on the abolition of past privileges or an unwillingness to follow policies were suppressed by the union. The workers were subject to indoctrination through the cooperative, the union, and possibly the workers' advisory committee. Potentially dangerous issues, including wages and hours, were, however, quickly forwarded to Havana for adjudication, and, toward the end of 1960, the regime was reportedly forced to accommodate localized unrest and pockets of resistance among organized workers.

Beginning in March 1960, following a reorganization and strengthening of the Ministry of Labor, several changes were made in the legal procedure for handling labor disputes. Conciliation by a "coordinator" appointed by the Ministry for all disputes of a social nature was made mandatory, and wages were apparently excluded as a matter for negotiation. In August 1960, a new decree was issued governing wages and industrial relations in enterprises wholly or partly owned by the state; most enterprises of any size were nationalized shortly after the decree was issued. The decree reaffirmed the practice of collective bargaining, but also empowered the government to fix wages. All agreements, moreover, were subject to approval by the Ministry. The law provided for the establishment of workers' Technical Advisory Councils in each enterprise to make recommendations on working conditions, methods of improving production, and the fixing of production norms. In January 1961, the Ministry called for meetings in all plants and factories to elect members to the Councils. The formation of these groups reflected the growing emphasis by the regime on increasing production and worker participation in governmental and semigovernmental organizations.

In April 1961, it was declared that all disputes in any business employing more than ten workers were to be heard in the first instance by committees made up of the workers themselves. It was improbable that disputes of any real importance, such as those dealing with wages, would be discussed. Two other groups were involved to some degree in labor relations at the local level: the Workers' Advisory Committees and the militia. After the Committees were established in January 1961, they quickly outweighed the union in importance; theoretically elected, they were in practice handpicked groups chosen for their willingness to follow government policy. One of their functions was to establish production norms; workers exceeding the norms were to be paid a bonus.

Considerable pressure was brought on workers to join the militia, with the implied threat that otherwise they would lose their jobs. Service in the militia, however, disrupted production and conceivably might offset the increased productivity for which the interventor was responsible. The existence of four people involved in labor relations at the shop level—the interventor, the union leader, the head of the advisory committee, and the militia leader—all with overlapping responsibility, was in one sense advantageous to the government: they all competed for favor, and they all could be used to promote central policy. On the other hand, it was possible that they all could join forces to safeguard their respective interests.

FOREIGN RELATIONS

CASTRO'S INITIAL POLICY STATEMENTS expressed his intention of honoring all Cuba's treaty obligations and remaining on good terms with all countries. His government was accordingly recognized by the United States and by all of Latin America within eight days of its accession.

Grounds for future difficulties, however, already existed—in particular, the belief of Castro and his supporters that the United States government had prolonged the revolution by supporting Batista and supplying him with arms. Great play was made in the Cuban press of bomb fragments marked with the handshake symbol of the mutual defense program. More generally, Castro's followers saw themselves as part of a continuous revolution against imperialism, beginning in the nineteenth century, but arrested by North American influence.

In the early weeks of 1959 there was no single official attitude on foreign affairs. That which gradually developed took into consideration both Cuba's economic and political interests and a series of ill-defined, emotionally-charged assumptions concerning future actions of the United States and the course of history in Latin America as a whole. By the end of 1960 these assumptions, fostered by direct Communist influence, had been fully integrated with current Communist doctrines on the worldwide progress of the anti-imperialist revolution. Foreign policy was further hardened by the regime's need of financial aid for which the Communist bloc appeared to be the only source. The climax of the trend came on May 1, 1961, when Castro described his regime as Socialist.

The unfavorable reaction to this description from many Latin American sympathizers with the revolution apparently prompted the government's vigorous efforts during May to disavow the implication of a Communist alliance and to associate itself with the cause of neutralism. Special diplomatic efforts were made to reach understandings with Brazil, Mexico, and the United Arab Republic. Cuba never held a strong bargaining position in international affairs, having always been in the position of a client among the nations of the world. After the establishment of the republic in 1902, the proximity of the United States and the value of the American domestic sugar market made the United States its principal patron. This dependence was intensified by a series of trading and fiscal agreements establishing and strengthening economic ties which lasted until 1960, by the explicit assertion of American political authority under the Platt Amendment from 1902 to 1934, and by the reliance placed on American influence by every Cuban government since 1902 unsure of its ability to retain power by manipulating internal forces. The foreign policy of the republic had accordingly been more a matter of organizing foreign influence, especially that of the United States, for use in internal politics than of pursuing a distinctive line abroad.

Since 1959 the government has established complex economic and political ties with the Soviet Union, China, and other Communist countries in an effort to assert its independence. It still remains a client among nations, however, dependent upon other countries for sugar outlets and for consumer goods; and it continues to exploit its relationships with other American countries, especially the United States, in an effort to strengthen its position at home.

Cuba and the United States (1933-1958)

After the abrogation of the Platt Amendment in mid-1934 and the arrangements made by President Roosevelt during the 1930's to restore the Cuban economy, the United States followed a policy of non-intervention in Cuban affairs, reiterated by each new ambassador. In practice the level of United States investments in Cuba, the volume of trade between the two countries, and the pervasive influence of American publications, opinions, and values were such that the United States, by simply failing to associate itself with internal forces tending to change, exerted a powerful conservative influence. It was strongly encouraged in this direction by the ruling political cliques and by American and Cuban businessmen who sought guarantees of political stability.

Although there was no major example of direct United States

intervention in Cuba during this period, the power to intervene did not lapse. According to Earl Smith, ambassador to Cuba from June 1957 to January 1959, "The United States, until the advent of Castro, was so overwhelmingly influential in Cuba that . . . the American ambassador was the second most important man in Cuba; sometimes even more important than the president." Many Cubans, aware of this influence, held the United States directly responsible for the actions of the Cuban government and accused it of intervention; others attacked it for not intervening to correct abuses.

The major concern of the United States in relation to Cuba, apart from the preservation of internal political stability, was the defense of the Western Hemisphere against foreign military and political attack. During World War II Cuba's strategic position in relation to the Latin American sea routes and the importance of Cuban exports to the United States war effort made it particularly important to incorporate the island in the continental defense scheme. Since the sympathies of a large number of Cubans of Spanish extraction lay with the Spanish Falange and, through the Franco government, with Nazi Germany, Cuba was also a base for German espionage activities directed against shipping in the Caribbean.

Cuba's entry into World War II in 1941 afforded the United States naval bases for antisubmarine patrols and the cooperation of the Cuban government against espionage. It also ensured that Cuban sugar was not sold to Germany. The army was mobilized but, although many Cubans served in United States forces, no Cuban units were sent overseas.

The war benefited Cuba considerably and President Batista still more. The United States bought the entire sugar crop and many of Cuba's normally unprofitable mineral deposits were exploited by Cuban and United States enterprises. As a result the economy rapidly completed its recovery from the prewar depression. Batista benefited from emergency powers enabling him to rule without reference to the legislature—some of these powers remained in force until 1959—and by cracking down on Falangist sympathizers, most of whom belonged to the old upper class, was able to strengthen the position of his own supporters.

After the end of World War II, the United States became increasingly concerned over the spread of Communist influence in Latin America, much of it channeled through the Soviet embassy in Havana. Like the Falange, the Communists were assisted by a well-organized movement within the island.

When Batista took over the government once again on March 10, 1952, during a period of social disturbance, it was essential for him to secure United States support. His first policy statements emphasized Cuban loyalty to the United States in any conflict that might arise with the Soviet Union. On March 21, two Soviet couriers were searched in Havana in violation of their diplomatic immunity. A week later the United States recognized the Batista regime. On April 3, the Soviet Union broke diplomatic relations.

The same year the United States and Cuba signed a Mutual Defense Assistance Agreement in accordance with the United States Mutual Security Act of 1951. Although ostensibly a purely military matter, this agreement, like those made with other Latin American countries, was intended to secure political cooperation and, by strengthening the position of the existing regime, to make Communist subversion more difficult. The Batista government gained approximately $1 million a year in military aid, and non-military grants from the United States to Cuba rose from $40,000 in 1950 to $176,000 in 1953 and $561,000 in 1958.

Cubans on both sides of the struggle between Batista and the opposition were eager to get American support and any public act by a United States government representative frequently was seized upon by both sides. In July 1957, Ambassador Smith witnessed the dispersal by the police in Santiago de Cuba of a parade of mourning women protesting the barbarities of Batista's forces (see Table 18). When, in response to persistent queries from the press he made an extremely cautious statement disapproving of police brutality, he was criticized by the Batista government for interfering in internal affairs, and Batista's opponents, including Castro forces, interpreted the statement as evidence of a new American attitude. Similarly the attendance of Secretary of State Dulles at a dinner at the Cuban embassy in Washington in November 1958, was treated as a sign of favor to Batista by both the government and the opposition.

Batista retained a United States citizen as public relations adviser and gave maximum publicity to events in which officials of the Cuban and United States military and diplomatic services participated jointly. Opposition representatives sought aid in Washington and pro-Castro pickets in New York and Washington publicized his cause. The rebel forces' sensational kidnapping in February 1958, of Juan Manuel Fangio, Argentine world champion racing driver, and in June 1958 of forty-seven United States servicemen and civilians from the Guantánamo base, attracted American public attention to the rebellion and to the fact that weapons made in the United States were being used by the Batista government.

In addition to the effort to influence public opinion and obtain diplomatic support, both sides needed arms. In March 1958 shipments of American military supplies to Cuba were stopped entirely. In July, however, Castro publicly complained of continued United States aid to Batista because 300 rocket warheads were shipped to replace a faulty consignment of the previous year. The cessation of arms shipments was a double blow to Batista, who needed both the weapons and the appearance of United States approval that the aid program provided. He complained frequently of United States government failure to prevent the smuggling from Florida of arms to the rebels. The sporadic efforts of United States authorities to prevent gunrunning to Castro forces—particularly the public arrest in Florida of ex-President Prío Socarrás—created a reserve of anti-American resentment among the opposition.

When in December 1958 the Batista regime was obviously tottering, several Cuban groups not affiliated with Castro sought to set up provisional governments. Their only hope was to obtain the backing of the United States which had already refused to recognize the puppet government of Rivero Aguero, a follower of Batista. Although American approval was also withheld from the proposed provisional governments on the ground that such approval would constitute intervention, the United States twice attempted to persuade Batista to retire in favor of a regime acceptable to the United States. Castro, however, had already, in August 1958, nominated Manuel Urrutia as president and after the flight of Batista on December 31, 1958, the new government was recognized by the United States on January 7, 1959.

Batista blamed the United States for undermining his position, and the Castro forces claimed that they had won despite the position of the United States. The first issue of *Bohemia* in January 1959 included an article heralding the departure of the United States ambassador, "Ambassador Smith: Servant of the Despot."

Cuba and Latin America (1933-1958)

International conferences of American states have met at intervals since 1889 when the International Union of American Republics was founded. The early years of the Union were also the years of the emergence of the United States as a world power, and the chief topic of discussion at these conferences was intervention, its definition and control. The United States through the Monroe Doctrine in 1823 had denied European powers the right to military intervention in the Western Hemisphere and President Theodore Roosevelt's reinterpretation of the doctrine in 1904 (the Roosevelt Corollary) reserved to the United States the function of an international police force in the area for the maintenance of order and the collection of debts. At first the Latin American republics welcomed United States protection, but later they claimed that the police power was used chiefly to assist expanding United States private investment.

Admittedly there was a need from time to time for some international machinery to settle disputes and to protect states from their neighbors and peoples from dictatorial regimes. The absence of language barriers in Latin America and the similarity of the economies, cultures, and social structures of the region made it easy for dissatisfied elements to make their way to neighboring countries and find support for intended revolts. The instability of Latin American governments made them vulnerable to small-scale insurrections encouraged from abroad and also motivated them to try to overthrow unfriendly neighboring governments. These alarms and excursions were always justified by appeals to justice and democracy.

At Pan-American conferences the principles of freedom, justice, and democracy were the basis for resolutions condemning intervention and deploring dictatorship—resolutions that were supported almost unanimously, even by republics which at the time were practicing dictatorship at home and intervention abroad. Cuban policy in Latin America, both before and after the overthrow of Batista, in this respect resembled that of several of the other republics.

In 1933, implementing the Good Neighbor Policy of President Franklin D. Roosevelt, the United States for the first time accepted the proposal that no Latin American state has the right to intervene in the affairs of any other. In 1938, at the Eighth Inter-American Conference, the delegates in effect reinterpreted the Monroe Doctrine to guarantee multilateral action against any aggression from outside the hemisphere. This resolution was implemented at succeeding meetings of foreign ministers in 1939, 1940, and 1942 to concert American action against Axis aggression. The 1940 conference, held in Havana, passed a resolution to the effect that any attack on an American state would be considered an attack against all and that collective countermeasures would be taken. This agreement was later strengthened by the Inter-American Treaty of Reciprocal Assistance (the Rio Treaty) signed at Rio de Janiero in 1947.

In 1948 the machinery of inter-American cooperation was entirely rebuilt at the Ninth International Conference of American States in Bogotá, Colombia, with the adoption of the Charter of the Organization of American States (OAS). The supreme organ of the OAS is the Inter-American Conference, normally convened every five years. The Pan-American Union is the permanent secretariat of the Organization.

Article 15 of the Charter states that:

> No state or group of states has the right to intervene, directly or indirectly, for any reason whatever, in the internal or external affairs of any other state. The foregoing principle prohibits not only armed forces but also any other form of interference or attempted threat against the personality of the state or against its political, economic, and cultural elements.

According to this definition it is possible to describe almost any act or even a failure to act as intervention. It was chiefly intended to limit the influence of the United States. Most of the Latin American republics have themselves been involved in charges of intervention and aggression since the signing of the Pact of Bogotá. Some of these incidents involved Cuba. In 1947 an assorted group of revolutionaries, including Castro, prepared an invasion of the Dominican Republic with initial, tacit support of the Cuban government headed by Grau San Martín. The Inter-American Peace Committee was convened in 1951 and 1956 to study Cuban charges against the Dominican Republic. In August 1958 Castro announced the headquarters of the government of the "Republic in Arms" as Venezuela and circulated copies of a "Caracas Pact" of anti-Batista groups. The Charter of the OAS requires that "all international disputes that may arise between American states shall be submitted to the peaceful procedures set forth in this charter before being referred to the Security Council of the United Nations."

The 1948 Conference also resolved to support the "essential freedoms and rights of the individual," but to several of the governments concerned, this emphasis on democracy was not so much a statement of internal policy as a reiteration of the principle of nonintervention directed against international Communism. This issue became increasingly important to the United States during the 1950's. At the Fourth Meeting of Foreign Ministers in 1951 and the Tenth Conference at Caracas, Venezuela, in 1954, resolutions were passed opposing intervention by international Communism. Most of the republics, however, regarded the danger of Communism as an internal matter for each state, not a justification for collective action by the OAS.

The Apparatus of Foreign Policy Under Castro

From the beginning the Castro regime displayed a calculated contempt for the usual conventions and institutions of international diplomacy, although from time to time it chose to make use of them. A basic premise of the regime was that the revolution of 1958 was the inevitable response of "the people" to an unjust situation imposed by the governing minority. As Raúl Castro said, "The revolution created a new type of diplomacy, a popular diplomacy."

The new government, describing itself as the agent of the popular will and therefore morally justified in all its courses, chose to define all problems of international relations in terms of a corresponding moral evaluation of the social and political situation existing in the countries with which Cuba had dealings. Governments favorable to Cuba were automatically described as representative of the popular will, motivated by just and rational impulses. Opposed governments were tyrannical agents of anachronistic economic monopolies and United States imperialism; in such cases Castro's government assumed the right to address itself to "the people," disregarding the legally constituted government and the normal restrictions of diplomatic activity.

The foreign minister, Dr. Raúl Roa, vigorously upheld Cuban interests at international assemblies, particularly those of the United Nations and the OAS. His chief concern was the public denunciation of the aggressive intentions of the United States. His accusations and appeals were presented in an excited tone consistent with the regime's melodramatic posture at home and abroad. Every event, even the refusal of the United Nations to entertain a Cuban complaint, was represented as a victory for Cuba and a demonstration of the cunning or the ineptitude of the United States. The Castro government's disregard for normal diplomatic procedure was complemented by Dr. Roa's personal disregard for conventional politeness which he saw in the context of international affairs as a hypocritical device to conceal political realities.

From early 1959 to early 1961 defections from the diplomatic service were frequent. Most of the defectors were well-educated, upper-class, professional men and women, usually lawyers, who became dissatisfied with the increasingly totalitarian character of a regime whose advent they had at first welcomed. A typical case was that of José Miró Cardona, a lawyer and first prime minister of the new government who, after his resignation in February 1959, was appointed ambassador to Spain. Following the rupture of diplomatic relations with Spain early in 1960, Miró Cardona was reassigned to the United States, but in July, before taking up his new post, he sought asylum and subsequently went into exile, later becoming the titular leader of anti-Castro forces in the United States.

On September 27, 1960, the Cabinet suspended for three years all legal provisions governing appointment and dismissal of foreign ministry personnel. Ambassadors would serve as before at the will of the president, all other personnel at the will of the minister. The Cabinet also authorized the establishment of an institute to train personnel within the ministry.

When relations with the United States were broken off in January 1961 many of the Washington embassy staff chose not to return to Cuba. The regime described all such defections as the revelation of the true color of opportunists and bribe-takers. Too many ambassadors, it was said, had been appointed for their diplomatic experience alone; in the future, younger men would be employed whose gift of revolutionary mentality would make up for their lack of experience.

In consonance with the people-to-people theme, much of the Castro government's representation abroad was carried on by organizations whose chief ostensible function was to represent popular opinion inside Cuba. The most important of these organizations was the Cuban Workers' Confederation (CTC), which organized the labor unions in conformity with official policy. The 1959 May Day celebrations of the CTC were attended by foreign representatives chiefly from Latin America. In 1960, after the CTC withdrew from the Inter-American Regional Organization of Labor (ORIT), the May Day celebrations were attended chiefly by Communist labor leaders, with Eastern Europe and Communist China strongly represented. CTC delegates from time to time attended similar gatherings in Prague, Moscow, Peiping, and elsewhere. CTC funds were reportedly used to assist leftwing unions in Latin America in strike operations.

Similar use was made of student congresses and student organizations abroad to establish unconventional channels of international liaison. The Federation of University Students (FEU) was reaffiliated with the Communist-controlled International Union of Students, which in May 1961 met in Havana. Maximum publicity was given to the resolutions of such congresses, the slogans of anti-imperialist riots, and the pronouncements of student and labor spokesmen, with headings indicating that "the people" or "the workers" of Mexico, Venezuela, or some other country supported Castro's policies. The exchange of cultural and professional delegations and expressions of solidarity between such organizations contributed to this type of propaganda.

Government pronouncements simplified all world problems into clear issues between good and evil. The United States, its allies, and all who expressed disapproval of Cuban policies were in the wrong, united in error by mercenary interests. The government went out of its way to associate itself with all causes—no matter how irrelevant to Cuba—that could be considered embarrassing to the United States, since the universal cause of right was held to profit thereby. Cuba declared its support, for example, for the admission of the Mongolian People's Republic to the United Nations. On the death of the Congolese leader Patrice Lumumba, Cuba declared three days of official mourning. Government spokesmen frequently expressed support for the Algerian revolt.

Within the general theme of anti-imperialism, propaganda dealt chiefly with the rights and prospects of workers and peasants, Negroes and American Indians. The Cuban view toward the American hemisphere was summarized by Radio Mambí, commenting on Foreign Minister Raúl Roa's withdrawal from the OAS conference in Costa Rica in August 1960:

> Roa was not alone when he left the hall, because with him went the Indians, the mestizos, and the Negroes of all America. . . . The fate of America will someday be decided on the Rocky Mountains and the Andes, when the Negroes of the North and the Indians of the south unite to break their chains. The United States workers will join their Latin American brothers and the United States farmers will join the Latin American farmers and all of them will achieve freedom, forming a truly new world in the New World.

A clear distinction was made between the "bosses" and the "people" of the United States. The people, it was assumed, only needed to hear Castro to start their own revolution. United States citizens, once classified as "humble" and "honest" or as "intellectuals," were treated with great friendliness. Efforts were made to attract United States tourists, especially Negroes, a United States public relations firm being engaged for the purpose. In Cuba, Castro asserted, Negroes would find no trace of race prejudice; Cuba was itself a mestizo, almost a Negro, nation. Instances of racial conflict in the United States attracted considerable notice from the press and radio. In every case the conflict was represented as one between oppressed Negroes and the Federal establishment, including the president, Wall Street, the FBI, and the Pentagon.

Although the Indian element in the Cuban population is negligible and Indian cultural traces virtually nonexistent, the government was at pains, particularly in 1960, to assert its leadership of Indo-America. This assertion was an effort to attract the support of existing Indo-American parties in Latin America, of which the oldest and strongest is the Popular American Revolutionary Alliance (APRA) of Peru, whose support for Castro could weaken the opposition to him in the governments of their respective countries. However, in February 1961 a meeting of Aprista delegates from various countries condemned the course of the Cuban revolution as anti-American and antipopular.

Another theme, sporadically sounded, was neutralism and the love of peace. This was clearly inconsistent with the belligerent posture of the regime, its statement of the need for armed defense against imminent United States aggression, and its support for violent revolution in Latin America and elsewhere. President Sekou Touré of Guinea was welcomed in Havana in 1960, and loud assertions of community of interest with other well-known neutralists were occasionally made, but in fact little community of interest existed. In late 1960, the Communist newspaper *Noticias de Hoy* denounced Yugoslavia for being too neutral to send aid to Cuba.

Cuba and the United States (1959-1961)

Relations with the United States, direct and indirect, have been the dominant foreign policy concern of the Castro government and are closely related to its domestic policies. Aggressive nationalism, one of the revolution's favorite poses, was justified by the assertion that the United States was responsible for the underprivileged status of a large proportion of the Cuban people under Batista and for the underprivileged status of Cuba in the community of nations. The national agrarian reform, the expropriation of foreign interests, the diversification of the economy, and the suppression of opposition were all carried out under the slogan, "Cuba, si! Yanqui, no!"

At first the open support for Castro in most of the United States press and the speedy recognition accorded the new regime by the United States government mollified the doctrinaire anti-Americanism of the Castro government. This comfortable mood scarcely lasted a week; the summary trial and execution of many followers of Batista aroused vigorous protests in the United States, to the surprise of Castro, who complained that there had been little protest against the atrocities for which Batista's men were being shot.

In April 1959 Castro visited the United States at the invitation of the American Society of Newspaper Editors. He defended the trial procedure, saying that only those who deserved it had been executed; declared that Cuba was not neutral, but favored the West and would remain in the Inter-American Mutual Defense Pact; denied any intention of confiscating foreign enterprise; and said Cuba wanted trade, not aid. According to Secretary of State Herter, Castro made no request for financial or other assistance during this visit. Although the visit was unofficial, Castro later expressed annoyance because he had not been formally received by the government.

During the next three months, internal developments contributed to a change in Cuba's attitude toward the United States. Many middle-class professional men who at first had associated themselves with the new regime resigned their positions, in some cases leaving the country. One of these, Pedro Díaz Lanz, once Chief of the Cuban Air Force under Castro, testified before the United States Internal Security Subcommittee that the Cuban government was being infiltrated by Communists. Overt Communist influence was apparent in the establishment in June 1959 of a New China (Communist) News Agency office in Havana.

On July 2, the government discovered a counterrevolutionary plot involving hundreds of the dissatisfied, chiefly members of the middle class. To Castro the existence of this opposition indicated the continuation of United States support for reactionaries, as in the days of Batista. The forced resignation of Provisional President Urrutia, who had expressed opposition to Communism in Cuba, was the occasion of statements by Castro that the revolution was only half won; that many Cubans, accustomed to a different form of society, did not yet understand what the revolution was; and that to be anti-Communist was to be counterrevolutionary. By September 1959 the Foreign Minister was advocating neutralism at the United Nations. Later that month an agreement to sell 330,000 long tons of sugar to the Soviet Union was concluded.

Counterrevolutionaries began to fly airplanes over Cuba, dropping leaflets and creating other disturbances. Castro charged that one such plane, flown by Díaz Lanz from a base in Florida, had on October 21 dropped bombs as well as leaflets on Havana. Officials and propaganda agencies repeated and enlarged this charge in ensuing months and implied "North American" responsibility for these actions, although they admitted there was no evidence of actual United States government intervention. "The most rigorous and elaborate system of controls ever adopted by the United States government in time of peace," was set up to stop illegal flights and described in United States memoranda to the Inter-American Peace Committee.

The Cuban government, however, showed no serious interest in constructive measures to help stop such flights. Even wilder charges were made concerning the attempts of "monopolists" to set fire to cane fields from the air as the sugar harvest approached, but a grand jury indictment returned in Florida accused several United States and Cuban citizens of arranging such a flight in complicity with officials of the Cuban government, to manufacture propaganda material.

In late 1959 foreign investors were seriously alarmed by the trends of Cuban policy. A number of enterprises had been taken over by the government, whose statements of plans included payment in twenty-year bonds equivalent only to the nominal, not the actual, value of the properties. The United States did not object to the nationalization as such, but to a procedure which dispensed with receipts and inventories. Further objections to the bond program were interpreted by Castro as a cynical and unreasonable demand for cash payment since United States interests were well aware that there was insufficient cash available. The chief of the Economic Department of the Ministry of Foreign Affairs stated in 1961, from his refuge in the United States, that, after the Agrarian Reform Law was put into effect in late 1959, officials began to discuss with the State Department the compensation to be paid expropriated Americans, but that Castro refused to allow such talks to continue.

Abusive remarks by Castro prompted the temporary recall of the United States Ambassador in January 1960. The semiofficial newspaper, *Revolución*, drew attention to President Eisenhower's visit to Spain as an indication of the Fascist sympathies of the United States government. When the United States terminated a minor military aid program in February, Castro promptly denounced the move as an aggressive act.

In March a French vessel, *La Coubre,* carrying munitions from Antwerp, exploded at the dock in Havana. A dockworkers' meeting attributed the disaster to careless handling; other explanations, none very satisfactory, were also offered. Castro, noting that the United States had been asking European nations not to supply arms to the Caribbean area, violently accused the United States of sabotage, openly basing his argument on inference rather than evidence. His charges were widely disseminated in propaganda literature including a brochure distributed to OAS delegates in May 1960.

Other pamphlets repeated indirect accusations of United States responsibility for bombings and the counterrevolutionary activity of "fugitives from justice who now, under the protection of political asylum, violate international law by launching new and criminal attacks against Cuba." Extradition proceedings for these fugitives were not instituted.

During May and June relations with the United States grew worse. At a May Day rally Castro decried elections as a bourgeois device to cheat the people and accused the United States of planning an invasion through Guatemala. Propaganda attacks increased in violence with talk of imminent hostilities. A United States submarine was chased in international waters by a Cuban gunboat; the incident was used by Castro to demonstrate the aggressive designs of the United States and the superior valor of the Cuban navy. United Fruit Company holdings were expropriated; in June one British and two United States oil refineries were seized after their managers refused to process Russian oil. Two United States attachés, described as Nazis, were expelled for conspiracy; in reply the United States expelled two Cuban representatives said to have been fomenting racial unrest in Florida.

In July the government, anticipating action by the United States to eliminate the Cuban sugar quota, authorized the expropriation of all United States properties unless sugar purchases were increased and the price raised. The inconsistency of this attitude with the routine denunciation of the existing system as slavery was not resolved. The President of the National Bank, Ernesto Guevara, had said in March 1960:

> The representatives of the sugar companies are trying to show that by selling to another country (USSR) we are enslaving ourselves, and they have never stopped to analyze what amount of slavery the three million tons of our sugar which we customarily sell at supposedly preferential prices to the giant of the north has meant and means for the people of Cuba.

On July 6, President Eisenhower eliminated the remainder of the Cuban quota for 1960, valued at about $92.5 million. This action was described as economic aggression in a complaint submitted by Cuba to the United Nations Security Council and later to the OAS.

Cuba retaliated on August 7 by nationalizing all major enterprises controlled by United States subjects, including Texaco, Esso, Sinclair, the Cuban Electric Company, the Cuban Telephone Company, and thirty-six sugar mills. More United States companies were seized during September and October, "because of their efforts to hamper the consolidation of the revolution."

After the Declaration of San José, in which the OAS condemned extracontinental interference, Castro publicly tore up the 1952 mutual defense agreement with the United States.

Castro personally headed the Cuban delegation to the United Nations General Assembly in New York in September 1960. The action of the United States in restricting him to Manhattan was interpreted in Cuban propaganda as indicative of a fear that, "If Fidel should ever speak to the United States masses the revolution would start at once in the United States." In retaliation the United States Ambassador in Havana was similarly restricted. Castro walked out of the downtown Manhattan hotel where he had lodged at first, charging unacceptable cash demands and other persecutions. Ignoring the United Nations' offer of free accommodation, he repaired to the Theresa Hotel in the Negro district of Harlem, where he ostentatiously introduced his Negro Chief of Staff, Juan Almeida, to Negro groups. "A humble hotel sheltered us," he said, and he had the name of a hotel in Havana changed to the Theresa, with a plaque commemorating the event. In the Cuban press, the oppressed New Yorkers, "the entire city," were reported as gathering around Fidel, shouting, "We want freedom!"

In a long speech before the General Assembly Castro described his country's relations with the United States. The first unfriendly act, he said, was the offer of hospitality to Cuban criminals, men who had murdered hundreds of defenseless peasants with weapons supplied by the United States, nominally for hemispheric defense. When the agrarian reform and other expropriations were undertaken there were conflicts with "United States monoplies." The State Department, disregarding Cuban problems, demanded "payment right now, in dollars." Countering charges of Communism Castro explained: "While the United States press was telling the world that Cuba was a Red danger ninety miles away from the United States, the revolutionary government had not even had a chance to establish diplomatic or trade relations with the Soviet Union. Then threats began against our sugar quota."

In the course of seeking new markets, Castro continued, Cuba made a trade pact with Soviet Russia, whereupon the United States, brandishing the economic weapon against the revolution, eliminated the Cuban sugar quota, in violation of regional agreements. "The Cuban government is always ready to discuss its problems with the United States, but the United States does not want to discuss problems with Cuba." Castro then charged that Swan Island was being used as the site of counterrevolutionary radio broadcasts and that the United States Naval Base at Guantánamo was creating tensions leading deliberately to war.

Outlining the pattern of United States investments abroad, he alleged that the case of Cuba was the case of all underdeveloped nations and warned that Latin America, the Middle East, and Africa would encounter similar problems. Castro condemned the manner of United Nations intervention in the Congo and concluded by associating the United States with reactionary and militaristic forces throughout the world.

During the remainder of 1960 Castro exchanged accusations with the United States on the subjects of aggressive intentions, the Guantánamo base, and the violation of agreements against nonintervention. Cuban officials frequently raised the Guantánamo issue, saying that the treaty ceding the base to the United States was an imperialist document violating the rights of the Cuban people, but emphasizing that if trouble arose the United States would be the responsible party. Three American citizens belonging to a counterrevolutionary unit were shot after conviction by a military tribunal; the United States protested against the circumstances of the trial. The United States prohibited the export to Cuba of all goods except food and medical supplies, but continued to permit the entry of Cuban products. In retaliation, Cuba expropriated 166 more United States companies.

A United States note to the OAS said that Soviet war materials were being stockpiled in Cuba to prepare the extension of the revolution to other countries. In October the militia was mobilized in response to reports, encouraged by the government, of an impending invasion from the United States. In December, President Eisenhower authorized $1 million in aid to Cuban refugees in the United States. Cuba and the United Arab Republic asked the Security Council to consider America's aggressive intentions against Cuba, but without response.

Counterrevolutionary preparations by Cuban exiles supported by the United States government in Florida, Guatemala, and elsewhere in the Caribbean area prompted the Cuban government in early 1961 to alert the militia for three weeks immediately preceding the inauguration of President Kennedy. The Castro government, which regarded the incoming Democratic administration in the United States as less reactionary than that of President Eisenhower, considered it likely that Eisenhower would force the hand of his successor by mounting an invasion against Cuba in the last days of his presidency.

On January 3, Cuba required the United States to limit the number of its personnel at the embassy in Havana to eleven, on the ground that the United States needed no more representatives in Cuba than the Cuban government had in the United States, and that the additional employees were engaged in espionage and counterrevolution. In fact, the Cuban government was concerned at the growing number of would-be emigrants, including many with much-needed skills, who were seeking visas from the embassy.

The United States regarded the move as having "no other purpose than to render impossible the conduct of normal diplomatic relations." It accordingly withdrew all its diplomatic and consular personnel, requesting the Swiss government to represent American interests in Cuba. The withdrawal was considered by the Cuban government as fresh evidence of aggressive intentions on the part of the United States.

After the demobilization of the militia Castro expressed cautious hopes that the new United States administration would revise the American attitude toward Cuba, Within a few days, however, he announced that President Kennedy, the "illiterate millionaire," was as reactionary as his predecessor. An increased appropriation for Cuban refugees was described as aid to war criminals. Increasingly violent charges of aggressive intentions were exchanged in the United Nations and the OAS. Cuban officials, noting that President Kennedy was a Catholic, spoke of a vast antipopular conspiracy involving Fascists, the Catholic Church, Wall Street, and the Pentagon. Several United States citizens captured while participating in counterrevolutionary activities were tried and sentenced by military courts.

During February and March increasingly authoritative reports were published in the Cuban and United States press regarding the training being given to exile military forces in Guatemala by United States advisors and of invasion preparations being made. On March 10 the formation of a Revolutionary Council—in effect, a government-in-exile—was announced in New York, with José Miró Cardona as coordinator-general. On April 15, 1961 three airfields were bombed by aircraft, one plane subsequently landing in Florida. United States authorities announced that the pilot described himself as a defector from the Cuban air force, but later reports in the American press indicated that he had taken off from a base outside the island, probably in Guatemala.

Some 1,200 men were landed at the Bahía de Cochinos on the south coast of Matanzas province on April 17. The invasion was reported to have been launched from Guatemalan bases, using a staging-area in Nicaragua. The United States provided military supplies and support facilities. The invaders encountered strong resistance and were defeated in a few days. The government described the invading troops as mercenaries in the pay of the United States and presented a complaint to the Security Council of the United Nations.

Cuba and Latin America (1959-1961)

Castro's victory sparked a series of disturbances in the Caribbean area during 1959. Some seem to have had the encouragement of Cuban officials if not the outright endorsement of the government. Others were undertaken privately by Cuban guerrillas, joined by members of the permanent Caribbean corps of would-be revolutionaries. These adventurers, mainly exiles from their own countries, had contributed to Castro's forces and saw in his success the beginning of an international movement to dislodge dictators and oligarchs.

In April 1959 a small force hired by right-wing Panamanian dissidents sailed from Cuba for Panama. The expedition came to nothing. No protest was lodged against Cuba by Panama. In May, dissident Nicaraguans invaded their own country from Costa Rica. Cuba was not at first involved, but objected to the investigation undertaken by the OAS on the ground that, since the invaders were Nicaraguans, the revolt was a domestic matter. Later the Nicaraguan army commander made unsubstantiated charges, denied by Castro, that the Cuban government had helped the rebels.

In July, the Dominican Republic, responding to an invasion attempt, accused Cuba and Venezuela of having planned the invasion with the connivance of the United States. Cuba denied the charge, declined to allow the OAS team to investigate the matter in Cuba, and with Venezuela countercharged that Trujillo violated human rights. Diplomatic relations with the Dominican Republic were cut; Cuba raised the dispute in the United Nations and later asserted that Trujillo was planning to invade Cuba. In August the Cuban government announced the capture of a plane said to have been carrying arms from the Dominican Republic to pro-Batista rebels in Cuba. During the same period the Cuban ambassador was accused by the Haitian government of subversion and of assisting an armed invasion launched from Cuba.

To discuss these difficulties the Foreign Ministers of the OAS met in Santiago, Chile, on August 12, 1959. Cuba and Venezuela insisted that human rights and democratic principles be included in the discussion, on the ground that nonintervention strengthened dictators such as Trujillo. The Declaration of Santiago, supported by Cuba, affirmed seven principles regarding human rights, including the separation of powers, free elections, equality before the law, and freedom of the press and radio. Intervention in support of these principles was not, however, considered acceptable.

Whether or not the Cuban government actively supported any of these armed attempts, its leaders undoubtedly believed that their revolution was the product of social conditions similar to those found in most other parts of Latin America and that, accordingly, similar revolutions would occur elsewhere. Castro, disavowing the intention of actively leading a continental uprising, has said, "Latin America will inevitably free itself. Nobody can have the slightest doubt on this point. It is a law of contemporary history." On another occasion he prophesied that uprisings would occur simultaneously in many parts of Latin America. The government assumed the responsibility for spreading the good news. Cuban agents, from late 1959 onward, made contact with revolutionary movements of all kinds, in almost every country. Diplomatic channels were used to distribute propaganda and advice, such as Ernesto Guevara's handbook on guerrilla warfare. Several Cuban diplomats were expelled for interfering in the internal affairs of the countries to which they were accredited. The official Cuban view, made increasingly explicit as 1959 advanced, was that all Latin American governments were dictatorships or pseudodemocracies run by politicians and businessmen in their own interests and in the interest of United States monopolies. Propaganda appeals and diplomatic contacts were accordingly made directly to "the people." The OAS itself was frequently denounced as "a lie," a capitalists' conspiracy, and as the United States' "Ministry of Colonies."

In November 1959, a Venezuelan government objection to a proposed visit from Raúl Castro and Guevara, on the ground that it might provoke leftist demonstrations, resulted in the recall of Cuba's ambassador and led to an eventual break in November 1961 between the two countries. By April 1960, Cuban propaganda was violently denouncing the leading liberal politicians of the region, including President Betancourt of Venezuela, President Frondizi of Argentina, Governor Munoz Marin of Puerto Rico, and the Chilean Aprista leader Victor Raúl Haya de la Torre. In May President Osvaldo Dorticós toured Argentina, Brazil, Uruguay, Peru, Venezuela, and Mexico to present the Cuban case in opposition to United States warnings of Communist inroads.

During 1960, several Caribbean countries were involved in the increasing tension between Cuba and the United States. Charges of aggressive intent were exchanged, particularly between Cuba and Honduras, Nicaragua, and Guatemala. Former President Arbenz of Guatemala, deposed in 1954 with the assistance of the United States, was ostentatiously welcomed in Havana and made speeches denouncing in advance any repetition in Cuba of the 1954 incident. Castro described the Monroe Doctrine as worm-eaten.

In the last week of July, Argentine police seized a Cuban diplomatic pouch containing Communist, Peronist, and pro-Castro propaganda, a manual of terrorism, and other subversive material.

Castro apologized to President Frondizi, but official propaganda continued to describe his government as the servile instrument of the United States and as worse than Peron's regime.

At an anniversary celebration on July 26, Castro said, "We promise to continue making the nation the example that can convert the Cordillera of the Andes into the Sierra Maestra of the American continent." In August the national coordinator for the Venezuelan 26th of July Movement, a pro-Castro group, was shot, and several Cubans were deported from Venezuela for their involvement in riots. In September 1960, Peruvian police seized thousands of leaflets, printed in Czechoslovakia, Cuba, Communist China, and elsewhere and consigned to the Cuban embassy. The Cuban Ambassador to Colombia established contact with groups advocating the overthrow of the Colombian government; the embassy helped to organize and finance public demonstrations by societies of Friends of the Cuban Revolution, and supervised the activity of Cuban agents entering the country as tourists.

In August 1960, Cuba and the United States submitted opposed memoranda to the Peace Committee of the OAS. Cuba accused the United States of economic aggression—the elimination of Cuba's sugar quota—and of fomenting counterrevolution. At San José, Costa Rica, later in the month, the Foreign Ministers of the OAS adopted a Declaration of San José which, without specifically mentioning Cuba, condemned Communist alliances within the hemisphere. The Cuban delegate, Dr. Raúl Roa, walked out of the meeting. A few days later Castro submitted a Declaration of Havana to cheering crowds in the Cuban capital, asserting Cuba's right to enter into alliances at will and, specifically, to recognize Communist China.

At Bogotá, Colombia, in September 1960, the United States submitted a plan for aid to Latin America which resulted in an agreement not signed by the Cuban representative. Cuban agents reportedly organized demonstrations in an attempt to disrupt the entire meeting. The Colombian government asked that the Cuban ambassador be recalled.

Minor uprisings occurred in Nicaragua and Guatemala in November. The respective governments appealed for United States aid against an invasion allegedly being prepared in Cuba. No evidence of Cuban aid to the insurgents was ever demonstrated, but United States ships and aircraft were ordered to patrol the Caribbean.

In the same period Venezuelan police discovered clandestine radios being operated by Cubans.

In late April, after the failure of the attempted invasion by Cuban exiles trained in Guatemala—in particular, its failure to excite counterrevolutionary enthusiasm in the majority of the people —the traditional anti-interventionist attitude of Latin Americans produced widespread comment in favor of Castro. This sympathy was reversed, however, when on May 1, Castro described his regime for the first time as Socialist, implying an alliance between Cuba and the Communist bloc.

Cuban spokesmen hastened to qualify the commitment to "socialism," indicating that the United Kingdom, for example, was also a socialist country. Carlos Olivares Sanchez, Roa's deputy, made an "unofficial" trip in late May to Mexico, Brazil, and Ecuador, explaining that Cuba had contracted no formal alliances outside the hemisphere and that the United States was responsible for any rift between Cuba and its natural allies in Latin America.

The Communist Alliance

Although diplomatic relations with the Soviet Union were broken off in 1952, trade between Cuba and the Communist countries, chiefly the Soviet Union, increased from a negligible amount in 1952 to $42.6 million (5.3 percent of total exports) in 1957. In late 1959 Cuba sold 330,000 long tons of sugar to the Soviet Union at slightly below the current world price, a transaction valued at approximately $21.4 million.

In the ensuing months the Castro regime increasingly revealed pro-Communist sympathies. In November 1959, for example, the Cuban Workers' Confederation voted to break its ties with the Inter-American Regional Organization of Labor and to promote a new Latin American labor organization which would exclude the United States and Canada. Russian observers attended this meeting. In December a National Peace Committee was set up as an affiliate of the Communist-front organization, World Peace Council. At this time United States intelligence authorities described Castro as not Communist but certainly not anti-Communist, and said that his extreme policies were being exploited by the Communists to the maximum extent.

During January 1960, Castro's nationalist indignation against the United States and other long-time allies of Cuba grew markedly violent. In February, the Deputy Chairman of the Council of Ministers of the USSR, Anastas Mikoyan, came to Havana to open a Soviet Industrial exposition and to sign trade agreements which represented the first major break in the restriction imposed by United States influence on trade between Latin America and the Communist bloc. The Soviet Union agreed to buy five million tons of sugar over a five-year period, 20 percent of the payment to be made in United States dollars and 80 percent in equipment and goods at prices determined by the Soviet Union. This exchange made the Soviet Union the second largest buyer of Cuban sugar. In addition the Soviet Union granted a credit of $100 million repayable in twelve years at 2.5 percent and promised technical assistance. The joint communique on the occasion "reaffirmed" the agreement in attitude of the parties toward international problems.

An agreement with Poland was signed in April, exchanging sugar and minerals for such manufactures as seagoing ships, steel foundries, machine shops, and textile factories. Poland also agreed to supply helicopters and light aircraft for crop dusting; the United States refused to supply such aircraft because of their potential military uses. Technicians from East Germany, the Soviet Union, and several Latin American countries arrived in May, their arrival coinciding with the resumption of diplomatic relations with the Soviet Union. Trade delegations were sent to Latvia, Czechoslovakia, and other countries of Eastern Europe. In June Núñez Jiménez, director of the National Agrarian Reform Institute, headed an economic delegation to Moscow and extended an invitation to Nikita Khrushchev to visit Cuba. Oil from the Soviet Union was refined in nationalized British and United States plants.

During July Cuban charges of aggressive American intentions and the abrupt nationalization of many United States properties created a tense international situation. On July 9, Khrushchev intruded into this situation by making the "symbolic" offer of Russian rockets in case Cuba needed help against the United States. The precise value of this offer was not determined, but in the ensuing months Cuban officials repeatedly referred to it as though it guaranteed Soviet military assistance. The argument was used in foreign policy statements and in reassurances to the Cuban people.

Raúl Castro toured Czechoslovakia and the Soviet Union during July 1960 and on his return observed, "Khrushchev is more like a Cuban than the pictures indicate." On July 22 the Soviet Union said it would buy the sugar Cuba was unable to sell to the United States. A $70 million trade agreement was reported between Cuba and Communist China. The head of the Chinese trade delegation in Havana pledged Communist Chinese support against imperialist aggression. In August an agreement was disclosed for trade with East Germany to the value of $3 million annually. Diplomatic recognition of Communist China was announced on September 2 and effected on September 24. At the United Nations General Assembly in New York, Khrushchev and Castro ostentatiously sought each other out and embraced. Each addressed the Assembly in favor of the position and policy of the other. Khrushchev visited Castro in his Harlem hotel but did not accept the invitation to visit Cuba.

Ernesto Guevara, then president of the National Bank, participated in October Revolution anniversary celebrations in Moscow in November 1960. During his trip he arranged for additional Soviet sugar purchases during 1961, and announced Cuba's wholehearted support for the resolutions adopted by the recent international conference of Communist parties in Moscow. "We are threatened every minute with American warships, planes, and marines," he said, "but the friendly hand of the Soviet Union, extended to us, shields us from the enemy as an invisible armor." The October Revolution was also officially celebrated in Havana. In April 1961, according to the State Department of the United States, military supplies received from Communist countries by the Castro regime totaled more than 30,000 tons.

TABLES

Table 1. POPULATION GROWTH, 1899-1953

Census year	Total population	Average yearly increase (by percent)	Density[a] (per square mile)
1899	1,572,797	....	35.6
1907	2,043,980	3.8	46.3
1919	2,889,004	3.4	65.3
1931	3,962,344	3.1	89.6
1943	4,778,583	1.7	108.0
1953	5,829,029	2.3	131.8

(a) Based on a total area of 44,218 square miles.

Source: Adapted from Antonio Núñez Jiménez, *Geografía de Cuba*, p. 184; and Republic of Cuba, *Censos de Población, 1953*, p. 1.

Table 2. DISTRIBUTION OF ETHNIC GROUPS BY PROVINCE, 1953

(percent of provincial population)

Province	White	Black	Yellow	Mixed
Pinar del Río	79.7	14.2	....	6.1
La Habana	77.0	11.4	0.6	11.0
Matanzas	77.7	12.1	.1	10.1
Las Villas	82.4	9.2	.2	8.2
Camagüey	78.2	13.2	.3	8.3
Oriente	59.1	14.6	.1	26.2

Source: Republic of Cuba, *Censos de Población, 1953*, pp. 49-62.

Table 3. **CUBAN SUGAR PRODUCTION**

(in long tons)

Year	Cuban production	World production	Cuban percent of world production
1951	5,668,187	36,137,188	15.7
1952	7,110,438	38,891,292	18.3
1953	5,077,690	38,615,763	13.1
1954	4,813,202	41,228,438	11.7
1955	4,456,113	41,024,431	10.8
1956	4,664,965	41,275,329	11.3
1957	5,581,640	43,615,610	12.8
1958	5,689,500	46,316,180	12.3
1959	5,788,154	n.a.	n.a.
1960	5,688,859	n.a.	n.a.
1961	(a)6,350,000	n.a.	n.a.

(a) Estimate.

Source: Adapted from Antonio Núñez Jiménez, *Geografía de Cuba,* p. 306; U.S. Department of Commerce, *Economic Developments in the Western Hemisphere 1959,* March 1960, p. 15; and Editora Mercantil Cubana, S.A., *Cuba Economica y Financiera,* XXXV, Nos. 416-417, 1960, p. 12.

Table 4. **AMERICAN AND CUBAN SUGAR MILLS, 1939 AND 1958**

	1939	1958
American:		
Number	66	36
Percent of total sugar output	55	37
Cuban:		
Number	56	121
Percent of total sugar output	22	62

Source: Adapted from U.S. Department of Commerce, Bureau of Foreign Commerce, *Investment in Cuba,* p. 37.

Table 5. LAND USE, BY PROVINCE

Province	Total land (in acres)	Total farm land (in acres)	Culti-vated	Pas-ture	Woods	Mara-bú[a]	Other uses[b]	Idle	Number	Average acreage
										Farms
			Use of farm land (in percent)							
Pinar del Rio	3,334,500	2,393,067	15.2	44.5	20.3	4.8	14.9	0.3	23,030	103.91
La Habana	2,030,587	1,628,286	23.5	34.5	22.8	1.6	17.3	.3	14,272	114.09
Matanzas	2,085,668	1,616,155	32.0	46.5	5.7	1.7	13.6	.5	12,486	129.44
Las Villas	5,288,517	5,021,982	20.4	43.9	10.4	4.1	20.7	.5	40,182	124.98
Camagüey	6,507,462	5,347,241	16.3	48.1	11.0	3.2	21.2	.2	18,541	288.40
Oriente	9,040,694	6,413,671	26.6	38.5	16.7	1.8	16.3	.1	51,447	124.67
Total	28,287,428	22,420,402	21.7	42.9	13.9	3.0	18.2	.3	159,958	140.16

(a) Includes roads, buildings, and unproductive land.

(b) Farms not cultivated.

Source: Adapted from International Bank for Reconstruction and Development, *Report on Cuba*, 1951, p. 87.

Table 6. VALUE OF PRINCIPAL PRODUCTS, 1958

(in millions of U.S. dollars)

Product	Value
Agricultural:	
Sugar cane	280
Livestock (on the hoof)	100
Coffee (decorticated)	36
Rice (decorticated)	33
Tobacco (unprocessed)	22.5
Industrial:	
Sugar	579
Meat and other livestock products	160
Cigars and tobaccos	103
Coffee (roasted)	60
Rice	45

Source: Adapted from Antonio Núñez Jiménez, Geografia de Cuba, p. 322.

Table 7. GOVERNMENT DEVELOPMENT LOANS (BANCA), 1953 AND 1958

(in millions of U.S. dollars)

	1953	1958
Private sector loans:		
To industry	1.7	133.0
To agriculture	5.6	19.6
To public utilities	1.2	236.2
To unclassified	....	7.1
Total private sector loans	8.5	395.9
To government institutions	2.1	8.1
Cuban bond purchases	20.4	55.3
Total	31.0	459.3

Source: Banco Nacional de Cuba, Revista, September 1958.

Table 8. PARTY REGISTRATION, 1948

Party	Presidential candidates	1948 registration
Auténticos	Carlos Prío Socarrás	790,327
Republicans	Carlos Prío Socarrás	282,154
Liberals	Ricardo Núñez Portuondo	357,469
Democrats	Ricardo Núñez Portuondo	188,610
Ortodoxos	Eduardo Chibas	164,875
Popular Socialists	Juan Marinello	157,283

Source: William S. Stokes, Latin American Politics, p. 381.

Table 9. OCCUPATIONS OF THE ECONOMICALLY ACTIVE POPULATION, 1953

(fourteen years of age and over)

Occupational groupings	Total	Male	Female
Technical and like professions			
Engineers, etc.	5,748	5,453	295
Chemists, pharmacists, etc.	5,144	3,376	1,768
Professors, teachers, scientists	42,571	7,726	34,845
Lawyers, judges	7,858	7,325	533
Doctors and related professions	10,577	9,156	1,421
Artists, writers, entertainers	9,914	8,477	1,437
Clergy and social workers	2,184	1,197	987
Other	1,913	1,621	292
Total	85,909	44,331	41,578
Managers, administrators, directors			
Public officials	6,135	5,132	1,003
Commerce	74,732	71,438	3,294
Other	12,795	12,049	746
Total	93,662	88,619	5,043
Office workers, etc.			
Typists	13,415	6,331	7,084
Accountants, conductors, etc.	24,424	22,044	2,380
Telephone operators	39,000	30,162	8,838
Other	64,490	47,147	17,343
Total	141,329	105,684	35,645
Salesmen, vendors			
Retail and itinerant	104,152	93,462	10,690
Other	19,088	18,065	1,023
Total	123,240	111,527	11,713

Table 9. (*continued*)

Occupational groupings	Total	Male	Female
Agriculture, fishing, etc.			
Paid agricultural workers, etc.	568,779	558,725	10,054
Farmers	221,939	220,479	1,460
Forestry workers	10,844	10,615	229
Fishing	5,952	5,896	56
Total	807,514	795,715	11,799
Mining, quarrying			
Total	6,168	6,063	105
Transportation			
Total	85,897	85,098	799
Artisans, factory workers, etc.			
Metal workers and mechanics	45,745	45,745	....
Woodworkers	42,326	42,076	250
Construction and maintenance	54,725	54,615	110
Clothing workers	53,835	29,570	24,265
Food and tobacco workers	80,342	60,757	19,585
Factory operatives and dayworkers	52,542	48,802	3,740
Other	31,979	27,471	4,508
Total	361,494	309,036	52,458
Manual and dayworkers			
Construction workers	23,796	23,571	225
Transport workers	30,119	24,057	6,062
Other	18,694	16,133	2,561
Total	72,609	63,761	8,848
Services			
Protective services	14,038	13,764	274
Domestic service	78,336	8,462	69,874
Personal service	16,743	11,456	5,287
Other	51,289	38,944	12,345
Total	160,406	72,626	87,780
Other	34,038	33,366	672
Grand total	1,972,266	1,715,826	256,440

Source: Adapted from Republic of Cuba, *Censos de Población, 1953,* pp. 204, 205.

Table 10. **MEMBERSHIP CLAIMED BY THE CONFEDERA-
TION OF CUBAN WORKERS (CTC), 1960**

Industrial federation	Number of affiliated unions	Membership
National Federation of Sugar Workers	243	502,072
National Federation of Workers in the Construction Industry	64	75,000
National Federation of Commercial Workers	91	70,000
National Federation of Transport Workers	100	(a)62,000
National Federation of Gastronomic Workers and Related Trades	63	62,000
National Tobacco Federation	207	(a)40,000
Workers' Federation of the Food Industry	62	35,000
National Maritime Workers' Federation	200	32,000
National Federation of Workers in the Cattle and Derivative Industries	38	(a)24,000
National Federation of Textile and Needle Industry Workers	44	(a)23,000
National Federated Railway Brotherhood	23	22,000
Industrial Chemicals Workers' Federation	26	22,000
National Federation of the Shoe Industry	34	(a)21,000
National Federation of Mine Workers and Similar Trades	26	17,000
National Federation of Graphic Arts	27	15,345
National Federation of Liquor, Beer, and Refrigerator Workers and Related Trades of Cuba	28	(a)14,200
Labor Federation of Electric, Gas and Water Plants	6	12,350
National Federation of Workers in the Metallurgical Industry and Related Trades	27	12,300
Federation of Workers in the Forestry, Wood and Furniture Industries and Related Trades	27	12,100
National Federation of Barbershop, Haircutting and Manicure Workers	46	12,000
National Federation of Medical Workers	23	11,200
National Federation of Petroleum (and Products) Workers	28	11,000
National Federation of Professions Auxiliary to Medicine	(b)20	(b)9,000
National Cinematographic Federation	10	6,000
National Federation of Insurance, Surety and Related Trades	8	5,300
Bank Workers' Labor Federation	6	4,500
National Federation of Musicians	23	4,200
Labor Federation of Telephone Workers	6	4,200
National Federation of Salesmen and Helpers	6	4,100
National Federation of Theater Workers	11	3,800
National Federation of Medical Traveling Salesmen	7	2,000
National Aviation Federation	7	1,500
National Federation of Cable and Radio-Telegraph Workers	5	650
Total	**1,542**	**1,152,817**

(a) Estimated.   (b) 1955 figure.

Table 11. BALANCE OF PAYMENTS

(in millions of pesos)

	1955	1956	1957	1958	1959[a]
Current account:					
Exports (f.o.b.)	607.8	694.5	844.7	763.2	675.3
Imports (f.o.b.)	−575.1	−649.0	−813.2	−807.5	−673.2
Foreign travel (net)	− 3.0	4.3	25.9	19.4	18.9
Transportation (net)	− 56.9	− 60.5	− 70.4	− 69.8	− 57.3
Investment income (net)	− 40.9	− 50.6	− 65.6	− 47.9	− 5.9
Other (net)	15.8	19.5	12.2	14.9	8.2
Capital account:					
Private donations and capital	57.7	33.9	43.2	− 20.9	102.8
Direct investment in Cuba	23.0	39.0	61.0	20.0	80.8
Official donations	....	.5	.6	.6	....
Official and bank capital	53.0	40.7	66.9	187.9	25.1
Loans to official banks	90.9	20.4	26.7	98.9	....
Monetary gold (decrease)	50.0	.1	.2	55.1	30.2
Other	− 81.4	13.7	51.7	79.3	− 39.8
Net errors and omissions	− 57.9	− 33.3	− 44.3	− 39.9	− 53.9

(a) Preliminary.

Source: Adapted from International Monetary Fund, *International Financial Statistics,* XIV, No. 5, 1961, p. 95.

Table 12.   VALUE OF PRINCIPAL EXPORTS, 1953-1954

(in thousands of U.S. dollars)

Commodity	1953	1954
Sugar:		
Raw	439,785	333,386
Refined	62,723	68,511
Molasses:		
Blackstrap	21,416	12,051
High-test	822	13,516
Invert syrup	3,726	4,063
Tobacco (unmanufactured)	34,540	34,311
Cigars	7,202	6,766
Nickel ore	14,119	12,756
Manganese ore	11,184	6,964
Copper ore	8,828	8,337
Iron ore	2,159	1,073
Chrome ore	1,093	123
Rayon tire cord	4,137	4,307
Rayon fiber and yarn	2,580	3,966
Yarn, other	2,248	494
Henequen fiber	1,449	1,298
Pineapples (fresh and canned)	3,107	2,696
Other commodities	19,226	24,430
Total Exports	640,344	539,048

Source: U.S. Department of Commerce, Bureau of Foreign Commerce, World Trade Information Service, *Basic Data on the Economy of Cuba*, March 1957, p. 18.

Table 13. COMPOSITION AND VALUE OF IMPORTS, 1954

(in millions of U.S. dollars)

Item	Amount
Consumer goods:	
Clothing	1.5
Household articles	34.7
Automobiles	25.6
Luxury	2.1
Foodstuffs	139.9
Medicines	11.1
Tobacco	1.1
Beverages	6.2
Other	4.2
Total	226.4
Production goods:	
Sugar industry	2.6
Other industries	51.2
Agriculture	13.4
Transport	12.8
Construction goods	17.7
Fuels	33.7
Raw materials	130.1
Total	261.5
Grand total	487.9

Source: Adapted from U.S. Department of Commerce, Bureau of Foreign Commerce, *Investment in Cuba*, July 1956, p. 140.

Table 14. BUDGETARY REVENUES AND EXPENDITURES, 1940-1958

(in millions of pesos)

Year	Revenues	Expenditures[a]	Surplus or deficit
Calendar			
1940	78.1	79.3	—1.2
1941	80.2	77.7	2.5
1942	106.3	101.7	4.6
1943	125.3	112.2	13.1
1944	148.4	133.2	15.2
1945	158.0	145.1	12.9
1946	201.0	174.0	27.0
1947	277.2	199.4	77.8
1948	241.9	288.8	—46.9
Fiscal[b]			
1949-50	229.6	228.6	1.0
1950-51	285.7	271.4	14.3
1951-52	326.8	324.5	2.3
1952-53	309.5	340.6	—31.1
1953-54	270.2	303.5	—33.3
1954-55	303.4	329.3	—25.9
1955-56	328.7	325.3	3.4
1956-57	370.8	357.9	12.9
1957-58	359.9	330.1	29.8

(a) Total ordinary and extraordinary expenditures.

(b) Fiscal year ending June 30.

Source: Adapted from U.S. Department of Commerce, Bureau of Foreign Commerce, *Investment in Cuba,* 1956, p. 120; United Nations, Department of Economic and Social Affairs, Economic Commission for Latin America, *Economic Survey of Latin America, 1957,* 1959, p. 181.

Table 15. MONEY SUPPLY, 1950-1958

(at end of year—in millions of pesos)

	1950	1951	1952	1953	1954	1955	1956	1957	1958
Total money	800	829	900	881	899	962	1,106	1,125	1,090
Currency	303	349	384	378	391	396	414	427	451
Deposits	497	480	516	503	508	566	692	698	639

Source: Adapted from International Monetary Fund, *International Financial Statistics* (Vol. XIII, No. 11), November 1960, pp. 98-99.

Table 16. ESTIMATED REVENUES, 1961

(in millions of pesos)

Taxes	500
4-percent industrialization tax	60
Profits of nationalized industry	400
Rents under urban reform plan	35
INAV (Savings and Housing Institute)	70
BANSESCU (Social Security Bank)	170
Seized assets of pro-Batista men[a]	4
Foreign credits, profits of commercial and agricultural activities, revenues from provinces and municipalities	120
Total	1,359

(a) Amount remaining in the Ministry for the Recovery of Misappropriated Assets.

Source: Adapted from *Revolución*, December 31, 1960, pp. 2, 14.

Table 17. ESTIMATED EXPENDITURES, 1961

(in millions of pesos)

Public investment		600
Industry	190	
Agriculture	200	
Other	210	
Public works		200
Roads, highways, bridges	35	
Housing (Urban Reform Program, National Institute of Savings and Housing and National Institute of Agrarian Reform)	95	
Schools and other	70	
Education		120
Health		70
Social security, etc.		200
Administrative costs		95
Other (public debt, internal security, defense, emergencies)		200
Total		1,485

Source: Adapted from *Revolución*, December 31, 1960, pp. 2 and 14.

Table 18.   **CHRONOLOGY OF EVENTS, 1957-1961**

Year	Month	Event
1957	February	Herbert Matthews publishes story of visit to Castro.
		U.S. ambassador witnesses police brutality in Santiago de Cuba.
1958	February	Prío arrested in United States.
		Fangio kidnapped.
	March	United States military aid stopped.
	June	United States servicemen kidnapped.
	July	Castro objects to rocket shipment.
	October	Batista buys British aircraft.
	November	Batista supporter Rivero "elected" president.
	December	United States attempts to set up caretaker government.
	December 31	Batista departs.
1959	January 7	United States recognizes government of Manuel Urrutia.
	January 9	Communist party declared free to operate.
	January 12	United States Senators deplore "bloodbath."
	February	Miró resigns; Castro becomes prime minister.
	March	Cuban Telephone Co. intervened.
	April	Castro visits United States.
	July 2	Plot crushed in Havana.
	July 14	Díaz Lanz testifies before Senate committee.
	July 17	Urrutia resigns.
	August 12	Declaration of Santiago.
	September 30	Cuba-USSR sugar deal.
	November 9	United States charges Cuba with creating hostility.
1960	January	Temporary recall of U.S. ambassador.
	February	Mikoyan in Havana.
	March 4	*La Coubre* explodes.
	March 16	Sugar sale to Britain.
	April 1	Cuba-Poland barter agreement.
	April 18	Cuba-Japan trade agreement.
	May 7	Cuba and USSR announce resumption of diplomatic relations.
		Cultural exchange agreements with Indonesia and Yugoslavia.
		Dorticós tours Latin America.
	June 4	Núñez in Moscow.
		U.S. note protests slanders.
		Democratic Revolutionary Front established in Miami.

Table 18. (continued)

Year	Month	Event
	June 24	Eisenhower requests authority to reduce sugar quota.
	June 29	Oil refineries nationalized.
	July 6	Sugar quota for 1960 eliminated.
	July 9	Khrushchev offers rocket support.
	July 22	Cuba-China $70 million trade deal.
	August 2	Cuba-East Germany barter agreement.
	August 6	Castro seizes 26 United States companies.
	August 28	OAS Declaration of San José condemns intrusion.
	September 2	Castro tears up Rio Treaty, announces Cuba-Communist China diplomatic link. Declaration of Havana.
	September	Castro and Khrushchev in New York.
	October	Guevara to Moscow.
	October 13	Four hundred private companies nationalized.
	October 25	One hundred sixty-six more companies expropriated in retaliation against United States trade embargo.
	November 16	Nicaragua and Guatemala charge Cuban aggression.
	December 31	Cuba accuses United States before Security Council.
1961	January 1	Peru breaks off diplomatic relations.
	January 3	United States breaks off diplomatic relations.
	January 6	Cuba mobilized against invasion.
	March 10	Cuba government-in-exile organized in New York.
	April 17	Abortive invasion by exiles.
	May 1	Castro declares Cuba socialist.

BIBLIOGRAPHY

BIBLIOGRAPHY

ABRAHAM, R. C. *Dictionary of Modern Yoruba.* London: University of London Press, 1958.

ACEBAL, SERGIO. *Mis memorias.* Habana: La Milagrosa, 1955.

AGRAMONTE, ROBERTO. "Estado actual de la Sociología en Cuba," *Revista Bimestre Cubana,* LXIV, No. 1-3 (1949), 17.

"Agrarian Reform Act, 17 May 1959," *Gaceta oficial; edición extraordinario especial,* No. 7 (June 3, 1959)

AGUILERA, FRANCISCO (ed.). *Handbook of Latin American Studies.* (Continued series.) Miami: University of Florida Press, 1954.

AITON, A. S. "Spanish Colonial Reorganization under the Family Compact," *Hispanic American Historical Review,* XII (1932), 269-280.

ALEXANDER, ROBERT J. *Communism in Latin America.* New Brunswick: Rutgers University Press, 1957.

————. "Communism in Latin America," *New Leader,* XLIV, No. 5 (1961), 15-19.

ALFARO, RICARDO J. *Diccionario de anglicismos.* Panama: Imprenta Nacional, 1950.

ALISKY, MARION. "Confused Cuba," *Nieman Reports,* XIV (April 1960), 12, 13.

————. "The Disappearing Cuban Daily," *Nieman Reports,* XV (April 1961), 5, 6.

————. "Havana Havoc," *Nieman Reports,* X (April 1956), 16-18.

Almanaque de la Caridad, 1957. Habana: n.pub., 1958.

ALTAMIRA Y CREVEA, RAFAEL. *A History of Spain.* Translated by Muna Lee. New York: Van Nostrand, 1949.

ALVAREZ ACEVEDO, JOSÉ M. *La colonia española en la economía cubana.* Habana: Ucar, García, 1936.

ALVAREZ CONDE, JOSÉ. *Arqueología indocubana.* (Publicaciones de la Junta Nacional de Arquelogía y Etnología.) Habana: 1956.

American Jewish Year Book, LXI. New York: American Jewish Committee, 1960.

American Universities Field Staff, Reports Service. *Castro Cuba in Mid-*

356

1960: Fidel of Cuba, By Voice and Violence. (Mexico and Caribbean Area Studies, I, Nos. 1-3.) New York: American Universities Field Staff, 1960.

AMES, DAVID W. "Negro Family Types in a Cuban Solar," *Phylon,* XI, No. 2 (1960), 159.

AMIGÓ, GUSTAVO. "La iglesia católica en Cuba," *Revista Javeriana* (Bogotá, Colombia), XXVIII, No. 138 (1947), 165-175; XXVIII, No. 140 (1947), 328-335.

Anglo-American Directory of Cuba, 1951. Marianao, Cuba: n.pub., n.d.

ANGULO Y PÉREZ, ANDRÉS. *Curso de historia de las instituciones locales de Cuba.* Habana: Cultural, 1943.

ARREDONDO, A. *El Negro en Cuba.* Habana: Editorial Alfa, 1939.

ARROM, J. J. *Historia de la literatura dramática cubana.* New Haven: Yale University Press, 1944.

ATKINS, EDWIN F. *Sixty Years in Cuba.* Cambridge: Harvard University Press, 1926.

AZCUY ALÓN, FANNY. *Psicografía y supervivencias de los aborígenes de Cuba.* Habana: n.pub., 1941.

BALL, M. MARGARET. "Issue for the Americas: Non-Intervention vs. Human Rights and the Preservation of Democratic Institutions," *International Organization,* XV, No. 1 (1961), 21-37.

Banco Nacional de Cuba. *Economic Development Program; Progress Reports No. 1 and 2.* Habana: n.pub., 1956, 1957.

BASCOM, WILLIAM R. "The Focus of Cuban Santeria," *Southwestern Journal of Anthropology,* VI, No. 1 (1950), 64-68.

————. "The Yoruba in Cuba," *Nigeria,* No. 37 (1951), 14-20.

BEALS, RALPH. "Social Stratification in Latin America," *American Journal of Sociology,* LVIII (1953), 327-339.

de BEAUVOIR, SIMONE. *France-Observateur,* April 7, 1960.

BEMIS, SAMUEL FLAGG. *The Latin American Policy of the United States.* New York: Harcourt, Brace, 1943.

BERLE, A. A., JR. "Cuban Crisis," *Foreign Affairs,* XXXIX (October 1960), 40-55.

BETANCOURT, JUAN RENÉ. *Doctrina negra.* Habana: P. Fernandez, 1955.

BINGLE, E. J. (ed.). *World Christian Handbook, 1957.* London: World Dominion Press, 1957.

BLANKSTIN, GEORGE I. "Political Groups in Latin America," *American Political Science Review,* LIII (March 1959), 106-127.

BLASIER, STEWART C. *The Cuban and Chilean Communist Parties: Instruments of Soviet Policy (1935-1948).* Ann Arbor: University of Michigan Microfilms, 1954.

BRENNAN, RAY. *Castro, Cuba and Justice.* Garden City: Doubleday, 1959.

BUENO, SALVADOR. *Medio siglo de literatura cubana (1902-1952).* Habana: Comisión Nacional Cubana de la UNESCO, 1953.

CABRERA, LYDIA. *Anagó, vocabulario Lucumí.* Habana: Ediciones E. R., 1957.

————. *El Monte, Igbo Finda, Ewe Orisha, Vititin Finda, etc.* Habana: Ediciones E. R., 1954.

————. *La sociedad secreta Abakuá.* Habana: Ediciones E. R., 1954.

CABRERA, RAIMUNDO. *Cuba and the Cubans.* Translated by Laura Guiteras. Philadelphia: Levytype, 1896.

CALDERÍO, FRANCISCO (Blas Roca). *Los fundamentos del Socialismo.* Habana: n.pub., 1943.

CANET, GERARDO, and ERWIN RAISZ. *Atlas de Cuba.* Cambridge: Harvard University Press, 1949.

CARPENTIER, ALEJO. *The Lost Steps.* Translated by Harriet de Onís. New York: Knopf, 1956.

————. *La música en Cuba.* Pánuco, México: Fondo de Cultura Económica, 1946.

CASTELLANOS, ISRAEL. *Medicina legal y criminología Afro-Cubanas.* Habana: Molina, 1937.

CASTRO, FIDEL. *History Will Absolve Me.* New York: Liberal Press, 1959.

————. *Pensamiento político, económico y social de Fidel Castro.* Habana: Editorial Lex, 1959.

Centro Asturiano, Habana. *Reseña ilustrada.* Habana: La Habanera, 1943.

CHACÓN Y CALVO, JOSÉ MARÍA. *Ensayos de literatura cubana.* Madrid: Editorial Saturino Calleja, n.d.

CHAILLOUX CARDONA, JUAN M. "Síntesis histórica de la vivienda popular," (Biblioteca de Historia, Filosofía y Sociología, No. 20.) Habana, 1945.

CHAPMAN, CHARLES E. *A History of the Cuban Republic: A Study in Hispanic American Diplomacy.* New York: Macmillan, 1927.

CHASE, ALLAN. *Falange.* New York: Putnam, 1943.

CHESTER, EDMUND A. *A Sergeant Named Batista.* New York: Holt, 1954.

CHRISTENSEN, ASHER N. (ed.). *Evolution of Latin American Governments.* New York: Holt, 1951.

CLAGETT, H. L. *The Administration of Justice in Latin America.* New York: Oceana, 1952.

CLARK, SYDNEY. *All the Best in Cuba.* New York: Dodd, Mead, 1956.

Commonweal, "Cuban Turmoil," LXXI (November 1959), 117, 118.

————, "Cuba's Uneasy Path," LXXI (February 1960), 536, 537.

"Constitution of the Republic of Cuba, 1901." In Willis Fletcher Johnson (ed.), *History of Cuba,* IV, New York: B. F. Buck, 1920.

CORBITT, DUVON CLOUGH. *The Colonial Government of Cuba.* Chapel Hill: University of North Carolina Press, 1938.

————. "Mercedes and Realengos: A Survey of the Public Land System in Cuba," *Hispanic American Historical Review,* XIX, No. 3 (1939), 262-285.

358

CRAWFORD, WILLIAM REX. A Century of Latin American Thought. Cambridge: Harvard University Press, 1944.

CREVENNA, THEODORE R. (ed.). Materiales para el estudio de la clase media en la América Latina. Washington: Pan American Union, 1951.

Cuba. Consejo Nacional de Economía. El programa económica de Cuba. Habana: Consejo Nacional de Economía, 1955.

——————. Dirección General de Estadística. 10 Años (1949-1958) de balanzas de comercio, balanzas de pagos, ingreso nacional. Habana: n.pub., 1960.

——————. La estimulación industrial en Cuba. (Publicaciones del Consejo Nacional de Economía.) Habana: n.pub., 1956.

——————. Ministerio de Hacienda. Anuario statistico de Cuba. Habana: n.pub., 1957.

——————. Tribunal Superior Electoral, Oficina Nacional de los Censos Demográfico y Electoral. Censos de población, viviendas y electoral, Enero 28 de 1953; Informe General. Habana: Tribunal Superior Electoral Oficina Nacional de los Censos Demográfico y Electoral, 1955.

CUYAS, ARTURO. The New Constitutional Laws for Cuba: Text of the Recent Measures for the Self-Government of the Island, With Comments Thereon. New York: Associated Spanish and Cuban Press, 1897.

DAVIS, HAROLD EUGENE (ed.). Government and Politics in Latin America. New York: Ronald Press, 1958.

DAVIS, J. MERLE. The Cuban Church in a Sugar Economy. New York: International Missionary Council, 1942.

Diario de la Marina, 1957-1960, passim.

DÍAZ AGUIRRE, MARIO. Cromos de ayer. Madrid: Artes Gráficas, 1958.

DRAPER, THEODORE. "Castro's Cuba: A Revolution Betrayed?" Encounter (March 1961), 6-23.

——————. "Runaway Revolution," Reporter, XXII (May 12, 1960), 14-20.

DUBOIS, JULES. Fidel Castro: Rebel, Liberator or Dictator. Indianapolis: Bobbs-Merrill, 1959.

DUMONT, RENÉ. "La Marche du Temps: Cuba," L'Express, September 22, 1960, 24.

DYER, DONALD R. "Urbanism in Cuba," Geographical Review, XLVII (April 1957), 224-233.

Economist (London), "Cuba in Mid-Revolution," January 7, 1961, 43, 44.

Economist Intelligence Unit. Three-Monthly Economic Review: Cuba, Dominican Republic, Haiti, Puerto Rico, Nos. 29-33 (February 1960-February 1961).

Bibliography

————. *Three-Monthly Economic Review, Annual Supplement: Cuba, Dominican Republic, Haiti, Puerto Rico.* May 1960.

ENTRALGO, ELÍAS JOSÉ. *Apuntes caracteriológicos sobre el léxico cubano.* Habana: Molina, 1941.

————. "El carácter cubano," *Revista Bimestre Cubana,* XXVII (March-April 1931), 267-294.

————. *Esquema de Sociografía Indocubana.* Habana: Molina, 1936.

————. "Un forum sobre los prejuicios étnicos en Cuba," *Nuestro Tiempo,* May-June 1959.

————. *La liberación étnica cubana.* Habana, 1953.

ESPINOSA, CIRO. *La evolución fonética de la lengua castellana en Cuba.* Habana: Echevarría, 1935.

ESTÉNGER, RAFAEL. *Cien de las mejores poesías cubanas.* (2d ed.) Habana: Ediciones Miraflor, 1948.

FABELO, T. D. *Lengua de Santeros, Guiné Góngorí.* Habana: n.pub., 1956.

FEBRES, CORDERO G. JULIO. "Balance del indigenismo en Cuba," *Revista de la Biblioteca Nacional,* I. (Series 2.) No. 4, 1950.

FERGUSSON, ERNA. *Cuba.* New York: Knopf, 1946.

FERNÁNDEZ DE CASTRO, JOSÉ A. *Esquema histórico de las letras en Cuba (1548-1902).* Habana: University of Habana, 1949.

FITZGIBBON, RUSSELL H. "Constitutional Development in Latin America: A Synthesis," *American Political Science Review,* XXXIX (1945), 511-522.

————. *Cuba and the United States, 1900-1935.* Menasha, Wisconsin: George Banta, 1935.

————. "Cuban Elections of 1936," *American Political Science Review,* XXX (August 1936).

————. "Revolution Next Door: Cuba," *Annals of the American Academy of Political and Social Science,* CCCXXXIV (March 1961), 113-122.

FORDE, DARYLL (ed.). *Efik Traders of Old Calabar.* London: Oxford University Press (for the International African Institute), 1956.

————. "The Yoruba-Speaking Peoples of South-Western Nigeria," Part IV in Daryll Forde (ed.), *Ethnographic Survey of Africa, Western Africa.* London: International African Institute, 1951.

FORDE, DARYLL, and G. I. JONES. "The Ibo and Ibibio-Speaking Peoples of Southeastern Nigeria," Part III in Daryll Forde (ed.), *Ethnographic Survey of Africa, Western Africa* (International African Institute). Oxford: Oxford University Press, 1950.

Foreign Policy Association. Commission on Cuban Affairs. *Problems of the New Cuba: Report of the Commission on Cuban Affairs.* New York: Foreign Policy Association, 1935.

FORTES, MEYER. *Oedipus and Job in West African Religion.* Cambridge: Cambridge University Press, 1959.

FOSTER, GEORGE M. "Cofradía and Compadrazgo in Spain and Spanish America," *Southwestern Journal of Anthropology,* IX (1953), 1-28.

FOY, FELICIAN A. (ed.). *National Catholic Almanac, 1960.* Paterson, New Jersey: St. Anthony's Guild, 1960.

FRIEDENBERG, D. "History Will Not Absolve Castro," *New Republic,* CXLIII (October 1960), 11-13.

GARCÍA CASTANEDA, JOSÉ. A. "La transculturación indo-española en Holguín," *Revista de Arqueología y Etnología,* 1949.

GEISERT, HAROLD L. *The Caribbean: Population and Resources.* Washington: George Washington University, 1960.

GILLIN, JOHN P. "Modern Latin American Culture," *Social Forces,* XXV (1946-1947), 243-248.

————. "Some Signposts for Policy." In Council on Foreign Relations, *Social Change in Latin America Today.* New York: Harper, 1960.

GÓMEZ-SICRE, JOSÉ. "Some Aspects of Art in the Caribbean Area." In A. Curtis Wilgus (ed.), *The Caribbean: Contemporary Trends,* III (Series 1), Gainesville: University of Florida Press, 1953.

GORDON, WENDELL C. *The Economy of Latin America.* New York: Columbia University Press, 1950.

GREENBERG, JOSEPH H. *Studies in African Linguistic Classification.* New Haven: Compass, 1955.

GRILLO SÁEZ, DAVID. *El problema del negro cubano.* (2d ed.) Habana: n.pub., 1953.

GRISMER, RAYMOND. *Vida y obra de autores cubanos.* Habana: Editorial Alfa, 1940.

GUERRA, *et al. Cubana.* Habana: Editorial Historia de la Nación, 1952.

"La Guerra de Guerrillas" (condensation of a book by Ché Guevara), *Army,* March 1961, 21-32; April 1961, 59-69; May 1961, 63-75.

GUERRA Y SÁNCHEZ, RAMIRO, *et al. Historia de la nación cubana.* Habana: Editorial Historia de la nación Cubana, 1952.

GUGGENHEIM, H. F. *The United States and Cuba.* New York: Macmillan, 1934.

Habana, City of. *Las Comparsas populares del carnaval habanero: cuestión resuelta.* Habana: Molina, 1937.

————. *Registro Social de la Habana, 1957.* Edited by Julio de Céspedes. Habana: Molina, 1957.

————. *Registro Social de la Habana, 1958.* Edited by Julio de Céspedes. Habana: Molina, 1958.

————. *Registro Social de la Habana, 1959.* Edited by Julio de Céspedes. Habana: Molina, 1959.

HANKE, LEWIS. *Modern Latin America: Continent in Ferment,* I. New York: Van Nostrand, 1959.

HARING, CLARENCE H. *The Spanish Empire in America.* New York: Oxford University Press, 1947.

HARRINGTON, MARK R. *Cuba before Columbus.* New York: Museum of the American Indian, Heye Foundation, 1921.

HENRÍQUEZ-UREÑA, PEDRO. *Literary Currents in Hispanic America.* Cambridge: Harvard University Press, 1945.

HERRING, HUBERT. *A History of Latin America.* New York: Knopf, 1960.

HOLME, J. G. *The Life of Leonard Wood.* New York: n.pub., 1920.

HUBERMAN, LEO, and PAUL M. SWEEZY. *Cuba: Anatomy of a Revolution.* New York: Monthly Review Press, 1960.

————. "Cuba Revisited," *Monthly Review,* XII, No. 8 (1960), 401-432.

HUMBOLDT, ALEXANDER. *The Island of Cuba.* Edited and translated by J. S. Thrasher. New York: Derby and Jackson, 1856.

International Bank for Reconstruction and Development in Collaboration with the Government of Cuba. Economic and Technical Mission to Cuba. *Report on Cuba: Findings and Recommendations of an Economic and Technical Mission Organized by the IBRD in Collaboration with the Government of Cuba in 1950.* Washington: IBRD, 1951.

International Cooperation Administration. Office of Labor Affairs. *Summary of the Labor Situation in Cuba.* (Prepared by the U.S. Department of Labor, Bureau of Labor Statistics). Washington: Department of Labor, December 1956.

International Financial News Survey, "Cuban Budget for 1961," XII, No. 6 (1961), 48.

International Monetary Fund. *International Financial Statistics,* XIII, No. 11 (1960); XIV, No. 5 (1961).

JAMES, PRESTON E. *Latin America.* (3d ed.) New York: Odyssey Press, 1959.

JENKS, LELAND H. *Our Cuban Colony.* New York: Vanguard Press, 1928.

JOHNSON, JOHN J. *Political Change in Latin America.* Stanford: Stanford University Press, 1958.

JOHNSON, WILLIS FLETCHER. *The History of Cuba.* (5 vols.) New York: B. F. Buck, 1920.

KANTOR, HARRY. "The Aprista Search for a Program Applicable to Latin America," *Western Political Quarterly,* V, No. 4 (1952), 578-584.

KANY, CHARLES E. *American-Spanish Syntax.* (2d ed.) Chicago: University of Chicago Press, 1951.

KENNY, MICHAEL. "Twentieth Century Spanish Expatriates in Cuba: A Sub-Culture?" *Anthropological Quarterly,* XXXIV, No. 2 (1961), 85-93.

362

Kirkpatrick, Eoron M. (ed.). *The Year of Crisis: Communist Propaganda Activities in 1956*. New York: Macmillan, 1957.

Krauss, Paul H. *Communist Policy in Cuba, 1933-1946*. New York: Columbia University Press, 1950.

Labrador Ruiz, Enrique. "Chinatown, Havana," *Américas*, IV, No. 8 (1952), 6.

Lachatañeré, Rómulo. *Manual de Santería: El sistema de cultos "Lucumís."* Habana: Editorial Caribe, 1942.

————. "Las religiones negras y el folklore cubano," *Revista Hispánica Moderna* (New York), IX (January, April 1943), 138-143.

Lancis y Sanchez, Antonio. *Legislación orgánica del poder ejecutivo*. Habana: n.pub., 1947.

Lanning, J. T. *Academic Culture in the Spanish Colonies*. New York: Oxford University Press, 1940.

Lavine, Harold. "Social Revolution in Cuba," *Commentary*, XXVIII, No. 4 (1959), 324-328.

Lazcano y Mazón, Andrés Maria. *Commentarios a la ley orgánica del poder judicial*. Vols. I, II. Habana. n.pub., 1955.

Leiseca, Juan Martín. *Apuntes para la historia eclesiástica de Cuba*. Habana: Carasa, 1938.

Lincoln, Freeman. "What Has Happened to Cuban Business," *Fortune*, LX, No. 3 (1959), 110-113, 264-274.

Lizaso, Félix. *Martí: Martyr of Cuban Independence*. Albuquerque: University of New Mexico Press, 1953.

————. *Panorama de la cultura cubana*. México-Buenos Aires: Fondo de Cultura Económica, 1949.

Llaguno y Ubieta, Pedro Pablo. *La masonería ante el momento político-constitucional cubano*. Habana: n.pub., 1937.

Llano Montes, Antonio, "Aún existen Indios en Oriente," *Carteles*, July 18, 1948, 28, 29.

Lockmiller, D. A. *Magoon in Cuba*. Chapel Hill: University of North Carolina Press, 1938.

Losada, J. "Batista: Master of the Coup d'Etat," *United Nations World*, April 1953.

MacDonald, Austin F. *Latin American Politics and Government*. New York: Crowell, 1954.

Mañach, Jorge. *Martí: Apostle of Freedom*. New York: Devin-Adair, 1950.

Mantirez Ortiz, Rafael. *General Leonard Wood's Administration in Cuba*. Paris: Dubois et Bauver, 1920.

Marcos Vegueri, Pascual B. *El negro en Cuba*. Habana: n.pub., 1955.

Marrero, Leví. *Elementos de geografía de Cuba*. Habana: Minerva, 1946.

Bibliography

————. *Geografía de Cuba.* Habana: Editorial Selecta, 1957.

MARTÍN, JUAN LUIS. *De donde vinieron los negros de Cuba.* Habana: Atalaya, 1939.

————. *Esquema sobre los factores alógenos de la población cubana.* Habana: n.pub., 1944.

MASSIP, SALVADOR, and SARAH E. YSALGUÉ MASSIP. *Introducción a la geografía de Cuba.* Habana: Fiallo y Hermanos, 1942.

MECHAM, J. L. *Church and State in Latin America.* Chapel Hill: University of North Carolina Press, 1934.

MEISLER, STANLEY. "Cuba's Frenzied Culture," *Nation,* December 24, 1960, 504, 505.

MÉTRAUX, ALFRED. *Voodoo in Haiti.* Translated by Hugo Charteris. New York: Oxford University Press, 1959.

MILLS, C. WRIGHT. *Listen, Yankee.* New York: Ballantine Books, 1960.

MINNEMAN, P. G. *The Agriculture of Cuba.* (U.S. Department of Agriculture, Foreign Agriculture Bulletin, No. 2.) Washington, 1943.

MITJANS, AURELIO. *Historia de la literatura cubana.* Madrid: Editorial America, 1918.

MONTAGUE Y VIVERA, GUILLERMO DE. "Judicial Organization in Cuba," *Journal of the American Judicature Society,* April 1949, 166-170.

————. *El poder judicial y la constitución y otros estudios.* Habana: Cultural South America, 1951, 171.

MONTERO DE BASCOM, BERTA. "Influencias africanas en la cultura cubana," *Ciencias Sociales* (Washington), V. No. 27 (1954), 98-102.

MORALES PATIÑO, OSWALDO. "Los indigenas en los primeros municipios cubanos," *Revista de Arqueología y Etnología,* 1951.

MORÁN, MARÍA VIRTUDES. "Church and State in Cuba." Unpublished master's thesis, Columbia University, 1950.

MURKLAND, H. B. "Cuba: The Evolution of Revolution," *Current History,* XXXVIII (March 1960), 129-133.

NELSON, LOWRY. *Rural Cuba.* Minneapolis: University of Minnesota Press, 1950.

NEWMAN, A. "Operation Truth: A Cuban Diary," *Reporter,* XX (February 1959), 27-32.

NIETO Y CORTADELLAS, RAFAEL. *Dignidades nobiliarias en Cuba.* Madrid: Ediciones Cultura Hispánica, 1954.

NÚÑEZ JIMÉNEZ, ANTONIO. "Con los últimos indios de Cuba," *Bohemia,* May 30, 1954.

————. "Las culturas indias de Cuba," *C.T.C.,* September 1945, 18, 19, 37, 41.

————. *Geografía de Cuba.* (2d ed.) Habana: Editorial Lex, 1959.

NZEKWU, ONUORA. "Masquerade," *Nigeria* (Lagos), Independence Issue, 1960, 135.

ODELL, EDWARD A. *It Came to Pass*. New York: Board of National Missions, Presbyterian Church in the U.S.A., 1952.

OLIVA PULGARÓN, LUIS. *Apuntes históricos sobre la masonería cubana*. Habana: n.pub., 1934.

OLIVERA, OTTO. *Breve historia de la literatura antillana*. Mexico: Studium, 1957.

OLMSTED, DAVID L. "A Note on the Dialect of Regla, Cuba," *Hispania*, XXXVII, No. 3 (1954), 293, 294.

DE ONÍS, HARRIET. "The Short Story in the Caribbean Today." In A. Curtis Wilgus (ed.), *The Caribbean: Peoples, Problems and Prospects*, Gainesville: University of Florida Press, 1952.

ORTIZ, FERNANDO. "Biografía cubana del café," *La Nueva Democracia* (New York), July 1951, 31, 64-71.

————. "Los cabildos afrocubanos," *Revista Bimestre Cubana*, XVI, No. 1, 1921.

————. *Las cuatro culturas indias de Cuba*. Habana: Arellano, 1943.

————. *Cuban Counterpoint: Tobacco and Sugar*. New York: Knopf, 1947.

————. "Dónde hay Náñigos?" *Bohemia*, October 22, 1950, 4, 5.

————. "Glosario de afronegrismos," *El Siglo*, XX, 1924.

————. *El hampa afrocubana: Los negros brujos*. Madrid: Librería de F. Fe., 1906.

————. *El hampa afrocubana: Los negros esclavos*. Madrid: Librería de F. Fe., 1916.

————. *El Huracán*. México: Fondo de Cultura Económica, 1947.

————. "Una moderna secta espiritista de Cuba," *Bohemia*, XLII, No. 3 (1950), 8, 9, 137-139.

————. "El movimiento africanista en la música cubana," *Estudios Afrocubanos*, II, No. 1 (1938).

————. "Los muertos sacaos," *Bohemia*, XLII, No. 11 (1950), 28-31, 112-115.

————. "Las negros y la transculturación," *Khana, Revista Municipal de Arte y Letras* (Bolivia), IV, No. 7, 8 (March 1955), 115-118.

————. "On the Relations between Blacks and Whites," *Points of View* (Pan American Union, Division of Intellectual Cooperation), No. 7 (October 1943).

————. "Origen geográfico de los afrocubanos," *Revista Bimestre Cubana*, January-June 1957.

————"El origen de la tragedia de los Náñigos," *Bohemia*, XLII (1950), 26.

————. "Orígenes de los Cordoneros del Orilé," *Bohemia*, July 9, 1950, 34-36.

————. "El Quinto Jinete del Apocalipsis," *Revista Bimestre Cubana*, LXVII, No. 3 (May-June 1951).

————. "La Religión en la poesía mulata," *Estudios Afrocubanos*, I, No. 1 (1937).

Bibliography

Padron, Alfredo F. "Giros sintáxicos en las hablas cubanas," *Revista Bimestre Cubana*, LXVII (January-February 1951), 34-48.

Page, Charles A. "Communism and the Labor Movements of Latin America," *Virginia Quarterly Review*, XXXI, No. 3 (1955), 373-382

Pan American Union. Division of Intellectual Cooperation. *Carreño.* ("Contemporary Artists of Latin America Series.") Washington: PAU, 1947.

————. *Fundamental Law of Cuba, 1959.* Washington: PAU, 1959.

————. General Secretariat. Organization of the American States. *Indices de precios al consumidor (costa de la vida) de las Naciones Americanas.* Washington: PAU, 1959.

————. Legal Division. Department of International Law. *A Statement of the Laws of Cuba in Matters Affecting Business.* 2d ed., revised and enlarged by Jesus Bugeda Lanzas. Washington: PAU, 1958.

Paredes, Angel Modeste. *Sociología americana.* Quito, Ecuador: Editorial de la Casa de la Cultura Ecuatoriana, 1953.

Pattee, Richard. *Catholic Life in the West Indies.* Washington: Catholic Association for International Peace, 1946.

Peaslee, Amos J. (ed.). *Constitutions of Nations,* I. The Hague, Netherlands: Martinus Nijhoff, 1956, 610-682.

Phillips, R. Hart. "Castro Gets the Bill," *Reporter,* XXI (October 29, 1959), 23-24.

————. *Cuba: Island of Paradox.* New York: McDowell, Obolensky, 1959.

————. *Cuban Sideshow.* Habana: Cuban Press, 1935.

Pichardo Moya, Felipe. *Los indios de Cuba en sus tiempos históricos.* Habana: Muniz, 1945.

Pichardo y Tapia, Esteban. *Pichardo novísimo, o diccionario provincial casi razonado de voces y frases cubanas.* (9th ed.) Habana: Selecta, 1953.

Pierson, William W. "The Establishment and Early Functioning of the Intendencia of Cuba." In William W. Pierson (ed.), *Studies in Hispanic-American History* (James Sprunt Historical Studies, XIX, No. 2), 74-133, Chapel Hill: University of North Carolina Press, 1927.

Poblete Troncoso, Moisés. *El movimiento obrero latinoamericano.* México: Fondo de Cultura Económica, 1946.

Ponte Domínguez, Francisco J. *El delito de francmasonería en Cuba.* Mexico: Humanidad, 1951.

————. *La masonería en la independencia de Cuba.* Habana: Modas Magazine, 1954.

Pool, Rose Goodwin. *Light in Yumurí.* Atlanta, Georgia: Home Mission Board, Southern Baptist Convention, 1954.

The Popular Socialist Party of Cuba. "A Program for Cuba," *Political Affairs,* XXXVIII, No. 6 (1959), 25-33.

PORTUONDO, JOSÉ ANTONIO. *Bosquejo histórico de las letras cubanas.* Habana: República de Cuba, Ministerio de Relaciones Exteriores, Departamento de Asuntos Culturales, Division de Publicaciones, 1960.

PORTUONDO LINARES, SERAFÍN. *Los independientes de color.* (2d ed.) Habana: Editorial Librería Selecta, 1950.

PRADO PÉREZ, LAUREANO. *Clasificación ocupacional de Cuba.* Habana: Tribunal de Cuentas, 1955.

RAMÍREZ OLIVELLA, GUSTAVO. *Ley orgánica del poder judicial de 27 de enero de 1909 con todas las modificaciones introducidas hasta abril de 1939, inclusive.* Habana: n.pub., 1939.

RAMOS, ARTHUR. *Las culturas negras en el nuevo mundo.* México: Fondo de Cultura Económica, 1943.

RAMOS, JUAN J. *Historia de la literatura cubana,* III. Habana: Cárderas, 1945.

Revolución, "Urban Reform Law," October 18, 1960.

ROA, RAUL. *15 Años después.* Habana: Editorial Librería Selecta, 1950.

ROMUALDI, SERAFINO. "Communists Control Labor in Cuba," *AFL-CIO American Federationist,* LXVI, No. 11 (December 1959), 26.

ROUSE, IRVING. *Archaeology of the Maniabon Hills, Cuba.* (Yale Publications in Anthropology, No. 26.) New Haven: Yale University Press, 1942.

ROWE, LEE STANTON. "The Reorganization of Local Government in Cuba," *Annals of the American Academy of Political and Social Science,* XXV (March 1905), 311-321.

RUBENS, HORATIO S. *Liberty: The Story of Cuba.* New York: Brewer, Warren and Putnam, 1932.

SÁNCHEZ ROCA, MARIANO. *Leyes orgánicas del tribunal de garantiás y de los Presupuestos.* Habana: n.pub., 1949.

SAPIR, BORIS. *The Jewish Community of Cuba.* Translated by Simon Wolin. New York: J.T.S.P. University Press, 1948.

SARTRE, JEAN-PAUL. *Sartre on Cuba.* New York: Ballantine Books, 1961.

SHAPIRO, S. "Castro's Cuba Revisited," *New Republic,* CXLIV (February 1961), 15, 16.

————. "Cuba: A Dissenting Report," *New Republic,* CXLIII (September 1960), 8-26.

SHERMAN, G. "Sixty Minutes from Miami," *Reporter,* XXII (September 1960), 17-20.

SMITH, ROBERT F. *The United States and Cuba: Business and Diplomacy, 1917-1960.* New York: Bookman Associates, 1960.

Sociedad de Beneficencia de Naturales de Cataluña. *Libro de oro.* Habana: Sociedad de Beneficencia de Naturales Cataluña, 1940.

STOKES, WILLIAM S. "The Cuban Parliamentary System in Action, 1940-1947," *Journal of Politics*, II (May 1949), 335-364.

————. "The Cuban Revolution and the Presidential Elections," *Hispanic American Historical Review*, XXXI, No. 1 (February 1951), 609-626.

————. "Economic Anti-Americanism in Latin America," *Inter-American Economic Affairs*, Winter 1957.

————. *Latin American Politics*. New York: Crowell, 1959.

————. "National and Local Violence in Cuban Politics," *Southwestern Social Science Quarterly*, September 1953.

STRODE, HUDSON. *Pageant of Cuba*. New York: Harcourt, Brace, 1934.

TABER, ROBERT. "Castro's Cuba," *Nation*, CXC, No. 4 (1960), 63-71.

TANNENBAUM, FRANK. "The Political Dilemma in Latin America," *Foreign Affairs*, XXXVIII, No. 3 (1960), 497-515.

TEJEIRO, GUILLERMO. *Historia ilustrada de la colonia china en Cuba*. Habana: n.pub., 1947.

THOMAS, ALFRED BARNABY. *Latin America: A History*. New York: Macmillan, 1956.

United Nations. Bureau of Social Affairs. *Report on the World Social Situation*. New York: UN, 1957.

————. Department of Economic and Social Affairs. Economic Commission for Latin America. *Economic Survey of Latin America, 1957*. New York: UN, 1959.

United Nations Educational, Scientific, and Cultural Organization. *Basic Facts and Figures*. Paris: UNESCO, 1959.

————. *Statistics of Newspapers and Other Periodicals*. (ST/S/4.) Paris: UNESCO, n.d.

————. *The Training of Journalists*. Holland: n.pub., 1958.

United Nations Statistical Yearbook, 1958. New York: UN, 1958.

U.S. Congress. 85th, 86th. Senate Committee on Foreign Relations: Subcommittee on American Republics Affairs. *United States-Latin American Relations: Compilation of Studies*. Washington, 1960.

————. 86th, 1st Session. Senate Committee on Foreign Relations: Subcommittee on American Republics Affairs. *United States-Latin American Relations: United States Business and Labor in Latin America*, Committee Print No. 4, January 22, 1960. (Prepared by the University of Chicago). Washington, 1960.

————. 86th, 1st and 2d Sessions. Senate Committee on the Judiciary: Subcommittee to Investigate the Administration of the Internal Security Act and Other Internal Security Laws. *Communist Threat to the United States Through the Caribbean*, Pt. 3, 5, 7, 9. Washington, 1960.

————. 86th, 2nd Session. House Committee on Foreign Affairs: Subcommittee on Inter-American Affairs. *The Communist Threat in Latin America.* Washington, 1960.

U.S. Department of Agriculture. Foreign Agricultural Service. *Food Balances in Foreign Countries.* (FAS-M-104, Pt. III.) Washington, November 1960.

U.S. Department of Commerce. Bureau of Foreign Commerce. *Basic Data on the Economy of Cuba.* (World Trade Information Service: "Economic Reports," Pt. 1, No. 57-15.) Washington, March 1957.

————. *Foreign Commerce Weekly,* LXIV, Nos. 6, 17, 19, 24 (1960); and LXV, No. 2 (1961).

————. Bureau of Foreign Commerce. *Investment in Cuba.* Washington, 1956.

————. *Economic Developments in Cuba, 1955.* (World Trade Information Service: "Economic Reports," Pt. 1, No. 56-26.) Washington, March 1956.

————. *Economic Developments in Cuba, 1956.* (World Trade Information Service: "Economic Reports," Pt. 1, No. 57-16.) Washington, March 1957.

————. *Economic Developments in Cuba, 1958.* (World Trade Information Service: "Economic Reports," Pt. 1, No. 59-42.) Washington, April 1959.

————. *Economic Developments in the Western Hemisphere, 1959.* (World Trade Information Service: "Economic Reports," Pt. 1, No. 60-9.) Washington, March 1960.

U.S. Department of Health, Education and Welfare. Social Security Administration. Division of Program Research. *Social Security Programs Throughout the World, 1948.* Washington, n.d.

U.S. Department of Labor. Bureau of Labor Statistics. *Labor Developments Abroad.* Washington, December 1960.

U.S. Department of State. Bureau of Public Affairs. Office of Public Service. *Cuba.* (Department of State Publication 7171, Inter-American Series, 66.) Washington, April 1961.

————. "Cuban Responsibility in Increased International Tensions in the Hemisphere," *Department of State Bulletin,* XLIII, No. 1105 (1960), 317-349.

————. *Department of State Bulletin,* XLIII, Nos. 1114, 1115 (1960); and XLIV, No. 1123 (1961).

VALDIVIA, ROBERTO. "Los aborígenes de Cuba? Viven todavía?" *Artes Blancas,* February 1946, 11-13.

VARONA, ENRIQUE JOSÉ. *Observaciones lexicológicas y gramaticales.* Habana: Academia Cubana de la Lengua, 1956, 58.

VERGER, PIERRE. "Nigeria, Brazil and Cuba," *Nigeria* (Lagos), Independence Issue, 1960, 112.

VERNENGO, ROBERT. "Freedom of Association and Industrial Relations in Latin America," Parts I, II. *International Labour Review*, LXXIII, Nos. 5, 6 (1956), 451-482, 592-618.

VIDAURRETA, JOSÉ L. "Ensayo sobre la música cubana," *Estudios Afrocubanos*, II, No. 1 (1938).

VILLAREJO, DONALD. "American Investment in Cuba," *New University Thought*, I, No. 1 (1960), 79-88.

VITIER, CINTIO. *Cincuenta años de poesía cubana (1902-1952)*. Habana: Dirección de Cultura, 1952.

VITIER, MEDARDO. *Los ideas en Cuba*, II. Habana: Editorial Trópico, 1938.

VIVANCO Y DÍAZ, JULIÁN. *Las raíces de la lingüística indígena de Cuba*. Habana: El Sol, 1953.

WELLES, SUMNER. *Relations between the United States and Cuba.* (U.S. Department of State, Latin American Series No. 7.) Washington, 1934.

WESTERMANN, DIETRICH, and M. A. BRYAN. *Languages of West Africa.* (Handbook of African Languages, Pt. II.) London: Oxford University Press (for International African Institute), 1952.

WEYL, NATHANIEL. *Red Star over Cuba.* New York: Devin-Adair, 1960.

WHITTAKER, A. P. (ed.). *Latin America and the Enlightenment.* New York: Appleton-Century-Crofts, 1942.

WILGUS, A. CURTIS (ed.). *The Caribbean: Its Culture*, V. (Series 1.) Gainesville: University of Florida Press, 1955.

————. *The Caribbean: Its Economy*, IV. (Series 1.) Gainesville: University of Florida Press, 1954.

————. *The Caribbean: Natural Resources.* Gainesville: University of Florida Press, 1959.

WOOD, LEONARD. "The Military Government of Cuba," *Annals of American Academy of Political and Social Science*, XXI (March 1903), 153-182.

World Today, "Can Cuba's Dictatorship Survive?" XIV (April 1958), 162-167.

————. "Cuba: A Peasant Revolution," XV, No. 5 (1959), 183-195.

World Health Organization. *Report of the World Health Situation, 1954-56.* Geneva: WHO, 1959.

WRIGHT, IRENE A. *The Early History of Cuba, 1492-1586.* New York: Macmillan, 1916.

WRIGHT, T. P., JR. "United States Electoral Intervention in Cuba," *Inter-American Economic Affairs*, XIII (Winter 1959), 50-71.

ZELINSKY, WILBUR. "The Historical Geography of the Negro Population of Latin America," *Journal of Negro History*, XXXIV, No. 2 (1949), 153.

INDEX

374